NORTH PLATTE COLLEGE LIBRARY
D1244077

OTHER KNOPF BOOKS ON CONSERVATION

THE NATIONAL PARKS: *What They Mean to You and Me*
BY Freeman Tilden

THE NATIONAL PARKS OF THE UNITED STATES
BY Luis A. Bolin

THIS IS THE AMERICAN EARTH
BY Nancy Newhall and Ansel Adams

WORDS OF THE EARTH
BY Nancy Newhall and Cedric Wright

A CONTRIBUTION TO THE HERITAGE
OF EVERY AMERICAN,
The Conservation Activities of John D. Rockefeller, Jr.
BY Nancy Newhall

STEVE MATHER OF THE NATIONAL PARKS
BY Robert Shankland

THE STATE PARKS

Their Meaning in American Life

Baxter State Park: Mount Katahdin

PHOTO BY MAURICE DAY

THE STATE PARKS

THEIR MEANING IN AMERICAN LIFE

BY

FREEMAN TILDEN

Foreword by CONRAD L. WIRTH

DIRECTOR, NATIONAL PARK SERVICE

Tilden, Freeman, 1883-
The State Parks, their meaning in American
life. Foreword by Conrad L. Wirth.
E160 .T53

RSN=00016952

NEW YORK ALFRED A. KNOPF

1962

L. C. catalog card number: 62-17547

THIS IS A BORZOI BOOK,

PUBLISHED BY ALFRED A. KNOPF, INC.

Manufactured in the United States of America, and distributed by Random House, Inc. Published simultaneously in Toronto, Canada, by Random House of Canada, Limited.

FIRST EDITION

FOREWORD

THE STATE PARK MOVEMENT in this country has grown tremendously during the past four decades. When the National Conference on State Parks first met in 1921 on the recommendation of Stephen T. Mather, the first director of the National Park Service, a few state parks existed, but in only nineteen of the states. All the states now have state parks. This recreation estate consists of nearly 2,800 parks, monuments, recreation areas, beaches, parkways, and waysides; embraces some 5.8 million acres; and is administered by over a hundred state park and historical agencies. Current annual expenditures run to $110 million and visitors exceeed 273 million.

Several factors have influenced this tremendous growth—increasing population, mobility, and income; the shorter work week; paid vacations; and the trend toward participation in outdoor recreation activities. Furthermore, as our resources are rapidly vanishing, the states have become increasingly responsive to the need for preserving the precious examples of their scenic, natural, and cultural heritage. They are aware of the urgency to acquire and preserve such areas before it is too late. The situation has already reached the now-or-never stage.

No comprehensive survey and report on the state parks has been attempted since the publication of Beatrice Ward Nelson's *State Recreation* in 1928 and Herbert Evison's *A State Park Anthology* in 1930. And, when these books were written, many of the states not only had no state parks, but had no well-based hopes of having any.

For some years there has been an evident need for an up-to-date, authoritative account of the state parks which would serve as a guide in state planning and development, in the establishment of appropriate policies and practices, and in the winning of public support. There is great value in being able to study in a single volume what other states have accomplished, how they have done it, and what attitudes have been encountered. This book, then, is directed toward legislators, conservation agencies and organizations, schools, and particularly the general public. It is hoped that it will provide an understanding of the meaning and purposes of state parks and will encourage the public to use and cherish its extensive recreation estate.

The seventy-four descriptive chapters include examples of all categories of parks, except the wayside, which are covered in the statement on "Suggested Criteria for Evaluating Areas Proposed for Inclusion in the State Park Systems" adopted by the National Conference on State Parks. The areas described were selected as outstanding examples of a variety of types. They are not offered as the "best parks"—no one is qualified to make such a distinction.

The interest of the National Park Service in promoting this book stems from the activities of its first director, Steven T. Mather, who recognized the value and need for strong state park programs and who lost no opportunity to further this cause. In 1933 this interest was substantially strengthened when the Service and the states cooperated in the CCC program, thus beginning a most significant period of growth in state park conservation. More recently, the success of the National Park Service Mission 66 program has stimulated the states in formulating long-range programs for their park systems.

Special acknowledgment is made to Jackson Hole Preserve, Incorporated, and its president, Laurance Rockefeller, whose interest in the ideals of park conservation is well known. It was their generous grant that made possible the preparation of this book.

Acknowledgment also is made to Resources for the Future, Incorporated, and its board chairman, Horace M. Albright, for encouragement in the study and support in publication.

Freeman Tilden was chosen as author because of his discerning mind and inimitable style. His human touch makes for reader delight. It is intended that this book will stand as a companion piece to his 1951 publication. *The National Parks—What They Mean to You and Me.*

CONRAD L. WIRTH

DIRECTOR, NATIONAL PARK SERVICE

CONTENTS

PART 3 : *THE SOUTH*

PART 4 : *THE MIDWEST*

PART 5 : *THE WEST*

PART 6 : *THUMBNAIL SKETCHES*

ILLUSTRATIONS

MAPS

PART 1

THE STATE PARKS

(I)

A STATE PARK MOVEMENT TAKES SHAPE

ON A DAY in January 1921 about two hundred conservationists met in Des Moines, Iowa, at the invitation of Governor W. L. Harding of that state. The word *conservation* covers a multitude of social ideals, all of them good. Within that wide definition, these conferees from many states, cities, and towns were *preservationists*, concerned with the best use of any given piece of land, specifically when that best use, freed from all commercial employment, might mean the creation of state or other parks for the recreation of a population swiftly becoming urbanized and separated from that vitalizing contact with nature which had once been so easy and implicit in the national life.

In calling together this epoch-making group, the hand had been the hand of Esau; but the voice was the voice of Jacob. And Jacob, in this instance, was none other than the Director of National Parks, the tireless and inspired Stephen Tyng Mather.

Beyond his belief that the time had come when the states should begin to do on a political level what the nation was doing upon the heroic scale, Mather also had a problem. The national park concept had caught the public imagination—in one respect only too ardently. Yosemite, Glacier, Yellowstone, Grand Canyon—tourists had begun to move toward these wilderness treasures in greater and greater numbers, and with new means of locomotion. Within these glorious preserves, and upon their fringes, a burgeoning industry showed signs of becoming profitable—the entertainment of the traveler. Besides, the very possession, within its borders, of a *national* park, was a plume in the crest of any state. "Why can't *we* have a national park, too?" The director was being embarrassed with offers of new national parks that did not seem to him to have *national* significance, excellent as many of them were.

It is true that the borderline between national significance and state significance may sometimes be a shadowy one. Indeed, some state parks now luring millions of visitors are fully of national-park caliber. But there is no reason to change their status since they are amply protected, wisely administered, and accessible to the people of the whole country.

Finally, this matter of relative significance becomes one of governmental decision. The Congress votes a national park into being; a President may proclaim a national monument. Similarly, a state legislature may decide that one of its scenic, historic, or scientific places must be preserved because it is an outstanding expression of the natural or the human aspect of its own particular heritage.

From that January meeting emerged a movement toward the creation of *systems* of recreation areas within the states which would be comparable in purpose, in choice, in administration, and in resultant benefits to what on the national scale was the purpose and achievement of the National Park System.

The result was the creation of the National Conference on State Parks. The sentence announcing the purpose of this incorporated body was long and rather involved, so I have taken the liberty of breaking it up as follows:

> To urge upon our governments, local, county, state, and national, the acquisition of additional land and water areas suitable for recreation, for the study of natural history and its scientific aspects, and the preservation of wild life, as a form of the conservation of our natural resources;
>
> until there shall be public parks, forests and preserves within easy access of all the citizens of every state and territory of the United States;
>
> and also to encourage the interest of non-governmental agencies and individuals in acquiring, maintaining and dedicating for public uses similar areas;
>
> and in educating the citizens of the United States in the values and uses of recreational areas.

It was a large order. Only such impractical people as preservationists could indulge in what were, in 1921, such patently interstellar aspirations. But the meek and the visionary do seem somehow to inherit the earth, and finally to provide sanctuaries for those practical people who have fallen victims of their own success.

We must not jump to the erroneous conclusion that there had been no solid achievements in the development of state parks before this vital meeting in Des Moines. There had been fine and courageous thinking; there had been notable triumphs. As early as 1885, the dedication of Niagara Falls State Reservation signaled the rescue of a great national wonder from spoliation. The people of the state of New York, appropriating their own money, had already preserved much of the Adirondack and Catskill lands. The New Jersey–New York Palisades had been rescued from destruction by commercial exploitation and were on their way to become a great interstate park. There were other fine achievements.

But when Stephen Mather read the roster of existing state parks at Des Moines, there were twenty-nine states that had no parks at all. California (imagine it! a state that now has close to 180 areas of high quality) had only one. Also with but one park were Idaho, North Carolina, Kansas, Michigan, New Jersey, and Pennsylvania. There were seven in North Dakota, a state that had shown a commendable cultural interest in preserving some of its historic possessions. Iowa had four parks; there were five each in Ohio and Texas; and six each in Minnesota and Wisconsin. Under various administrative authorities, New York already had gone furthest, though as late as 1924 there were no parks on the east side of the Hudson; and in Long Island, now crisscrossed with parks and parkways, there were as yet but 200 acres of park, on Fire Island. Connecticut (ah, that fortunate state had Albert Turner and George Parker!) already had twenty-two parks, and though none was of great size, they preserved some of the quiet loveliness which was the original dowry of the little commonwealth.

Yes, something had been accomplished: in a few cases, the achievements had been very great. But there was need of (call it what you choose) a spur, a dramatization, a coherent drive instead of the here-and-there valiant efforts of idealists, a dynamic movement that would stir the grass roots and rise therefrom into the legislative bodies. Nobody at Des Moines contemplated miracles. The point was to get something underway. The National Conference on State Parks was the galvanic device.

THERE WERE MEN AND WOMEN OF VISION

There had not been a lack, the country over, of men and women who could look into the future and devote themselves, facing apathy and narrow self-interests—and the lack of popular grasp of the imperative need—to the acquisition of recreation sites while there was yet time. Sadly we look back upon that date, 1921, when for a pittance, or even by unchallenged entry and appropriation, long stretches of the seashore could have been preserved for public use; much virgin forest and stream and lake still remained undeflowered. But in the way stood the pioneer assumption that our national physical assets were inexhaustible!

These farseeing men said no; time was of the essence. Locke Craig in North Carolina said to his legislature: "The upper part of Mount Mitchell must be saved from lumbering." William E. Carson in Virginia, Percival Baxter in Maine, James Scrugham in Nevada, Peter Norbeck in South Dakota, Ellwood Chapman in Pennsylvania were pleading with refractory and doubting legislatures to initiate coherent park planning in their respective states; and sometimes, as in the case of Scrugham and Baxter, their efforts invited political chagrin.

There was Colonel Richard Lieber in Indiana, with a tart tongue and an impatience of stupidity that yet somehow never seemed to nullify his efforts; and the vigorous Lieber had younger men about him, like Charles Sauers, who later were to accomplish much in the recreation field. Congressman Kent in California was to spend his own funds in acquiring a precious and threatened stand of the coast redwood giants, near San Francisco. Henry Fairfield Osborn, John C. Merriam, and Madison Grant started the Save-the-Redwoods League, an infant hopeful, with a few dollars of contribution; it was to become one of the greatest agencies of preservation the world has ever known, and by the extension of its efforts into statewide acceptance, was to forward California's superb system of scenic, scientific, and historic parks, as well as the recreative beach areas that line its coast.

There was in Palisades Interstate Park the great engineer William Addams Welch, who not only saw the lands donated by Rockefeller, Harriman, and others on the outskirts of our greatest population center as a haven for the urban millions and the underprivileged, but was quite unabashed in his proposal that these millions should fully enjoy these unspoiled natural surroundings and should refreshen their minds and souls by contact with the animals, birds, flowers, and trees, even with the humblest forms of organic life. Welch did not wince at the word *education,* for he knew that gaining knowledge firsthand is not a chore but an adventure and a pleasant holiday. The result was Bear Mountain Museum and nature trails and the early efforts of Bill Carr in a kind of interpretation that would be unlabored and attractive to children and adults alike.

Many other names should be here, if only there were space in this hurried and foreshortened review—the Dean Coulters of Indiana, the Wilbur Nelsons of Tennessee, the Tom Wallaces of Kentucky, the Theodore Wirths of Minnesota—some of them mild and persistent, some capable of wielding a literary sledge when needed, as when Wallace, for example, standing nearly alone among a whole commonwealth of newspapers in his editorial pulpit of the Louisville *Times*, thundered like Jove in behalf of the threatened Cumberland Falls, day in, day out, until his voice was heard and obeyed.

Also not to be forgotten are those able men in the fields of landscape architecture and park planning. Frederick Law Olmsted, Jr., in his classic California State Park Surveys, laid down the principles which should guide that state, or any state, in determining the areas to be included in an ultimate, comprehensive park system. These principles are, briefly, that such areas should be sufficiently distinctive and notable to interest people from distant parts of a state in visiting them; that they contain scenic and recreation resources of a kind not likely to be preserved and made available under private ownership; that they be so geographically distributed as to comprise a wide and representative variety of types, a reasonable assortment of them accessible to people in each part of the state.

Many other landscape architects, appalled by the increasing ugliness of a fast-growing urbanization, also hailed the coming of the National Conference on State Parks and made fine contributions to the yearly meetings of the organization, usually held in later years within the boundaries of some outstanding state park, cross-country from Vermont to California. There were even some highway engineers who, thanks to the ripening of experience during the lifetime of the Conference, gave up the notion that nature should be fitted to the drawing board, instead of being delicately wooed and accommodated.

Steve Mather used to tell of a great sugar pine in California which was left standing but sliced away on its side for a third of its diameter because the alignment of a scenic roadway required it! But one has only to drive over the recently constructed parkways of New York to realize that the spirit both of the artist and of the naturalist has slowly made its way into the cold and mathematical blueprint.

DEFINITIONS WERE SOMEWHAT VAGUE

We look back and wonder what the talk was, during that memorable meeting in Des Moines. They had gathered there to set in motion a movement that would result in the development of a park system in every state. But what did each person present mean when he uttered the words "state park"? Curiously enough, owing to a misguided enthusiasm that became translated into a phrase, in its first days the Conference was saddled with the odd slogan: "A State Park Every Hundred Miles." Somebody has said that the notion originated with a Texas delegate who was dazzled by his reception of the new gospel. This enthusiast may have misinterpreted something that Stephen Mather had said to the assembly: "I believe we should have comfortable camps all over the country, so that the motorist could camp each night in a good scenic spot, preferably a state park. . . . I hope that some day the motorist will be able to round up his family each night on some kind of public land."

This was an end to aim for; it is now fast becoming a realization. But Mather had said *preferably* a state park, and it was obvious that he was thinking about the more scenic states of the country.

The salty Yankee who was such a moulding influence in the development of Connecticut state parks, Albert M. Turner, told at a Conference meeting at Clifty Falls in 1929 about his long association with George A. Parker, one of the three or four men in his state who prodded the legislature into creating a state park commission. But though the two men agreed in so many ways, Parker would many times say to Turner: "You can make a park *anywhere.*"

Turner would reply: "You *can't* make a state park *anywhere.*"

You *can.* You *can't.* How could two associated and able men have had such a polar difference of opinion? There could be but one explanation; they were not thinking of the same thing. *State park* must have represented to one a resting place for the people, an open-air haven for urban citizens, an uncommercialized spot where children of all ages could gambol and picnic and camp and stretch and grow in the light of the sun. This had long been a loud imperative for human health and happiness, and such a need for physical recreation grows beyond any contemporary supply.

But Turner saw much further than that. He was thinking along the same lines as Lieber. And the insistent Lieber was saying: "Our parks and preserves are not merely picnicking places. They are rich storehouses of memories and reveries. They are bearers of wonderful tales to him who will listen, a solace to the aged and an inspiration to the young. . . . A state park cannot be planned *until it is found.* . . . Speaking for myself, I would not be at all interested [in state park work] if the function of parks and recreation would merely be to provide shallow amusement for bored and boring people. Folks so disposed should be referred to bingo or any other of the abounding inanities."

I have remarked that Colonel Lieber had a sharp tongue. But don't misunderstand him; his bark was not a bite. He knew as well as any man that there was a crying need for places suitable for physical relaxation and simple romping. But he did not want *that* to be mistaken for the sole, or even the paramount, requirement.

Lieber was the author of the challenging remark that "state parks are meant to be the show windows of a state." But again, do not misconstrue him. *Show window* may suggest a merchandising dodge. Nothing was further from the mind of this great promoter of culture. So, remember that he had added quickly: "But, more than that, state parks are a dedication of the soul of the land. Without vision, a land would die. Without inspiration, we remain disconnected from the immortal order of all things. Our state parks preserve the sources of our inspiration."

One begins to see that, from the beginning, earnest men might be thinking of two very different things when they spoke of state parks. In one way, there was no harm in this. Both concepts were good, desirable, vital. But, in the Lieber sense, there could not be a state park every hundred miles. The sites just don't exist.

In New York there is Jones Beach—a boon beyond price to the citified millions—and there are Letchworth and the Adirondack parks; and in the last two you are conscious of the earth-mother and her children, and of the consummate beauties resulting from the way nature has employed her forces of change. In such places "indoor man comes for air and quiet; the athletically inclined for sport; teacher and preacher for inspiration and knowledge; the nature student for the museum and the wild." Gold is where you find it. The state park (in this conception) is where you find it—and *save* it for future generations, before it is obliterated.

DEFINITIONS OR NOT, THE VISITOR KNOWS

Not long ago, a friend of mine expressed the difference between these two types of recreation areas in a way I had never heard before. He said: "When I go to one of them, I know just what I am going to do. I want to fish, I want to swim, I want to boat, I want to bask on the sand; I know why I am there; there is no surprise. When I go to the other, it is sheer adventure. I don't know what may turn up, what I may see, what my feelings are going to be. I may have plans, but they are never followed. Nature overpowers me and makes me do things I never dreamed of—even, in the redwood forest, to utter a prayer of thanksgiving."

There is no reason for the pattern of a state park system to be perfectly parallel to that of the National Park System; nor, from the very nature of the governmental units, could it be so. Yet, in fundamentals, the concepts are not far apart. The National Park System does not emphasize the purely physical side of recreation, though the possibility of it is to be found naturally almost anywhere within its stewardships.

"The National Park Service has consistently maintained," says *A Study of the Park and Recreation Problem of the United States,* made in 1941, "that its dominant purpose has been the refreshment of mind and spirit; that the purpose could be accomplished with the utmost satisfaction only if the inspirational qualities of the areas it administers, whether based upon natural scenery or scientific, historic, or prehistoric values, were safeguarded to the utmost; and that provision of physical recreation was permissible only to the extent that it did not impair those qualities."

But this is only one side of the picture. There is not a single state, even among those which are not regarded as having *scenic* spots, as the average traveler understands the word, which can afford to be without its "show windows." Some will be more spectacular than others. That is not important. The possession by the people of, let us say, Kansas, of a preserve to which in all time schoolchildren and thoughtful adults may resort to see, in unspoiled natural condition, at least something of what their forefathers saw in bison days as the nation marched westward (with a little of everything that the land then bore)—this is what Colonel Lieber meant by a "show window." That is the cultural state park, spectacle or not. There is the educational asset (why should we fear that word?), the satisfaction of honest pride, the meditative opportunity for heart and soul. Could there be any use of land superior to this? If not, why require a multiplicity of purposes, when this one end is obvious?

The National Park Service itself periodically has to meet this threat of dilution. Its reply must always be categorical. Why talk of "multiple use" when the best use of the land has already been determined and accepted by the people?

All this, however interesting, does not bring us nearer to the answer to the question: What *is* a state park? Turner and Parker could not agree: they were not talking in exactly the same language. Perhaps if Richard Lieber had been referee he would have said to them, as he said later to a large audience: "Remember that we deal in two separate values: parks and recreation. Keep the promotion of the two separate in their own interest. Parks offer recreation of one kind, recreation centers of another. Recreation centers may be built wherever needed. Between the two stands the state recreation park, an area of lesser scenic value but of wider opportunity for sports and play."

I have gathered information in many thousands of miles of travel, during which I visited and studied many outstanding state parks; and my answer to the question, What is a state park? would be: A state park is any area of any size set aside for any type of recreation purpose, or as a historic memorial, or to preserve scenery or a natural curiosity, and *called* a state park. The reader is justified in retorting: "You are actually telling me nothing. You are merely announcing that a state park is a state park. I am not a dullard. I could have guessed that much."

But I shall take refuge in the fact that if you were to ask a state park director the same question, he would probably reply: "As a generalization, I can't tell you. I can tell you what the designation means in *my* state. I can tell you what I personally think of as a state park; that is to say, what my ideals are. I can't even promise you that you will find those ideals practiced in my own bailiwick. I'll have to refer to the statement of *Suggested Criteria for Evaluating Areas Proposed for Inclusion in State Park Systems*, adopted by the board of directors of the National Conference on State Parks at one of our sessions."

This statement, defining the objectives that state park executives wish to work toward, represents the policies of Colonel Richard Lieber as expressed in the light of present-day thought and conditions.

CLASSIFYING STATE PARK AREAS

For the purpose of this evaluation, which was the result of long and painstaking effort on the part of an able committee, the possible areas are placed in six classifications: parks, monuments, recreation areas, beaches, parkways, and waysides. As a criterion for selection, then, the answer to the question, What is a state park? is: "It is a relatively spacious area of outstanding scenic or wilderness character, oftentimes containing also significant historical, archeological, ecological, geological, and other scientific values, preserved as nearly as possible in their original or natural condition and providing opportunity for appropriate types of recreation where such will not destroy or impair the features and values to be preserved. Commercial exploitation of resources is prohibited.

"A state monument is an area usually limited in size, established primarily to preserve objects of historic and scientific interest, and places commemorating important persons or historic events. The only facilities usually provided are those required for the safety and comfort of the visitors such as access, parking, water, sanitation, interpretive devices, and sometimes facilities for picnicking and other recreation facilities.

"A state recreation area is one selected and developed primarily to provide non-urban outdoor recreation opportunities to meet other than purely local needs but having the best available scenic quality. Hunting and some other recreation activities not usually associated with state parks may be permitted. Commercial exploitation of resources is usually prohibited.

"State beaches are areas with frontage on the oceans, lakes, and streams designed primarily to provide swimming, boating, fishing, and other waterfront activities. Other coastal areas acquired primarily for their scenic and scientific values (such as Point Lobos Reserve in California) are included in the classification 'state parks.'

"State parkways are elongated or 'ribbon' parks featuring a motor road for non-commercial traffic, connecting parks, monuments, beaches, and recreation areas, or otherwise affording an opportunity for pleasant and safe driving. Access is controlled by the administering agency and is provided only at designated intervals, and roadside developments are controlled to prevent undesirable uses. As an adjunct to the motor road, appropriate facilities such as turnouts, picnic areas, and other recreation developments are frequently provided where space permits.

"Finally, state waysides. These are relatively small areas along highways selected for their scenic or historical significance and providing opportunity for the traveler to relax, enjoy a scenic view, read a historic marker, or have a picnic lunch. These areas should be administered by a highway department; however, the larger and more scenic waysides may sometimes be administered as units of state park systems."

Now, these are ideals, very nearly attained in some states, in others very far from fact. It must be remembered that the natural conditions not only differ but overlap; and in the end each state will be the judge of how far those ideals may be attained. A generalization can serve only to set a desirable mark to shoot at. The fact is that there are as many kinds of actual performance in the development of state parks as there are states involved. But there are principles to which all conform, or try to. With an exploding population, the greater emphasis will justly be on more and more recreation areas, as good as they can possibly be, but at least in increasing numbers. As "Cap" Sauers, the remarkable superintendent of the Forest Preserve District of Cook County, which encircles Chicago with its lifegiving air and sunlight, dryly said to me: "I used to be more of a 'purist' than I am now. Nowadays I'll take any reasonable offer of land and put it in my bank."

During its early years, the infant National Conference on State Parks was guided by two able executive secretaries—Miss Beatrice Ward (later Mrs. Wilbur A. Nelson) (1921-29) and Herbert Evison (1929-33). Then, in the depression days, when the Conference was faced with insufficient funds, it had the good fortune to make an arrangement with the American Planning and Civic Association by which the latter's secretariat would serve both organizations. This brought into the picture Miss Harlean James, whose devoted service extended through a long period of years. No matter how far she had to travel, alone or accompanied, there were no sessions of the Conference at which this energetic lady did not appear with her crisp and businesslike report.

HELPING HANDS TO THE STATES

Director Mather, when he initiated the Conference, had promised the co-operation of the National Park Service in a number of ways. There has not been a time since when directors of the federal agency were not ready with whatever degree of sympathetic and active assistance they could supply. Assistance; not interference. As Director Conrad L. Wirth stated in a talk at Little Rock in 1957: "It is axiomatic that the initiative, direction and guidance of the state park programs can be furnished only by the states themselves. The National Park Service is glad to assist in planning to the extent that it can, and *when asked to do so.*"

Enactment by the Congress in 1936 of the Park, Parkway, and Recreation-Area Study Act, on the recommendation of the National

Park Service, was another milestone in strengthening the relationship between the Service and the states. This legislation directs the Service to make a comprehensive study of the park and recreation-area programs of the United States to provide data that would be helpful in "developing a plan for coordinated and adequate public park, parkway, and recreation-area facilities for the people of the United States." It also authorizes the Service to furnish consultative and advisory assistance to the states and their political subdivisions.

In the late thirties, under authority of this Act, the Service assisted forty-six of the states and the Territory of Hawaii in developing a plan for statewide park and recreation areas. Thirty-seven of these plans—some quite preliminary in nature—had been completed at the time the work was suspended soon after our involvement in World War II. The 1941 report, *A Study of the Park and Recreation Problem of the United States,* was based to a considerable extent on the findings of the state studies.

Work on these co-operative studies with the states was resumed in 1956 as an important part of the Service's Mission 66 program. Since the establishment of the Outdoor Recreation Resources Review Commission in 1958, the Service co-operated closely with the Commission and made its planning data available to that group.*

A PUSH FROM CIRCUMSTANCE

Only a decade after the meeting at Des Moines, federal assistance was to give the development of state parks an impetus that neither Mr. Mather nor anyone else could have envisioned.

The high-flying economy of the middle and late 1920's in the United States came to an abrupt end and was succeeded by a tragic period that we now look back upon, perhaps too dimly, as the depression. After a blithe interval during which the present and the future were enjoyed simultaneously, the technological machine had stopped on dead center. It was calamitous for the whole population, but perhaps the hardest hit were the young people who emerged from primary and secondary schools to find the employment gate padlocked.

* Following issuance in January 1962 of the Commission's report, *Outdoor Recreation for America,* a Bureau of Outdoor Recreation was established in the Department of Interior to implement one of the Commission's major recommendations. A number of functions relating to co-operation with other Federal, state, and local agencies, as authorized by the 1936 Act, have been transferred to the new Bureau.

NORTH PLATTE COLLEGE LIBRARY
NORTH PLATTE, NEBRASKA

The national emergency was met through the use of the federal powers of spending on a scale such as no country had ever known. The "alphabetical" agencies incidental to general relief—WPA, CWA, PWA, FERA, and the like—are now only vaguely remembered except by those who were associated with them; and more than a whole generation has come to maturity since those buzzing times. The CCC (Civilian Conservation Corps) is most vividly recollected, since its activities penetrated most deeply into family life. At its peak, there were 2,635 CCC camps operating on projects in the United States, 561 of which were assigned to national, state, and local parks. As hundreds of millions of dollars were poured into the field of conservation, it was fortunate that, in the National Park Service, there was already at hand an organization admirably suited in skill and experience, though not staffed for such a burden, to direct the efforts into channels that would secure lasting benefits.

Whoever said that "in ten years of the CCC there was performed park-conservation work that would have taken fifty years under ordinary conditions" was employing very moderate language. In truth, without this impetus some of the states would have had little recreation acreage in the present century.

Conrad L. Wirth, later to become director of the National Park Service, was assistant director (Branch of Planning) under Arno B. Cammerer when the emergency projects began to call for the talents of that organization. He subsequently became Department of the Interior representative on the Advisory Council of the CCC. From the very nature of his experience in the greatest of park systems, he was able to see the job as one that went far beyond "taking the boys out of the streets." He felt that it was a golden opportunity to bring before the people of the country the need for and the value of a sound and active conservation program. He was also aware of the fact, so well demonstrated among the career people of the National Park Service, that the very nature of conservation work, and the contact with nature it affords, lifts the individual beyond the normal daily round of chores. To Wirth, then, this was not merely a relief program, but a program of conservation and preservation.

Of the vast sums expended through the National Park Service, the greatest proportion went to nonfederal park development—that is, to the state, county, and metropolitan park agencies. Virginia is a typical example of the assistance rendered states toward the achievement of a park system. In 1933 this state had only one state park. Through the aid of the CCC, by the middle of 1942 eleven areas

25592

had been developed; these were well distributed geographically from coastline to mountains, with a total acreage of nearly 20,000. Road systems, water supply, power lines, and necessary structures had been provided in six principal areas. There were now three dams for recreation purposes, with bathhouses and beach facilities. And, in that year of 1942, nearly half a million people visited the eleven parks.

As today one visits the parks in states where the CCC made its contribution, it is truly astonishing to see how skillfully the program was planned and executed. Walking the fine trails, perhaps accompanied by a park employee, you learn that "this was laid out in CCC days." The cabins built at that time are nearly all still in use; so are thousands of other structures. There were mistakes, naturally; some things didn't materialize as envisaged in the rapid thinking of the times. The marvel is that so much of it is functioning today; and one may add soberly that, if it were not, there would be in many cases a distinct lack of facilities for the public.

For it must be said that just as the Great Depression was not an unmixed evil—as a result of it much conservation work was accomplished which otherwise would have remained in the imagination of enthusiasts—so the great and sudden advances in state park development were not an unmixed good. Some of the states, true, have gone ahead nobly under their own steam. In others, there are unmistakable signs that, whatever competent park directors and the general public might think, legislatures have done little on their own.

There was never any defined contract that the states would take up the burden where the federal relief work left off. But the *Study of the Park and Recreation Problem of the United States* delicately hinted at a reasonable amount of self-help in the states when it remarked: "The possession of such physical facilities . . . entails public responsibility for their proper maintenance. . . . The states and local communities were expected to assure such financial support."

Even, for example, in North Carolina—a state with a well-conceived and ably managed park system—I find its director saying in 1952 that "had it not been for these federal agencies the development of the North Carolina state parks would now be little better than it was when Mount Mitchell was established 37 years ago."

(II)

WAYS AND MEANS TOWARD RECREATION

CURRENTLY, and belatedly, the promoters of adequate facilities for human recreation are enjoying what publicity people call "a good press." The city editor and the periodical publisher are at last finding the subject a matter of news. We now are asked to view with concern the fact of a megalopolis that stretches from Portland, Maine, to Norfolk, Virginia—a linear city, as it is sometimes called—either devoted to commercial ends or pre-empted by cottage owners who were fortunate and clever enough to find themselves on a front of sea and sand. However, the family that craves a day at the seashore now finds itself cut off from it. Similarly, the lake and river fronts within reach of an increasing population have been exploited, cut into front-foot real estate speculations, and occupied. A quiet haven in natural and beautiful surroundings is now more desirable than ever.

The patient and persistent preservationists who have labored so long in the recreation field might now say triumphantly: "We told you so. For fifty years we have been saying that this is precisely what the country was headed for. But when we asked that the public be informed, an editorial eyebrow was raised and the comment made: 'This is very interesting, very. But it is something for the conservation publications. It lacks reader appeal. Besides, to tell the truth, aren't you exaggerating a little?' "

Well, no matter. The preservationists are not saying this. They are cheered by the fact that at last recreation is "news." For, in spite of the great advances in the acquisition and management of state parks, the movement has not at any time been on quite a sound basis, except possibly in a handful of states. John D. Rockefeller, Jr., when making contributions to the cause of conservation, wisely offered to match funds, either with the government or with other donors. He wished, as he said, to "broaden the base." For the spread of understanding, he realized, ten contributions of a thousand dollars each are better than a single gift of ten thousand.

The number of state parks which have originated in gifts of land or money is remarkable. All to the good, of course. But for the security of the program it is better that parks originate through public demand and understanding, through the appropriation of taxpayers' money. Therefore, the preservationist sees, in the present surge of recreation publicity, a rift in a clouded sky.

WHAT KIND OF RECREATION?

This brings us directly to the question, What *is* recreation? A great deal of effort has been expended in the attempt to find a satisfactory definition of the word *recreation.* But this word is understood by so many different people in so many different ways that it has become an abstraction, like *truth, justice, love, beauty.*

One thoughtful writer defines recreation as "the pleasurable and constructive use of leisure time." But that won't do. Recreation is not necessarily either pleasurable or constructive; it may be utterly disappointing or destructive. What the writer meant was that *ideally* it would be pleasurable and constructive. That is not a definition but a hope.

Someone else refers to it as the "creative" use of leisure. But this definition requires another definition, and so ad infinitum. If you say that recreation "is any use of leisure with the *expectation* of enjoyment," you will be nearer the truth, though this definition is also to some extent unsatisfactory.

Leisure must then be defined. Somebody has labored with this mountain and emerged with a large mouse—but a mouse nevertheless. "Leisure is that segment of time in the life of any individual, separate and apart from the time spent as necessary for his personal care, sleep and securing the necessities of life for himself and those dependent upon him and the accumulation of surplus wealth." There is a mouthful for you! Let's just say that leisure is the time people have when they are not sleeping or working.

But the truth is that *recreation* is one of those words you need not define. Just as the French child learns gender by hearing his mother or his nurse *use* gender, so people approximate a knowledge of this word by experience and association. I will gladly dispense with definitions in exchange for more good public reserves where the thing itself may be found. Whether it will prove creative, constructive, or enjoyable will be in the lap of the gods, who provide the mood, the weather, the capacity, and everything else.

Indeed, if after reading the descriptions of outstanding state parks which are given in this book, the reader does not know fairly clearly the almost infinite variety of forms that recreation can take, then no definition would help him.

Since this book is being written to present a picture of the park reserves the states now possess, to show the variety in their conception and administration, and to consider the problems and dangers that beset them, rather than to look into the future, the discussion of the crisis the American people must meet will here be brief. But crisis it is—make no mistake about that. If the opportunities for recreation that knits up the raveled sleeve of a care incident to a leaping technology should not prove equal to the minimum demand, we face vast social and psychic unrest. All contemporary thinkers are agreed on that.

You do not have to adopt the extreme pessimism of Friedrich Georg Juenger (*The Failure of Technology*) to view with some apprehension the effect of the machine upon the man, and even the effect of the machine upon natural resources from which man's life must derive. Juenger sees it as a sort of devil's dance in which the technologist has become a hapless victim of his own successes; and the machine, "a hungry and pitiless consumer" instead of a producing agent, has abolished the equilibrium between man's work and his leisure, and between man and nature.

You don't have to go that far. But if you consider that Stanley Coulter was saying back in 1925 that "we live in a swiftly moving age, fiercely driven by the machines we have invented—more rapidly than we have developed the power to use them wisely"—and then add thirty-five years of remarkable technical discovery to that, with no commensurate education in the use of the resultant leisure time, you must have at least some sense of alarm. Perhaps our "purist" park enthusiasts were not altogether wrong, after all, in proclaiming that areas of mere physical recreation, however valuable, would not be enough: that only contact with a natural, tranquil scene can truly heal.

In brief, it is estimated that there will be twice as many people in the United States in the year 2000—no distant period—as there were in 1950. People will have much more money to spend, perhaps twice as much in 2000 as in 1950. The work week of 2000 is estimated at about 28 or 30 hours. We can assume that people will then travel many thousands of miles a year. "We don't *know* that these estimates will be exactly as projected," says Marion Clawson in his well-studied paper on *The Crisis in Outdoor Recreation*, published in 1959, "but we can be sure that all the above four forces are pushing in the same direction."

DONATIONS AND PUBLIC MONEY

As we have seen, many of the existing state parks originated as a result of generous donations from private persons and sometimes from corporations. Of the first sixty-four Michigan parks, fifty-nine were started by means of such gifts. The fourteen state-owned areas that fan around the city of Detroit for a radius of fifty miles came to the people from the Dodge brothers and from Howard Bloomer, and even the facilities in most of them were provided by the donors. In New York, the most notable contributions from families of great wealth were in the neighborhood of the metropolis—for the Palisades Interstate Park and the great outdoors tapped by its parkway. The superb chain of recreation places along the Taconic State Parkway was partly acquired through such donations, though these were greatly amplified by purchases out of legislative appropriations. In Iowa, many of the state parks were gifts, as were also some of the finest in Washington, Wisconsin, and Minnesota. The Indiana system, particularly in the Dunes, where the donations were so fortunately timed, benefited greatly from private contributions. The matching of state funds with equal amounts of private money made possible the salvaging of the incomparable stands of redwoods and of other California treasures that now rival even the jewels of the National Park System itself.

In addition, the states have acquired parks through bond issues, by exchange of school lands for equivalent acreages of the national forests, through direct and specific legislative appropriations and transfers from the federal government, by special tax levy; also by such means as the increment from fish and game revenues. This does not exhaust the roster of means used to establish parks but will indicate their variety.

No doubt the only answer to the question, What is the best way to acquire state parks? would be still, as it was in the past: Any way possible, where the quality of the areas indicate that they should be acquired. However, the comment of Beatrice Ward Nelson in her book of reference on *State Recreation,* published by the National Conference on State Parks in 1928, would seem still to be valid. In summing up the means by which state parks had come into being, she said:

> This is the only major activity that has consistently accepted gifts of money for carrying on a state function. In a way, this has hindered the establishment of recreation as a definitely recognized function of state government, since many states seem to look upon the provision of recreational opportunities as a semi-governmental activity which they are *willing to supervise.*

In other words, private donation is too narrow a base. The creation of a state park system is more soundly grounded on what the people of the grass roots have demanded and got through the use of their own moneys, which therefore they will the more zealously guard. States like New York and California and some others, have made considerable contributions of their own. They accept gratefully the donations given them, but without sparing their own efforts. But Texas may be taken as an example of what can happen when enthusiasm for a state park system is not coupled with a well-developed plan. Partly as a result of Steve Mather's Des Moines Conference in 1921, Texas became fired with the idea of state parks. A newly formed State Parks Board toured the state spreading the gospel and as the result of its charm and persuasiveness secured gifts of fifty-one areas for parks. But most of these areas had to be returned to the owners; they were not by any measure suitable for state parks.

FINANCING THROUGH BOND ISSUES

The matter of acquisition brings us to financing through issuance of bonds. Financing of the modern state park systems in California and New York was originally initiated with funds derived from bond issues. A number of other states are now resorting to bond issues to meet the growing crisis.

New York pioneered this trend when in 1960 its voters ratified overwhelmingly a $75 million bond issue for the acquisition of park and recreation lands. This issue had been promoted with a "now or never" slogan. Of the total amount, $35 million was earmarked for state purposes, including $20 million for state parks. And $40 million was designated for grants to state and local agencies on a matching basis, 75 per cent given by the state and 25 per cent by local governments. In the same year, Kentucky voters ratified a $100 million bond issue, $10 million of which is for the establishment and development of state parks.

The New Jersey Green Acres Bond Act of 1961 authorizes a $60 million bonding program for recreation and conservation lands and for assistance to the state's political subdivisions on a 50 per cent matching basis. In the same year, New Hampshire authorized a $10 million bond issue to acquire new state parks and to enlarge existing ones. It is interesting to note, too, that Wisconsin in 1961 authorized a $50 million ten-year program for the development of outdoor recreation and resources, including $33 million for state parks and forests.

In 1962 the New York legislature passed a supplemental $25 million bond issue, which will be placed before the voters for ratification at the next election. In Pennsylvania the legislature overwhelmingly passed a $70 million bond issue for acquisition of park and recreation lands, including matching grants to local governments; it will be effective when passed again by the next legislature and ratified by the voters. The same year, a $150 million bond issue was passed by the California legislature for the purpose of acquiring and developing recreation lands and providing matching grants to local governments; however, ratification failed by some 100,000 votes. Further action is being considered.

In recent years the use of revenue bonds has been tried out in a number of the states. True, this program is aimed at the development of facilities within existing state parks rather than the acquisition of new and desirable areas. But it has been so widely discussed that the National Conference on State Parks asked the National Park Service to make a study and prepare a report for the guidance of the states that were considering the issuance of such bonds. Such a study and report have been made by Ernest E. Allen, of the Regional Office in Santa Fe, New Mexico. There could not have been a better choice, since Allen was director of Oklahoma state parks at the time such bonds were pioneered and sold in that state.

Allen finds that such revenue bonds, which necessarily serve to finance only a part of the over-all state park program, have both advantages and disadvantages. My impression is that Allen feels that the disadvantages tend to outweigh the benefits—though the study is impartial and proceeds on the assumption that what would be good for one state might be harmful for another. The report indicates that such financing furnishes the means for a rapid development that otherwise might be long delayed. The cost of facilities so obtained would be borne by the visitors who use them. They do "tend to upgrade the local economy, increase the scope of the park program and the responsibilities of the state park agency."

The fear is that a psychology of great and sudden wealth may result from the bond sale. The number of visitors may not have reached the point where expensive developments can pay out. The director and his staff may find themselves in a position subservient to the operation of the facilities. Most important of all, the original purpose for which the park was established may be relegated to the background in the pressure to meet payments of capital and interest.

So far, eight states (Kentucky, Louisiana, Michigan, Minnesota, Oklahoma, South Carolina, Virginia, and West Virginia) have issued such revenue bonds. Three other states have authorized such issues but have not proceeded further. At the present time, on the basis of the returns, it may be added that bond-investment firms do not yet regard such financing as a prime investment risk.

SHOULD STATE PARKS BE SELF-SUPPORTING?

When Richard Lieber was developing the Indiana state parks, he said on many occasions that such areas should be self-supporting. Later, judging from his public talks, he modified his views to "as nearly self-supporting as possible, or else the cost will have to be put on the tax duplicate." To quarrel with anything Lieber has said upon the subject of state parks requires temerity; yet I cannot conceive that state parks, viewed as whole systems, could ever pay their own way; or that they should be expected to do so. True, Colonel Lieber had in mind mainly Indiana parks, which are virtually self-supporting. And at the time the inflationary surge had not yet gotten underway. Admissions to his parks were ten cents a head, reflecting consumer prices that we shall not see again. Metropolitan newspapers were one or two cents a copy, and the subways and electric cars were hauling passengers long distances for five cents.

There are ways, of course, in which a particular state park could pay its way, or even turn a profit. The states could operate amusement spots, more sanitary and on a higher plane than the privately operated ones, and make them profitable. But the states were never considered by park-minded people to be properly in such business. If anyone wishes to know to what extent the state parks the country over are actually self-supporting, he can obtain an approximate idea from *State Park Statistics*, compiled by the National Park Service. In 1961 the total cost of operating and maintaining the state parks amounted to nearly $61 million; revenues received from operations (accruing from facilities, concessions, entrance and parking fees, and so on) exceeded $23 million. This indicates self-support of about 38 per cent.

In some states there are no entrance or parking fees. In others, there are parking fees only. No charge, or a reasonable charge, is made for camping, picnicking, or other uses.

In New Hampshire—fortunately this is almost the only instance of it—successive legislatures have insisted that the state parks "pay their way." Nature provided this state with some of the most thrilling and satisfying scenery in the country; it has never been a problem to find suitable natural areas that measure up to the most exacting criteria of the ideal state park. Yet, the insistence upon self-support has forced a director of ability and discrimination to resort to "attractions" that are obviously incompatible with the grandeur of the parks.

To be fair, however, the reasons for this situation should be mentioned. New Hampshire was in the tourist business long before state parks were conceived. The same geological changes that made it, except for pockets of alluvium, a hardscrabble agricultural region endowed it with a beauty and significance that enabled it to count on income from visitors as a regular means of livelihood. Natives, or old-time visitors, bequeathed beauty spots for preservation. Therefore, the feeling for state parks based upon cultural values, population needs, or pride in saving from delapidation the finest of its natural scenery for posterity, remained mostly in the imaginations of a few idealists. At the moment of writing, a federal interstate highway, wide and fast, is projected to traverse the world-famous Franconia Notch; it will impair the qualities of one of the world's best-known scenic sites. The federal authorities are not to be blamed for this situation. They were willing to accept whatever route the state proposed. The preservationists were appalled, but they are few in number. "It would be good for the tourist business" ended the discussion.

THE TOURIST AND HIS MONEY

This brings us to a consideration of the "tourist industry," as it has come to be called, and its relation to the conception and development of state parks as social instruments for the mental and physical health, enjoyment, education, and spiritual well-being of the people of the states. How does the tourist industry affect the states, and how do such travelers affect the whole nation?

Charles Sauers, in his forceful talk, *The Order of Parks,* delivered at a meeting of the National Conference at Lake Hope State Park, Ohio, remarked that "neither state nor national parks are in the tourist business." In the sense "Cap" Sauers had in mind, he was absolutely right. You see what he meant when you read his next words: "Rather, they are responsible for properties that are a great cultural factor essential to the well-being of all of us." But in a different sense, both the national and the state parks *are* in the tourist trade, whether they want to be or not.

When Kenneth Chorley, as president of Colonial Williamsburg, thought it worthwhile to journey to Little Rock and talk to the National Association of Travel Organizations, he was acknowledging the fact that John D. Rockefeller, Jr.'s great restoration of a colonial capital—a venture motivated solely by cultural aspirations—is in one sense decidedly in the tourist trade. Colonial Williamsburg operates at an annual deficit of three quarters of a million dollars—an amount which, if appropriated for state parks in some states, would make the director reel as though intoxicated—and Rockefeller intended that his venture should have a deficit. But Colonial Williamsburg, as Chorley told his audience, "is a proof that *history can be sold,*" whereas "I understand that there are some people in the travel industry who believe that the public will buy only sun, sex, and sports." (State park directors who vainly try to make their legislatures believe that there is more to be derived from a state park than physical exercise might quote that succinct remark of Chorley's.)

The sweetness and healing qualities of wilderness places can be *sold,* too. (I don't quite like this use of the word. But it is applicable.) They can't be had unless people get to them; and the means of getting there, of eating and sleeping, of moving around and getting home—this is the travel industry in operation.

Colonial Williamsburg, however, was not restored with the slightest intent that it benefit the travel industry. The Library of Congress, the New York Public Library, and other similar repositories of printed contributions to learning were not projected with any idea of improving the fortunes of booksellers and publishers. The American Museum of Natural History and the Smithsonian Institution were not founded to promote travel. We are looking at an effect, and a beneficial one; not at a purpose.

Admittedly, when the acquisition of a desirable recreation area comes before a legislative body, the park director will use almost any persuasion to further the appropriation. Incidentally, he cannot be blamed for looking with a slight squint at volunteers, like myself, who are ready with ethical principles and advice. In most cases he knows all that the volunteer knows, and much more. And he faces reality when he comes to his desk every Monday morning. He has his ideals, but he knows that the acquisition of a new area will take that land out of the range of taxation; that there are private interests which will voice objections to the creation of a state-owned site that seems to impinge upon commercial interests. Hence, when the question arises whether such an establishment will bring in tourist money, he is prepared, with perfect honesty, to show that it will. It always has: presumably it will do so this time, too.

The fact remains, however, that the state parks are not established as tourist attractions. And it is unfortunate, though apparently often necessary, to becloud the issue at a time when the need for recreation opportunities has become imperative for sounder reasons.

WHAT STATE PARKS ARE FOR

What purposes do state parks serve? First, the salvation of the last-remaining spots of beauty and scientific and historic meaning, which should be preserved for posterity and put to the highest possible recreation use. These need not be places of transcendent loveliness—the scenery of "Oh" and "Ah" quality. Years ago the landscape architect Harold Caparn advised: "State parks should not necessarily be confined to the rare and most beautiful scenery. They might with great advantage also preserve examples of the average or characteristic scenery of each state." Or they may be areas of beauty and significance, though not in the highest degree, which also offer opportunities for physical recreation to the inhabitants of nearby centers of population. Hillsborough River State Park in Florida is an example of such a combination. It lacks the superb natural qualities of the state's Highlands Hammock and Myakka River state parks, but it offers beauty, and nooks of repose and study.

Second, the preservation of clean, readily accessible, enjoyable beaches and lake shores and life-giving woodlands such as, for instance, the Long Island State Park Commission has been so actively developing for the crammed millions of New York City and neighboring urban centers.

Finally—to reduce the types of recreation areas to a mere three—the preservation of places of historical importance in the life and march of the state's story; and often acreage is available nearby to afford picnicking and hiking facilities. For hardly less important than the saving of the historic scene itself is the maintenance, unspoiled, of its surroundings.

These are good reasons for preserving and maintaining sites for recreation of all kinds; and no other reasons are needed. The emphasis on the tourist trade is evidence of our having mistaken the part for the whole, a frailty which Ralph Waldo Emerson declared to be possibly the greatest of all human errors. If public understanding of the necessity for a greatly enlarged program of state recreation facilities is a basic requisite of their acquisition, any purely commercial occultation of the primary purposes is harmful.

"Every tourist is worth a bale of cotton, and he is twice as easy to pick," said somebody at a meeting in a southern state, when the talk was of the need for parks. We need not take too gloomy a view of this statement, which in print has a rawness that may not have been intended in a half-jesting afterdinner talk. The decision—to rate the tourist as superior to a bale of cotton—is not an irrevocable one, anyway. If at some future time the tourist should wear out through overuse, it will always be possible to return with the same hearty handshake of hospitality and welcome to the cotton bale.

Tourists seek change, rest, escape from deadening technology, active and passive play and fun, a chance to forget themselves—any of a thousand things, *not excluding,* as has been so beautifully said, "a deepening of their experience, a renewal of their acquaintance with the roots of their institutions, and occasionally to encounter those rare moments of understanding and insight that regenerate our strength." And for whom are the state parks intended? Is it true that, just as the national parks are for the whole people of the nation, the state parks are for the people of the state, the county parks primarily for those of the county, and so on, down through the units of the government? If this is not altogether so, it is not very nearly an acceptable view? The director of state parks and his chief engineer in one of our greater states have both affirmed to me in the bluntest terms: "Our parks are for the people of this state. Visitors from other states are welcome, of course. We like to have them come. They spend money here, which is fine. But our parks are aimed at the needs of our own millions."

In what I have said of the tourist industry, I hope not to be mistaken. The cart should not get ahead of the horse; the animal should do the pulling. And there are some good brains in the tourist and travel business. The best audience I ever had was the Virginia Travel Council, to whom I was asked to speak while I was working on a study of the philosophy of interpretation as carried out in parks, museums, and the like. I feared that such a subject might not be as vital to a group that was confessedly commercial as it was to me. Not so. They knew that whatever is best for the parks, whatever affords the tourist the finest experience during his visit, is also beneficial to them. The travel business, they realized, is a result, not a cause.

MANY OPERATING AGENCIES

The state park movement has had, because of the nature of its short life and the complex forces involved, a Topsy-like growth. It has responded to whatever nutritives were available. Hence, the student of park administration finds himself involved with a maze of agencies, known by diverse names, often with limited powers, and curbed by competition. On the whole, the central authority represents conservation in its most general application.

This authority may be a department of conservation, a department of natural resources, a state park and recreation board, a state park and forest commission, a board of land commissioners, a forestry, fish, and game commission; or it may be known by some other designation. In New York, under a Conservation Department, the Division of Parks is such a bewildering aggregation of subordinate agencies that at first glance it would appear hopelessly chaotic. Yet the various state park commissions, under a strong Council of Parks, have performed admirably. The quality and devotion of the people involved, combined with a powerful overseeing hand and mind, have resulted in the phenomenal growth of the New York system. But the setup could hardly be recommended for any other state, even by those who have seen it prosper in New York.

The defect of subordinate park direction is readily apparent when the chief of the general conservation department, though a high-minded and excellent public servant, is not receptive to the concept of the preservation of land for park use because that is the one best use of such land. He sees forests not as an unspoiled haven but as an economic asset to be judiciously managed—and "let people enjoy them at the same time." Good forestry; but he is not thinking of *parks*.

"Department of Game, Fish, and Parks," as a designation, sounds appropriate; but what is the local concept of *parks*? "Division of State Parks and Recreation" tells a story, but you must visit the state to discover what is meant by *recreation* and what by a *park*. I am not quarreling with words, but showing how impossible it is to make a generalization that will not become an absurdity across the state line.

HISTORICAL PARKS

Almost, if not equally, important to the states is the preservation of scenes of historic events and of memorials to great men and women. (The naturalist would say *almost* and the historian would say, probably, *more*.) This includes, of course, the remains of the life and work of prehistoric dwellers upon our continent. The question commonly arises: Should the agency responsible for the administration of recreation areas also administer the historic monuments?

In most of the states, a single agency administers both parks and historic sites. This arrangement has certain advantages since many problems are common to both types of areas, for example, land acquisition, construction of facilities, protection, maintenance, interpretation, and public relations. It also permits employment of a wider range of technical personnel, makes possible the application of coordinated policies and practices designed to preserve and make available to the public the state's natural and cultural resources, and provides a broader base of public support.

There are a few notable exceptions. In Colorado, the historic sites are administered by the State Historical Society of Colorado; in New Mexico, by the Museum of New Mexico; in New York, by the Division of Archives and History of the Education Department; in Ohio, by the Ohio Historical Society; in Wyoming, by the State Archives and Historical Department; and most of those in North Carolina, by the Historic Sites Division of the State Department of Archives and History. Certain advantages also can be cited for this arrangement. For instance, the staff may concentrate its attention on a narrower field of specilized activity and its energies then are not diffused. Moreover, this arrangement avoids the possibility that the historic sites may become subservient to parks, or vice versa.

In at least seven of the states, the park agency administers some of the historic sites, and one or more separate historical agencies administer the others.

The National Park Service is charged with the administration both of natural and scientific and of historical areas. But the great national system, with its complex organization, does not offer a good comparison. Here again only the test of years of experience will give the answers. "Do you think," asked the manager of a state historical area of me one day, "that the historic properties should be operated by the same agency as the parks?" I dodged politely: "Well, of course my experience has been pretty much confined to the National Park Service." This didn't fool the lady. "You don't want to answer my question," she said. "All right. But I can tell you that in my state the park board has no interest in history. I can't get any money to operate properly." What could I say, except to comment feebly that what might prove successful in one state might not be suitable to another state?

(III)

PRINCIPLES, POLICIES, AND PROBLEMS

THE STATE PARKS, like the national parks, are never free from threats of adverse uses that would destroy, or at least impair, the very qualities which led to their preservation for recreation purposes. Not less so; rather, the state parks, except in rare cases, are much more vulnerable to attack. The national parks have behind them a great body of ardent conservationists, coast to coast, who on many occasions have set off an explosion that reverberated in the national capitol. There is no such solidarity in the defense of state areas. Resistance must come almost wholly from protectors within the commonwealth itself. Outside its borders, friendly forces shake their heads and commiserate, but they add: "After all, it's the affair of the folks over there."

When commercial interests—or even apparently benevolent promoters—want to make their way into a preserve setup the one best use of which had been determined to be human recreation, they employ some interesting devices. The hardest to combat is smoggery.

Smoggery is the artful ruse of diverting attention from the point at issue to an entirely unrelated proposition by means of an inky cloud. The squid and cuttlefish adopt somewhat the same plan of defense. But their purpose is to escape. The aim of the smoggist is to remain, and to retain control of the argument. Let us see how this verbal trick is worked.

We start with a simple instance. You say children should be taught discipline. Your opponent, whatever his reason for opposing you, replies, in accents of shocked morality: "Ah, then, you don't like children." You are now on the defensive; smoggery has risen around you like a sticky haze. To attempt to achieve an intelligent debate along such lines will find you floundering in meaningless babble. You have been smogged.

A similar psychological device is used in advertising. The price is \$49.95, just five cents less than \$50. But what you see is the figure 4. This suggests forty, not fifty. That this trick is in constant use would seem to imply that people like to be taken for imbeciles. But that is not the point. To use an example in the park field: when Tom Wallace, in Kentucky, was heroically trying to save the beautiful Cumberland Falls from destruction by the power interests, smoggery moved in. "Then you are *against having Kentucky prosperous, Mr. Wallace.*" Tom now faced an issue that was not even remotely related to anything he had said.

A university wishes to invade the priceless Cook County Forest Preserve. "Cap" Sauers says: "No, that is not what this preserve is intended for." "Ah, then, Mr. Sauers, you *don't* believe in college education."

In World War II an attempt was made to raid the virgin forests of Olympic National Park for Sitka spruce, to be used, I believe, in airplane construction. Certain lumbering interests on the West Coast thought this a very good idea, since any invasion of the park would set a precedent for further exploitation. The director of the National Park Service demurred in strong terms. If the survival of the nation depended on this, very well. But this fact must be proven. And it was not proven; suitable wood was found elsewhere. But when the director first objected to the proposal, he was smogged: "Ah, Mr. Drury, so you are *not in favor of winning the war!*" It happened that the director had been in the advertising business and knew the trick well. He just ignored the verbal shift and reiterated his original statement till the cloud blew away.

Not all the adverse threats come from commercial interests, however. After Director Drury left Washington and returned to his native state to become park director there, smoggery on one occasion emerged from an unexpected source. It was proposed that a school building be erected in one of the choicest state park areas. Drury in this painful situation—because some of his good conservationist friends were among the promoters of the plan*—may have recalled what Frederick Law Olmsted said, back in 1895, at a hearing on a proposal to erect a cultural building in New York City's Central Park.

"Mr. Olmsted, are not fine buildings, statues, monuments, great additions to a park?"

* "My friends are legion," said the wise Aly ben Hassan, "and my heart is overflowing with affection for them; but what a pity it is that so few of them ever understood what I was trying to do."

"Nay, they are deductions from it."

"Do they not add greatly to the value of Central Park?"

"Nay, they take much from its value as a park. They would be worth more to the city if they were elsewhere."

The school building was not erected in the California park. The courts backed the director. "But, Mr. Drury, we never thought you would be *against education*," lamented a smoggist.

The unimaginative highway engineer makes plans for a fine new road. Unfortunately, the route he designs goes through a park or other sanctuary. He regrets this, but of course you want highways, don't you? Or are you *against* fine highways?

Or, you state your opinion that, except under the most exceptional conditions, which must be determined by expert nonpartisans, there should be no hunting in state parks. See how quickly smoggistical adeptness shifts the point at issue. "So you don't wish people to get out in the open air and indulge in the sport of their pioneer ancestors, eh?"

It is awkward, in a time of "cold war," to say anything that might seem to reflect on the wisdom of any measures taken by the nation's armed forces. Congressmen occasionally make comments that imply less than complete belief in military omniscience, but they have a degree of immunity from the smoggistical retort: "Then you want to see the Communists take over the country, do you?" If the existence of the free world depends upon locating an airstrip where it will render almost useless a state park that has given recreation to millions of people, then this fact, proved, cannot be gainsaid. Too bad for the park. If stark national necessity demands the sacrifice of the Wichita Mountains National Wildlife Refuge, set aside by President Theodore Roosevelt in 1905 and said by qualified judges to be not only precious historic ground but also a remarkably fine recreation resort—if this land is required as an artillery range or else the country will be defenseless against enemies, then so be it. But it is only fair to ask whether this is indeed so.*

On the credit side may be listed the honest and intelligent efforts of the Navy to deal with the problem of the Laysan albatrosses of

* Great Britain has her invaders of preserves, too. In the early days of World War I the British Airboard tried to requisition the British Museum for headquarters and had actually begun to clean out the treasured collections of that hallowed institution. Sir Arthur Evans and others raised such a tempest of speeches and letters to the press about "this monstrous proposal" that the Airboard quickly discovered that "it did not need the building after all."

Midway Island. They are a danger to aircraft, and aircraft are often fatal to them. Yet the birds have refused to accept any other home. The Navy will have made an effort, however, and apparently has not resorted to smoggery.

No form of invasion could be more prejudical to a state park set aside to afford tranquillity in association with wilderness than the exploitation of its mineral wealth, actual or fancied. Evidences of prehistoric or pioneer workings within the area may be of great interest to the visitor and offer the chance of valuable interpretation. But an operating mining venture—with the necessary rough buildings, the defacement of landscape, the inevitable dust and smoke and tailing dumps, to say nothing of the proximity of a smelter with fumes fatal to vegetation—is a thrust at the very heart of a primary purpose. "Then you are against providing pay-envelopes for workmen?" In a later chapter we shall see how that question was answered in the case of Michigan's superb Porcupine Mountains State Park.

A final word to preservationists who may be enveloped in the murk of smoggery. Stick to the original statement. Insist: "*This scheme has no place in the park.*" When the gloom lifts, the smoggist will be seen rounding the bend, muttering: "Damn the fellow! He has sales-resistance."

COMPLEXITY OF THE PROBLEMS

In all I have written about state parks, I have been constantly reminded that my approach has been halting in one respect. I have been tempted at times to use such expressions as "a *real* park," or the "*ideal* state park." But who am I, indeed, to make such a designation? The best minds in the state park field are unable to agree on such distinctions. The National Conference has made a statement of "criteria"; it has earnestly attempted to describe wildlife policies and good plans for the management of vegetation. But the problems that arise are myriad and complex.

Robert Shankland has described a visit that Steve Mather and Gilbert Stanley Underwood made to Coney Island. Mather had said: "I want to show you an object lesson of what we do *not* want in national parks." They spent a day in the hurlyburly of a perspiring humanity frantically trying to find surcease from humdrum and cramped urban living. They ate hot dogs and raw onions and swigged soda pop. They sat elbow to elbow on a crowded beach, and threw baseballs at targets for prizes. Afterwards, Underwood said: "Who can enjoy this kind of place?"

However that may be, Bob Moses and the State Council of Parks in New York have provided havens for the people of the state. These are clean and hygienic, free from litter, well but not officiously policed, and furnished with many kinds of play. Assuredly this is a boon. But is it as good as a woodland lake resort where there are opportunities for meditation among wild creatures, where men can sense a kinship with their elder brothers, the trees, and with the younger annual wildflowers?

Who is to say what is better for *you*? All I know is what is better for *me*. When I describe either a fine playground or the natural and scenic loveliness of repose, I do so with a difference. Of the playground I have only good to say—but also *little*. "Having wonderful time. Wish you were here."

But . . . the state park! I sit beside my tent, watching the moon rise at the lake end, silvering my tent stakes. A loon laughs madly. I entertain a chipmunk who craves the welfare state of tourist crumb; or a fox daintily walking along a wall; or a charmingly dressed skunk who will mind his own business if I do likewise. Here are beech trees with lovers' names carved on them years before I was born (the ancient Romans used the beech and popular for the same purpose). An evening with a naturalist interpreter in a little amphitheater where the seats are hewn logs; blissful sleep in the aroma of hemlock instead of the stinking fumes from a motor exhaust—well, why try to name it all? But is this not recreation of a superior order?

Even after the best minds in the field of state parks agree that *this* is the essence of the state *park*, they must then try to arrive at principles of management for it. And that is not easy. For the state park, except in unusual cases, is not large enough to be an ecologic whole—and even in national parks there must be wildlife management, though as little as possible, ideally. And management, alas, calls for more management.

WILDLIFE AND OTHER MANAGEMENT

In most of the eastern state parks, there are no large mammals, except deer and a few bears. In all of them we still have the smaller creatures, and they delight the visitors who have no other opportunity of seeing them. The ambling turtle, the wood-duck mother with her brood crossing the road in single file (let traffic stop!), the singing birds with the occasional display of migrating numbers, the aquatic birds along a stream—you don't really need grizzlies and kodiaks, and panthers and wolves.

That delightful bit of philosophy came from a magazine editor, James Speed, at a meeting of the National Conference on State Parks. "Everyone agrees with the remark that 'it's wonderful how tame animal life becomes when it is properly protected.' In reality sanctuaries do not tame the animals; but they do tame men and women. Wild life is wild only because it has been forced to fear man. Really, these reservations should be called 'sanctuaries for the taming of men and women.' "

In the state park, wholehearted recreation is not possible without the mingling of wildlife and people. That raises immediate problems. For one thing, only the native species should be there. For another, the animal life, when protected, tends to become too abundant. Where reforestation with native trees is being carried out, the deer can be fatal to young trees. The porcupine ravages. There must be a reduction in animal numbers; but should it be left to sport and trophy hunters?

The park managers have to deal with these things. And, along with wildlife problems there are problems of vegetation management. "Use" areas must be set aside for visitors. That cannot be helped. It is frequently unavailing to move the campgrounds to another spot. That spot will only meet the same fate.

There may be a fringe zone of vegetation between the heavily used sections and the wilderness—if in any given park it could be called that. Exotic plants do not belong here. Grazing by domestic stock, it is suggested, should not be permitted; though as to this I cannot refrain from quoting the always provocative Albert Turner:

"The axe, the bush-hook and the gasoline clipper are about equally abominable in the sight of nature, and fortunately they are about equally footless in the back pasture . . . the sheep are as yet unorganized and are willing workers. They are true artists in that they make their own rules as they go along, and their confirmed habit is such that even the lunch hour does not interfere. . . . " But Albert was ever the roguish nonconformist.

A more spectacular problem results from the amazing multiplication of the camping humans. Where to put them? In many state parks the tendency is away from cabin and cottage accommodations although those that exist are being retained and toward increased camping space, whether on bare ground, on platform, or in the form of shelters. People have gone camp-minded; in addition, the creation of facilities for the camper requires no such capital outlay as does the cabin, which these days, must have modern conveniences.

Just as some motel keepers and other caterers to the traveler inveigh against a given state park "because it takes away their legitimate business," others do not accept the fact that the camper *wants* to camp. He may be able to afford a motel, but he does not want it. Witness the late-model, expensive automobiles that drive into state parks with camping equipment atop them. The camper is even willing to forego television in favor of raw nature. We hope nature is duly grateful for this testimonial of esteem.

THE QUALITY OF PUBLIC USE

Aldo Leopold, whose *Sand County Almanac* is a missal—that is to say, a calendar of devotions—for all those who strive to understand the natural world of which they are a part, has said: "The principal function of administration of recreational areas is to improve the quality of public use."

In order to realize fully the importance of Leopold's statement, it is necessary to know what kind of "recreational area" he had in mind. For it is obvious that he was not speaking of an area used purely for physical exercise, no matter how valuable that is. He could not have had play areas in mind, although there is room for improvement in these, too. More sports may be offered; the physical area itself may be enlarged or changed; the fishing may be improved. But these things do not improve the *quality of public use.*

It is not necessary for me to elucidate what "quality" Leopold had in mind. This has been amply done by William D. McClintock in a report he prepared for the Department of Conservation in Indiana. "The enjoyment of nature does not come naturally except to a few persons," he began. "Most have to be trained; all can increase this enjoyment by taking thought." A place to take thought in is, though it may sound trite to say so, a fine state park. "Natural scenery enjoyed is one of life's greatest joys. It is restful, prevents worry, increases our sense of beauty and wonder . . . opens for us the 'spirituality of the visible universe.' "

So, McClintock suggests, you should go to the park in the right state of mind, to look, to feel, to put yourself in nature's hands. Leave your old philosophies behind, make your mind a blank sheet; nature will write upon it. I am not quoting McClintock now; I am paraphrasing. Leave *sports* behind, for a while. Be alone a little. Don't talk much. You can talk later, after you have come back from a stroll. Always *walk*, where you can. And slowly. Get into the silent places and sit on a fallen log. Listen to the birds. Look at the wide landscape and then shift your view to the small things—organic, inorganic. Don't compare what you are seeking with something somewhere else. Nature never repeats, parrotlike. Don't look, in Nebraska, for what that state does not possess. Each spot of earth has its own special beauty. You may think the flat plain, or the desert, lacking in thrill. You will find yourself mistaken, if you remain awhile and give yourself up to *what is here.*

Thus far, McClintock, you see, is trying to establish a fruitful mood. "Take a little food along—a sandwich and cheese and an apple—and munch quietly as you see what the gentle creatures about you will be doing. It will add to your enjoyment."

THE PLEASURES OF INTERPRETATION

I don't know of any sager counsel for posing the simple mood in which the owner—part owner—of a state park should enter his domain. The quality of its use, so far as you are concerned, has already been improved, because you have heightened your own perceptions. But now, to go beyond that. A thousand things you see in your fine state park do not explain themselves to you. Beauty needs no interpreter; You carry in your own mind and soul the capacity for sensing beauty; it is yours, your very own. But the naturalist, the historian, the archaeologist, or some other trained mind can carry you further into the search for answers if you wish to make that journey. And this task, performed for you and your children *if you wish it,* we call interpretation.

Interpretation, the National Park Service believes, should be available in every area—scenic, scientific, historical, prehistorical—for those who ask for the service. It may be offered through guided trips, self-guiding trails, museums, pictures on a screen—through any and all suitable devices.

Early in the history of the national parks it was realized that without some such unpressured service to the vistor the park would not be fulfilling its purpose. It is a pity that the limitation of this book, a necessary one, does not permit a descriptive chapter telling of the wonderful interpretive work done in a county park like that which encircles the city of Chicago. If anyone asks whether people want, and make use of, naturalist service and interpretation, I need only refer them to the activities in the Cook County Forest Preserve. Wherever an interpretive program is offered in a state park, it is eagerly accepted by some of the visitors. How many? I do not know. Who knows, except where the park management has kept a record? How many visitors to any park do any given thing, or accept any particular opportunity?

Does the interpretive effort reach only a few visitors? In some park areas, perhaps. Would improved facilities for interpretation increase the number? In any given spot, who knows? But why should the experience in state parks be notably different from that in the national parks? In a survey conducted in Maryland, park visitors were asked to state which activity among a considerable number they especially liked. Sixteen per cent mentioned nature trails or some similar interpretive service. This seems a fairly high percentage; it might even be unusual. But suppose it were no more than ten per cent, countrywide. You are dealing with the "cream of the crop," providing what must be considered the highest quality of public use.

Of course, full interpretive services will not be available immediately in all state parks. Many states have needs that must be met before this educational function can become a reality. Too, in states that have had recreation places only for a short time, where therefore the spirit is manifestly for play, the higher uses will wait. In those states that have long had interpretive services, nobody would easily relinquish them. Perhaps that tells the story as well as anything can.

QUALITY OF PARK PERSONNEL

While these state park journeyings were being made, the Federal Civil Service System celebrated its seventy-fifth birthday. The event was proclaimed by the President of the United States:

"A strong civil service, based upon the merit principle, is now recognized as an essential factor in stable, responsible government....

"The seventy-fifth anniversary of the Civil Service Act is an appropriate time to salute the Civil Service . . . and to increase public knowledge and understanding of its importance in our system of self-government."

Dwight D. Eisenhower thereby called upon the people to observe this anniversary . . . and upon the heads of the federal departments and agencies, governors, mayors, and other public officials . . . to study federal, state, and local civil service systems with a view to their continuous improvement in every way possible. . . . In witness thereunto the President set his hand and caused the Seal to be affixed.

It happened that I had recently been talking with the general manager of the Taconic State Park Commission, who administers a "ribbon" park comprising a lovely parkway which widens now and again into famous recreation refuges used by the crowded urbanites of the northeast. I knew already, of course, that New York State operates under civil service rules. But the manager gave me the multigraphed sheet which is attached to all applications for employment in his region, and this paragraph held my attention:

"The Taconic State Park Commissioners do not have a personal or political interest in the appointment of any applicant. They have delegated to me the responsibility to carry out policies and to the General Manager the authority to enable him to administer our affairs with the greatest possible efficiency. The Taconic State Parks and Parkways cannot properly be developed and maintained in accordance with the highest standards on any other basis."

For the Taconic and other regions of the great New York system, this announcement means exactly what it says. Behind it lies the reason, or at least one of the reasons, for the high quality of career men, from desk to field, that are found wherever New York has a state park; or, for that matter, any other cultural institution. And what is said here of New York is applicable to the other states that operate under like conditions—either with the protection of civil service for the career man, or with a so-called "merit system" that measurably achieves the same end.

In the proclamation quoted above, the President said that the civil service system is operated on the "merit principle." The states that have a "merit system" are not, strictly speaking, under civil service. There are local differences as to what is comprehended by the term. In Florida, for example, some departments have a merit system and some do not; this is optional with the departments. But the trend is toward such a system throughout.

Wherever there is a merit system, there is a fair degree of protection from political pressures and changes. One park director told me: "Under our merit system, if a man is performing an unsatisfactory job we can prefer charges and have him discharged. As long as he does a good job, he is reasonably assured that there will be no political interference with him and that he can make it a career."

The difference in employment tenure becomes fairly evident as one visits the country's state parks. On the whole—admitting a few exceptions—the highest type of personnel, the most efficient management, the best service to the public, will be found in those states where a change in political party will not mean a change in the management of the park. In Indiana, as a park manager expressed it, "the county chairman brings the new man around and introduces him." Strange, indeed, it seemed to me that Indiana could continue operating its most excellent parks under the spoils system, and do it so well. This is perhaps due to the fact that the friendly ghost of Richard Lieber still hovers over the fruits of his labors, and also that the able state park director and some of his staff have managed miraculously to weather the political hurricanes over many years. Other states that pursue the spoils system are not so fortunate.

It is not the business of this book to tell the states what they should do in the field of state parks. It can only indicate what has been done, how this has been achieved, and what the public enjoys in any given area. It can quote experienced minds upon many phases of the work, and so it has. No good park official, director, or enthusiast has yet felt that a personnel subject to political turnover can devote itself to constructive thinking and beneficial activity with the same intensity as career people who foresee a lifetime of work in a field they love.

At the time this is being published, there are nearly 2,800 state parks and related types of recreation areas, containing some 5.8 million acres, visited by more than 273 million persons annually, and administered by over a hundred state park agencies. In whatever Valhalla the preservationist retires to when he bows out from this scene of beauty and wonder, a part of which he was so eager to preserve for succeeding generations, there must be rejoicing that his effort has borne ample fruitage.

In the total acreage devoted to state park preserves, the leading states are New York, California, Maine, Michigan, and Pennsylvania. New York's superior domain is due, naturally, to its Adirondack and Catskill parks. The Anza-Borrego desert park and the precious redwoods of California account for much of that state's holdings. In Maine, Percival Baxter's gift accounts for by far the greater part of the acreage. Other large parks are Custer of South Dakota, 72,000 acres; Allegany in New York, 58,420 acres; Porcupine Mountains of Michigan, 58,167 acres; Palisades Interstate Park of New York–New Jersey (most of the preserve being in New York), 53,814 acres; and Itasca of Minnesota, 32,214 acres.

In the ensuing chapters we shall visit together a considerable number of the country's state parks. The *best* parks? No; the word has no place in our vocabulary. Outstanding state parks these certainly are, but the *best* park for any given individual is the one he likes best, the one where he finds his taste and enjoyment satisfied to the greatest degree.

(IV)

A LONG JOURNEY IN STATE PARKS

IT MAY INTEREST the reader to know how I was guided in my selection of places to visit. Without expert advice, I might have spent a lifetime of gypsying, pleasurable but hardly to the purpose—which was to describe representative examples of the various types of parks and the development of the special recreative opportunities of each.

When this study was being projected some years ago, the regional directors of the National Park Service (for better results, the administrative work is divided among five regional offices) * were asked to indicate which of the state parks within their observation in their opinion *must* be included in the schedule of travel, and which they considered *worthy* of inclusion if space permitted. The state park officials themselves were also consulted, of course. In nearly every instance I have followed this listing. It should be added, however, that no opinion is infallible and it may well be that many a splendid preserve, just as worthy as those I have described, has been passed by.

The state parks described in this book are, for the most part, those which most nearly measure up to the criteria adopted by the National Conference on State Parks, as stated in a preceding chapter. Some chapters deal with what, for lack of a more precise description, may be called "recreation areas." These include parks which lack the scenic, scientific, and over-all inspirational qualities of the ideal, but which offer, or could offer, valuable interpretive services. Other "recreation areas" are those created by multiple-purpose reservoirs, which offer exceptionally fine opportunities for fishing, boating, swimming, and various kinds of play.

Both sea and lake beach parks are described. The present recrea-

* The National Park Service has since established a sixth regional office to administer the parks in Washington, D.C., and vicinity. This unit was formerly designated as National Capital Parks.

tion crisis calls particularly for the acquisition of more such areas—and promptly—for available locations have been so commercialized by private interests that, as has been shown in the National Park Service brochure *Our Vanishing Shoreline* and other reports covering the Pacific Coast and the Great Lakes, there is little left for preservation as state parks.

Not forgotten are other recreation areas, such as those which came into existence during the depression, when the federal government, through emergency programs, converted submarginal farmlands into playlands. Forty-six such recreation demonstration projects, with a total acreage of 400,000, were developed under the sponsorship of the National Park Service in twenty-four states. The fine results—happy men, women, and children enjoying the outdoors where only starveling farmers and mangled forest growth existed before—can be seen, for instance, near Raleigh, North Carolina. This state has shown its appreciation by going beyond mere physical recreation and providing rewarding interpretive services.

In the course of this study I have visited some of the best historical and prehistorical parks in the country. Ohio alone has 58 of these parks; North Dakota, 54; Illinois, 38; Pennsylvania, 31; and California, 36. Many of these parks, besides being priceless memorials of the life and works of man, are sufficiently spacious to permit gracious enjoyment of their natural qualities.

There could be no more cheering excursion into the realm of human happiness than this which I have made. If I am asked whether all the ideals, including those in the hearts of the park directors, have been attained, I must answer no. Perfection could hardly be expected. There are disappointments, defects. Yet, in such a far-flung bright picture, these are forgotten. There is yeast and fermentation in most of the states, and the future is bright.

PART 2

THE NORTHEAST

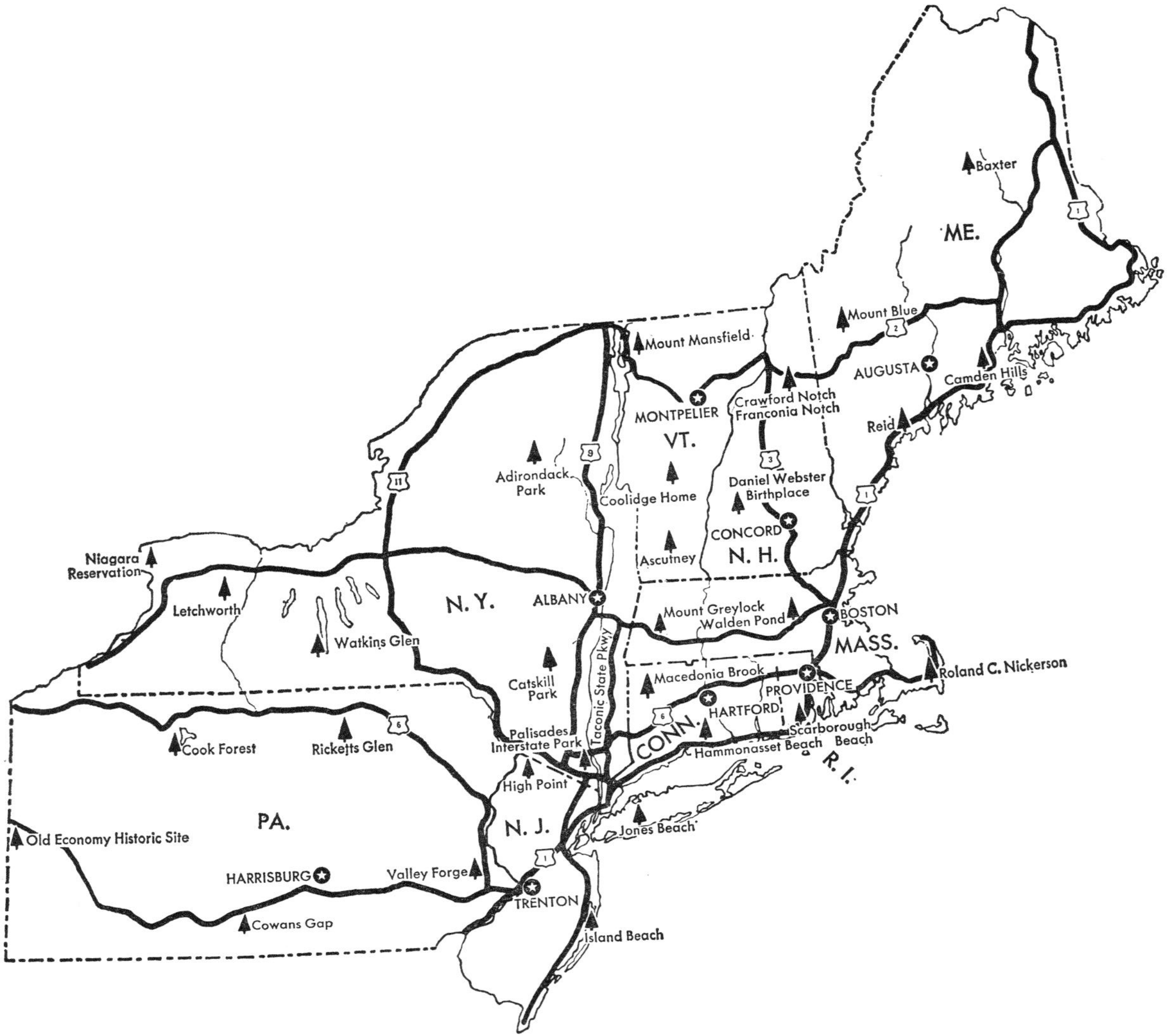

Baxter
ME.
Mount Blue
AUGUSTA
Camden Hills
Mount Mansfield
Crawford Notch
Franconia Notch
MONTPELIER
VT.
Reid
Adirondack Park
Coolidge Home
Daniel Webster Birthplace
CONCORD
N. H.
Ascutney
Niagara Reservation
Letchworth
N. Y.
ALBANY
Mount Greylock
Walden Pond
BOSTON
Watkins Glen
MASS.
Catskill Park
Taconic State Pkwy
Macedonia Brook
PROVIDENCE
Roland C. Nickerson
HARTFORD
Scarborough Beach
Cook Forest
Ricketts Glen
Palisades Interstate Park
CONN.
Hammonasset Beach
R. I.
High Point
Jones Beach
PA.
N. J.
Old Economy Historic Site
HARRISBURG
Valley Forge
TRENTON
Cowans Gap
Island Beach

(I)

ADIRONDACK AND CATSKILL PARKS AND THE FOREST PRESERVE

NEW YORK

May be reached from Highways 3, 8, 9, 10, 19, 28, 29A, and 87

SOME FACTS OF HISTORY may be merely bleached bones: others certainly are not. The following is not. By a coincidence that means immeasurable welfare to the people of the nation and to those of the state of New York, the month of March, 1872, saw the establishment of Yellowstone National Park by act of Congress, and the introduction in the New York Assembly of an act "to inquire into the expediency of providing for vesting in the State the title to the timbered regions lying within the counties of Lewis, Essex, Clinton, Franklin, St. Lawrence, Herkimer and Hamilton, *and converting the same into a public park.*"

Admittedly, this was a promissory note, issued at the insistence of a group of idealistically minded people. It was a declaration of purpose. There were to be some years of foot-dragging, political skullduggery, and despoliation of public forests before legislation with sharp teeth was enacted. So it was even in great Yellowstone in the first years. If we are to believe the accounts, curio hunters swooped into that incomparable treasure house to carry off anything portable. The question in both cases was whether public opinion would honor the promissory note.

Not until 1885 did the ardent New York conservationists get encouragement and begin to see daylight at the end of a long, sometimes very dark tunnel. In that year a Forest Preserve and a Forest Commission were created, and a policy of forest protection and supervision inaugurated. This would have been the first state move of its kind; but enlightened California a few months before had created the first State Board of Forestry.

The New York Legislature then passed an act with two important provisions. First: "All the lands now owned or that may hereafter be acquired by the State of New York within the counties of [here naming the fourteen counties north and south of the Mohawk Valley] shall constitute and be known as the Forest Preserve." Second: "The lands now or hereafter constituting the Forest Preserve shall be forever kept as wild forest lands. They shall not be sold, nor shall they be leased or taken by any corporation, public or private." The original act made no distinction between the northern and southern counties, but later the reservations were distinguished as the Catskill Preserve and the Adirondack Preserve.

Was conservation then triumphant? Not at all. So little stock did the legislature put in these projects that an initial request for one million dollars with which to buy forest lands was greeted with derision. Fifteen thousand was reluctantly voted to keep the Forest Commission breathing. But in 1894 the people of the state spoke with a ringing voice. By referendum they wrote into the Constitution an amendment that so far has resisted all efforts (even some well-meant ones) to change that deliberate resolve.

We have been speaking of the preserves. The creation of parks within those preserves came later. The Adirondack and Catskill parks are not the same as the preserves. The setup is rather baffling to the outsider. There are forest-preserve lands outside the famous "blue line," but they are not part of the parks. The state lands within the "blue line" are part of both the preserve and the park. The private lands within the "blue line" are part of the park, but not of the preserve.

You probably will not find this epoch-making "blue line" on your automobile road map. But it is one of the classics of conservation for public welfare, mental and physical health, and happiness. Today the boundaries of the parks enclose more than 6.3 million acres, of which more than 2.3 million are state-owned, with by far the greatest part being in the Adirondacks. Perhaps for our purposes it would be better to ignore the legislative and administrative technicalities and call these precious areas parks or preserves, as you please. Your camping, hiking, or canoe trip will be as enjoyable even though you are unaware of the fine distinctions. The important point is that

New York has preserved a part of its natural inheritance—some of the finest vacation lands in the world—and is slowly and prudently developing them for the benefit of the millions who *must* at times commune with nature or perish.

Many of us, on seeing the words "the Empire State" have shrugged a little and murmured something about "chamber-of-commerce boasting." But it isn't altogether so. A people who can rescue so much of the natural beauty and spiritual stores of their state—and do it by deliberate vote—may indeed have something of the stuff that makes a *lasting* empire.

It seems ungracious to try to tell the story of these New York preserves and parks in a single short chapter. Only the wide scope of this book could excuse such impertinence. How fine it would be to go back over the years and name the valiant humanitarians who labored unselfishly that these jewels should survive! As the years pass, the names will perhaps be forgotten. But the impact of what these people did will not perish.

Let us begin, then, with the Catskills, because in the usual comparisons with the mighty wildness of the Adirondacks the gentler beauties of the preserve south of the Mohawk is in danger of being considered tame. The comparison is not fair. The Catskills have a charm all their own, quite different from that of its northern neighbor. And curiously enough, until a later date than you would suppose, it was thought that the Catskill peaks were higher than any in the Adirondacks.

The interior of the Catskills was a remote wilderness for longer than most people imagine. As late as 1918, we are told by William D. Mulholland, assistant commissioner for the New York Conservation Department, "a writer referred to the summit of Slide Mountain as 'but a few hundred feet from Winnisook Lake' "; and John Burroughs, who knew and loved these mountains-of-the-sky, tells about his party's first attempt to ascend Slide Mountain, starting in Woodland Valley, and being able only to reach the summit of Wittenberg. But in recent years this region has become much more accessible.

"Onteora," as the Indians called the Catskills, is now at the backdoor of Greater New York, and is visited in addition by millions from other centers of population. Except on the higher slopes, the forest of Catskill Preserve today consists preponderantly of hardwood. Once it abounded in hemlock, perhaps a more suitable dwelling place for the Great Spirit: for the Indians knew He lived there and trod this land with awe.

Despite the yearly invasion of humans, the Catskills are still far from tame. The Wittenberg-Cornell-Slide Trail, ending at an elevation of 4,180 feet, still offers a panoramic view that has few equals. And if you "want to get away from it all," and prove to yourself that you are still young enough to do a bit of rugged climbing, try the Pine-Hill-Eagle Mountain West Branch Trail, over the summits of Belleayre, Balsam, Haynes, Eagle, and Big Indian. All those who are elated when they hear of the continued existence of some portion of the white man's wilderness will thrill at the mile-square stand of virgin spruce between Cornell and Slide Mountains.

When you move northward into the Adirondacks, you are conscious of the very different natural conditions resulting from different geologic history. The Catskills have mountains with flat summits and valleys with precipitous sides. There are outcropping of shales and sandstones, and many of the summits are a tough conglomerate. The core of the Mountain Belt of the Adirondacks is older—old beyond our imagination. When we say it is "pre-Cambrian," we are describing an unknown and prodigious passage of time. These Adirondack rocks are associated with the Laurentian system, once (but no longer) thought to be the oldest on earth.

On the lower slopes of the Adirondacks are the forests of broad-leaved trees—the beech-birch-maple association of northern hardwoods, the kind that go ablaze in the autumn. On the middle slopes are the dark-colored evergreen cone-bearing forests, mainly red spruce and balsam fir, with a dash of yellow and white birches throughout. Above these are the treeless areas, with low shrubs, mosses, and lichens: the home of the Alpine flora, where, sometimes at the inhospitable peak of the mountain, you may find delicate flowers among clumps of furtive and resistant plants. You are reminded that once a great ice sheet passed over all this country—in no less than four advances and four retreats—and that mayhap we are living even now in a warm cycle of an ice invasion not yet ended.

"Whether your ambition be to climb ragged mountains, negotiate mile after mile of sparkling water in canoe or guide-boat or simply to pack your duffle in the car and camp on the shore of a lake, in the Adirondacks it can be realized to the fullest." So says the Conservation Department recreation circular. And this is exactly what the state offers. Since there is within the "blue line" a great amount of privately owned property, your vacation may be as formal and luxurious as you wish; but then you will not be a guest of the state, except in a very indirect sense. "Recreation circulars" are available for those who want to know the public campsites, the trails to Mount Marcy, the canoe routes, the rules and regulations governing public use of the forest preserve, the state-owned islands of Lake George, and the information necessary to enjoy the Catskill region.

Certainly since the days when the Iroquois Nations were prosecuting their bitter feud with the Algonquins, and the Adirondack mountains were the scene of both animal chase and human struggle, the toll of the lumberman has been ravenous. True, only the wealthy and the pioneers and the hunter-hermits who came into the region in the old days knew a wildness of a perfection that will not again be realized in our times. But so much still remains that the camper can have his fill and enjoy as rugged an experience as he wishes. The hundred largest lakes of the Adirondacks have a combined area of 242 square miles!

Mount Marcy is the highest peak in New York, and the principal lure of the climber. The view from it is a not-to-be-forgotten experience. Longstreth, who knew the Adirondacks, said it was "like being on top of the biggest bubble in a boiling cauldron." Old Mountain Phelps, a picturesque character of the early days, described his feelings, when atop this peak, as of being "heaven up-h'istedness." With all due respect to the statesman whose name the peak now bears, let us remember also the Indian name of Tahawus, which means "he splits the sky." It is by no means certain, however, that the Indians called the mountain anything in particular. Tahawus may have been the invention of Charles Fenno Hoffman, the student of Indian languages.

On the southwestern slope of Mount Marcy lies the pond-source of the Hudson River, the stream which becomes an estuary below Albany and under whose broad reach so many commuters read their newspapers every day.

The human history of the Adirondacks—that is, the white man's side of it—from the time when northern New York was divided into the two enormous counties of Tryon and Charlotte to the time of the creation of the forest preserve and the park makes fascinating reading. "My camp in the Adirondacks" may have meant in this century either the private park and mansion of the millionaire, or the humble dwelling of a man like John Cheney, the gentle Nimrod who, in thirteen years of wilderness hunting, totaled his game bag at 600 deer, 400 sable, 19 moose, 48 bears, 7 wildcats, 6 wolves, 30 otter, 1 panther, and 1 beaver. The wolves and the panthers are not there any more; you may see one of the last of the big cats in the state museum in Albany. But note that John Cheney, the professional hunter, was obviously a sportsman. He shot *one* panther—and that was the result of a chance encounter where it was touch-and-go; yet he must have seen many such cats.

July 1858 was the date of a memorable gathering of notable men—including Ralph Waldo Emerson—on the shore of Follansbee Pond. William J. Stillman, artist, journalist, and lover of this New York wilderness, was probably the instigator of what the Adirondack guides with sly humor called "the philosophers' camp." Besides Emerson, look who was there: James Russell Lowell, Louis Agassiz, Judge Ebenezer Rockwood Hoar, Jeffries Wyman, John Holmes; these, and other Bostonians who ventured forth from their urban or suburban ease to taste the real wilderness. A watercolor sketch now in the Concord, Massachusetts, Library, done by Stillman, depicts an after-breakfast scene at the camp.

Stillman had tried to get Henry Wadsworth Longfellow and Oliver Wendell Holmes to be of the party. Holmes couldn't imagine that the wilderness would interest him much. Longfellow asked: "Is it true that Emerson is going to carry a gun?" Stillman admitted that there was such a plan. "Then someone will get shot!" was the reply. Nobody got shot; probably Emerson finally came unarmed. But the sage of Concord, a nonsmoker, gallantly agreed to try smoking a pipe, as a woodsman should—and paid with nausea the penalty for being a good fellow.

Out of this "philosophers' camp" came a poem by Emerson, "dedicated to my fellow travelers" and called "The Adirondacs" (Emerson's own spelling of the name). It may not be a great poem; nor even one of Emerson's best. But some of the last lines have not only a philosophic charm but also a touch of that elfin humor that lay deep in the grave, contemplative character of the man. See if *you* have ever felt this way, at the end of your holiday in the wild:

The holidays were fruitful, but must end;
One August evening had a cooler breath;
Into each mind intruding duties crept;
Under the cinders burned the fires of home;
Nay, letters found us in our paradise;
So in the gladness of the new event
We struck our camp and left the happy hills. . . .

Or, in other and less poetic words: "We have had a swell time; it'll be nice to get home."

All except Stillman. He left with the philosophers, but he came right back to his beloved wilderness. He was an Adirondacks man.

(11)

ASCUTNEY STATE PARK

VERMONT

Off U.S. 5, between Windsor and Ascutney; four miles from Windsor

Mount Ascutney, not far from the Connecticut River, which forms the boundary line between New Hampshire and Vermont, is called by the geologists a "monadnock." The phenomenon is an engaging one, for the word describes a mountain of considerable height that has no association with a range or chain. The peak actually named Mount Monadnock, in southern New Hampshire, is of course the type example.

Apparently these monadnocks are resistant rock remnants of a flat plain which existed long ago in this part of New England—a so-called "peneplain" that has been eroded down from a former much higher elevation, leaving these tough stumps as isolated peaks. Ascutney, 3,144 feet above sea level, rises abruptly from a general elevation of about 600 feet. Composed of a pinkish quartz-syenite rock which welled up in molten condition into a covering sedimentary deposit, long since weathered away, this mountain affords a magnificent panorama of a large extent of the region. Like all such peaks, it is visible from any slight elevation for great distances.

In a great range of mountains such as the Presidential of New Hampshire it is often difficult to identify any particular peak, such as Mount Washington, among so many comparable heights. You must be familiar with the range, or you must see it from the right perspective. But these friendly forested monadnocks, standing majestically alone, are colorful personalities. "There's Ascutney!"

says the New Hampshire man when he tops a hill and looks into the west. It is a landmark as definite in character as anything in his own back yard.

Like all such peaks, Ascutney bears on its exposed rock the scars of the great ice sheet that passed this way in what, geologically, were recent times. However, except for such bare patches, the whole mountain is covered with trees, and its lines are sleek and—may we say?—feminine.

Of this mountain 1,530 acres are owned by the state and constitute the park. An excellent surfaced automobile road winds its way for four miles up to a large parking area near the summit. On this road no grades are over fifteen per cent, but the visitor will miss much if he does not pause at the picnic areas and at the overlooks on the ascent. Magnificent as the view is from the top, the forest growth is almost as alluring, even though none of it is virgin. On the way down, the prudent motorist will obey the sign: "Use Low Gear." It is surprising how the eye can be deceived when one ascends a mountain highway; One gets the whole truth in descending.

Many of the Maxfield Parrish pictures (with the blue sky, remember?) which were so popular some years ago were painted on, or originated from, Mount Ascutney. The artists of the Cornish colony, on the New Hampshire side of the Connecticut, had Ascutney for a daily model. And the story goes that when Lafayette visited the United States after the Revolution the eager citizenry of the Ascutney region cut a trail and built a granite shelter where the general could be entertained. Alas! The general never got there.

Two picnic areas are available in this park, and there is a camping area with tent platforms. Otherwise, except for hiking trails, there are no developments—just the forest, the view, and you—on the whole, vastly rewarding and memorable.

(III)

BAXTER STATE PARK

MAINE

Twenty-six miles northwest of Millinocket

THE STORY of Baxter State Park is the story of Percival P. Baxter, so we may as well start with the man.

Now that he is old in years and accomplishments, stories and legends about this Maine philanthropist begin to accumulate. And rightly so. Anything concerning a man who has performed outstanding service to his time and to his people is of interest; we want to know how he came to be what he is and do what he has done.

The story about Percival Baxter which I like best has a double edge. From the time Percival was four years old, he went on camping trips with his father in the Maine woods. When the lad was seven, they went to the Rangeley Lakes. On the last day there James Phinney Baxter said to his son: "For every trout five pounds or over you catch today, I will give you ten dollars a pound." A squaretail, a real speckled beauty, obliged; he was worth $80 to the boy who landed him in the boat.

"Now what are you going to do with all that money?" asked Percy's father.

"Put it in the savings bank," was the reply.

That was what he did, seventy-odd years ago. The interest has compounded. The eighty is now more than a thousand. It has always been in a separate account—"the trout account." When Governor Baxter goes into the bank, he often inquires: "How is my trout account? . . . Fine! Take good care of it."

This was Baxter's thrift—one kind of thrift. Not Jacob's, with an eye to pied lambs. Just the simple Maine kind, with an understanding of the nature of compound interest. Baxter knew a nobler thrift, too. This takes the form of a gift, to one's own fellows and to posterity, of a piece of lovely and historic wilderness

> forever to be held in trust in its natural wild
> state for the benefit of the people . . . and as a
> sanctuary for wild beasts and birds.

The trout money, or its equivalent, was destined to make possible these gifts. As I heard this story, I thought that Ben Franklin would have loved the frugal-minded young Percival. Ben, as a child of seven, spent a sudden fortune on a whistle—and thereafter made a homily of his shame: "Don't give too much for the whistle."

Baxter's Thrift, as it may be called (actually it is only one of Baxter's many benefactions), takes the form of a state park of nearly 200,000 acres. At present, to be exact, it is 193,254; but the ultimate aim is the round number. Only three state parks in the nation are larger than this: the Adirondacks and Catskills of New York, and the Anza-Borrego Desert of California.

Drawing upon his own early-cultivated love of wilderness and of animals both wild and domestic, and upon his persuasion that nerve and soul restoration is to be found in such wildness, and above all perhaps on his belief that it is shameful for any state not to perpetuate something of its native, original condition, Percival Baxter, as early as 1905, when he was a member of the Maine legislature, proposed the acquisition of this Mount Katahdin country as a state park. Young Baxter, the earnest legislator, had something to learn about the altruism of legislators. Whatever they may be as individuals, as political bodies they are remote from idealism. They respond to idealistic pressures, yes; a vociferous, determined band of conservationists can drive them to cover, and has done so. Unfortunately, young Baxter stood alone. From the time the project was first broached to the last effort lies a span of twenty years or so; but the legislature would have none of it, even when Baxter was governor—and a respected governor, too. You will probably not be surprised, after the story of the banked trout-money, to hear Baxter's own account of his record as state chief. "My administration was not spectacular. We paid our bills, kept the state's affairs operating satisfactorily, left money in the bank, and had no scandals." The statement has the crispness of Cal Coolidge.

But Baxter did not succeed in getting the legislature to make an appropriation for the creation of the state park of his dreams. There was only one way to attain this end, Baxter finally concluded. He must do it himself, with his own money and by his own effort and such help as he could obtain from the owners of the desired land. Even good friends thought him overly idealistic, at least on this subject; and the lumber and water-power interests, in business to get rather than to give, suspiciously asked: "What's the racket?" How often a clear, straightforward idea in our complex world seems to carry concealed weapons—much the way a single sober man in a party of inebriates will appear drunk to them.

At any rate, Baxter State Park came into being at last, deeded to the state of Maine, administered by an authority set up for that single purpose, and legally secured against future despoliation and abuse or overuse. There are few state parks like it. It delights the wilderness lover just to read about it; the true camper revels in it; but of course such a park is the despair of the tourist bureau and the chamber of commerce because, forsooth, there is "nothing to do when you get there." Nothing, that is, other than to enjoy being there, under the conditions the park was established to preserve: that is, nature, beauty, wildlife, repose, understanding, reverence, contemplation.

That is Baxter State Park, and this is the way it will continue to be if Governor Baxter has succeeded in protecting it as well as he thinks he has.* This is no reflection whatever upon any other state parks, or upon their management or their value to man. The wilderness quality of Baxter State Park will not be tramped out of it, because there won't be enough people there. The bobcat is going to have his say. There are going to be a lot of animals and birds; the virgin timber on the slopes of Katahdin will remain so; there will be no roads except the simplest and slowest.

"Baxter State Park is a cross-section of interior Maine," said Governor Baxter to me. Precisely that: lake, stream, mountain, some virgin growth, moose, deer, foxes, beavers—a cross section, that is exactly it. And along with the natural features there will be preserved the memory of the rugged, salty past of the Maine woodsman, as Henry David Thoreau saw him more than a hundred years ago, when the classic primeval white pines were being ruthlessly cut.

Thoreau, who was always a little different from most folks, called

* Since this was written, Governor Baxter has achieved his acreage goal by giving the state another 7,764 acres. He also gave approximately $500,000 "to provide income for the care, protection and operation of the park." Thus he has put it a little farther from the reach of those who might at a later date clamor for uses the donor regarded as adverse.

the grand granite monolith which is the crowning glory of the park *Ktaadn*. But Sockbasin, the Penobscot Indian from whom William Willis got his definitions and pronunciations of the Abnaki dialect, pronounced it *Ka-tah-din*. Thoreau, by the way, climbed the mountain on a day of heavy, boiling clouds and did not get to the top of the monolith, now Baxter Peak. He did reach the strange, wide tableland which cannot be seen by anyone viewing the mountain from below.

Here on this mountain is one of the finest exhibits of the work of the great continental ice sheet of the Pleistocene. The ice passed completely over the peak, planing off part of the top; it tore off and dropped countless boulders; and in the ensuing centuries during which the ice clung to high elevations, cirques of spectacular dimensions were formed. Mountain ice cut back into Great Basin till only the narrow rim of the Knife-Edge remained to connect the massive rounded peak of Pamola with the rest of the mountain.

Pamola: by that name the Indians knew the highest point, where a guardian deity lived. When Charles T. Jackson was working on his study of the geology of Maine, and when before him Charles Turner, Jr., climbed Katahdin in 1804, they found their Indian guides chary of disturbing Pamola in his rocky mansion. Pamola punished intruders.

If Baxter had preserved only the integrity of the mountain itself, he would have deserved perpetual gratitude. For it is the most famous of all the mountains of the country, if one may judge from all that has been written about it. Here, as everyone should know, is the northern terminus of that Appalachian Trail which can be hiked from Maine to Georgia. The annotated bibliography of Katahdin, issued by the Appalachian Trail Conference, consists of 82 pages of references—a "literature" unequaled by Mount Washington or any other of our famous landmarks.

Indeed, though Thoreau's visit and description enhanced Katahdin's fame, he only followed a long list of climbers who knew it well. The Reverend Marcus Keep opened up the first trail in 1848; it started on the old Wassataquoick (pronounced Was-sa-ta-cook) tote road. Keep was a lover of this wilderness and the huge mile-high mountain of Pamola, and for thirty years and more he induced fellow clergymen to climb it with him. One of them preached a sermon on the summit, demonstrating that Pamola was merely an Indian superstition and that Katahdin was created on the sixth day —a final touch to an important job. In 1784 the Reverend Manasseh

Cutler of Ipswich, Massachusetts, had concluded, after climbing Mount Washington, that the small fir trees in the upper zone had been "growing ever since creation," though they were only inches high.

Mention of the tote road from which the Reverend Keep began his trail reminds us of another tote road, on which there is a painted sign that could have come from no one but Governor Baxter:

THIS IS THE
SOURDNAHUNK TOTE-ROAD.
IT IS
WINDING AND NARROW
AND IS TO REMAIN AS A
WILD FOREST TOTE-ROAD.
IT IS NOT A PARKWAY
OR A BOULEVARD.

And that is just what it is—a winding and narrow road. There is room on it for an automobile and a half, which means that when another driver is approaching, you must turn out. It is not a scenic road, but a slightly modernized way to get from one place to another on your "tote." And that is the way Governor Baxter wants it to be. One day, he tells me, he saw some highway machinery bound into the park from Millinocket. When he asked where they were going, the reply was that they were "going to improve the Sourdnahunk tote-road." "Oh, are you indeed?" And Baxter headed for the nearest telephone where he could reach the state capitol. The road has not been "improved"; but it is a nice cheerful road, and no driver need fear it. The kind of people who like Baxter State Park like the tote road.

When you travel this narrow road, you observe the truth of the often-quoted remark of Thoreau: "the mountain seemed a vast aggregation of loose rocks, as if it had some time rained rocks. . . ." Was there ever such a rock pile as this, superimposed on rock? Everywhere you look—boulders. The great glaciation made mincemeat of Katahdin's upper surface and strewed the boulder hash far and wide, besides adding erratics that originated at other places.

Imagine what this Katahdin country must have been when first the king's "broad arrow" was put upon the giant white pines, marking them for masts and spars! These choice trees had to be a foot in height for each inch of diameter. Actually, few were ever cut here for such a purpose. It merely pleased his majesty's vanity to know that he could have the best. The demand for lumber for a fast-growing urban northeast began the white-pine ravage noted by Thoreau—as early as 1828, on the west branch of the Penobscot. Thus started the days of the long-log drivers whose saga has been often and rightly chanted. Finally, the search for pulpwood also made inroads. What contempt the old driver had for the pulpmen—even for himself when he was forced to become one of them! Baxter State Park stands astride this story of past and present timberland. I recall a wooden cross (still there, I believe) not far from the bridge across the west branch, marking the grave of one of the old long-log men. His companions buried him by the roadside and hung his caulked boots on the arms of the crossbar, but the bears soon found the boots and ate them with great relish.

It looks like a wonderfully easy country for the tenderfoot to get hopelessly lost in. I asked my pleasant guide, Helon Taylor, the superintendent of the park, about this. "No," he said, they hadn't had any trouble that way for several years. No doubt one reason is that the kind of people who want to pitch camp in this wilderness (there are two campgrounds that you have to *pack* into) are not the kind that get lost. Maybe they have that sense of direction that Thoreau's guide, Joe Solis, possessed. Thoreau tried to find out from Joe just what the secret was, and Joe tried to give reasons; Thoreau found that Joe was *inventing* explanations. The fact was simply that he *knew* without knowing how he knew.

There is a story, to be sure, which tells about the Indian who protested that he was *not* lost. "Indian no lost. Indian here; wigwam lost." The storyteller should not have made his character an Indian, but a camp counselor from the Bronx.

To my surprise, I found on my first visit to Katahdin that approached from the south the mountain seems to be a huge monadnock, somewhat like Ascutney in Vermont, but much bigger and higher. When you get to the west or east of it you begin to see it as part of a *range*; and, at last, you realize that it is really the triumphant culmination of *two ranges*.

There was once a dispute as to whether the first point of land in the United States to catch the sunrise was the top of Katahdin or the top of Cadillac on Mount Desert Island. I heard that the weighty question was referred to the Geological Survey, who promptly dodged it, probably fearing a chamber-of-commerce trap. If the reader is a good mathematician, he might figure it out; but I imagine the decision is a little difficult to make.

Governor Baxter bluntly said to me: "The Park doesn't need any advertising." And I judged from what he added that he is not in favor of increasing either the number of campgrounds or the facilities for camping. At present the camper must make reservations, with a deposit which is forfeited if he fails to show up for any but a reason of emergency. During the height of the season, people who have not made such reservations drive in to find every space taken; and "driving in" means no small drive, usually.

This state park is administered by an authority quite separate from that which directs the other Maine state parks, an authority composed of the governor, the forest commissioner, the commissioner of inland fisheries and game, and two residents of Maine, one of whom must be from either Greenville or Millinocket. And this park quite deliberately discourages *numbers.* It invites the elite of the camping world, and not too many of them.

Some will quarrel with this concept of Percival Baxter's. I assume, however, that before expostulating too hardily, they may recall that it was *his* idea from the beginning and that it was carried through with his energy and his money. Without a tinge of sarcasm, permit me to suggest that anyone with a different concept is free to acquire another park of 200,000 acres and dedicate it to such use as he sees fit. There is still plenty of land in Maine.

At Thoreau Spring, on Katahdin, is a bronze plaque reading:

> Man is born to die. His works are short lived. Buildings crumble. Monuments decay, wealth vanishes, but Katahdin in all its glory forever shall remain the mountain of the people of Maine.

These simple words, the affirmation of a man of clear vision, are signed P. P. B.

(I V)

CALVIN COOLIDGE HOME

VERMONT

In Plymouth

THE DICTIONARY says that a *hamlet* is "a little cluster of houses in the country." That perfectly describes what one visits at Plymouth Notch. Exactly, this is a hamlet. On August 2, 1923, the population was, by unofficial census, 12.

No; on that momentous day, the population *happened* to be 14, for Vice President Calvin Coolidge and his wife were "home" from Washington. Warren Harding, the President, was in San Francisco. That night, following their usual habit, Calvin and Grace had retired about nine o'clock. It was muggy dog-day weather; but the summer nights in Plymouth Notch are never too oppressive.

About midnight there was an emphatic knocking at the door. John Coolidge, father of the vice president, responded to the thumping and was told the news that President Harding was dead and that by Constitutional succession Plymouth Notch had a President of the United States asleep upstairs in this house.

There followed one of the strangest scenes in our political history. The event itself—the notification of a vice president that death had brought him to the highest office—was not unique. Theodore Roosevelt, vacationing on Mount Marcy in the Adirondacks, had received a similar message, and had made his famous midnight trip down the mountain road to a railhead. But here in Plymouth Notch, in the early morning hours, was enacted a scene that has no counterpart.

The succession of a vice president upon the death of the President is a practical fact but not a legal certainty until the oath of office has been administered. At two o'clock in the morning in Plymouth Notch, Vermont (population 12), who could perform this legal function? You probably know the answer already: Colonel John Coolidge, father of the new President, was a justice of the peace and a notary public.

Calvin, awakened, took his shaving mug down to the kitchen and shaved. Vermonters are not emotional people, but they observe the decencies. Grace Coolidge brought in another kerosene lamp and put it on a table in the "front room." The visitor sees this room today just as it was on that sultry morning. There is a wood stove at one end of the room, with a stovepipe crossing the room to the chimney at the other end. This is no accident. On a frigid winter day, such long runs of stovepipe shed heat that would otherwise hug one end of the room.

The family Bible, open, was on the table beside the kerosene lamp. Calvin repeated the oath after his father, ending with "so help me God." Then he turned to his wife; she looked at him, and they both said good night and retired again. Anywhere but in Vermont, and especially in Plymouth Notch, this behavior might have seemed too casual. Not here. This was a great moment. But to Calvin Coolidge, a Vermonter who knew full well the implications of that moment, it was natural to say: "Well, we may as well get our sleep."

President Coolidge was not born in this house. He was born in a house just across the street, the front part of which had been the "general store" kept by Colonel John. The store is still there, still selling Crowley cheese made in Healdville and maple syrup from nearby sap-gathering pails. On the corner, by the old road that came in from Bridgewater Corners, is the Wilder House, where Calvin Coolidge's mother was born. The state of Vermont owns this building also, and it is operated as an inn where a visitor might dine or stay overnight.

Though the dramatic event of 1923—the taking of the Presidential oath by the son before the father in the kerosene-lamplight—is surely worth remembering, the Plymouth Notch hamlet *as a whole* is, to my mind, the major attraction. Here is preserved a way of life, a truly *living* past. This is Vermont, if you will; the very heart of a conservative, thrifty, self-contained people.

It is not just the house where Calvin Coolidge lived as a boy; or even the house where he was born. It is the hamlet itself—those two houses, the Wilder house, the church, the cheese factory—all of it.

And, mark this, it is not a restoration. Plymouth Notch is as it was. How fine it would be if the cheese factory could operate again—on a profit basis, of course.

It is difficult to describe, because you are dealing with human essence here. However, some of the flavor of Plymouth Notch was caught by President Coolidge in his description. He said, and he was not exaggerative: "The neighborhood was made up of people of exemplary habits . . . they had no mortgages on their farms. If debts were contracted, they were promptly paid. Credit was good and there was money in the savings bank. The break of dawn saw them stirring and their industry continued until twilight. . . .

"It would be hard to imagine better surroundings for the development of a boy than those which I had. Country life does not always have breadth, but it has depth."

That is so true. Coolidge knew that there were narrowing influences intrinsic to this rural hamlet existence. The visitor, seeing Plymouth Notch as a whole and living with it imaginatively for a quiet two hours, perceives that life here would have depth. He realizes why Calvin Coolidge, thirtieth President of the United States, came to be what he was. The saltiness of his youthful environment still has savor.

Apart from the many visitors who come here, the population of Plymouth Notch hamlet is still, I should think, about 12.

(V)

COOK FOREST STATE PARK

PENNSYLVANIA

Seventeen miles northwest of Brookville, on Clarion River, via Highway 36

THIS IS THE Black Forest of the time of William Penn, the Quaker. Indeed, you may here walk trails that will take you among pines and hemlocks that were growing before William Penn was born, and before his father was born. Most of us are probably accustomed to associate the great Quaker merely with Philadelphia and the eastern part of the Keystone State. But the grant from King Charles II was for a domain of 26,000,000 acres—nearly the equivalent of what is now the state of Pennsylvania.

Samuel Pepys, the great diarist, referred to Sir William *Pen* (he spelled the name thus) as a "base raskall." Sir William was controller of the King's Navy when Samuel was its secretary. And both gentlemen were ambitious. It was the custom of the period to seek gratuities, and Sir William managed to get the king into his debt for about sixteen thousand pounds sterling. The debt, which was bequeathed to son William, was canceled by a grant to Penn of a "charter." Charles had only a hazy idea of the location of the land; he was not certain even that he had the right to give it away; and a million acres, to say nothing of twenty-six million, was quite beyond the imagination of a prince who could not comprehend how an apple gets inside an apple turnover.

We have only a limited idea today of what that virgin forest of northern Pennsylvania looked like in 1681. Rough and shaggy as much of the region still is, 250 years of lumbering, and of cutting and burning for agricultural crops, have left only small islands of the original forest growth. Penn himself never saw these northern woods. So the visitor to Cook Forest today has the advantage over the first white owner: he can see at least something of that virgin growth. And what trees they are! Three and four feet in diameter; a few reaching the height of two hundred feet; a single specimen of white pine, we are told, "capable of resulting in 5,000 board feet of lumber."

A few years ago, after a small tornado that swept through part of this virgin stand, some wind-thrown giants were salvaged for commercial use, with results that amazed even the foresters. Fortunately no other cutting is done within the forest, though the basic policies of management would seem to allow it. When I visited the area, a forester told me, with a smile, that "the conservation feeling around here is pretty strong."

At all events, the visitor to Cook Forest today has no reason to be dissatisfied, even if he is a purist. Nature is being allowed to pursue her way, to a delightful degree. This park offers wonderful pleasures to those who are willing to use their feet or the feet of a horse. The trails were planned with understanding and imagination. While I was there, arrangements were being made to receive 500 boys from Pittsburgh out on a group camping holiday. It was a joy to listen to the conversation between the park superintendent and an assistant on the one hand and the boys' camp committee on the other: the cheerful desire to accommodate this little army (and 500 boys constitutes no small problem) and to make this the richest possible experience for them.

Nature has been especially generous to this section of the state lying south of the Allegheny National Forest. The deeply cut, winding, and steep-sided valleys worn into the rainbow-sandstone rock furnish both a shelter from strong and cold winds and an easily warmed porous soil that permits rich growth of tree, shrub, and flower. On Birch Trail, for instance, one looks down into a rhododendron thicket in the swampy area bordering Tom's Run, a jungle of growth through which one would have to cut one's way—and a gallant sight in the time of bloom.

In undergrowth like this, deer aplenty may find food. Small animals are abundant—black, gray, and red squirrels; cottontail and snowshoe rabbits; and that happy low comedian, the raccoon. The black bear abounds in greater numbers than the visitor suspects, for his shyness has not yet given way to the panhandling tactics of more sophisticated bears in other parks. The tomtom noise on the garbage can at night is more likely to mark a visit from Br'er Coon than from a bear. There are beavers, too; they have built several dams in Tom's Run.

Whence the name *Cook* Forest? John Cook, the son of a German immigrant who came to the colony of North Carolina before the Revolution, elbowed his way along the Clarion River (named Tobeco by the Indians for the alders that grew along the banks) in 1826, when the state of Pennsylvania was looking for a location for a canal that would form part of an east-west navigation system. The road he chopped through the wilderness, to lead his oxen along, was still visible only a few years ago. Cooksburg, now the headquarters of the park, was named for this pioneer, whose resourcefulness, muscular strength, and hunting prowess are remembered in legend. It is of either John or his father Daniel that the story is told that on a trip to Pittsburgh he was seen to lift a barrel of whisky by the staves projecting beyond the head, raise it to his mouth, and drink from the bunghole. This tale is a classic of the early days when muscles were muscles.

On a single day in 1830, it is said, John Cook killed seven deer, one panther, one wolf, and fifty wild turkeys. He supposedly kept so many hunting dogs that when visitors came it was necessary to clear the house of dogs so that the guests could come in. Certainly Penn's Black Forest abounded in game and was a great hunting ground of the Indians.

The primeval trees began to fall early in the nineteenth century. The Clarion River was the raftway over which the giant logs, usually hewn square, were floated to market when the spring freshets came. Many of the 100-foot timbers found their way to England, for shipbuilding purposes.

Interesting to note is the fact that in the slaughtering of the American forests the only real profits were made by those who skimmed the cream and went out of the business quickly. Almost all those who stayed in the lumber business found themselves out of timber sooner or later. The inexorable law of diminishing returns caught up with them. "Even if I could have stolen the trees, I would have gone broke sooner or later," was the rueful remark made to me by a man who had in his day floated millions of logs down the Connecticut to the pulp mills. The great successful lumber companies of today's Northwest are scientific croppers, not skinners.

The first move to preserve what was left of the virgin growth near

Cooksburg, and to set aside the fine green spot as a public park, is said to have been made by Major McCreight of DuBois. As early as 1911 he took the idea to the legislature, but without result. Usually the promoters of reservations for public use are a group of enthusiasts who have talked the prospects over many times. But we can be precise about the first move for the preservation of Cook Forest: in December 1926 the Cook Forest Association was formed to get the project underway. The owners of this land were asking $650,000—no doubt a reasonable price. In 1927 the legislature of Pennsylvania appropriated $450,000, with the understanding that the Cook Forest Association would raise the other $200,000. This was done, and the original 6,055 acres were acquired. Subsequent donations have extended the boundaries.

As we have suggested, the ideal way to enjoy Cook Forest State Park is to walk the trails. Even the names of the trails are inviting—Longfellow, Seneca, Deer Park, Mohawk, Joyce Kilmer. Longfellow is the main trail, beginning at the parking space and picnic area and passing through one of the larger stands of virgin white pine and hemlock. Tom's Run Trail is one of the most appealing. This one follows the old log road up the run and through the evergreens that border the little stream. It leads away from the main part of the park into a region with the truest feeling of wilderness.

The newest trail, Nature Trail, has been developed by the Bureau of Parks in conjunction with the Open Air Club of Clarion College. This "self-guiding" hike of two and a half miles has labels marking the various shrubs and trees. Of this trail a nature lover has written: "It carried us through birch groves, sunny mountain meadows and deep pine-scented ravines. In the open stretches we saw many varieties of wild flowers; deep rose mallow with heads bending over the chuckling brook; sun-yellow ladyslippers dotting the tall grass with brightness, and many more that we could not name but could only enjoy . . . there was a sign pointing the way to a small cave housing a family of porcupines."

The bridle trail is a recent addition. This one enters the forest from the road above the Mausoleum and follows Henry's Run northward through one of the richest stands of trees, ending at the dirt-road above.

For those who are unable to travel afoot or on horseback, a leisurely drive along the roads—park and highway—is the next best thing. The River Drive follows the north bank of the Clarion through younger but equally charming growths and connects with the Troutman Run Road. Another pleasant drive is along Lookout Road, which crosses the Seneca Trail near the Lookout Tower. Here the car may be parked; a short walk through the woods brings the visitor to the great weathered rocks known as Seneca Point, with the winding Clarion and Hemlock Island below.

Set in a semicircle on the site of an old Indian campground are some comfortable cabins—rustic buildings that blend into the background. It was near these cabins, on a little bridge, that I passed two attractive damsels busily carving their initials on the log railings. This is a mild kind of vandalism, but one that the parks can do without. I thought I would try a little irony on the girls, and said, pleasantly: "Well, isn't that just fine! A hundred years from now some visitor will see that and think it was done by the Seneca Indians." Alas, I was too subtle. One of the girls looked at me with a flush of pleasure and replied: "Do you *really* think they will?"—and went on with renewed vigor and a new high purpose.

Nearby is a spacious trailer and camping lot. And if the visitor wants a bit more luxury, the accommodations at the Cook Forest Inn are excellent.

(VI)

DANIEL WEBSTER BIRTHPLACE STATE HISTORIC SITE

NEW HAMPSHIRE

Four miles southwest of Franklin, off State 127

NEARLY eighty years ago George B. Elliot of Boston, refurbishing an office, discovered in a trash barrel a painted tin sign. In gold lettering on a black background was the name:

D. WEBSTER

It was the shingle of a famous lawyer, one of New Hampshire's greatest sons, which had once sat under the window of his office in Scollay Square, Boston. The little tin sign, thus accidentally rescued from the public dump, can now be seen in the much-visited birthplace in Franklin, New Hampshire, a historic site in the keeping of the state. Without unduly emphasizing the importance of this particular relic, one does wonder, in looking at it, how many mementos of our great Americans have vanished in such a manner. Such men of course did not lack great fame and respect among their contemporaries. But there was a failure to realize that posterity would treasure every reminder of their public and private lives.

Daniel Webster emerged in an age when oratorical powers counted far more than they do today, or perhaps ever will again. He was one of a great trio of orators in the Senate; an announcement of his coming speech was enough to fill the galleries. And, as with the other two, Clay and Calhoun, it was Webster's tragedy that his devotion to the Constitution cost him the good will of many of his friends and followers. He could perhaps have been President. A historian, writing of him not long after his death, said that "he was decidedly the favorite of a large portion of the people . . . many thousands at the polls voted a ticket headed by his name, knowing that he was dead."

Daniel Webster was caught in the maelstrom of the bitter slavery dispute that was to end in a terrible civil war. The gentle sage of Concord, Ralph Waldo Emerson, was so captivated by the mind and voice of Webster that he allowed himself to speak of him as "godlike." But the time came when Emerson joined the Abolitionist fold, and the philosopher's former hero became a strayed sheep, even a fallen Lucifer.

"Sir," said Daniel Webster in the Senate, "my object is peace—my object is reconciliation. My purpose is not to make up a case for the North, or to make up a case for the South. My object is not to continue useless and irritating controversies. I am against agitators North and South; I am against local ideas North and South, and against all narrow and local contests. I am an American, and I know no locality in America. This is my country. My heart, my sentiments, my judgment, demand of me that I shall ever pursue such a course as shall promote the good, and the harmony, and the Union of the whole country. This I shall do, God willing, to the end of the chapter."

Webster was spared the anguish of witnessing a divided and fratricidal nation. He died in Marshfield, Massachusetts, in 1852, at the age of seventy.

Webster was *not* born in a log cabin. He himself said so, maybe with a roguish tinge of irony at a time when it was politically advantageous to have been so ushered into the world. "But my elder brothers and sisters were born in a log cabin, raised amid the snowdrifts of New Hampshire at a period so early that, when the smoke first rose from its rude chimney and curled over the frozen hills, there was no similar evidence of a white man's habitation between it and the settlements on the rivers of Canada."

Log cabin or not, this part of New Hampshire where Webster was born was no land of milk and honey. The visitor who comes up from Concord and turns off upon the road leading to the memorial soon puts behind him the more fruitful soil of the valley bottom of the Merrimack, and climbs into a lean terrain of glacial drift, peppered with erratic rocks, fit indeed to raise the fine white pine that roots upon it, but making one wonder how Ebenezer Webster,

Daniel's father, could have raised enough on it to support a family. Indeed, if you approach this part of what was Stevenstown in the early days by the back road from Warner, you see much of "Poverty Plain," so dubbed by the settlers who enjoyed a better soil.

The fact is that Ebenezer Webster, who hailed from Kingston near the sea, took what he could get. His patron, Colonel Stevens, a "developer" of thirty-six square miles of land in this region, gave the young Ebenezer 225 acres to start him on a laborious career. The deed was from one Ebenezer to another. No doubt Colonel Ebenezer Stevens felt that the Ebenezers should stand together.

Webster's father, by oxcart, toiled up an old Indian trail that followed Punch Brook from the valley to the wilderness and built a log cabin, long since rotted away, near the spot where the birthplace can now be seen. On Punch Brook, at a point where freshets pour down between ledges of mother rock, Ebenezer Webster, according to contract with the "proprietors," built a sawmill. Part of the old up-and-down saw blade may be seen today at the birthplace; otherwise nothing remains of that sawmill, later also a gristmill, which operated for many a year.

On a hot summer day the visitor to this memorial can have a picnic lunch by Punch Brook. Indeed, visitors will find picnic tables scattered about the birthplace grounds, tucked away in charming nooks with a sense of privacy. Just because this is a lean and hungry soil for crops, don't think it is not a country of subtle charm. Nature knows how to clothe herself prettily under any circumstances: she has a varied wardrobe.

Somehow you feel, here at the Webster Birthplace, that it is as much a memorial to the father as to the illustrious son. For Ebenezer Webster, a six-foot swarthy man, of Yankee grit and resourcefulness, was one of Rogers' Rangers and later fought valiantly in the Revolutionary War, becoming Colonel Webster and Squire Webster—a man who could disperse a mob by looking them in the eyes and saying: "I command you. . . ."

Ebenezer had not been on this land long before he planted elms. What a weakness our ancestors of New England had for this rugged individualist among trees, the elm! No two of them alike, each going its own sweet way. One of these trees, at least, is still there—a noble onlooker of two centuries. It has lost many a limb to storms, and so fumbles around somewhat like a great octopus, but it seems to be still strong and vigorous. Ebenezer—Daniel—the elm—kindred stout hearts of healthy core: you have a sense of the solid virtues that created the nation and kept it inviolate.

Ebenezer became prosperous enough to use some of his up-and-down sawed boards to build this house that faced down the hill toward his mill. No great prosperity was indicated: he probably did most of the work himself and bartered for what he could not supply. Look at the structure from the downhill side: very plain, only two rooms with an attic above, but the proportions are, as always with the early builders, good. The wellsweep furnishes a touch of grace. Here Daniel Webster was born in the year 1782.

The black-haired youth—"Black Daniel" he was called in his young manhood—showed promise. The Reverend Samuel Wood, minister of nearby Boscawen, offered to prepare the boy for Dartmouth College. "How could my father afford it, in such narrow circumstances and with so large a family?" thought the youth. In later years the statesman recalled, in touching words, the night, and the very place, when riding in a sleigh with his father he was told that the dollars would be found to send him to Dartmouth. "A warm glow ran all over me, and I laid my head on my father's shoulder, and wept." A little later, at fifteen, Daniel came into Hanover town on horseback, carrying his feather bed behind him: the other children were sleeping on their straw pallets in the attic of the home by Punch Brook.

It had to be Dartmouth, of course; for though Ebenezer Webster lacked education himself, he had been chairman of the legislative committee which in 1789 had recommended the Dartmouth College Land Grant of 42,000 acres.

Nothing in American history is finer, and more affecting, than the story told in Daniel's autobiography of the sacrifices made by his parents to give their children an education. One day Daniel came home from college and was disturbed to see his brother Ezekiel, whom he loved, toiling on the farm. "Why should I get a college education, and he not?" Dan offered to leave Dartmouth for a spell and teach school, if by that means Zeke could have his chance. The father talked it over with the boys. Ebenezer said that "he had but little . . . that to carry us both through college would take all he was worth; that for himself he was willing to run the risk, but that this was a serious matter to our mother and two unmarried sisters . . . if their consent was obtained, he would trust to Providence and get along as well as he could."

The "mother," Abigail Webster, mind you, was not Daniel's mother but his stepmother. Yet she said, when the proposal was made known to her: "I have lived long . . . and have been happy in my children. If Daniel and Ezekiel will promise to take care of me in my old age I will consent to the sale of all our property at once, and they may enjoy the benefit of what remains after our debts are paid." Golden words! It is reassuring to find the statesman writing from Washington, after he had become famous: "Take care of my mother's garden [at Elms Farm] and keep it in good order, even if it cost you the wages of a man to do it."

Though crowds seldom come to Webster Birthplace, the flow of visitors is pretty constant during the season when the house is open —from Memorial Day until October 15, when the brilliant foliage of the northern trees usually begins to fade. Most of the visitors are—unfortunately, I think—from outside the state. It is fine, of course, that those should come. The more the better. But primarily this memorial is for the people of New Hampshire; it is a leaf of the book of *their* heritage. It is excellent to attract tourists, and benefit from their spending. It is far wiser, and better, to know your own history, and to feel a kinship with the men and women of your origins.

(VII)

FRANCONIA NOTCH STATE PARK

NEW HAMPSHIRE

Eight miles north of North Woodstock, via U.S. 3

WHEREVER the forces of nature have sculptured rock shapes, people have exulted in finding likenesses. A bishop's mitre, an old-fashioned sugarloaf, an Indian with feathered headdress, a baby's shoe—the variety is interminable. Occasionally a similarity is seen by many people and agreed upon; more often the imagination suffers a severe sprain.

Of all the rocks that have dared to be so imitative, it is safe to say that one is pre-eminent; one alone is nationally and even internationally famous. This one is the chief—but he is far from the only outstanding feature of Franconia Notch State Park. This is the Great Stone Face, otherwise known as the Old Man of the Mountains.

Nobody has ever questioned this resemblance to a human face. From the time that it was first seen by white men, probably somewhere between the years 1800 and 1810, when a road through the Notch was being cleared, up to the present moment when a cloud of visitors are gazing up at it, it has been unquestionably a face. As to *whose* face—that is something else. A legend has it that one of the white discoverers nudged his companion and exclaimed: "Look! There's Jefferson!" Another early viewer thought it was the very image of Benjamin Franklin. And so on.

No doubt it was Nathaniel Hawthorne who gave the Old Man the first push toward world fame. His *Great Stone Face* is a sort of lay sermon in short-story form. There is some doubt as to whether Hawthorne had actually seen the rock when he wrote. And if you reread the story, in *Twice-Told Tales*, you may wonder exactly what the author meant. But what a piece of unconscious advertising it was!

As this is being written, a crew of workmen happens to be up on Cannon Mountain in yet another effort to keep the Old Man from disintegrating. About 1915 a climbing parson named Guy Roberts called attention to the danger of a rockfall that would destroy the face; the state anchored the projections of the ledge. But erosion, and the pull of gravity, constantly threatens the granite blocks. An impassioned legislator stated that the face must be preserved even at the cost of a million dollars. "It is worth that, and more, to the state," he proclaimed.

The legislator was right. The Old Man is an intrinsic part of the Granite State. It is the inheritance of every child born to the cultural and spiritual resources of New Hampshire.

It is rather amusing to note that Charles Hitchcock, the geologist who surveyed New Hampshire in 1870, studied the Stone Face carefully and wrote that "the pieces are liable to fall at any time." Hitchcock noted that "the profile is made of three jutting masses of rock (an ordinary granite quite friable from decomposition) in different vertical lines; one piece making the forehead, the second piece making the nose and upper lip, and the third the chin." "I would advise any persons who are anxious to see the *Profile* to hasten to the spot, for fear of being disappointed," warned Professor Hitchcock about eighty-eight years ago. You might grin at this prediction. The chances are that the Old Man with the stony visage will be with us a long time; yet . . . well, one never knows . . . perhaps you should get to Franconia Notch and see him this year.

Since geologists are not overly sentimental about rocks that resemble other things, it is significant that not only Hitchcock but a much earlier state geologist, Charles T. Jackson, were at great pains to make the Old Man known. Perhaps because he felt that the face might not long exist, Hitchcock devoted a whole page in his report to a line drawing indicating what the profile was like and how it appeared when one shifted from the straight line of observation either to the left or to the right. Jackson, after stating that it was held to be "one of the greatest natural curiosities of the State," became more prosaic: "It is a proper subject for romantic legends, but there is no proof that it has been known more than forty or fifty years [he was writing this in 1840] by white men, nor does it seem to have been specially observed by Indians."

But the visage no doubt was well known to the Indians. It may have had religious significance, in which case they didn't talk about it. Possibly they merely commented that it looked like one of their sachems.

Franconia Notch is a deep defile that lies between the Kinsman Range on one side and the Franconians on the other. Rugged as are the surroundings, nothing could be more lovely and inspiring than the view from the Old Man observation point. There the towering mountain, rising a sharp 1,200 feet, is mirrored in the lovely Profile Lake at its foot; Echo Lake, a little farther on, is another bit of limpid perfection. Of still another silver-blue sheet of water, nestling in the side of the mountain itself, Charles Dudley Warner said years ago that it is "a mirror for the sky and the clouds and the sailing hawks."

Almost as widely known as the Great Stone Face is the Flume. Along the flank of Mount Liberty for 800 feet the visitor may make his way up a cleft in the mother rock, by means of a boardwalk, with vertical walls rising 70 feet above his head. Though in times of freshet the stream at the bottom of the chasm roars impetuously through it, the side walls do not give the impression that rushing water could have been the scouring agent that created the Flume. Jackson thought it was clearly a fracture that had been deepened but not widened very much. When he first saw it, and for many years afterward, another phenomenon was connected with it which can no longer be seen.

Pictures taken in the Flume before 1883 show a huge boulder wedged between the walls of the cleft. After the glaciation theory of Louis Agassiz had finally been accepted by the scientific world, no geologist could doubt how the boulder got there. But, though the receding ice that invaded New Hampshire left boulders aplenty strewn upon the denuded surface of the land, it was rare chance that deposited one of these boulders into the narrow Flume in such a manner that it remained securely wedged in the upper part.

Securely wedged? It would appear so, since the boulder must have been in the Flume between fifteen and eighteen thousand years. Thousands had walked beneath the boulder with the assurance that it wouldn't drop. But nothing in nature endures. In June of 1883, following several days' rain which ended with a cloudburst, the Flume became a thundering raceway. The guests in the Flume House, recently opened for the season, heard the roaring, and some thought they heard a mighty blast. When it became possible once more to get near to the gorge, it was seen that the great erratic had fallen from its perch. As Dr. Hitchcock said of the Great Stone Face, it had been "getting ready to fall anytime"—anytime, that is, these last few thousand years.

More than two million people have made the ascent to the top of Cannon Mountain in the enclosed cablecar. From the observation platform on the 4,200-foot crest, one looks down upon the valley floor and around at the folded, forested peaks of the White Mountains. Far below these folks who take the easy way to the sky will be hundreds of happy campers in the beautifully kept campground called Lafayette. Here is a recreation building with showers and laundry and comfort rooms; and when the tent sites are filled—and they are very quickly during the season—the considerate rangers will try to find a temporary place for your tent somewhere nearby. Here, too, the desire of people to get back to nature is markedly apparent. No matter how fast the facilities of the camping parks are increased, they continue to fall behind the demand.

Lafayette is, naturally, a favorite with the campers. This is a region of trails that lead not only through wonders of natural history but through marvels of human occupation and pioneering as well. For, one remembers, this was tourist country when the territories of the United States west of the Mississippi were still unmapped, and when great Yellowstone, for example, was known only by tall tales that nobody believed.

Indeed, when one goes, for instance, to Franconia Notch and finds that the state has no naturalist to make the visit a more enriching experience, one must recall that New Hampshire was well in the tourist business before state parks were even heard of. For this reason it is difficult here to dissociate the idea of state parks with that of a paying business. Add to this the fact that *gifts* of land and structures account for nearly every preserve the state possesses, and the picture begins to emerge. But I am told that a more understanding attitude is developing.

A little off the highway in the Notch is an oddly shaped enormous boulder set down by the ice at such an angle that under one side of it a dozen people could easily take shelter. There is a somber story connected with that boulder—known as Boise Rock. In the

A scenic gorge, Watkins Glen State Park, New York

Wilmington Notch, Ausable River, Adirondack Park, New York

Jones Beach State Park, New York

Washington's winter headquarters at Valley Forge,
Valley Forge State Park

Sunken granite coastline in Maine's Reid State Park

Palisades Interstate Park Commission,
Harriman State Park, New York

The Genesee River Gorge at the "Big Bend,"
Letchworth State Park, New York

Middle Falls, Letchworth State Park

A stretch of the Taconic State Parkway, New York

High Point State Park monument, near which the boundaries of three states meet, as seen from Lake Marcia, New Jersey

The Calvin Coolidge Homestead, Vermont

*Niagara Falls: the American Falls on the left,
the Horseshoe or Canadian Falls on the right;
Niagara Reservation, New York*

Hemlocks and ferns along the Mohawk Trail,
Cook Forest State Park, Pennsylvania

Relics of the Rappite Colony, a mid-nineteenth century experiment in communal living, preserved at Old Economy Historic Site, Pennsylvania

The Rappite Colony's granary at Old Economy Historic Site

A section of the Flume, Franconia Notch State Park, New Hampshire

early days, when the road through the Notch was not much more than a trail, a lone horseman was making his way in the gloom of a cloudy day. The impending blizzard struck around him at a point near this rock; he had the wit to realize that he could not go on. The temperature was dropping rapidly; even if he could find shelter under the rock, he might not survive the cold. Boise made a fast decision. He killed his horse, skinned it, dragged the still warm hide into the shelter of the glacial boulder, and wrapped himself in it. When a search party found him, the traveler was alive but tightly frozen in!

(VIII)

HIGH POINT STATE PARK

NEW JERSEY

Highway 23, three miles south of Port Jervis, New York; eight miles northeast of Sussex

JUST A short distance from the place where the states of New York, New Jersey, and Pennsylvania have a common meeting, and where the Delaware and Navesink rivers mingle their waters is a height called High Point. (The Navesink, by the way, is sometimes spelled Neversink, owing to what Naoh Webster would call a colloquial pronunciation, but by any spelling it is the same snaky stream.)

There are two other places in New Jersey called High Point. As they are both near the ocean, their altitude is relative—the height of a sand dune compared with the adjacent beach. But from High Point State Park, on this summit of the Kittatinnys, one looks westward across the valley of the Delaware into Pennsylvania, to the ridges of the Poconos; to the Catskill Mountains of New York in the northeast; to the farmlands and woodlands of Sussex in the southeast. Enthusiasts with enviable eyesight or rapturous imagination make out the U of the Delaware Water Gap, many miles distant.

Visitors who wish to see more and more and farther and farther may climb the 220-foot monument that stands upon the highest point of the ridge. And that is just what one out of eight visitors does. It is a stiff climb, and there is a nominal fee for this last footage of satisfaction. The philosopher may wonder what further mysteries of distance are revealed there—but, then, the philosopher remains at the base of the granite shaft (which was quarried in Vermont but lined with Kittatinny quartzite), looks up, and walks away with legs that tremble—at the very thought of this great height.

High Point State Park, consisting of over 11,000 acres, was given to the people of New Jersey by the late Colonel and Mrs. Anthony R. Kuser of Bernardsville. The monument is dedicated to "the Glory and Honor and Eternal Memory of New Jersey's heroes by land, sea and air in all wars of our country." It was a noble gift; and a humanitarian one, as the growth of the recreation needs of an increasing population will demonstrate. For this delightful park is only 65 miles, an easy two hours, from Metropolitan New York, and will play a vital role in assuring the outdoor enjoyment of urban folk. When you consider that Bear Mountain and Harriman parks are only twenty miles nearer to the greatest population concentration in the country, High Point seems another example of interstate amity such as the Palisades Parkway.

High Point is farther from Philadelphia, but at risk of intruding Pennsylvania into a chapter devoted to New Jersey I must mention the inspiring trip up the incomparable Delaware Valley. It happens to have been the way I approached High Point; and I can vouch for the fact that the next best thing to the enjoyment of a fine state park is a lovely scenic prologue on the way there. From Riegelsville our road paralleled the old Easton-Bristol Canal, one of the water-traffic facilities that mushroomed in eastern Pennsylvania before the railroads came. This canal was operated to some extent up to the early part of the century, and the section I saw apparently is still in good condition. Pennsylvania has wisely acquired this long section of the canal, and created Roosevelt State Historical Park around it. This strip reaches down to the river in some places, offering cool green shade and quiet for picnicking millions to come. Perhaps some day the canal will again be put to use, as the C & O Canal has been, for barge trips offered by the National Park Service.

Route 611 pulls away from the river above Easton. Following it, we soon saw the famous notch in the mountains known as Delaware Water Gap. Here, on the New Jersey side of the river, the Garden State (aptly named, in spite of its great industrial development) owns 6,000 acres of magnificent woodland right down to the Delaware bank. From the highway, in that great green slope, not a structure can be seen, though hidden in the forest cover there may be some dwellings. On the Pennsylvania side the mountains form a similar sweeping slope; the Keystone Department of Forests and Waters is acquiring, by the use of oil royalties, tracts of this fine forest as fast as possible.

Here is the famous Gap itself! Some geologists believe that this surprising cleft in the Kittatinny Ridge resulted from a breakthrough of the impounded waters of the great lake which once lay above it. Another explanation is that the Delaware, then flowing slowly along a surface that was almost level, and having already secured its bed on that plain, began to cut into the rocks of the ridge deeper and deeper as the land mass slowly rose—the same phenomenon is said to account for the canyon of the Colorado in the southwest, and for other natural wonders. At any rate, the result is one of the great scenic attractions of the East. The Indians called this gorge "Minisink" (where the stones are gathered together).

Six or seven miles above Minisink a prospective dam, intended partly for flood control and partly to create a water supply, will incidentally provide a highly significant area of recreation. The resulting lake will be a mile wide, and of course very deep, at the dam; and the impoundment will reach up to Port Jervis, in New York. Since the changes in water level are not expected to be very great, public ownership of the charming woodland mountainsides by both New Jersey and Pennsylvania will insure the finest of recreation advantages.

But it is time to get back to the many attractions of High Point State Park. Let us look at what is to my mind its most valuable asset, one which the generous Kusers of Bernardsville may have held less precious than the patriotic granite monument, but which will prove a priceless boon in years to come.

About a mile north of the lodge, fifteen hundred feet above sea level, is a swamp. Swamplands at that altitude are not rare in the lands over which the glacial ice flowed during its Wisconsin stage. But if you have an interest in unusual plant associations, do not miss this one at High Point. You would expect to see the white cedar, the arborvitae, in the pine barrens of the southern part of New Jersey; and red spruce you would look for considerably farther north, or at least at a much higher elevation. They do not belong together. Yet here they grow side by side. Not only that: there are masses of rhododendron, laurel, stately pine, and hemlock. Around the swamp circles a good road, but not the kind on which one may speed. It was engineered with the idea that the visiting public would rejoice in a leisurely, curvy course.

Those who would like to know more about this exceptional bit of plant ecology can refer to *Past and Present Vegetation of High Point,* written by William A. Niering, of the Botany Department of Rutgers, in New Brunswick, New Jersey.

The park has only two cabins for public occupancy. However, there is also a lodge with sleeping accommodations; in the summer meals may be had at the nearby inn. Other visitors shift for themselves under canvas. For them the environs of Sawmill Lake, a twenty-acre segment of sparkling water, is a quiet haven. Each campsite is complete with either a platform or camp space, and wood is furnished in *long lengths.* That means the camper brings an ax and whets his appetite—which is as it should be.

At present, most visitors come to High Point from the metropolitan area on the Hudson, or from Long Island, but Philadelphians are already looking eagerly in this direction. Currently the number of visitors is more than four hundred thousand a year. There is a brisk competition for picnic space—in spite of the many tables scattered in charming locations—so that a time rule is enforced on the busiest days. The limit is four hours at an ordinary table, and three hours for tables with fireplaces. Naturally, on days when there is ample space for all who come, the time rule is not enforced.

Sawmill Lake has a good bathing beach, but an even better one exists at a lake of similar size, spring-fed, cool and tonic in the hot weather: Lake Marcia. There is a third body of water within the park, bearing the quaint Dutch name of Steenykill.

For the nature hiker there were formerly good trails throughout the park, but I have been informed that these trails are no longer well kept. Nor is there a museum, nor any naturalist service, which is a pity, because this park lends itself ideally to that kind of educational enjoyment. The superintendent said that he would like to install a museum in a now-vacant building that was erected in the heyday of the twenties. The geology, botany, and wildlife of this park call for just such an introduction.

High Point State Park, then, is scenically charming and well kept and administered, but, like so many other parks, it fails to realize its educational possibilities.

Bordering High Point State Park on the south is the Stokes State Forest, a magnificent tract of 12,428 acres given to the people of New Jersey by Governor Edward Stokes. Here, too, is a most desirable spot for the camper. Some of the sites are near the roads, others deep in the woods. A neighboring forest like this should be primarily an added protection for the state park. Unfortunately, the huntsman fraternity, having been allowed to kill within the forest, have now succeeded in carving 5,000 acres of shooting privilege from the formerly protected park domain.

Five thousand acres is about half the park. It makes one squint and wonder. I don't know whether the line of demarcation—the animals' Mason and Dixon line—has been clearly pointed out to the deer and other game. No doubt the concession was made within the wilder section of the park, where visitors would not be endangered. But it remains doubtful whether a state park can be maintained half as a preserve of natural organic life and the other half as an open hunting ground.

(IX)

JONES BEACH STATE PARK

NEW YORK

On Wantagh Parkway, thirty-three miles southeast of New York City

HOME-HUNGRY servicemen returning in army transports from the battlefields of Europe in the forties scanned the horizon and saw, not the familiar skyline of Manhattan, but a tall water tower modeled after the Campanile of Saint Mark in Venice. Many of them knew it well, for they had drunk from its water and basked at the beach in its shadow, when the marine dining room of the west bathhouse was their U.S.O. lounge. Jones Beach! Home!

To say first of all, in relation to this greatest of all physical recreation areas of the seashore, that its water tower has a capacity of 316,000 gallons is to begin with what sounds like a sticky and prosaic bit of statistic. But the fact is significant, for a recreation area that calls for a facility of these proportions must itself be the result of colossal planning and performance. Let statistics help, then, to project an adequate idea of it.

In Jones Beach State Park, on a peak day, 215,000 persons are accommodated, and 47,000 automobiles are parked. More than 10,000,000 men, women, and children visit the Atlantic Ocean here each year. The two bathhouses contain 15,000 lockers and dressing rooms. The nine parking fields cover 122 acres of ground and can handle 20,000 cars at a time. The park has a marine theater that seats more than 8,200 spectators. During a summer season 1,400,000 hot dogs, 600,000 hamburgers, and 2,000,000 servings of ice cream are dispensed. At peak periods during the summer months 1,000 park employees are at work: of these, 150 are lifeguards. The park contains 2,413 acres, with six miles of the finest white sand beach and a bay frontage of half a mile for still-water bathing. Is "colossal" too pretentious a word for all this?

I have stressed the dimensions of Jones Beach deliberately, knowing full well that enormous size can be a drawback, and that other factors can be far more important. But here, remember, size responded directly to need. This place is within a few miles—a very few miles, indeed, in an age of fast transit—of the world's largest concentration of people, whose longing for a day at the seaside could not be satisfied in a site of lesser proportions. Indeed, the need grows and grows.

This is the place to quote Robert Moses, president of the Long Island State Park Commission:

> We could, of course, have developed a plan which was less ambitious, with cheaper buildings and facilities of poor design and flimsy construction. By keeping down the number of employees and not insisting on the highest standards of order and cleanliness; by ignoring the need of future expansion, we could reduce our charges. *We do not wish to be associated with this kind of an enterprise. Doubtless commissioners can be found to do this sort of thing.* . . . When we first announced our program there was great skepticism expressed . . . as to the kind of parks we would run, and there was a lot of talk about litter and waste, and hordes of filthy people. We believe this fear has been dissipated, and that it has been shown that there are plenty of people who want the kind of parks we are trying to give them.

The italics are mine, to emphasize that this is Robert Moses speaking. Moses can be even more acid than he is in these words; frequently he has been. He is, I suppose, what has sometimes been referred to as a "controversial character." At any rate, when you go to Jones Beach State Park and enjoy its order and cleanliness, its range of accommodations for recreation needs, and the consummate planning it exemplifies—including the parkways by means of which the millions of visitors get there and back—when you observe these riches, you will have met Moses.

Moses's accomplishments are to be seen not only at Jones Beach. Moses has been longtime chairman of the State Council of Parks of New York; in traveling along these parks, I have found traces of him everywhere. I would not make comparisons among the devoted men who have developed the nation's parks and recreation places, and those who have preserved them for the people. But these men must possess certain characteristics in common: planners and executors like Steve Mather and Colonel Lieber and Charles Sauers and Robert Moses—to mention a few from a brilliant roster—armed with integrity, drive straight toward their goal, refuse to acknowledge defeat, are determined and true to their purpose. They are capable of decisive action when needed; otherwise they wield a tight grip under a soft glove.

And now to Jones Beach State Park itself, and the two areas that may be considered a part of it: Captree State Park and Fire Island State Park.

What the visitor to Jones Beach now sees is a long stretch of gently sloping white sand beach that looks precisely as though the Atlantic Ocean had washed it up in a leisurely manner. It looks that way, but it is not. The entire beach, as well as most of the surrounding parking lots, facilities for healthful recreation, and even a few natural-looking dunes anchored by vegetation, is manmade.

Among the recreation facilities are handball courts, deck tennis, shuffleboard, a rollerskating rink, archery ranges, an 18-hole pitch-putt golf course, softball diamonds, picnic areas, a fishing dock, outdoor dancing, and a two-mile boardwalk. Special sports programs are also available. A sample "contest day" for children under fifteen years of age included, on the day of my visit, archery, hole-in-one, and shuffleboard tournaments, a "talent" showing, a quiz contest, and even a spelling bee! On occasion there are also setting-up calisthenic exercises on the beach. What doesn't the beach offer? Not least important, at least in the eyes of mothers, are diaper-changing rooms with booths and electric bottle-warmers, and kindergartens "for the slightly older tots." Whatever is done here is done well. Justly, some private enterprises may boast of their precision and efficiency; but this is a public service which can make equal claims.

The marine theater, whatever else one may think of its inclusion in the list of entertainments, was a novel idea and was carried out in the grand manner. The forestage is on the mainland; the larger stage is on an island in Zach's Bay; and between the two is open water where "Viking ships," "Venetian gondolas," or other seagoing craft come gliding out of the darkness into the glare of lights.

Zach's Bay! Who was Zach? Zachariah James was an early landowner here, and he certainly never dreamed of anything like this when the area was merely a maze of shoals and bars and tidal creeks. So difficult to approach was this stretch of Long Island shore that a man in neighboring Wantagh described it thus: "An excursion to Jones Beach was always planned as a full-day outing and the day chosen so that the voyager went out with the ebb tide and came back with the flood. All-night sojourns on the sand flats were not infrequent . . . the late Judge Seaman said that he spent more time out of his boat than in it." Which, translated for the landlubber, meant that he was continually shoving off a sandbar.

In 1924 there was just one state park on Long Island. This was Fire Island. The automobile was beginning to carry thousands out of the crowded metropolis, and already the traffic congestion was such that only the hardy relished the attempt to get out to the open country or the salt water. True, there is still sometimes congestion on the great wide highways and parkways that give access to Jones Beach today. On a peak day it is necessary to barricade the approaches against incoming cars until parking space is available again. But where there were thousands, now there are tens and hundreds of thousands who get to the ocean.

The state park plan, published in 1924, said that "the program which is proposed on Long Island will protect the landscape, provide for the public and prevent private owners from being overrun, by making adequate provision for public facilities." The plan has been carried out, more magnificently than could then have been foreseen. With the Palisades Interstate Parkway linking the great metropolitan area to the parks up the Hudson, and with the parkways that afford access to Jones Beach, Captree, and Fire Island (the latter reached by ferry from Captree), a great urban population has unparalleled opportunity to enjoy a "day in the country."

It was in 1926 that the first engineering survey stake was driven into the sands of Jones Beach, at the very place where the water tower now stands. Forty million cubic yards of sand had to be dredged and pumped to create what appears to the visitor today as perfectly natural scenery—the developed Jones Beach area, the Ocean Parkway, the causeways to the beach. Fortunately, this dredged material was ideal beach sand, most of it; indeed, over the years of geologic time it had been a beach more than once. If man doesn't take steps, the Atlantic Ocean will change the shoreline at a whim. Where the east bathhouse now stands there was, not many years ago, an inlet through which boats passed from bay to ocean. The Wantagh Causeway at one point replaces what was formerly a tidal creek. There was a nine-foot channel at a spot where the Ocean Parkway now runs.

The visitor takes for granted what he now sees and enjoys at Jones Beach. But it was achieved for the public only by devoted effort and superlative imagination. At the outset the vast plan was regarded by many as fantastic; indeed, the initial appropriation by the legislature for the east bathhouse was barely enough to build the foundations. There were frustrating delays, moments of uncertainty. Alfred E. Smith, then Governor of New York, was one of those who believed. Himself a product of the big city, he never faltered in his faith in such park projects and his keen sense of the needs of the people. His political skill and administrative ability were invaluable. But there were discouraging times. Commissioner Moses once had to borrow $20,000 from his mother when the causeway contractors were unable to obtain funds to continue their work. And there was constant opposition. There were lawsuits. There was the time when a group of sportsmen sued to halt the park development because it would interfere with their goose and duck hunting—regardless, says a writer, of "whether the shots they took at well-fed and almost tame ducks and geese hit their mark or hit a park visitor."

Within the park the wildlife is of course protected now. One asks a natural question: how can wildlife of any kind adjust itself to the presence of so many millions of people? For, assuming just five peak summer days, there would have been seen in that time more than one million visitors to Jones Beach. Apparently the small animals like coons, rabbits, and oppossums manage not merely to survive—they flourish. But the aquatic wildfowl positively insist on their oldtime habits of resorting and nesting, Jones Beach or no. The gulls, terns, skimmers, egrets, and other birds are far from dispossessed. There are difficulties, of course, both for the birds and for the managers of the parks. A flock, suddenly swooping across the highway among the automobiles, can be disconcerting.

Somebody once had the idea of discouraging the nesting of birds at certain unfavorable spots by laying down a thick cover of woodchips over the sand. But the birds dealt with that impediment forthwith; they scratched the chips aside till they hit the sand. In fact, they rather liked those chips: they helped make a more comfortable place for eggs.

And now, because we are curious as to how state parks got their names, who was Mr. Jones? He was Major Thomas Jones, who, in 1692, was one of the biggest landowners on the south shore of Long Island. Major Jones and his wife, Freelove Townsend, owned a whaling station on the outer beach near where the present park stands. Jones died in 1713, and himself composed his epitaph, containing the line:

This Seat He Chose, and Here He Fixed His Name.

(X)

LETCHWORTH STATE PARK

NEW YORK

Entrances at Portageville, Castile, Perry, and Mt. Morris

A SENECA INDIAN warrior, on the way from his snug northernmost town at Avon Springs to attend a council meeting of the Iroquois Nations at Caneadea in the final years of the eighteenth century, would have followed a well-worn trail up the fertile valley of the river he called the Gen-nis-he-o. Little changed in pronunciation, this stream is now known as the Genesee.

All along the riverside were prosperous cornfields and orchards—the tokens of a sound economy that gave the Six Nations the right to refer to the Algonquin Indians as "ratirontaks," or tree-eaters. Hence the name Adirondacks. It was a plain sarcastic reference to the fact that their ancient enemies were merely forest rovers, barbarians.

Soon our Seneca traveler would have arrived at Da-yo-it-ga-o, or "the place where the river comes out of the hills." Now he would cross the Gardeau Flats, described not many years later by that indefatigable traveler Timothy Dwight, president of Yale, as "large and very rich intervals . . . perhaps the best in the world." Mary Jemison, the famous white girl captive of the Indians, later became the owner of those flats, and brought up her half-blood family there. But of Mary we shall hear more later.

The wolf and the panther were here then. They held no terrors for our Seneca, but Timothy Dwight heard the wolf at night and didn't like the sound. They had been known, he said to "tree" travelers in the woods at night, and keep them there till daybreak. They did not attack in the daytime, he had been told. Also, Timothy was informed that just above the Gardeau Flats there was a tremendous chasm "through which the river passes over three sets of falls, said to have a descent of 180 feet in the whole."

Had the good Dr. Dwight followed the Indian trail, he would have recorded one of the finest scenes in the eastern United States. He would have looked down several hundred feet of cliff, cut into rock that was laid down as an ocean sediment long before the Genesee came into existence. He would have seen at the lower falls, where the Indian trail left the river and climbed for the great portage, a spot where the whole flow of the stream pours through a narrow flume that leaves one wondering how such a thing can be possible. Following the eastern ridge, he would have gazed in astonishment at the great middle falls, set in such forest beauty as would have made joyful his refined eye. He would have seen ribbon-like brooks leaping the cliffs to spray upon the river far below. In brief, he would have seen Letchworth State Park.

Not exactly as the visitor sees it today, true. That was a virgin growth of forest then, everywhere the vision roved. But the whole picture, as sensed by today's visitor, is little changed: as you look across from one of the towering cliffs to the other, the forest growth might well be uncorrupted, for all one can perceive.

Some feverish comparer has referred to Letchworth, and the great chasm of the Genesee, as "the Grand Canyon of the East," with reference, of course, to the Grand Canyon of the Colorado. No slogan could be less apt. This jewel of consummate loveliness is no more like the Arizona canyon than the ocean is like a sylvan lake. The Grand Canyon of the Colorado is the geologic history of the world in one lesson. It is a colossal demonstration of natural forces that smites the egotism of man as if with a poleax. You can no more feel an intimacy with that western canyon that you can with the fossil skeleton of a dinosaur. True, both canyons are examples of the powers of erosion. But the charm and beauty of Letchworth do not humble you. You can feel a kinship with all that surrounds you there. You can feel yourself a partner of it, instead of a spectator. For the canyon of the Genesee has its own incomparable qualities.

Speaking of the Grand Canyon of the Colorado, it surely is an interesting fact that Major John W. Powell, the first explorer of that Arizona wonder, was born in Mount Morris, at Da-yo-it-ga-o, "the place where the river comes out of the hills." The doughty one-armed major must have known and loved this New York gorge in his boyhood rambles.

At the upper end of the seventeen-mile winding gorge, a railroad crosses on a steel trestle high above the river. Although it cannot be said that this work of man adds to the superb scenic qualities of the area, the bridge at least has historical interest. When originally built of heavy wooden timbers taken by sturdy axemen from the handy source on the spot, the bridge was such a source of pride to the Erie Railroad that it issued handbills to its passengers, announcing: "This train will in a few minutes pass over Portage Bridge . . . the highest wooden bridge in the United States, if not in the world, and one of the grandest rivers on the Western Continent." It took many acres of primeval trees to create the structure, and it was certainly a masterpiece of American knowhow.

The gorge of the Genesee offers an instructive lesson in the shaping and reshaping of the surface of the earth in New York and wherever else the great ice sheet flowed in Pleistocene times. There is little doubt that before the glaciation—or at least before its fourth stage—the Genesee flowed through the valley that now lies between the deep chasms adjacent to Mount Morris and Portageville. The retreating ice choked this valley with gravel and boulder material, creating a high-level lake to the south. From that lake, at first, meandered a stream that found itself a lazy course through loose material, till it finally got down to bedrock. After that, it continued in the same direction, carving the present winding trail.

For lovers of birds and wild plant life, Letchworth is supremely inviting. One naturalist has said of it: "In many respects this charming retreat surpasses any other in its attractions for the naturalist. The flora is more abundant and varied, while the songbirds are here in greater numbers than in any other locality in the State."

Some years ago George V. Nash found, near the lower falls, a grove of trees that appeared to be a virgin stand; large hemlocks, maples, and tulip trees. Professor Clausen of Cornell discovered here a species of succulent plant, roseroot, the roots of which have a perfume like that of roses. He considered it a relic of the glacial period. Rare, too, are the vetchling and the butterwort, but, as one professional botanist has said, "no good purpose is served by informing the general public of their location." Too true, that cynicism. Some day, though, we hope and believe, the general public will be content to feast its eyes and leave the plants for others to view where they grow.

In the year 1858, while the lumbermen were still tearing at the heart of this place of extraordinary beauty, a successful young merchant in Buffalo experienced a longing for a house in the country. His name was William Pryor Letchworth. On one of his scouting trips, he stopped at the Portage station of the Erie and walked out upon the wooden bridge that spanned the Genesee gorge. It was a case of love at first sight—not an infatuation, but a passion to use his business ability and taste to rescue what was left of this noble victim of felonious assault. He saw a collection of shacks and a hungry sawmill surrounded by ugly stumps. He saw two gorgeous falls; the third he did not glimpse until later. But, to use the words of the great Mormon leader at Salt Lake, Letchworth concluded, with no shadow of doubt: "This is the place!" Then he returned to Buffalo, where he was already engaged in a humanitarian effort to help certain unfortunates on the fringe of society: juvenile offenders, epileptics, the insane. As I write, I have a picture of this man before me. If ever there was a face with character stamped on it—here it is.

In 1859 William Letchworth took possession of a spot overlooking the Middle Falls, where the sun-and-water magic of the 107-foot leap creates a great rainbow in the mists. "Glen Iris" he called the home he built there. All told, he acquired a thousand acres, which finally were given to the state for the enjoyment of posterity. More than twelve thousand acres have been added to the park since that bequest; and there is a strange aspect to those additions, for each time they were the result of the threat of a dam. Four different times this menace presented itself, and each time an agreement was reached by which the park was enriched and its interests promoted.

The home of Dr. Letchworth (it was a well-deserved honorary title, but the modest man never used it) became the Glen Iris Inn, where visitors are now accommodated. Not far from the inn is a museum with exhibits dealing with the Indian and pioneer history of the region: the way of life of these people as seen in the implements they used. You go out from the inn to the edge of the gorge and find a simple plaque:

WILLIAM PRYOR LETCHWORTH LLD
HUMANITARIAN-CONSERVATIONIST
DONOR OF GLEN IRIS AND HIS ESTATE
COMPRISING THE ORIGINAL 1000 ACRES
OF THIS PARK INCLUDING UPPER,
MIDDLE AND LOWER FALLS
SO THAT THIS GORGE MIGHT REMAIN
A PLACE OF INSPIRATION AND BEAUTY
FOREVER

William Pryor Letchworth did more than preserve the natural beauty of the gorge of the Genesee. He was a preserver of natural integrity, but he was interested in people, too. And *people* meant not only white people, but the regional Indians that the march of progress had expelled from their lands and scattered to the mercies of an inhospitable world.

The old trail that wound its way around the Upper Falls went on for several miles to the last Seneca "castle" and to the council house that had escaped the torches of Sullivan's army in 1779. Built of well-hewn logs, nicely dove-tailed at the corners and chinked with clay, this parliament house had known the oratory of Red Jacket and Cornplanter, Little Beard and Tallchief. It had heard the counsel of the great Mohawk Joseph Brant. It was still standing, but Letchworth found that the owner was about to tear it down. Forthwith, our conservationist proceeded to take it carefully, log by log, to his estate and re-erect it on the hill above his home.

In this salvaged historic building, at the invitation of Letchworth, the Indians were to meet once more and for the last time, in a pathetic kind of council. It was on the first day of October 1872.

One of the speakers was Thomas Jemison, grandchild of the white woman of the Gardeau Flats, Mary Jemison, who as a child had been captured by the Indians and had become one of them by adoption and marriage.

"Brothers," said this Thomas Jemison with the wrinkled face and snowy hair, "I am an old man, and well remember when our people lived in this valley. I was born in a wigwam on the banks of this river. I remember when our people were rich in lands and respected by the whites. Our fathers knew not the value of these lands, and parted with them for a trifle. The craft of the white man prevailed over their ignorance and simplicity. We have lost a rich inheritance: but it is vain to regret the past. Let us make the most of what little is left to us."

And another said: "We have raked the ashes over our fire, and have closed the last council of our people in the valley of our fathers."

The last speaker of all turned to Letchworth and said: "You have warmed your heart toward us: in our weakness you have not forgotten us: from this time you will be one of the Wolf Clan of the Senecas, and your name will be Hai-wa-ye-is-tah." It was a well-chosen name. It means "the man who always does the right thing."

Appropriately near to the Seneca council house stands the bronze statue of Mary Jemison, the "white woman of the Genesee." Having become fascinated by her strange, but not unique, experience, Letchworth not only had her remains moved from an Indian burial ground in Buffalo back to her longtime home, but engaged a sculptor to figure in bronze the likeness of a girl captive trudging the long trail from the Ohio country to the homeland of the Seneca tribe.

A strange, appealing, and typically Indian ceremony took place at the dedication of this bronze statue. A descendant of Mary Jemison handed a young maiden two ears of squaw corn. He bade the girl cast four handfulls upon the grave of Mary, and then said: "This is the corn that so often *you* cultivated . . . it is a symbol that as it dies only to spring up anew, likewise we shall live again. The birds eat it from the ground where we place it, and fly again to the skies. This is like the body that tarries on the earth to eat of its fruits, but flies upward when the Great Wisdom knows it is time."

The story of Mary Jemison's capture in a raid on her parents' frontier farm; the saving of her life by two Seneca squaws and her adoption into the tribe as their sister; her two marriages and subsequent colorful life: this tale has been published and has run to twenty-two editions; Dr. Letchworth spent the last days of his life preparing still another revision of the book, which can be purchased at the park museum.

In this park of natural and historic significance there is plenty of room and ample facilities for just plain relaxation and play. Seven picnic areas, with hiking trails radiating from them; a modern concrete swimming pool and bathhouse; shelters and ample parking space. Besides the accommodations at Glen Iris, overnighters will find small and large cabins and deluxe lodges. Look anywhere you chose in Letchworth—all is snug, well-protected, adequate.

(X I)

MACEDONIA BROOK STATE PARK

CONNECTICUT

One mile north of Highway 341 via town road, near Kent

IT HAPPENED, on this sweltering midsummer day, that the park ranger was off duty. Near headquarters I found a thickset, swartish laborer and a gangling youth with bright eyes standing beside a pickup truck just getting ready to go up the mountain road to look at the campers and picnickers, and probably to collect the very nominal camping charge that the state assesses. I told the thickset man that I was associated with the National Park Service. He had never heard of such an organization, and eyed me with a touch of suspicion, since I was obviously neither camper nor picnicker, and might, therefore, be a city slicker of the kind that could toss a live cigarette into dry underbrush.

Nor did my first question serve to grease the social axle. I asked: "Why do they call this township *Macedonia*?"

There was a touch of scorn in the man's voice when he replied, chopping his words in good nutmeg fashion: "Haven't you ever heard of Macedonia, in Greece?"

"Certainly I have," I responded. "And I particularly remember that 'a vision appeared to Paul in the night: There stood a man of Macedonia, and prayed him, saying, Come over into Macedonia and help us.' "

"Huh! I guess that's from the Bible." From a changed look in those challenging eyes, I realized that my display of vast erudition and piety had struck twelve. But I did not at that moment know that this park laborer and I would be bosom and understanding friends before four hours had passed.

Yet, I haven't yet found out why the locality was called Macedonia. He didn't know. He only knew that when his father came there from Bavaria, that's what it was called then. He said that his house was so near the New York State line that if a flood took out the underpinning he would be slid into New York taxes *just like that.*

Macedonia Brook tumbles down between two ridges of an uplift just north and west of the little town of Kent. At the time of my visit the water was low, but I could easily imagine the freshets rolling and bouncing the glacial boulders of the brook bed after a period of rains. To ascend to the north end of the park, where it ends in an open space, where a sign reading "Amenia, N.Y." points along a dirt road, and where a weathered picnic shelter is reminiscent of CCC days, it is necessary to cross and recross the brook many a time.

The geologists say that the falls along Macedonia Brook and the other streams of western Connecticut are "fine examples of the disturbance of the drainage line by the ice invasion." Some of the falls plough through white marble before the creek joins the Housatonic River. There are two peaks, locally known as "cobbles," which reach an elevation of 1,400 feet.

Here is a park where the camper and the picnicker can set themselves down wherever they can find a footing. They are on their own here. When the White Memorial Foundation of Litchfield (funds left to Alain C. White and his sister by their father, whose will stated that a portion of the income must be devoted to conservation) gave the land to the state, it was with the understanding that there would be no hunting, and that so far as possible natural conditions would be maintained. The promise has been kept. This is not a large park—less than two thousand acres—but the conditions for the visitor are just about what you find in the great Baxter State Park of Maine.

Rough camping? Decidedly, in the sense that if you want a fire place of your own, you gather up some boulders and prepare it. For water, you take your bucket to the brook or to some spring. You bring a Coleman lantern with you, or you sit in the dark, looking up through the hardwood trees, and meditate on the starry universe. Indeed, so far as I could see, Macedonia Brook is ideal for the campfolk who do not aim at absolute solitude but still want their vacationing neighbors at a fair distance. The park is used regularly, but it is not crowded, even on weekends.

I said to my guide, the son of a Bavarian immigrant who has become all-Yankee in his speech and outlook: "I like this. There's a marvelous sense of freedom here." He looked at me, nodded, and said nothing.

As we footed it along over a stretch of road, every now and then he would stop and challenge me. "Do you know what kind of tree that is?" I passed the examination. In fact, I scored heavily, by good luck, when my guide pointed at a shrub and said: "I wonder if you could tell me what that is." "Yes, that is the wild prickly gooseberry." My reputation was established. I'm not sure that he wasn't overly modest about his knowledge of plant life. He looked on nature not as a botanist but as its kinsman, and he was full of lore about plants. He told me about a woman neighbor who had shown him "a poison elderberry growing in an old cellarhole." Has anyone heard of a "poison elderberry"? He certainly was not confusing it with the poison sumac, because he knew the sly Borgias of the *Rhus* gang like a professional.

And he knew, too, the history of the Macedonia woodland. He pointed out the remains of two old forges at the lower end of the park, where crowbars, wagon tires, and other iron products had been produced over the years. He had heard somebody say that Ethan Allen, of the Green Mountain boys, had once run a blast furnace in this neck of the woods. Did I know whether that was so?—I did not.

Truly, this whole western edge of Connecticut was another of the virgin forest wildernesses ruthlessly destroyed in the early days to make charcoal for ironworks. The original forest of the land that is now the state park was probably gone as early as 1748. Two thousand bushels of charcoal a day went into the furnaces of Kent. Second growth went the way of the first. You are surprised to learn that in spite of the rich Mesaba sources of ore in Minnesota, the Kent Iron Company was operating its works as late as 1890. Whatever the virgin timber here might have been, there is now a noticeable lack of volunteer conifers on these rugged hills. Those conifers you see now—red pine, spruce, larch, and arborvitae—are plantings that were made after 1918, when the park was established.

But for the park's purposes the present forest is ample, and even surprisingly dense and wild. It must have been a sorrowful sight in the 1840's when the iron company was bustling about with teamloads of ore, lime, and charcoal, and the hillsides were "coaled off."

This, of course, was Indian country. My park guide didn't know much about Indians, except that it was very common to find relics of their occupancy in the area that is now park. But as we were talking of Indians, a big owl crossed the roadway from one tree to another, just ahead of us. "That just somehow reminds me, that bird," said my companion . . . "I like *old* names for things, don't you? I like Indian names, and names like *Bog Hollow.*"

I said I did, too.

"I said Bog Hollow," he went on, "because that's what came to my mind when I saw that bird. A city feller bought himself a place down here, and he didn't like the name Bog Hollow, so he said after this it would be called Chickadee Valley."

"So you call it Chickadee Valley now," I suggested, unsmilingly.

"Who? Me? I do not. Leave be the old names, I say."

As I mentioned, this was favorite Indian country. At the brookside, the Scatacooks used to take trout. Possibly Macedonia Brook was once called Scatacook, and the Indian subtribe got its name from the stream, for "cook" in Algonquian referred to a brook or small river. Anyway, this Scatacook tribe was brought together by one Gideon Mauwehu, who originally was the sachem of a small band living at the lower end of the Housatonic River.

Mauwehu was a man of talent, apparently. He invited members of the Pootatucks, Waramaugs, and some Mohegans from the Hudson River area, and then got the Moravian missionaries to Christianize the group. About a hundred and fifty of them were baptized, and a church built, and a flourishing congregation established. It is a tale often forgotten when we think of our early Indian relations: all was not scalping and warfare by any means.

There was the Reverend John Sergeant in Stockbridge, for instance. John, laboring to keep his bronzed disciples from backsliding, in 1743, notes the fact that Umpachene, number two sachem, once an addict to whisky, had so been converted to sobriety and righteousness that he was elected a selectman of the town. But Umpachene, unfortunately, fell off the abstinence wagon with a bump just as the Reverend John was "beginning to conceive good hopes of him."

When the Revolutionary War came, one hundred warriors from the Mauwehu band in the vicinity of Macedonia Brook volunteered for service with the patriot army. It is said that these Indians established a signal system from the shore of Long Island to high points along the Housatonic River, so that messages could be sent as far as Stockbridge, Massachusetts, in a couple of hours. There is still a small Indian reservation a few miles south of the state park.

Despite the absence of soft living, and though it is far from crowded at any time, Macedonia Brook State Park is sufficiently attractive to lovers of quietude—mostly from New York, Connecticut, New Jersey, and Massachusetts—to have accommodated more than 11,000 campers in 1958, and 33,000 day visitors. And I was told that each succeeding year the figures would be higher.

If you long to see wildlife in Connecticut, this is probably the most favorable location. The deer population is ample, and no doubt there are a few bobcats, too, though only by chance would they be glimpsed. Of gray squirrels and raccoons there are many; and I heard, without seeing, some ruffed grouse take to the air.

Looking in on one of the campers, who gave me a cheery greeting, I smiled at the sight of a well-supplied rack of provisions—bacon squares, breakfast foods, canned goods, flapjack flour displayed beside the tent. I thought how the bears in the Great Smokies and Yellowstone would like this display of provender. Alas, the bears of Scatacook days have long since migrated to safer haunts!

(XII)

MOUNT GREYLOCK STATE RESERVATION

MASSACHUSETTS

South of North Adams and northeast of New Ashford

As LONG AS the roads can be kept open on sleek Mount Greylock, the highest point in Massachusetts, whose 3,491 feet of elevation are set among surroundings of long-relished beauty, visitors may have shelter and refreshment in a building known as Bascom Lodge. It is near the summit tower that was erected by the state in memory of its World War dead. But who was Bascom?

I went into a news shop in Williamstown and asked the proprietor, who looked like a native of long residence: "Did you happen to know Dr. John Bascom?" He nodded. "I remember him. He was the last man I ever knew to wear sideburns in this town."

Such is fate! The scholar who had been president of the University of Wisconsin fom 1874 to 1887, and later was on the faculty of Williams College as professor of political science for more than a decade, should really be remembered for something other than the type of whiskers he wore. Especially in Williamstown, and in the surrounding territory, for John Bascom so loved Mount Greylock, so promoted it as a spot where man could rejoice and be cleansed, so strengthened the links that made it almost a possession of several generations of students of the college, that it seems no one could forget him for these achievements so long as Greylock resists the erosion of time.

He must have been a salty character, this Dr. John, and when he wrote, which was not often, he hammered out the words so that you would not misunderstand him. He had some ideas about the use of natural beauty, and the dangers that always beset it, which are worth putting down. "This countryside," said Dr. John, "is destined to become a recreation resort. There is nothing better than to make fully available this magnificent scenery. When the Greylock Park Association was formed, liverymen and hotel men were active in it, as a business venture. Sound as is this view, we do not care to dwell on it. We trust the time is remote when strangers will elbow out the native of Berkshire [the county in which Greylock is situated] or send him upon a lackey's errand. We would be hospitable . . . but we would command our own house. We would wish rather to enforce the sentiment, Massachusetts for the men of Massachusetts, Berkshire for the men of Berkshire, and Greylock our daily pleasure, our constant symbol, our ever-renewed inspiration, for *all who have fellowship with nature.*"

Maybe at first glance, this sounds a little parochial. Dr. Bascom was not at all ignorant of the fact that "liverymen and hotelmen" for the most part justly and honestly perform a useful service in feeding and lodging the visitor who comes to reap the "ever-renewed inspiration" of the lovely countryside of this northwestern corner of Massachusetts. What he was trying to express was his feeling that the commercial advantage is merely a result; that the preservation of beauty is the primary end. "The camping ground has the magic touch with which to take weariness from the brain and pain from the bones," in the words of Dr. John Bascom. "The object should not be to civilize the mountain, but to bring the over-civilized men of the valley [his own Housatonic Valley] into complete and appreciative contact with it."

Long before Professor Bascom's day, the college men of Williamstown knew the gracious qualities of Mount Greylock and sought to make use of them for simple recreation. As early as 1841, Professors Albert Hopkins and Tutor Griffin whipped up interest in a "farmer's bee"—similar to the old New England "church-raising"—with the result that a fair road to the summit was made and a tower built thereon. Not a tower like the modern one, but one with a first story of solid logs, then two recessing 20-foot stories of framed timber. Then, as now, Greylock's very top was bald, showing glacial scratches and grooves where the arctic ice had ground boulders over it, but this baldness is not apparent from lower elevations.

There is a hearty tradition that when the "bee" was in progress,

Williams students lugged loads of dried codfish and crackers to the volunteer workers. Simple fare: but perhaps there were huckleberries for dessert, for one of the sports that has endured in this Greylock region is berry picking. Sport? Well, maybe a form of therapy, for I know a good old country doctor who insists that huckleberry picking is the sovereign alleviator of nervous ailment. Some prefer the more adventurous feats, though, and this is notably a country of trails for hiking. Camping on Greylock, or even a day's picnic, is a perfect way to become acquainted with a region of almost flawless sylvan mountain beauty.

Looking down the broad valley of the Housatonic, you have on the left the rugged Hoosac Range and on your right the classic Taconics. Geologically, the Hoosacs (or Hoosics or Hoosicks, all variations on the same Indian syllables) may be a continuation of the Vermont Green Mountains. I'm not sure, and I don't think the detail important to your enjoyment of these hills; but some will find revealing the fact that there are lake-shore benches on Greylock at an altitude of about 1,000 feet. Compare these with similar benches in the Manchester-Pownal Mountains of southeastern Vermont, and you can visualize a vast lake that existed here in glacial times, when the water courses were blocked by ice and debris.

A countryside you cannot rush through, certainly. The college town of Williamstown is as beautiful today as it was when the master planner in landscape architecture, Frederick Law Olmstead (the senior), beautified it with funds furnished by cable magnate Cyrus Field. Driving in from North Adams through the sheer loveliness of the 250-foot-wide main street, you know why the poet Bryant and the author Hawthorne considered this the "gem of Berkshire."

And what history has unrolled in this northwestern tip of the Bay State! At the time of the French and Indian warfare the settlers thought first of a fort on the Hoosac heights, then settled for one in the valley of the Hoosic—Fort Massachusetts, so named; but it was a short-lived bastion, for it was captured and demolished just a year after it was established.

Massachusetts has state parks and it has state forests, and in addition it administers "state reservations," of which Greylock and Wachusett are examples. You could almost call these reservations *county* parks; yet they are so only in the sense that a commission consisting wholly of county residents controls them. As they were purchased with state funds, and as the commission is appointed by the Governor, they may well qualify for our purpose here as state parks. Greylock, for instance, was acquired about 1897, when the legislature appropriated the money to buy "not over 10,000 acres" adjoining the mountain's summit, once a dense primeval forest of hardwood interspersed with conifers, mainly spruce. In inaccessible places there may be yet a little virgin growth; at any rate, the present forest is luxurious.

Good reason for calling attention to the region rather than to the single peak is that this corner of Massachusetts, where, as has been said, the Taconics seem to put up a fence to keep the New Englander in, is jam-packed with recreation areas. Coming in from the East, over the "Mohawk Trail," just west of the town of Charlemont, you find at the very roadside the camping and picnic grounds of the Mohawk Trail State Forest. Too near the highway, in truth, even though as lovely a tenting spot as you will ever see. But it is hoped that funds will be available for a new campground on the other side of the Cold River, a tributary of the classic Deerfield, along which the highway climbs. The name of this highway is no misnomer, be sure. This *was* the trail, or trace, used by the redoubtable Iroquois tribe on their eastern raiding trips. Sit at a picnic table, or beside the pool that was created by damming an icy little stream rattling in a boulder bed, and look up at the slope of Todd Mountain, high above you. Along that ridge came the Mohawks who had hiked across the Hudson, up the Hoosic River, over Hoosac Mountain, and on toward the valley of the Connecticut—circumspectly choosing the high ground for their march, and camping at just about this point on a flat where afterwards arrow points could be found aplenty on the surface of the ground.

Mohawk Trail State Forest was the first forest reserve acquired by Massachusetts.

To folks from west of the Mississippi, distances in this little corner of the country must seem short. Next-door neighbor, then, to the fine Mohawk Trail State Forest is that of Savoy Mountain. This is one of the state's largest forest preserves: 9,000 acres of upland country in the Hoosac Range, best reached from North Adams. The North Pond section includes an attractive picnic area, with beach and bathhouse. At South Pond are some single-room log cabins, and tenting and trailer facilities are ample.

Also near North Adams is Clarksburg State Park. Apparently the only difference in management between these forests and parks is that no hunting is allowed in the areas denominated as parks. There is almost constant pressure to open both parks and reservations to hunting. But the fish and game organizations of this state are unusually intelligent in their general conservation views, which of course makes them all the more formidable in legislation.

As you ascend the east flank of the Hoosacs, the Mohawk Trail becomes steeper, the brooks leap more tumultuously, and the visitor sees a country hardly to be expected in such a long-settled state. At Whitcomb Summit, 2,300 feet in elevation, a view opens out which can without exaggeration be said to be one of the finest in the country, not excluding anything in the Great Smokies of the southern Appalachians. No comparison can fairly be made with the sharp-edged scenic points of the Rockies, because this is entirely different scenery. This is all greenwood, all lush field and meadow, all soothing and smooth. And before one reaches Whitcomb Summit there is a turnout from the highway, with a sign pointing downward through the forest: Hoosac Tunnel.

This is the east portal of this famous engineering project, which was so bold in conception that most state inhabitants thought it stark mad. The idea originated in canal days. Canal building was a fever that finally reached New England. How could any canal, planned to connect with the Erie, conquer these massive Hoosac Mountains, which walled off Massachusetts with seeming finality? The undaunted Yankees of 1825 actually planned a five-mile tunnel under the mountains, which would be converted into an underground river for canal barges! And they might have made the project a reality, too; but before that could happen, the railroad arrived, offering a new means of transportation.

In 1851 the work of boring through the rock was begun, but not till 1873 was the tunnel opened to traffic; and the intervening years were filled with frustrations, small scandals, legislative despair, and a whirlwind of pamphletry of which I recently saw a yellowed sample entitled, "The Agony of the Great Bore." I suppose only freight trains now use this elderly phenomenon, but lively are the memories of several generations of New Englanders of their first trip through Hoosac Tunnel, choking with sulfurous smoke, their ears assailed by racket, their spines tingling with fear at the thought that they were more than two thousand feet in the belly of the rock of the mountains—and how could a little gopher tube like that fail to come down and make a pancake of the train?

Before one arrived at the east portal of the tunnel, one stopped at a little station named Zoar. Seldom did anyone board or leave the train at Zoar, but a mailbag was dropped or taken on. Pious passengers knew that the name was a Biblical one. It gave them strength, no doubt, to meet the challenge of the dark tunnel adventure.

(XIII)

NIAGARA FRONTIER

NEW YORK

Near Niagara Falls, in Erie and Niagara Counties

> FOUR LEAGUES *from Lake Frontenac* [*Ontario*] *there is an incredible Cataract or Waterfall which has no equal. The Niagara River near this place is only the eighth of a league wide, but it is very deep in places, and so rapid above the fall that it hurries down all the animals that try to cross it, without a single one being able to withstand its current. They plunge down a height of more than 500 feet* [*overestimate*] *and its fall is composed of two sheets of water, with an island sloping down. In the middle these waters foam and boil in a fearful manner. They thunder continually, and when the wind blows in a southerly direction the noise they make is heard for more than fifteen leagues. Four leagues from this Cataract, or fall, the Niagara river rushes with extraordinary rapidity especially for two leagues. . . .*
>
> —First description of Niagara Falls and River
> by Father Hennepin, 1683

ON the handsomely printed brochure issued by the Power Authority of the State of New York, very cleverly, against a cover with a background of a dark slate color, the title drapes itself down the sheet in precisely the double curve made by the water that pours over the falls of Niagara. The wording is: NIAGARA POWER AND.

If you don't know what is happening, at top speed, in the vicinity of those falls that made honeymooning popular, this title is cryptic. "Niagara Power" you can readily understand. But the word "AND"?

What is the meaning of that? I suspect that the formidable Robert Moses got a good deal of rougish satisfaction from the title of the brochure.

For, ever since Moses was induced to accept the chairmanship of the Power Authority of the State of New York, the AND was a foregone conclusion. Those who thought otherwise just hadn't studied their lessons. The man who had gained the support of the wise Governor Alfred E. Smith back in 1924 for his ideas of conservation, and who has bowled over all opposition since, was not going to miss a chance like this.

Just this morning, as I sat down to write, in came a newspaper article by Raymond Moley about Robert Moses, paying full credit to "the incredible drive and imagination" of the man, but concluding that his ways are, after all, those of dictatorship. There is a shade of truth in the charge. Moses is the kind of dictator Steve Mather showed himself to be when he blew up the Great Northern Sawmill in Glacier National Park. Steve just wasn't going to allow the sawmill to mar the beauty of the area. Moses, probably one of the toughest conservationists in this country, has never let slip an opportunity to offer sunlight, beauty, and nature to his New York millions.

And what an opportunity this power development was! What I saw at Niagara Falls was brobdingnagian machinery moving earth (these contraptions could probably move heaven, too, though I trust they won't) to create the generating plant, the forebay, the surge basin, and the other vast units of the enterprise. What I did not see, but it shall as surely be realized, is the Niagara Parkway and the new park facilities that despite all opposition and all major impediments will offer a great new access and pleasure drive for millions of people. If the plans for a parkway require a small thing like the removal of the mainline tracks of the New York Central Railroad, depend on Moses.

Prospect Park, shabby in some details and outgrown in others, will be enlarged and improved. There will be a new elevator leading to the Maid of the Mist. Included in the plan is a community building for the Tuscarora Indians. The architects' drawings show a structure that should make any Tuscarora glad that his ancestors came up from the Carolinas and joined the Five Nations. One suspects that the displeasure of the Tuscaroras may have been in part fired by interests that do not appreciate Robert Moses as much as do conservationists; and, in truth, Moses's cocksure bluntness has pained many a conservationist, too. As an example of the keen joy with which Moses can lacerate the tender susceptibilities of those with whom he disagrees, I offer this quotation:

Among the commodities we can dispense with are dogmatic, theoretical pseudo-scientific standards governing the precise size, equipment and personnel of future city playgrounds, the cubic footage per child and adult and the elements of elaborate regimented play. The best advice is to grab for parks and playgrounds every possible piece of land . . . dreams of green belts and counsels of perfection don't produce outdoor fresh air, rest and exercise.

And here is a statement about the Niagara Frontier plans:

As I stated at the St. Lawrence Ground Breaking, *we do not aim to be popular here*, but we do expect to win your respect long before the project is completed.

This is, I realize, a great deal about Robert Moses in a chapter aimed to describe the present and future Niagara Frontier. My excuse shall be that, just as John Muir said to Ralph Waldo Emerson: "You yourself are a sequoia," it may be said of Moses, after this great digging at Niagara is done and the land's face is healed: "You yourself are a generating plant."

But there is more to this great Niagara Frontier system of parks and parkways. For example, there is the charming small park on Buckhorn Island, at the north end of Grand Island in the Niagara River. Here I found absolute silence; a sanctuary for wildlife. The public may visit, but the accommodations are such as to discourage all but a few. A state employee showed me a pen of 500 mallard ducks and another pen of several hundred pheasants which he would release when they were ready.

"We are raising them for people to see. Sure, most of them will stray off the reservation and get potted. But they're pretty clever, too. Anyway, people like to see these wild things in the parks."

The new Niagara Parkway is planned to come from the North Grand Island Bridge, at the village of La Salle, follow the river northward to the great power plant, thence continuing to Fort Niagara State Park. It will pass under Rainbow Bridge, thus providing easy access to Niagara Falls Reservation, the oldest park in the state, dating from 1885; the old traffic congestion in the city of Niagara Falls will be but a memory. The pedestrian will have an unchallenged loafing pace over the Goat Island Bridge, because a new bridge will carry the motor traffic.

Not far from Fort Niagara is a historic spot known as Four Mile

Creek. Nowadays this is but a swampy embayment, with wooded hills on both sides; it is ideal for the extensive camping areas so much needed in the Frontier Region. But in time past it was a cove of Lake Ontario, and it was here, in 1759, that Brigadier Prideaux, an Englishman with a French name, lay up his fleet of small craft in preparation for the attack upon the French stronghold. Prideaux did not live to enjoy the capture of Fort Niagara. He was killed by the premature explosion of one of his own shells, from a "coehorn" mortar.

In after years, the winds that blow from the Canadian side of the lake have put up a barrier of sand at the mouth of the former cove. This planned development at Four Mile Creek will not be a new state park, but will constitute an annex to Fort Niagara. Campsite development at Four Mile, with a boat harbor and other waterside facilities, will be a boon to some of the six million people who resort to the Frontier parks every year. Two million live within fifty miles!

In this congeries of Niagara Frontier recreation spots, Beaver Island State Park, at the head of Grand Island in the Niagara River, is the most fully developed. It has at least 1,000 picnic tables for the day users, who have numbered 25,000 on a Sunday in recent years. Here the Boy Scouts have their "camporee"—five hundred of them at a time—on ample acres for games, with a bathhouse and boardwalk. The big casino is a product of the depression and is, to be frank, a white elephant. The Buffalo Symphony Orchestra plays here on occasion. Perhaps the casino will finally serve as a golf clubhouse. There is a good beach on this piece of land, which is separated from Grand Island by Beaver Creek, but it is a manmade beach that has to be constantly renewed on account of the relentless wash of the river current.

Latest of the regional recreation developments is Evangola State Park, containing somewhat more than 500 acres on the shore of Lake Erie, twenty-six miles west of Buffalo. "Evangola" sounds like a musical Indian name, but is really the result of a newspaper contest. Evans–Angola: merge the names of two adjoining towns and you get the present title. This is a typical waterfront state park, devoted to bathing and picnicking on a large scale. It was only three years old when I saw it, and considering the land it was created out of, the landscaping promises a charming seasonal resort for the future.

Incidentally, one is constantly surprised at the numbers of game animals seen in all these state reservations which are so close to great concentrations of population. On Buckhorn Island, for instance, we saw twenty-one browsing deer in one group; and along the thruway, west of Buffalo, the motorist is constantly apprised of "deer runs." As the breeder of mallards and pheasants said: "People like to see these wild creatures."

Finally, there is Old Fort Niagara, at Youngstown. This outstanding historical preservation, so well maintained and managed by the Old Fort Niagara Association, to which it is leased for a token sum by the state, presents a clear reason for calling all this pleasuring ground the Region of the *Frontier*. A frontier post this surely was, from the day when keen-eyed La Salle selected it as a strategic spot and erected a light palisaded post there. Out upon the narrow peninsula where the Niagara River, rushing away from the falls, churns into the lower lake, the fort commanded the portage between Erie and Ontario. Whoever controlled this bastion had the fur trade of the western wilds in command. After La Salle, Dentonville realized it and garrisoned a large fortress on the spot. "The cradle of civilization on the Niagara Frontier," it has been called.

As the visitor enters the fort grounds, he passes through the "Gate of the Five Nations." François Pouchot, the last French commander to hold this post, named it thus in a vain attempt to conciliate the Iroquois; but these powerful tribes were not able to forget the defeats they had suffered at the hands of Champlain and his Algonquian allies.

Pass, stranger, through the gate and over the drawbridge, and you are back in the year 1759. If your imagination is not palsied with modernity, you begin to sense the epic struggle of England and France for possession of a rich new world. Ah, there is so much to see, and it is all so nobly shown! As a museum, the area is superbly kept, and it offers admirable interpretation services.

Can you not see before you, and *feel*, the drama of that seige? Prideaux, the attacking commander, killed by accident; Sir William Johnson taking personal charge; Aubry rushing aid to this priceless stronghold with French reserves hastily gathered at Detroit and Erie? The Indians, pro-French and pro-English (but most of them, properly enough, pro-Indian at heart, for whoever wins, *they* will eventually be the victims) challenge each other with whoops and ear-jarring yells. The reinforcements of Aubry are shattered by Johnson and his British regulars and Indians. There is a Highland regiment, with skirling pipers; there is stupidity on the part of the British engineers, who laid out the besieging trenches so that they were easily raked by the fort guns, and Allan Macleane cries upon them:

"They are fools and blockheads, goddamn them!" But Johnson takes Fort Niagara: the way to Montreal and Quebec is open. The next act takes place upon the Plains of Abraham, with the death of two valiant men, Wolfe and Montcalm.

There is so much to see, so much to feel, about that crucial struggle at Fort Niagara! It cannot be more than faintly suggested on these pages. The visitor would do well to read a historian like Francis Parkman before he visits Fort Niagara. At least, perhaps he will feel the urge to do so after he gets home.

The French Castle, the oldest, largest, and most important of the pre-Revolutionary buildings at Fort Niagara, is a fine example of skillful preservation and interpretation. This "stone house" was designed and built by Louis XV's chief Canadian engineer Gespard Chaussegros de Lery. It was constructed to resist any attack, though it is said that while it was underway the French were at great pains to deceive the neighboring Indians into believing it was to be merely another and larger trading establishment.

Certainly that subterfuge was not altogether a deceit. The trade room, which fascinates most visitors, was once a colorful and busy scene—the Indians bringing their pelts to barter for bright cloths and beads, cooking utensils, and powder and shot; yes, and unfortunately also for "firewater," which the American Indian never learned to handle with discretion.

There is an example of the value of patient research here. It had long been wondered whether the castle, built to house a hundred or more soldiers and officers, had ever had a source of fresh water within it. It seemed a likely provision, but no well had been found. But some years ago, plans of the castle were discovered in Paris, and photocopies were brought back to the Fort. They showed a fine deep well, which was sealed up by the British after they captured the place; they feared that the water might have been poisoned by the defeated garrison.

(XIV)

OLD ECONOMY HISTORIC SITE

PENNSYLVANIA

Near Ambridge, off State 88 in Beaver County

THE TRAVELER, let us say, has just emerged from some lovely spot in western Pennsylvania—from the perfume of flowers, the joyous warbling of birds, the dignity of trees. Suddenly (because much is sudden when one travels in an automobile) he finds himself on the road that ascends the Ohio River toward Pittsburgh, in a hill-hemmed valley which in pioneer days must have been good to look upon. What a transition—and what a shock!

All that man can do in the pursuit of sheer ugliness is represented on this road. It does not seem possible that it could exist by mere accident. It is more like the careful planning of some expert with a master's degree in Landscape Devastation. The great steel mills along the shore of Lake Michigan, though they may belch choking fumes, at least have something colossally awful, something cyclopean, about them. They have that "bad eminence" ascribed to Satan by John Milton in his *Paradise Lost.* This scene along the Ohio is merely a hodgepodge of the unpleasant. If the business structures of the closely packed towns should collapse some day into the streets, the debris would blend fittingly into the surroundings.

The traveler finally arrives at Ambridge. He doesn't know where he is, and is beginning not to care. He is in a region where the perfume is not that of flowers, and the birds have not the heart to sing. But, finally, getting his direction from some kindly passer-by, he turns down a side street toward the river and drives to the end of it. Surprise! He is facing a charming oasis—not desert palms, but more akin to a cathedral close, a beautiful enclosure open to the sky, with fine sturdy buildings of simple elegance, and a glimpse of a spacious garden, coolly inviting on a summer day. The traveler has arrived at Old Economy, third and final home of one of the greatest social experiments in American history.

This site is of national as well as state importance. The German peasants of the Harmony Society, led by the remarkable character named George Rapp, set the model for a type of humanitarian thinking which led, in the United States of the nineteenth century, to the formation of hundreds of communities of similar aspirations—Oneida in New York, Amana in Iowa, Brook Farm in Massachusetts, and a swarm of Fourieristic "phalansteries" that rose like mushrooms. Most of these communities were destined to perish speedily; a few of them, to live healthily for many years.

Of all such experiments in communal living, the Harmonist one was the most successful, the longest-lived, and certainly the richest in terms of property. In the days when Old Economy was at the height of its prosperity, the Harmonists here owned 3,000 acres, extending for five miles along the Ohio in Beaver County, and their wealth was estimated variously at between ten and thirty million dollars. This present historic site preserves the "home" of the Harmonists—their central quarters—but their various establishments and factories once extended widely beyond what the visitor now sees.

The reader will perhaps remember that when Brook Farm—a pale blue-stocking imitation of the Rapp colony—was projected, Ralph Waldo Emerson was invited to become a member. He declined, saying dryly that he thought he would prefer to own real estate in Concord. Emerson knew (though he was sympathetic with their ideals) that Brook Farmers were doomed to fail. He wondered "whether such a rereat does not promise to become an asylum to those who have tried and failed, rather than a field to the strong." In those words Emerson pinpointed the reason for the collapse of this and other similar groups. He was well acquainted with the history of the Rapp Harmonists, and he knew what had made them successful—unquestioning discipline, religious devotion, untiring industry. Yes; and perhaps the practice of celibacy—for the man or woman without children to strive for could well bend all efforts for the common good.

The poet Byron knew about the Rappites, too. In his *Don Juan* he indulged in some humor about them, not unmixed with high praise:

When Rapp the Harmonist embargo'd marriage
In his harmonious settlement, which flourishes
Strangely enough as yet without miscarriage, . . .
Why call'd he "Harmony" a state sans wedlock?
Now here I've got the preacher at a dead lock.

Because he either meant to sneer at harmony
Or marriage, by divorcing them thus oddly.
But whether reverend Rapp learn'd this in Germany
Or no, 'tis said his sect is rich and godly,
Pious and pure, beyond what I can term any
Of ours. . . .

The truth was that Rapp's scheme of the "community of goods"—the foundation stone of the colony—was taken from a verse in the New Testament (Acts IV:32): "And the multitude of them that believed were of one heart and one soul: neither said any of them aught of the things which he possessed was his own; but *they had all things in common.*"

George Rapp and his followers, at first numbering six hundred, had fled Germany because of petty persecutions arising from certain views that opposed those of the state religion. They were prosecuted for their beliefs, but the enlightened ruler in Wurttemberg had freed them, saying: "If they are law abiding, let them believe what they please." However, they lived uneasily among their orthodox neighbors, and finally they emigrated in a body, Rapp at the head, and settled near Zelienople, Pennsylvania, in 1805. They called the settlement Harmonie, or Harmony. With their unflagging industry, they cleared 150 acres the first year, and two years later a visitor to their community wrote of their "remarkable success . . . arising from their unity and fraternal love."

Successful as the Harmonists were near Zelienople, their keen leader realized the disadvantages of being twelve miles from the nearest point of navigation. Besides, the German peasants longed to cultivate all kinds of fruit, and their first holdings were not well suited for it. So George Rapp's adopted son Frederick went westward to scout all the lands bordering the Ohio. He chose a rich tract on the Wabash River, above what is now Evansville, Indiana. There the Harmonists bought 20,000 acres of government land and 10,000 acres of adjoining improved farms.

Unity, discipline, and devotion prove as fruitful in one place as in another. New Harmony, as the second colony was called, was a communal success such as had never before been seen. Visitors who had no sympathy with the central idea, or were even suspicious and antagonistic, had to admit the prodigious material performance of the Rappites.

There was stark jealousy in reports that circulated: Rapp was a tyrant; Rapp held his people in bondage; Rapp resorted to tricks to demonstrate his partnership with the Almighty; the peasants were stupid and sheeplike. Rugged individualists certainly would have been unhappy in this Eden on the Wabash, and, truly, security may be bought at too high a figure. But slanders to the effect that the Rapp flock were overworked, unhappy, or downtrodden were patently nonsensical. A group of field workers who marched to their hoeing behind a brass band, and were played to by the band while they plucked weeds; a bountiful table for the innerman; a knowledge that the humblest member could take his grievance or tribulation to the "father" and be treated with kindness and understanding—these are not the ingredients of misery. No; the Rappites were only guilty of shaming drones.

"In the orchards of New Harmony there were tables and benches, and on each machine in the factories stood a vessel filled with freshly cut flowers." Page John Ruskin!

Curiously enough, the Rappites had a great distillery, converting surplus grain into strong liquor, though they drank none of it themselves. Their neighbors acknowledged both the quality and the quantity of the Rapp whiskey.

Ten years of this unqualified success, and then the Rappites were ready for a third and last venture. It is not known just why they wished to quit Indiana. One suspects that the shrewd leader found his flock getting out of hand, or becoming soft: some new pioneering would be a natural cure for that. Anyway, they sold out, lock, stock, and whiskey barrel, to Robert Owen, the Scotch philanthropist mill-owner, who had been yearning to put some of his revolutionary social ideas into operation. Owen's sons came over to close the deal, though the mill-owner himself did not arrive till long afterward.

Thus the Rappite colony became the Owen colony. And what a difference! The Rappites were deeply religious. Owen was openly scornful of belief; his savior was political economy, though, in truth, he had a very shadowy concept of that quasi-science. Together with the brilliant but eccentric William Maclure, Owen and his sons proceeded to demonstrate how a communal group, starting with vast material advantages, can fail miserably.

The Rappites were a stupid lot of peasants, if you choose so to believe: the Owenites gathered to themselves the most sparkling coterie of natural scientists America had yet seen in one group—Thomas Say, Charles Alexander Lesueur, Constantine Raffinesque, Gerard Troost—men whose works are basic in their fields—and still the experiment staggered and decayed. Like all such attempts based upon purely economic principles, Owen attracted not only the intellectual lone wolf, but also the lunatic fringe and the congenital and self-made failure. Emerson had seen the trap: "*You* have failed, and *I* have failed; perhaps if we band together we shall marvelously prosper."

No, no; it won't do, it is pure delusion. The Rapps had the secret: discipline and industry and no pretentious *talk*.

Father Rapp and his flock moved back to Pennsylvania, not far from where they had first settled. Once more they chose wisely. In Ambridge, at the scene of this fine restoration by the state, you will visit seventeen surviving structures that amply tell the story of the third venture—the Great House, where Rapp and his elders lived and governed the far-flung affairs; the Feast Hall, the storehouse, the general store; everywhere are examples of the craft skills that the empire rested upon. Beautiful silks; cottons and woolens; a famous light blue glassware, made at Beaver Falls; wines (their wines were famous, and I believe they now most temperately drank a small glass with dinner, themselves). One of their favorite wines was made from quinces; it sounds appetizing. And these resourceful people concocted a widely sold "elixir" that would cure everything from coughs to housemaid's knee.

Here you will see the print shop, with a handpress that dates from about 1820, and some of the types that were used in printing books both in English and in German. The books themselves are preserved; the bindings were of their own handiwork. Indeed, these people produced practically everything they used. Never were there more self-sufficient folk. And such craftsmen! Whatever they did was well done.

A serpent came to dwell among these people of the third empire, and nearly wrecked them. One Bernhard Muller, styling himself Count Maximilian de Leon, injected himself into the colony with the pretence that he was devoted to the communal life. This smooth adventurer captured the hearts of many of the simple people, probably slyly introducing into their heads the notion that celibacy had its unjoyous aspects—and the younger ones especially were targets for such a message. There was a schism, a crisis, the first the Rappists had faced. A vote was taken: "Are you with Father Rapp, or are you with the count?" When hands were counted, 500 stood with the Father, 250 with the count. So a swarming took place; the dissidents were paid off and left for Louisiana with their new leader. Their money was soon gone; the count absconded; the colonists who had remained with Rapp could congratulate themselves on their good judgment. Imagine, though, the solvency of the group at this crucial time, when Rapp and his elders could find $105,000 to pay off the departing third.

As happened to the Shakers, the rule of celibacy finally became a deadweight upon the Harmonists. It was, of course, not the sole reason for the decline and extinguishment of the society. Prosperity, and the human vanity that comes with it, were factors. Discipline within the walls became more difficult to maintain when contacts with the outside world and its lack of discipline made for restlessness and peevish rebellion.

In 1905 the society was officially dissolved. It had lived a whole century. It had had a few dark moments, but had never owed a dollar it could not pay. On the contrary, Old Economy at Ambridge had in its heyday supplied capital to build railroads, to drill for oil, to build industrial plants.

To visit Old Economy is to learn much of a generous aspiration toward life's "good way"—a magnificent experiment of a sort which mankind will try and try again, always hoping to succeed.

(X V)

PALISADES INTERSTATE PARK AND PARKWAY

NEW YORK AND *NEW JERSEY*

Orange and Rockland Counties

ON AUGUST 28, 1958, the Palisades Interstate Park Commission of New York and New Jersey issued a handsome brochure, *Completion Story*, commemorating in modest terms the opening of the last section of an experiment in humane engineering that constitutes a true drama. Indeed, even the love interest is there, represented by the love of devoted people for nature, for beauty, and for the well-being of their fellow men and of the generations to come.

The eleven and a half miles of the Palisades Interstate Parkway in New Jersey were completed in 1957; the remaining thirty and a half miles, in New York, are now in use, making possible direct access to the New York park areas on the west bank of the Hudson for the millions of the great metropolitan population. The cost? In money, no less than $47,000,000. Of course, much more than money was involved. High skill, imagination, the strong will to overcome obstacles, and the willingness of two sovereign states to co-operate for a common end—all these and more. Still, money was the catalyst, and it takes nothing away from idealism to say that without the grand donations of wealthy philanthropists, and without the great resources of two rich states, this grand design could not have been accomplished.

This chapter will deal with two sections of what may be considered one great park with an integrating parkway—the Harriman and Bear Mountain regions. Either the Harriman area or the Bear Mountain area may be called a park, and both are sometimes so designated. The important point is that the parkway and the parks are inseparable components of a consummate plan to supply the best possible physical, mental, and spiritual recreation for an urban population that in 1975 is expected to number 19,000,000 persons. Obviously, the parks and parkway came not a whit too soon!

We must begin, then, not with the Palisades Interstate Parkway, but with the Palisades themselves. For it was the rapidly proceeding desecration of that tremendous fault-scarp on the west side of the Hudson estuary which initially planted the seed that was to flower so strangely and so happily.

Verrazzano, the Florentine sailor who entered the North River in 1524, described these beetling cliffs of diabase. The Indians called them "we-awken," meaning "rocks that look like trees," as indeed the columnar formations did. At one point the top of the Palisades is 540 feet above the river. To both professional and amateur geologists the picture presented here is illuminating. At the foot of the traprock can be seen the horizontal layers of red sandstone into which the molten material was intruded as a "sill," so long ago that the time makes little difference. You can see the zones of baked rock, where the heat of the intrusion changed the sandstone.

Along the top of the Palisades there was in Revolutionary times a heavy forest, and in fact up to the year 1895 more than 11,000 acres of this rather inaccessible stand remained uncut. This was considered one of the finest belts of timber in New Jersey.

Until the middle of the nineteenth century nobody would have dreamed that the rock palisades might have commercial value, or that consequently they would ever be attacked other than by natural forces. And even when the fallen rock at the cliff foot began to be used as ballast for ships, the amount taken for this purpose hardly altered the appearance of the shore. It was when traprock became urgently required for the burgeoning era of concrete construction that the Palisades appeared as a convenient supply.

Then it was that the dynamite began to jar down in rock avalanches the beautiful hexagonal prisms of diabase that had been so great a part of the scenic adventure of the Hudson. Though enterprisers were quarrying northward to Verdreitege Hook, the major defacement was between Edgewater and Englewood Landing and especially at a big quarry near Fort Lee, where 12,000 cubic yards of rock were being blown out every day.

How do you stop a thing like this? The country had for years been destroying a great deal of its natural scenery: it was part of the normal development. Traprock, just like any other natural resource, you "get where you find it." But the New Jersey Federation of Women's Clubs, which believes that traprock for construction costs too much in terms of ultimate human welfare, called a halt.

It was a very small voice that said "stop it," but it was an insistent one. In 1899 the ladies got a bill through the legislature empowering the Governor to look into the situation and take action. In New York there were other disturbed spirits, including those of Andrew Green, "father of Greater New York," and Theodore Roosevelt, just then Governor and beginning to show an active interest in conservation.

The rub was: even with the appointment of an interstate commission to contrive to salvage the Palisades, could the two states agree? Most of the Palisades were in New Jersey. Yet, in a long-range plan for recreation development, most of the benefits would accrue to the people of crowded New York City. New York saw the clear gain that could be derived from buying land in and together with a neighbor state, but was it constitutional? Strange to say, the question has never been raised, nor the law contested. The New York legislature appropriated $400,000 to be spent in acquiring the land "lying between the top of the steep edge of the Palisades . . . between Fort Lee and Piermont Creek." Fort Lee is in New Jersey, Piermont barely over the state line in New York. Unexampled and intelligent co-operation!

Christmas Eve, 1900, is an unforgettable date in the story of the interstate development. With a gift from the elder banker J. P. Morgan, the blasting at Fort Lee was forever stopped. The urgency of the case was pointed out to Morgan by George W. Perkins, whose understanding of the needs of the people, added to great business judgment, was to mean so much in the future. It is interesting to note that the appeal to Morgan for aid led directly to an invitation by the famous banker that Perkins become an associate in the firm. Not all conservationists are starry-eyed, nor considered so by "practical men." Perhaps Morgan judged that stewards who have been "faithful over a few things" would make good "rulers over many things." To the end of his life, George W. Perkins was "the mainspring of the Interstate Commission."

Great gifts and small gifts began to accrue in this mighty work. In 1933 John D. Rockefeller, Jr., presented to the park 700 acres of land along the top of the Palisades, extending nearly twelve miles. The land had cost Rockefeller, whose interest in the Palisades had been keen since his young manhood, almost $10,000,000. In his offer of the gift, Rockefeller said that he hoped to see "a strip of this land developed as a parkway."

Another gift of magnitude was that of the Harrimans. Edward H. Harriman, the developer of railroads, had been for many years acquiring forest land west of Bear Mountain to the extent of 30,000 acres. That he had had the idea of dedicating some of this tract to public purposes was made clear after his death, when Mrs. Harriman conveyed to the state of New York 10,000 acres and a million dollars in cash. She told Governor Hughes: "This fund should be used . . . to acquire other parcels of land adjacent to the above mentioned tract. . . ."

Thus, with gifts great and small, and appropriations by the legislatures, has been welded together a giant body that offers the sorely needed breathing space for millions of urban dwellers, as well as for those who live in the surrounding counties.

Briefly, then, this integrated park and parkway on the west side of the Hudson River comprises the following: the New Jersey section of the Palisades, a 12-mile stretch with picnic and camping areas, motorboat basins, trails and scenic drives; Hook Mountain State Park, open to hikers and scheduled for further improvement; Blauvelt State Park, with fine bridle trails, but awaiting greater development; Bear Mountain and Harriman State parks, to be described later on; Storm King State Park, with scenic views and picnicking; High Tor State Park, for hiking and a wildlife sanctuary; and, finally, the Stony Point Battlefield Reservation, a small but notable historic area, with a museum devoted to the Revolutionary period, and with picnic groves and trails.

The parkway, swinging westward from the river near the state border, ends at the Bear Mountain Bridge. There are other roads, of course, that make accessible to the motorist the various units of the whole park. As so many millions of drivers know, the parkway is a triumph of "understanding" engineering, besides being technically brilliant in modern design. Beautifully studied are those unnoticed but so-important touches that produce harmony and exciting beauty of landscape instead of the dullness of mere locomotion. The planning should be unnoticed, of course, by the traveler. Therein lies its art. The engaging way in which Tiorati Brook runs between the parkway lanes for several miles is just one of many eye-delighting devices. And, too, the surrounding country is exceptionally charming. These are friendly mountains and sweet valleys.

Herbert Evison's *A State Park Anthology*, published in 1930, contains a wise and amusing contribution from the pen of William H. Carr, at that time by co-operative arrangement with the American Museum of Natural History, an "interpreter naturalist" at Bear Mountain State Park. It begins: "As we sit here in the Trailside Museum writing, we can look out into the large room and see many people who have come from a considerable distance to visit Bear Mountain." How many people? Remember that it was a period when the common access to the park was by the delightful but slow excursion on the river boats from Manhattan.

The Bear Mountain Inn, then quite a novelty in a state park, was being described as "a heap of boulders and huge chestnut logs assembled at the base of Bear Mountain by the hand of man, yet following the lines of such natural proportions as to resemble the eternal hills themselves." The inn is no less cheerfully comfortable today than thirty years ago. The chestnut logs are still there—but chestnut trees of that dimension, of any dimension, are almost extinct.

Carr noted that in the years 1927-30 his nature trails and Trailside Museum had been visited by "more than 200,000 people." This was indeed a goodly number. It looks small when we consider that on a Sunday now in the Bear Mountain–Harriman Park there may be 30,000 people concentrated in a single area! But these early experiments in the art of what is now called "interpretation" were a real achievement. This was only a few years after the initial study made by a group of educators, with a view toward an educational program for the national parks. It may be said that Bear Mountain was among the very first areas where the valuable spadework was done.

And how is it now? In the midst of the truly marvelous developments for physical recreation—swimming, boating, archery, ice and roller skating, softball, basketball, square dancing—that have been created with such planning and technical skills throughout the park, it is good to know that the trails are still used and that the museums still evoke the curiosity, the "desire to know" that leads to an understanding and love of nature. Bear Mountain still does its excellent interpretive job.

If the major emphasis is upon the varied kinds of purely physical exercise, it is a response to clear needs; and where have the needs been satisfied better? Besides, this balancing of the educational and the non-educational leads us always into unknown territory. The softball player of one visit may be the hiker of the next: he may be both on the same day. No poll is possible. All one can ask is: "Do the trails and museums still attract their share?" They do; and on weekends to almost bewildering capacity.

The supplying of physical recreation to ever-increasing numbers is big business and no mistake about it. By necessity, everything is wholesale. If it's a cafeteria, it must be a cafeteria bigger than anything you ever saw, with every last device known to the science of feeding, and with absolute safeguarding of health. If it's a man-created bathing beach on a man-created lake, it must be on such a scale as to accommodate the population of a town, all at once. There may be doubts about how far one can go, in the effort to bring people to the nature they so much crave, without defeating the very purpose. How to manage such terrific concentration? How to give with one hand without taking away with the other?

But one thing is certain. In the magnificent Palisades Interstate Park—considering the access and the areas as a whole—the people can enjoy the very finest recreation without the taint and squalor of crowded, privately owned resorts. These public preserves are not only better, safer, lovelier in aspect, but they are the people's own—operated for them with a devotion to public service.

So whether it is camping on Lake Welch, named in remembrance of the first general manager and chief engineer, Major William A. Welch, or bathing in the two spacious pools at the Anthony Wayne area, beside the parkway in Beechy Bottom Valley, or at Sebago Beach in the Harriman section—no matter what or where, no accommodations in the world are finer or more adroitly planned to meet their purpose.

Superb management is found wherever New York State has a public park. Here, at Bear Mountain–Harriman, when you are told of the day-after-day concentrations of human beings—a good-sized city being abruptly dropped into the care of the managers—your first instinct is to shudder and say: "It just can't be done." But it is done. If it is winter and no snow has fallen, machines are busy making artificial snow for the skiers. Not just one kind, either—the kind best suited for Bear Mountain slope is not the same as that made for the lower elevation.

Policing such a population of visitors? When the season is in full swing, forty or fifty extra policemen are required. For this duty it has been found that schoolteachers, other qualifications being equal, are best, "because they know how to get along with youth." Seven thousand group campers have to be sheltered, five turnovers a summer—35,000 in all. It requires 800 regular employees to manage this great integration of pleasure parks. But aside from an accident now and then, all moves as smoothly as a good motor.

There are no less than one hundred miles of hiking trails in the park. The famous Appalachian Trail comes across the Hudson and into Bear Mountain, and on this path may be seen the fine Jo Davidson statue of Walt Whitman, distinctly the poet of the open road. On one of these trails I noted what seemed to me an innovation. At least I had never seen it elsewhere. The identifying labels on the trees were as usual, but posted just behind each label was another one, with an accurate picture of the tree's *leaf*. Since most "average visitors" are likely to use the leaf as their means of identification, this seemed a very excellent device in trailside interpretation.

But to come back, for a moment, to that fraction, whatever its dimension may be, of people who come to the parks to merge themselves a little with the natural surroundings—to seek to understand by contact their place in the natural world. An odd thing, a comical thing, came under my view as I was making the rounds with A. K. Morgan, the general manager. We reached a trailside place where a group of hiking youths, with perhaps aching muscles from a stiff jaunt, were taking a breather. Every one of the group was perusing a copy of a so-called "comic," his eyes fixed upon the color blobs with incredulous intensity.

I turned to my companion and remarked, simply: "Comic books!"

"Yes," said Morgan. "It is incongruous. They hike into the bosom of nature, and bring the funnies along with them." Then he told me that he had once brought this to the attention of the school authorities, suggesting that if the boys were coming out to learn something of nature, it would be better if they left their "funnies" at home.

What do you think was the reply to this observation? The school psychologists inhaled deeply, took somber thought, and gave the opinion that suddenly to change the regular "comic" habit might be upsetting to the youthful psyche. If they were to be weaned, it must be slowly and deftly—almost clinically—managed. It may be; it may. On the other hand, it could be that psychologists have a sort of protective coloration. They may be, even unconsciously, defending an addiction of their own.

(X V I)

REID STATE PARK

MAINE

Leave U.S. 1 at Woolwich on Route 127; at Five Islands, turn right at sign

If you will spread out your automobile map of the state of Maine, you will observe that U. S. Route 1 roughly parallels the sea coast from the Kittery Bridge to Lubec. You will also notice that all the way there are short state roads hanging from this notable main highway, on the Atlantic side, much as the gardener ties strips of cloth to a line over his strawberry bed in a rather vain hope to keep the robins from nipping his largest berries. You can conceive of this remarkable coastline as resembling the tattered edge of the bed sheet that the overfrugal motel owner sent to the laundry just one time too many.

Following an air route, the distance between the extreme points of the Maine coast would be about 225 miles. If you follow the actual water edge, however, you would travel at least 2,500 miles. Nowhere in the world is there such an erratic shoreline of such extent. For the greater part of its distance, it is just a succession of rock-faced peninsulas daring the rowdy ocean to do its worst.

One of these peninsulas juts out from the mainland at Woolwich, with the estuary of the Kennebec on one side and the waters of Boothbay on the other. Follow it down through old Georgetown, and you come to a perfect gem of a state park, named Reid. I call it a gem, because though it is not a large park, having 785 acres in all, it is as perfect an expression of the spirit of coastal Maine as you will find. Mount Desert, with its magnificent Acadia National Park, is the same, but on the grandest scale. Reid does the thing in little, in cameo. But it is all there, and because it *is* little, the drama of the sunken or drowned shoreline is perhaps more readily comprehended.

For this *is* a coastline that was invaded by the sea. Whether the land mass subsided, or whether the ocean level rose, would make no difference so far as the result is concerned. But in truth it was both. The prodigious weight of the ice field, a mile in thickness, which came down over this part of the continent in a succession of invasions during a period of a million years of alternating warmth and cold, could not fail to depress the land beneath it, even though that surface was seemingly irresistible rock. At the same time, the general melt of arctic ice, poured into the ocean, would raise the ocean level in relation to the land.

At Reid State Park try a little experiment and see how good your imagination is. Look seaward and make believe that the ocean has receded several miles, instead of just the ordinary twelve feet it fluctuates between the tides. Further, try to consider that the sea has receded for a time long enough so that, instead of beds of kelp and rocky ledges clothed in the green marine vegetation, the plant life of the land has come in, and there are grasses and shrubs and trees in the valley bottoms and on the hillsides before you.

Well, in your mind's eye, then, you are looking at the Maine coast as it was before it was sunk. The estuary of the Kennebec was just a deep valley between two high ridges. The islands you are looking at were the tops of hills. Where fishes are now swimming, land animals once browsed and grazed. And what you can thus imagine here is true for that 2,500 miles of coast which forms the edge of Maine. The serrated coastline is simply the old land contour line which the ocean has reached in its present relation.

What is not too common along this rocky coast are two sandy beaches on this peninsula at Reid State Park, one a mile long and the other about half that length, with fine dunes behind them. It was the third day of August when I was there; a bright clear forenoon with such sharp visibility that a mile of distance over the sparkling blue water seemed close at hand. The temperature of the water, being duly checked by the park ranger that morning, was forty-six degrees. Yet he confided to me that there was need of more bathhouses, that the present two were not enough. I told him he needed no more so far as I was concerned; I would not crowd in; I would be content to bask. But indeed, there were plenty of adults and children in the water, and since this was mid-week, I had to believe that on a weekend the bathhouses were worked to capacity. Forty-six degrees Fahrenheit! It needs to be seen (and felt!) to be credited. Most of these bathers were Maine folk; a hardy race!

A stroll through Reid Park is a revelation even to one who is not unfamiliar with the Maine seacoast. Where do pasture roses look pinker and breathe more fragrance than here? When can you see a greater variety of flowers in a healthier state? Actually I counted sixteen different kinds of flowers, all in lusty bloom, on a pocket of soil not more than two yards square. It is a short season for plants, and the plants know it, and say: "A short, but a merry one!"

Here, too, as all along the coast, the trees come down to the very edge of the sea, wherever they can find soil enough to nourish themselves. In well-filled pockets the spruces grow to quite astonishing size. Yet everywhere are rounded, and sometimes still polished, ledges that still show the gravings of the ice sheet that went over them, using imbedded rock fragments for scratching tools.

Many Maine boys, reared under the rigorous conditions imposed upon these people by coastal soil and climate, have left home to become either famous or prosperous, or both. Among these was one who had been born and reared in little Georgetown, Walter E. Reid. This industrialist, mindful of the beauty and the historical significance that had helped to form his youthful character, began to acquire the parcels of land which, in 1947, he presented to the people of Maine for the state park that now bears his name.

History there is in plenty in this vicinity, in addition to the usual amount of folklore, which even when not reliable is still entertaining. If you wish to believe that the Vikings, nearly a thousand years ago, visited this coast, there is no harm in doing so, and it is certainly a possibility. What is more probable is that the fishing in these cold waters had invited Basque and Breton, Spanish and Portuguese before Columbus landed in the West Indies. Cabot was at the nearby outlier, Monhegan, in 1498.

The famous battle between the British warship *Boxer* and the *U. S. Enterprise* was fought somewhere between Monhegan and Seguin. Many of the trees at the foot of this peninsula were peppered with grape shot, and several pieces of the chain shot used to cut rigging were found on these beaches.

Apparently this famous combat was not quite what our childhood histories led us to believe. Louise Dickinson Rich, in her "informal history" of the *Coast of Maine*, gives a persuasive and spirited account of the affair. It would seem, from her recital, that the "hostility" between the Crown and these Maine colonials was not, at that moment, the real thing. "When a shipment of English goods was destined for a Maine port, there was sometimes a gentleman's agreement that it should be allowed to pass unmolested . . . occasionally the British even furnished a convoy to protect it from the zeal of any who might not be 'in the know.'" The British *Boxer*, commanded by young Captain Blythe, was convoying the *Margaretta* with a cargo of wool from Halifax to Bath, at the same time making believe that it was pursuing the American ship as a smuggler. The *Margaretta* "escaped" into the mouth of the Kennebec and the British crew of the *Boxer* casually boated ashore and picked blueberries. That was all very jolly; but while this make-believe was going on, young Lieutenant William Burrows, commander of the brig *Enterprise* was lying in Portland harbor, eager to take on a British warship at a moment's notice. The *Margaretta* affair being reported to him, he sailed out to meet the *Boxer*.

By this version, the encounter appears to have been something of a sporting affair on the part of two young commanders who possessed both courage and skill. It ended in the death of both of them; and what gives color to this fresh point of view is the extraordinary double funeral in honor of Burrows and Blythe which took place in Portland, when "the bells tolled, the guns boomed, and everybody wept." The two gallant commanders were buried side by side in the old Eastern Cemetery. There is also to be found the grave of a young midshipman, Kervin Waters, who received "a mortal wound" in this naval encounter and "languished in severe pain; and died with Christian calmness and resignation." Age, eighteen years.

One has the feeling, in visiting this delightful state park, that it could be easily overdeveloped. It seems to have just the number of facilities required for public use, thus leaving the public elbowroom and a sense of restfulness. To be sure, the demand for public recreation in places of this sort is constantly growing. On the other hand, there must be similar locations all along this coast which would also supply spiritual and physical health for future generations. Mr. Reid generously provided this one. But is it wise for the states always to await the appearance of Reids?

(XVII)

SCARBOROUGH STATE BEACH

RHODE ISLAND

On Ocean Road near Point Judith, off U.S. 1

THIS STATE, sometimes affectionately called "Little Rhody," has a land surface of only 1,067 square miles. If you should drop it down in Brewster County, Texas, you would have to send an expedition to find out what had become of it. But if Texas had devoted as much of its land to recreation, proportionately, it would have more than two million acres so employed. This, of course, is not to say that Texas *should* devote any such area to state parks. It is noted here merely as a way of calling attention to what the smallest state in the Union has accomplished.

After the Civil War, Alexander H. Stephens, who had been Vice-President of the Confederacy, wrote a history of the United States. Of Little Rhody he was pleased to say, though he could not have been supposed to wax emotional about his late enemy-at-arms: "She is distinguished for the virtue, intelligence and thrift of her people, the learning and eloquence of her divines, and the ability of her statesmen." In the field of recreation activities, her statesmanship has not gone into eclipse.

But first, you should know (and a good many residents of Rhode Island may be surprised to learn this) that *Rhode Island* is not the official designation of this state. Accurately, when you are at Scarborough State Beach, or in any other of its beautifully kept recreation places, you are a guest of *Rhode Island and Providence Plantations.* That illuminating title is official, and when you realize it you are turning a page of our colonial history. You are face to face with that brave spirit Roger Williams, who so believed in religious freedom for himself and for others that he had to flee from the unbending piety of puritan Salem and take refuge in a wilderness. You see the gentler Pilgrims of Plymouth, not really unsympathetic with him but fearing to antagonize their rigid neighbors north of Boston, asking Williams to please move a little farther away from their border. So this gallant minister (who, to be sure, was not without fault) went to the other side of Narragansett Bay and founded a colony to which all protestants (here meaning all those who *protest*) could resort, and piously called it Providence. Later, when other victims of bigotry appealed for sanctuary, Williams persuaded the Indians to give them the island—later called Rhode Island—on which the city of Newport stands. Thus, you see how there came to be both Rhode Island *and* the Providence Plantations; and so it has been ever since.

It must be confessed, at the outset, that the title of this chapter is somewhat misleading. It would take only a paragraph to describe Scarborough State Beach, this Point Judith stretch of sand upon which, in WPA days, was built a staunch bathhouse of cut stone, with a parking lot in back of it. The title, however, will serve well enough as an invitation to view the whole effort of a resolute commonwealth toward making the best use of its natural resources in a highly civilized way.

Point Judith, of course, is famous. This is the place where the side-wheel passenger boats of the good old days, coming out of Fall River and Providence and bound for New York City, emerged from the landlocked bay shelters and came abruptly into the clutches of the open sea. There are many nostalgic recollections among our older citizens of those cheerful night trips. Can *you*, possibily, recall how you were sitting at dinner on the smoothly gliding craft when suddenly the dinnerware began to slide and bounce and your appetite ended in a vague alarm? The waiter explained: "Yassir, we is now gittin' off Point Judith."

Well, still the Atlantic Ocean hammers at this spot on the Rhode Island coast, and in late July and August the breakers come rolling in and give the lifeguards plenty of work to do. These lifeguards of the Rhode Island State Park System are picked men. It takes three years of training to qualify for the rugged work on this strip of coastline. Nor is that all. By state law the Division of Parks and Recreation is empowered to see that even private beaches have guards of proven experience. Scarborough is no place for the showoff who wants to parade his swimming ability against that power of the sea.

But just around the Point is another and safer recreation spot, within what is called "the harbor of refuge." This one the Rhode Island park people call "our family beach." As is well remembered, the West Indian hurricanes of 1938 and 1954, departing from their usual romp across Florida and roaring up the northeast coast instead, hit the Rhode Island shoreline with frenzy. The bathhouse and recreation facilities on Block Island were wiped out and the erosion damage along the sands that faced the open sea was colossal.

At Sand Hill Cove State Beach, in the Harbor of Refuge, the Division of Parks and Recreation has built a new type of structure planned to meet and defeat the power of a hurricane-driven ocean. Raised upon pilings, with a flooring that will admit abnormal high waters and let them flow out freely, it seems to supply the answer; however, nobody relishes the idea of a test, for even when the structures stand, the beaches themselves still are fragile things.

It is true that Rhode Island, like so many other states, has seen the greater part of its shoreline absorbed into private ownership. In the "Shore Recreation Index" of the state highway map, fifty-nine salt-water beaches are listed, and only a few of them are public reserves. Nobody is to blame: the explosion of population, with its attendant soaring national income, leisure, and fast travel crept upon us while our eyes were fixed on other things.

There is still an opportunity, however, for Rhode Island to acquire a five-mile stretch of beach on its western side. Little development has been done here. Most of this land is owned by Charlestown, a South County town which had large ideas of increment from an exploitation that failed to materialize. A few years ago the town wanted to have the state take half of this fine stretch, where people who love to walk a long uncrowded beach could enjoy that experience, provided the town could have the other moiety. Very properly the park folks said no; all or nothing. A deal like that sounds good enough. But park officials know only too well what happens; the state pays for something which is immediately surrounded and submerged in a welter of private promotions. There are now favorable signs that Rhode Island may acquire this whole precious strip; but it must be done reasonably soon. Opportunity for the ownership of white sand is becoming scant.

And it is curious, when you come to think of it. The other day somebody was declaiming, in relation to the establishment of the Cape Cod National Seashore, that such interference, or competition, with private enterprise was "socialistic." Now, as to that, it is of interest to look back into history about two thousand years and see what the Roman people thought. If there ever existed a more hard-boiled assembly of "business" people than the early Romans, we don't know about them. These folks on the Tiber were so far to the "right," as the saying goes in politics, that the left was not visible. Yet, when the Roman law was overhauled and codified in the reign of Justinian, one of the early laws which was retained was the one that said:

> By the law of nature, certain things are common property, for example the air, running water, the sea, and consequently the *shores of the sea*. . . . By the law of nations the use of the seashore is public . . . the shores are understood not to be the property of any individual but are viewed as like the sea itself.

Had you told the early Romans that this declaration was "socialism," they would have been rather surprised. They would have referred you to nature herself, who made a vast amount of land and ocean surface and a very small portion of seacoast; and they would have added (and again I quote their law): "As to farms, edifices, etc., we abstain from trespass, but no person is prohibited from approaching any part of the seashore."

The state parks of Rhode Island are not expected to "pay their way"; they are regarded as a public service akin to a public library, art museum, or other cultural device. For a few special services a charge is made, as would be expected, but as a rule these charges are lower than one finds elsewhere. For instance, the golf fee at Goddard State Park is fifty cents a round. There is what is called a "65 Club." Anyone sixty-five years of age or more is entitled to play golf without charge.

The state furnishes free swimming instruction for both children and adults. There are free skating lessons in the season, and likewise instruction in fishing technique, such as flycasting. There are free band concerts at Scarborough State Beach. The Division of Parks and Recreation employs an oceanographer who predicts the water temperature for the next day, the height of the breakers, surf conditions, tides, and other data; and this information goes out over the radio and through the newspapers.

All these services, long continued, have been possible because successive legislatures in Little Rhody have been willing to appropriate funds to operate the system of state parks and beaches as a legitimate function of the government. There is no play for tourist money. The parks have little income, and it makes no difference whether the visitor is a native or a stranger.

The roadside areas, usually managed by highway departments, are here a part of the park setup. They are among the finest in the country, both in their ample size and in the beauty of their location—some among pines, some in hardwood, some with little streams of water coursing through them. As in National Capital Parks in Washington, D.C., the Division here has its own police force.

How did Rhode Island come by this generous conception? It may date back many years to the time—1904, the year was—when the General Assembly set up a Metropolitan Park Commission "to consider the advisability of laying out ample open spaces for the use of the public in Providence and the cities and towns in its vicinity." The Public Park Association had a ready-made comprehensive plan, for among them was Henry A. Barker, who in his college days had observed the beginning of the splendid Minneapolis park development, as well as that of metropolitan Boston.

Obviously, the Rhode Islanders have become increasingly park-minded, and this has led to a generous attitude on the part of the legislature. In a state as small as this, as heavily populated (yet you may travel for miles along a lovely South County road where you begin to wonder "whether anybody lives around here"), the jump from the metropolitan to the state system was not a great one. Really, the point of departure was in 1927 when R. H. I. Goddard and his wife gave to the state 472 acres of their beautiful estate on Greenwich Bay.

From the very nature of its origin, Goddard Memorial State Park presents a formal landscape; it is very fine, and it has an outlet upon salt water. Some idea of the intensive use made of it may be gained from the number of picnic sites, each with its fireplace and table. There are 223 of them. Besides the golf course and the bridle trails, the salt water bathing beach has its bathhouse. There are eleven playfields.

Since the Division of Parks and Recreation operates under civil service rules, it is not really necessary to say that these career men in Rhode Island and Providence Plantations take the long view in their performance. They say, too, with some pride: "Our parks don't try to take in money. They aim to give our people service."

(X V I I I)

TACONIC STATE PARKWAY

NEW YORK

In Columbia, Dutchess, Putnam, and Westchester Counties

As one travels the northerly section of the Taconic State Parkway,* the exquisitely beautiful product of an imaginative landscape architect, there comes to mind a speech made by Thomas H. Benton of Missouri in the United States Senate in the year 1850. The discussion concerned a proposed highway across the nation from Atlantic to Pacific.

"It is a mistake," said Senator Benton, "to suppose that none but men of science lay off a road. There is a class of topographical engineers older than the schools and more unerring than the mathematicians. They are the wild animals—buffalo, deer, elk, antelope, bears—which traverse the forest not by compass but by an instinct which leads them always the right way—to the lowest passes in the mountains, the shallowest fords in the rivers, the richest pastures in the forest, the best salt springs, and the shortest practicable lines between remote points. . . . These are the first engineers to lay out a road in a new country; the Indians follow them, and hence a buffalo road becomes a warpath. The first white hunters follow the same trails in pursuing their game; and after that, the buffalo road becomes the wagon road of the white man. . . ."

Perhaps Emerson, in Concord, read this Benton speech, for, at about that time, he wrote a retort to the sneerers who said that the streets of Boston were "laid out by cows." "Well," said Emerson,

* Since this chapter was written, administration of the Taconic State Parkway (not including the adjacent parks) has been transferred to the recently established East Hudson Parkway Authority.

"there are worse surveyors. Every pedestrian in our pastures has frequent occasion to thank the cows for cutting the best path through the thicket and over the hills."

Lest, in connection with the Taconic State Parkway, we should overstress the acumen of cattle and become a trifle ridiculous, it is well to state quickly that this lovely adventure in landscape and locomotion has two very practical and primary objectives. It takes the increasingly impossible load off U. S. Highway 9, which emerges from Manhattan and heads for Rouses Point and the Province of Quebec. Further, it serves to provide easy access, for the crowding millions of the metropolis, to the many fine parks of what New York calls the Taconic Region. Or, the other way about, the up-stater who longs for a day at the white beaches of Long Island is offered a route that will make his venture a joy instead of a traffic battle.

But there is more to the Taconic State Parkway, in its upper reaches (it has already been completed to a point some hundred miles from the New York City line), than these wholly practical considerations. It is a cultural asset. For the New Yorker who has not realized the beauty, and even the occasional wildness, of those southern counties so close to the vast populations of the lower Hudson, travel on this parkway should be a revelation. I can well imagine him saying, as view follows view along the sweeping curves and easy grades till finally the bold and bolder shoulders of the ancient Taconic Range are on his left or right: "This is *my* beautiful state. I never realized. . . ." Cultural? Is that word an overstatement, when one considers what ordinary highways are so likely to become—junkyards surrounded by urban, suburban, and sometimes even rural slums?

"You may consider this parkway as a ribbon park," said the general manager of the Taconic State Park Commission. How obvious it it that there are values here that transcend the important element of getting somewhere and back. The parkway widens a number of times into parks like Fahnestock, James Baird, and Lake Taghkanic. Sometimes a narrow ribbon, sometimes wide. But always a park.

The Taconic State Parkway is expensive. To the unimaginative highway engineer it is almost sinful. He squints and asks, in mental anguish: "Why do you have to do *that?*" Give him his due. He is a competent fellow in his way, and not all roads are parkways nor are they intended to be. Nor in many states can they be *afforded,* though it should be recorded at once that this parkway was built out of current tax money and is paid for: no mortgage. But to engineer a road like this I suppose you should be—if I may say so without offense—one part engineer, one part artist, and a third part one of Senator Benton's buffaloes!

If you were to start, with an observant eye, at the southern end of Taconic State Parkway in Westchester County just south of Valhalla and go to the present termination, several interesting things about the building of roads would be impressed upon you. At first, you would be motoring along a formal four-lane road that represented the thought—perhaps the possibilities—of the years 1927-28. For, as someone has said of those roads in the metropolitan area which are not sufficiently wide, "the wonder is, not that they are not wider, but that we were able to build them at all." Anyway, with every new reach of construction, Taconic has blossomed with new ideas, till finally the median strips become a sample of the region's physical offerings, rock, tree, flower, a show window of the smiling land through which you pass.

All this would hardly have been possible had the parkway followed any earlier roads. The scars would have been permanent, and the costs of acquisition too formidable. For the most part, Taconic is built upon lands acquired for the precise purpose twenty years or more before the present construction.

There are no advertising signs, naturally; there is an economy of signs of any kind. The parkway right-of-way varies in width from point to point, and is usually of ample protective width; but in addition, it is against the law to place commercial signs within 500 feet of the parkway line, wherever it may be. I stopped at just one point where an advertising sign was visible from a turnout. Some rebellious realtor had stuck it up. I could see the signboard but not the lettering on it, so if the owner really has something important to say to me he will have to supply me with binoculars on my next visit.

Clarence Fahnestock Memorial State Park is a "wide spot" in the ribbon parkway, but fifty miles from Broadway and Forty-second Street. A mere fifty miles—yet if you were blindfolded and set down in Fahnestock, you might well think you were in part of the Adirondacks. Indeed, the elevation at the high point here is the same as that of Lake Placid. There are 3,400 acres in this park, with camping, fishing, picnicking, and winter sports.

Now, to go northward upon the ribbon of revelation, by way of James Baird State Park, called "the golf widow's dream." Here you are only seventy-five miles from New York City, and this is a famous 18-hole course; in addition, there is every kind of recreation facility you can imagine, even archery and bowling on the green. If Mrs. does not play golf there will be no bored moments, provided she likes physical recreation at all. I was at James Baird on a day when the temperature was well over ninety degrees, and the "humidity index" (evil phrase, invented and quickly expunged by the meteorologists a few years ago) was high. But the golfers were undeterred, and there were as many as the links could accommodate.

A hundred and fifteen miles from the metropolis is Lake Taghkanic State Park. Taghkanic—Taconic—two different spellings of the same Indian word. The Indians didn't spell anyway; they put syllables together to make words. But this park is going to be *Taghkanic* in perpetuity. When the state acquired Lake Charlotte (as it had been called for time out of mind), the agreement was that if the word Taghkanic (preferred by the last owner to Charlotte) were ever changed, the property would revert to its past owner. The Livingston Patent, with a lake whose bed—that is, the land beneath the water—was the only one not owned by the state of New York, came in by gift.

A description of the Taconic State Parkway leads naturally into a consideration of the development of this very modern type of specialized road. Just what is a parkway? How does it differ from the ordinary highway?

Ideally—and in many cases as an actuality—the parkway is a kind of park. It may be called an "elongated park," or a "ribbon park." Its purpose is the accommodation of automobile traffic, and this it shares with all kinds of highways. But there the likeness ceases. The parkway is administered with all the public controls inherent in "park law," and we have a concise statement by Stanley W. Abbott as to what this implies:

"Along a parkway the public owns all the frontage property. Therefore, the roadside cannot be exploited for business development nor advertisement by billboards. Instead, the beauties of the American roadside are maintained, and adjacent historical and cultural interests are preserved and interpreted for the public. At intervals along many parkway routes the land acquisition is enlarged to include areas of special scenic interest, and these may provide a setting for picnic areas, camp grounds, recreation facilities, and any necessary tourist accommodations.

"No city streets are incorporated into the parkway route, which usually bypasses the towns and cities. There are relatively few entrances and exits, and these are designed for the motorists' safety, and there are no trucks on the parkway."

In its essence, the modern parkway may perhaps be regarded as the extension and application of an ideal that was in the minds of early metropolitan park planners. Many years ago in Central Park in New York and in the Park District of Boston, provisions were made for getting away from the commercial traffic and following a cheerful winding road lined with trees, grassy plots, and shrubs, in a horse-drawn vehicle, or pedaling a bicycle. Indeed, this very idea of slow-paced travel, conducive to observation and peace of mind amid the odor of balsam and spruce, was in the thought of John D. Rockefeller, Jr., when he built the charming carriage roads of Acadia National Park. Travel by automobile can never hope to capture the repose and tonic quality of those ambling movements of older time. But it can supply an inspiring experience through charming countryside, a fluid sampling of nature's handiwork, with safety and the chance for restful pauses—and this the parkway does.

How interesting it is that the first parkway in the modern sense came into existence by what could almost be called a happy accident! The little valley of the Bronx Rixer, flowing through Westchester County in New York into the borough of the Bronx, had become a dumping ground that resulted in a sanitation problem. Something had to be done about it. The county and city acquired the land; and, having come into possession of a restored, naturally pretty valley, the authorities accepted the suggestion that it would be a good place for a road. Thus was born the Bronx River Parkway. The other Westchester parkways—Hutchinson River, Saw Mill River, and Cross County—were developed later by the Westchester County Park Commission. Now, as the parkway concept began to develop, the highway engineer and the landscape architect pooled their talents. For those early achievements there were men like Jay Downer and Gilmore D. Clarke, the latter afterwards consultant on the Mt. Vernon Memorial Highway in Virginia and the Garden State Parkway in New Jersey.

While these Westchester County parkways were being built, the Long Island State Park Commission began the development of its network of parkways leading from New York City to the various Long Island state parks. Partly as a project of the CCC days, the Genesee State Park Commission, in western New York, started the construction of the Lake Ontario State Parkway, to form a connection between Rochester and Hamlin Beach State Park. This 30-mile road will eventually continue onward to Niagara Falls.

After the Hutchinson River Parkway had been completed to the Connecticut state line, the next step was inevitable. Connecticut now offers the motorist a beautiful parkway eastward almost to Hartford—the Merritt Parkway as far as the vicinity of New Haven, and, beyond that, continuing as the Wilbur Cross Parkway. And, of course, one of the finest instances of parkway development, as well as one of the most recent, is the lovely Palisades Interstate Parkway, from the New Jersey side of the George Washington Bridge to Bear Mountain Circle, forty-four miles to the north. Of all the state parkways, the Garden State Parkway of New Jersey is by far the longest. From Cape May it runs to the New York boundary to connect with the New York Thruway, a distance of 173 miles.

Parkway design has greatly influenced the design of freeways and express highways. These, while permitting commercial traffic, have incorporated many of the parkway principles such as wide rights-of-way, flowing alignment, controlled access, elimination of grade crossings, and landscaped roadsides.

It is natural that most of the parkways thus far built by the states have been based upon traffic requirements and a predicted increased use. The two great parkways of the National Park System—the Blue Ridge Parkway, connecting Shenandoah National Park with Great Smoky Mountains National Park, and the Natchez Trace Parkway, running from Nashville, Tennessee, to Natchez, Mississippi—are in themselves in the nature of recreation developments.

The Blue Ridge Parkway, 478 miles long, takes the motorist along the highlands of the southern Appalachians through a virtual wilderness where no road had ever been. Here, owing to the sparseness of the population, scenic control was almost wholly possible. This is a *rural* parkway, averaging from 800 to 1,000 feet in width, with extensive facilities for picnicking and camping and with many foot trails suitable for intimate contact with the infinite variety of nature. The historic interest—the revelation of the remote lives and folkways of the mountain people—is notable.

Lacking the consummate scenic thrill of the Blue Ridge, the Natchez Trace Parkway is even more an adventure into our early history. The 450 miles of this road, when it is completed, will take the visitor on the route along which the boatmen of "Kaintuck" toiled homeward after floating their lumber rafts to New Orleans, and through the Indian country where the tribes took sides with French and English by turns when the destiny of the Great Valley was in the balance. This "elongated park," too, has ample facilities for physical recreation and the study of nature and history.

Colonial Parkway was designed primarily to provide a connection between Jamestown, Williamsburg, and Yorktown—Virginia's historic triangle. Although only twenty-two miles in length, it is one of the loveliest of the parkways.

(XIX)

VALLEY FORGE STATE PARK

PENNSYLVANIA

Northeast of Philadelphia, on Pennsylvania Routes 23-83 at Pennsylvania Turnpike Interchange

William Penn, out of the vast land holdings that came to him from the British crown, gave his daughter Letitia 7,800 acres situated about twenty miles from his City of Brotherly Love. We may imagine what that land looked like then: virgin forest upon it, clearings for planting just being made; land of good heart for agriculture; the whole face of the country of challenging beauty. It was a bountiful gift.

Of that dowry, 2,048 acres now comprise one of the nation's most beautiful parks, and the most significant historically. Here is commemorated in a charming countryside those dark days of the Revolution when George Washington, with almost superhuman patience and skill, maintained throughout a terrible winter the faint hopes of liberty for the colonies.

The country has many treasured shrines. There is something about Valley Forge, however, which makes it entirely different from all the rest. This was no triumph of arms; this, no spectacular conflict of armies, no winning of glory at the cannon's mouth. This is the story of the greatest valor—that of emerging from defeat into victory through self-discipline, and of a fortitude in misery almost without parallel.

There was a *Mount* Misery on this campground. One might think the name came from that winter of distress. No; Penn the Quaker had given the name to one hillock, and had called another one

Mount Joy, for some reason we do not know. For Washington's men, joy was almost a forgotten element of living. Yet the fruit was final victory, and, as the English historian, Sir George Otto Trevelyan has written: "Nations, like the readers of fiction, love a sad story which ends well; and the name of Valley Forge will never cease to be associated with the memory of suffering quietly and steadfastly borne, but not endured in vain."

When the mellow days of spring come to the lush western suburbs of Philadelphia, a million people flow into Valley Forge State Park to witness the miracle of the flowering of waxy white bracts upon the dogwood trees. It is perhaps the greatest of all outdoor flower shows. Automobiles roll over the park roads sometimes bumper to bumper, filled with admirers of this storm of beauty that signals the end of winter and the beginning of a new cycle of life. Dogwood, dogwood everywhere, from every point of vantage, as far as the eye can see. It is an inspiration: but the visitor will do well not to end with this. He should stand with bared head before the great arch and read again those words graven there:

> Naked and starving as they are, we
> cannot enough admire the incomparable
> patience and fidelity of the soldiery.

Those were Washington's words, uttered with a sigh, as he looked about him at the suffering men whose tatters he could not mend and whose hungry mouths he could not feed. No thought of dogwood bloom then. "Our sick are naked; our well are naked."

This was indeed a crisis in the march toward freedom. Brandywine had been an honorable defeat; Germantown a miserable failure; "Mad Anthony" Wayne had lost at Paoli. Washington's enemies (he was far from being the "Father of his country" in those somber moments) were actively intriguing against him at the moment when he was camping with his beaten army at Whitemarsh. He was being urged toward another attack upon the British which he knew he could not make. It was vital to go into winter quarters to re-equip, to train, to restore morale. He could not go too far from Philadelphia, where Lord Howe was preening himself in comfort among his well-billeted soldiers. The Pennsylvania Council threatened to quit the tottering confederacy if he should go farther inland to a safer place.

So Valley Forge it was. "Valley Forge" the location had been called, because, as early as 1751, there had been an iron mill set up on the creekside in the ravine between Mounts Joy and Misery. Here wrought iron had been shaped for many years, till its product at the outbreak of the Revolution was urgently needed for munitions. And for that very reason General Knyphausen's Hessians had burned the "forge" just a few months before General Washington pitched his marquee under a blackgum tree on the night of December 19, 1777, and the ragged army began the memorable winter of privation.

Twelve feet of silt covered the ruins of the forge when, in 1929, the park superintendent dug up the undershot wheels, the trip hammer, and the other units of the mill, lying among charred timbers. The larger sections of the forge remain still as the hostile wreckers left them. The Valley Forge Park Commission hopes to restore the old forge, not only as part of the historic scene, but also as an example of the rude methods employed by the early iron-masters.

The building of the winter camp was no haphazard operation. Washington himself, with both military and pioneer knowledge, drew up the specifications. He had with him, among those other European military men who had joined the colonial effort from sympathy or because they were soldiers of fortune, a young French engineer named du Portail. To him went the task of laying out the camp. The original plans he made are still in the archives of the Historical Society of Pennsylvania.

From the ample forests at hand 900 huts, regularly placed in brigade and company streets, were built. The rugged troops from Connecticut, Massachusetts, New Hampshire, New York, North Carolina, Pennsylvania, Rhode Island, and Virginia were no strangers to the ax and adze. The tree logs were chinked hopefully with clay against the blasting winds; thatching was with boughs, straw, tent cloth, or anything that would serve; and in a week most of the men were under cover. Under cover, but that was about all. The bare legs and shoeless feet with which many of them had made the grim march from Whitemarsh were still numb with cold. Washington pleaded with the Continental Congress for clothing and food, with meager results. It seemed almost as though they were forgotten men.

Looking back upon it from our modern luxurious comfort, and even from the viewpoint of present warfare, the wonder is that anyone in that shivering, all-but-abandoned army survived the ordeal. Winter can be on occasion rather mild in this region; but the winter of 1777-78 was not. Despite the heroic service of the doctors and surgeons under Bodo Otto, starvation rations, lack of sanitary arrangements, and the bitter weather took a sad toll.

Curiously, the thirty-one replicas of the soldiers' huts which have been built on the original site look rather comfortable on a pleasant day, when the visitor, comfortably clad, gazes upon them. They were quite otherwise that winter. They merely spawned rheumatism, dysentery, and amputations of frozen feet. Even smallpox broke out. About 3,000 of the men died and were hastily returned to the earth without a marker; in later years the burial grounds were known by metal buttons and other equipment that resisted decay. Of those 3,000 men who died at Valley Forge, the identity of only one is known—John Waterman of Rhode Island, and a granite obelisk marks his grave.

At the base of Fort Huntington, in the park picnic grounds, is the grave of an unknown soldier whose death was not heroic; merely a gruesome reminder of the callousness that went with the times. A farmer who lived near General Wayne's quarters came to "Mad Anthony" with a complaint that a soldier was robbing him of chickens every morning. The general, his mind on other matters, seemed not to be listening. Finally, to the complainant's impatient question as to what he should do, the general simply retorted: "Damnit, shoot him!" And this is precisely what the farmer did. The homicide seems to have been received placidly enough.

So much of Valley Forge has withstood time that the question "What can I see?" cannot be adequately answered in brief. True, the original soldiers' huts disappeared soon after the army left the camp. But of the more substantial buildings that were used as headquarters by Washington and his generals, and even of the varied units of the military works, there are plenty.

Naturally one turns above all to that house of the Quaker clergyman Isaac Potts, which became Washington's headquarters. Preserved in fine condition and furnished as of the period with delightful discrimination and restraint, here is a shrine indeed!

Washington, after a week in his marquee, moved into this house, then tenanted by the Widow Hewes. (And he paid rent, too!) Here, within these walls, the commander conferred with Lafayette, Knox, Sullivan, Wayne, von Steuben, de Kalb, and the rest of his generals.

Von Steuben, by the way, was the inspector-general charged with the job of drilling and teaching the way of war to an army of individualists who were tolerant of suffering and privation but were probably not quite so tolerant of discipline. They were no saints, these men here encamped, and the great Washington knew it and was often lenient in his judgments of weakness. But von Steuben, that winter, well earned the statue that was later erected here to his memory, and also those linden trees near his statue, grown from seed from the trees of the Unter den Linden in Berlin.

However it may be with others, to me the figure of Martha Washington, the first First Lady, has always been rather a shadowy one, no doubt because the strong personality of her husband has so dominated the Revolutionary scene. That second-floor front room of the Potts-Hewes house, a bed chamber seemingly identical in furnishing with that she would have known, somehow brought Martha into reality for me. I could see her sitting here with Lady Stirling and Mrs. Knox, knitting socks and making other things for the comfort of the soldiers. For she was here from late February of 1778 until the evacuation of the camp on the nineteenth of June. Colonel duPonceau, von Steuben's aide, said of Martha that "she possessed always a mild, dignified countenance, grave yet cheerful . . . her presence inspired fortitude." Without reservation, we accept the statement. Her presence during those hard days must have been a great help.

Though Valley Forge is primarily a historical and military park, it offers much also for the visitor who seeks the relaxation and enjoyment of nature. The state has provided ample picnic areas, a good tourist camp where upwards of 800 persons with tents or trailers can register and stay for as long as two weeks in the summer season. On the slopes near the Wayne equestrian statue there is usually good skiing and tobogganing in Winter.

There are both hiking and bridle trails, too. The well-known Horse Shoe Trail, with its chain of American Youth hostels, starts at the tourist camp and goes westward for 125 miles to join the Appalachian Trail—that great footpath which extends from Maine to Georgia. There are no charges for services in this park, except a reasonable fee for special tours with guides.

Twice in recent years the National Boy Scout Jamboree has been held in Valley Forge State Park. The average park superintendent may justly shiver at the mere thought of entertaining 57,000 boys, not to mention thousands of admiring parents and relatives. In most places it simply could not be done. The water problem alone, and the requirement of open space to deploy such an army, would forbid it. Fifty-seven thousand scouts! This is about the population of Passaic, New Jersey, or Port Arthur, Texas. It is no less than a military operation—indeed, on the first occasion about half the boys came down with ivy poisoning. By the time the second jamboree was held, an ivy-elimination program, undertaken at great expense, had eliminated the problem.

Army engineers put in an amphitheater and created a great stage for the scouts. When you consider that a sea of pup tents must have covered the place, and when you think of the mere physical impact of the hands and feet of 57,000 vigorous urchins, you are impelled to ask, as I did: "What did it look like when they left?" Admittedly, it showed wear and tear. But nature licks its wounds very successfully in this terrain. The park is willing to try it still again.

There is certainly no question that the boy scouts could have no more inspiring place to go. A handsome and well-written booklet on the Valley Forge story was given to each lad at the expense of an anonymous donor. There could not have been a wiser investment.

(XX)

WATKINS GLEN STATE PARK

NEW YORK

On Highway 14, at Watkins Glen

To ENTER this state park the visitor needs only to take a few steps off the main street of a rather populous town. This, certainly, is not as park planners would in these days contrive. But Watkins Glen was a famous resort—a *must* in the itinerary of sightseeing tourists—long before anyone dreamed of state parks.

When Generals Sullivan and Clinton were sweeping into the country of the six Iroquois Nations in 1779, in a scorched-earth progress that eliminated the only effective confederacy the North American Indians had ever evolved, some of their officers found time to look at the countryside at the southern end of the lake now called Seneca.

"Col. Hubley went to view the beauties of the glen and was in raptures over its picturesque waterfalls." If Colonel Hubley really put it in those words, he was the author of a remarkable understatement. In the first place, *glen* means "a narrow depression between mountains or hills." Glens are as common as huckleberries. This was actually an astounding gorge, or series of gorges, cut by glacial torrents carrying abrading rock into a tough shale, with nineteen leaping cascades, no two resembling each other. Picturesque? In a sense, yes. It is surely photogenic. But this description is a bit modest for a scene that has over the years brought millions of people to marvel and meditate upon an extraordinary example of erosion.

One wonders how Colonel Hubley and his fellow officers happened to stray over here and see the gorge. There is little doubt that they had heard of the place from their Indian guides, for the people of the Six Nations had legends about it. One of them concerned a naughty dog who had picked up cusswords from the white man—there being none extant in the Indian tongue—and this bad language infuriated the Great Spirit. Bolts of punishing lightning opened a great cleft in the side of the mountain. As for the dog, the experience cured him and his progeny. Ever after, when Fido feels like cursing, he wags his tail in expressive pantomime, but remains silent.

The Great Spirit's thunderbolt, or it may be the torrents that accompanied the melting of the mile-thick field of glacial ice, in addition to the erosion that has gone on during the 15,000 years since the polar grip was loosened, present to the visitor's eyes a cliffing that reaches heights of from 100 to 300 feet above stream bed, and some bewildering rock forms and shaping. One footbridge is 165 feet above the creek!

The Devonian shale through which the gorge is sculptured is a mud deposit of an inland sea, later buried under great succeeding sediments. In time both lateral and horizontal pressures resulted in two lines of rock weakness nearly at right angles to each other. Thus the gorge has been carved in a most unusual manner. Photographs of the sidewalls really offer a feeble impression of the phenomenon. One must take the trails and see it. As would be expected in such a defile, where the sun appears for only a short period or not at all, the plant growth offers the botanist, or the amateur, much to study.

The Indians of the "long houses" had been dispersed less than two decades when white men from farther east began to move in and take possession of the rich lands around the Finger Lakes. Two Connecticut Yankees purchased 350,000 acres which nearly surrounded Seneca Lake. Known as the Watkins and Flint Purchase, it included what is now this state park. But the newcomers were not interested in scenery. The amphitheater into which the visitor nowadays goes from the main street of the village looked to the Watkins brothers like an ideal place for a grist mill and blacksmith shop. The rest of the gorge, referred to as "the gully," was useless land. The fancy name of Salubria was used to give tone and invitation to the real estate speculation. Near Sentry Bridge, on the north side, the flume that was cut through the rock to harness the water power can still be seen.

The two pioneers passed on; another Watkins, Dr. Samuel L., was probably the first to sense that there was something more here than water for a gristmill. It was he who laid out the village, built a hotel, started a bank, and conceived the idea of a public park to display the natural wonders of the mountain cleft. He called the settlement Jefferson. Jefferson it remained till later in the century, when the name was changed again, first to Watkins, and finally to Watkins Glen.

It was a New England newspaper man, Morvalden Ells, who became to Watkins Glen what John Muir became to the Sierra. In both instances it was a case of love; a passion that took the form of talking and writing about its object on every occasion. Ells haunted the gorge in every leisure hour. Every waterfall had its own lovely individuality for him. He named them all. If the names were sometimes banal and hackneyed, no matter. There were, of course, a Rainbow Falls and a Jacob's Ladder. One couldn't get along without a Lovers' Lane and a Pulpit Rock. Strange to say, the Devil never got into the picture here; a real phenomenon, when you consider that the areas of the National Park System are heavily weighted with memories of Lucifer—Devils Tower, Devil's Slide, Devil's Almost Everything.

Americans, in the mass, were already beginning to see in their native landscape something more than limestone and traprock to be blasted, coal fields to be horribly strip-mined, and agricultural lands to be coveted for their fertility. Not that there had not always been a few who looked on their land forms from the aesthetic and educational aspects. Ells, though, had a feeling that Americans, becoming more mobile, would rejoice in what this stupendous gorge had to offer. A back-to-nature man himself, he sensed a trend.

Ells was right. He had constructed wooden staircases and railings in the gorge, made paths, and even perched a small "Swiss chalet" on a shelf near the end of the present suspension bridge. He saw Watkins Glen taking its place beside the White Mountains, Mammoth Cave, Saratoga Springs, and Niagara Falls. He was right, too; for though the Glen never dimmed the glory of the other tourist attractions, and perhaps was not quite so great as his passion saw it, it became one of the lures of the horse-and-buggy days. "When the railroads came to Watkins Glen," says its historian, "the streets were black with hacks to take the guests to the various hotels."

The Glen was always far better than its promotion, as is inevitably the case where a significant scenic or scientific area is in private hands. The ideal of preservation, without blame to anybody, readily gets submerged in a welter of unimportant distractions. So it was a relief to preservationists when the 103 acres (what it then was; it has grown to about 600) were acquired by the state of New York and "forever reserved as a state park for the purpose of preserving it in its natural condition and for free access to all mankind, without fee, charge or expense to any person for entering or passing to or from any part thereof."

At first, the park was placed in the hands of the American Scenic and Historic Preservation Society. In 1911 its administration was handed over to the Watkins Glen State Park Commission; and finally it was placed under the jurisdiction of the Finger Lakes State Parks Commission, where it now rests.

These regional park commissions, nine in number and operated by unpaid regional commissioners with long, overlaping terms and a State Council of Parks composed of the heads of these regional commissions, are peculiar to the state of New York. The system resulted from a state park plan evolved in a 1922 report of the New York State Association, when Alfred E. Smith was governor—and put his wholehearted support behind it—and Robert Moses was secretary. Certainly the plan has functioned magnificently in New York.

It is not often that a park deer gets a place on the front pages of the newspapers and holds it for several days. Watkins Glen had a deer which did. Somehow the animal managed to land itself in an impossible position on a cliff edge near Savern Cascade. How it got there nobody knew but the deer; and there it was. It would have been a good publicity stunt; but it was more than that. Eagerly people all over the country, and even some abroad, followed the dubious fortunes of that deer. "Anything new about the deer at Watkins Glen?" The radio commentators kept their audiences in touch with the situation. When the deer escaped from its peril there was rejoicing. It is cheering to discover that the life of a wild animal can so evidently be a matter of genuine human concern.

Two years afterward, a cloudburst sent floods down the gorge and demolished the ledge on which the deer had stood. This flood of July 7, 1935, did a great deal of fortunate damage in the glen. Practically all of the unsuitable concrete steps, trails, and iron railings were washed out. With rebuilt steps, trails, and parapet walls of native stone which harmonize with the surrounding rocky cliffs, the natural beauty of the park has been greatly enhanced.

At the southern entrance of the park there is a large shelter pavilion on the steep hillside facing the glen. On the north or glen side the hill slopes down in terraces and meets broad trails that connect with woodland trails on each side of the glen. Below is the lily pond and a footbridge which crosses the ravine to the Indian trail on the north side of the gorge.

Picnicking, children's playground facilities, and tent camping sites are also available in the vicinity of the south entrance. There are no cabins or swimming facilities in the park. However, at the end of the gorge trail, near the upper entrance, there is a picnic area.

PART 3

THE SOUTH

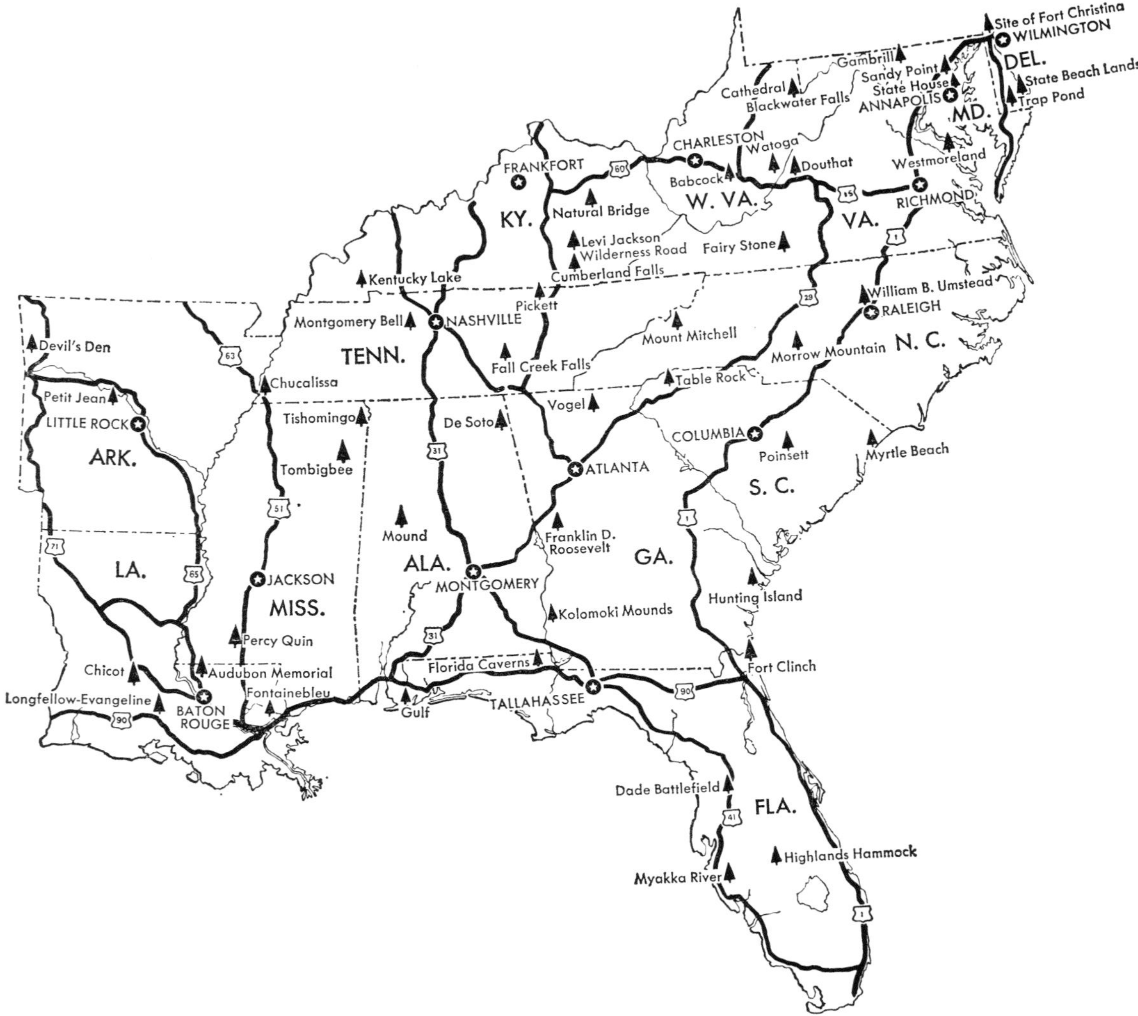
Site of Fort Christina
WILMINGTON
DEL.
State Beach Lands
Trap Pond
Gambrill
Sandy Point
State House
ANNAPOLIS
MD.
Cathedral
Blackwater Falls
CHARLESTON
Watoga
Douthat
Westmoreland
FRANKFORT
60
Babcock
W. VA.
15
RICHMOND
KY.
Natural Bridge
VA.
Levi Jackson
Wilderness Road
Fairy Stone
1
Kentucky Lake
Cumberland Falls
William B. Umstead
Pickett
29
RALEIGH
Montgomery Bell
NASHVILLE
Mount Mitchell
Devil's Den
63
TENN.
Morrow Mountain
N. C.
Fall Creek Falls
Chucalissa
Table Rock
Petit Jean
Vogel
LITTLE ROCK
Tishomingo
De Soto
COLUMBIA
31
Poinsett
Myrtle Beach
ARK.
Tombigbee
ATLANTA
S. C.
51
1
Mound
Franklin D.
Roosevelt
71
GA.
LA.
ALA.
65
JACKSON
MONTGOMERY
MISS.
Hunting Island
Kolomoki Mounds
Percy Quin
31
Florida Caverns
Fort Clinch
Chicot
Audubon Memorial
Longfellow-Evangeline
Fontainebleu
90
BATON
ROUGE
Gulf
TALLAHASSEE
90
Dade Battlefield
FLA.
41
Highlands Hammock
Myakka River
1

(I)

AUDUBON MEMORIAL STATE PARK

LOUISIANA

In West Feliciana Parish, four and a half miles southeast of St. Francisville, on Highway 965

A LOUISIANA friend of mine, who happens to be a university professor, shocked some northern friends once by declaring, in stout tones, that his state was not really part of the Union, but was actually an outpost of the Latin American banana republics. He was exaggerating. Still, behind the jest there was truth. There is an exotic flavor in Louisiana that you find nowhere else in the country in such a marked degree.

I am not referring to New Orleans. New Orleans, in my opinion, is greatly overrated. Whatever it once was, it is now just another big city attracting tourists with its French Quarter tradition recommended by Duncan Hines.

To realize what some hundreds of years of occupancy or exploitation by the Spanish and French left behind in the way of customs, attitudes, and even physiognomy, you must visit those smaller units of government which in most states are called "counties" but here are known as "parishes." Just why the Spanish imprint is not so remarkable as the French, I do not know. There is much Spanish blood here. But consider the names of some of the state parks, alone: Chicot, Chemin-à-Haut, Lake Bistineau, Fontainebleau. Yes; and even *Audubon.* John James Audubon did not consider himself French, of course. Neither did a biography of him published in Paris in 1862, for this book called him, in its title, a "naturaliste Américain." But John James must have felt quite at home in West Feliciana Parish when he came there in 1821. He spoke French and Spanish, as well as English.

In Oakley the state of Louisiana has preserved one hundred beautiful acres of the plantation, including the exceptional colonial mansion, where this incredible man, illustrator of American birds, lived for a few months. The name Audubon has come to be almost synonymous with "bird protector"—a rather humorous fact when you know about him and his unerring gun. The current Audubon enthusiast uses a pair of binoculars, which I take to be a very charming way of finding out what a *live* bird is like. But a fig for moralizing about it. Audubon was—Audubon. The world would have been poorer without this strange, violently determined, exasperating, protean crack shot and consummate artist.

I was surprised, at Oakley, when I asked a custodian what I supposed would be a painfully trite question: "I suppose a great many bird watchers and Audubon people come here?" The answer was no, not very many. I wonder why. True, I *saw* very few birds of any kind on the late February day when I visited Oakley. But it may not have been the right season. Still, Audubon, the incomparable Audubon, actually lived in this house and taught Miss Eliza Pirrie, the daughter of the owner, how to draw and paint a little, at sixty dollars a month. He climbed these very staircases, and in these surrounding lovely woods he roamed as only tireless, fast-footed John James could do.

Then there are the live oaks. Where will you see finer ones? Or finer crape myrtles? Or a more completely restful scene? In West Feliciana Parish, even this very day, time is nothing. *Dolce, dolce far niente.*

You never saw such a planter's mansion as Oakley, built in 1799. You may have seen something *somewhat* like this three-story plantation home, with its jalousied galleries that brought cooling air into the living rooms—but Oakley was built by Ruffin Gray according to his own ideas of comfort in such a climate as this. The lines are simple and dictated by utility rather than for the classic effect, but it conquers by being perfect to its purpose, and even seems stately. Not much decoration, but what there is, is delicate.

Ruffin Gray was a Virginian who had transplanted himself to Natchez on the Mississippi. He got the land grant for the plantation from Spain and had the house begun, but he did not live to enjoy it.

His widow married James Pirrie, a Scotsman. Until 1947, when the state bought it, the place was never out of possession of the family.

Mrs. James Pirrie had met Audubon on a trip to New Orleans. It was one of the many moments in the artist's life when, as a result of his single mindedness, which so often met with contempt, he was ill-fed, frustrated, up a blind alley. The suggestion that he come to Oakley and teach drawing to the young lady of the family was a rift in the heavy clouds. Up the Mississippi to the mouth of Bayou Sara came Audubon. He arrived on a hot, sultry day. Let him tell it in his journal:

> The aspect of the country was entirely new to me and distracted my mind from those objects which are the occupation of my life. The rich magnolias covered with fragrant blossoms, the holly, the beech, the tall yellow poplar, the hilly ground and even the red clay, all excited my imagination. Such an entire change in the face of nature in so short a time seems almost supernatural; and surrounded once more by numberless warblers and thrushes, I enjoyed the scene. [There were not so many warblers and thrushes there after John James unpacked his trusty gun.] The five miles we walked [up from the river] appeared short . . . we were received kindly.

The restoration of the plantation house to which Audubon came on that sultry day in 1821 has been carried out with taste and exemplary restraint. Most of the funds were obtained by legislative appropriation; and the furnishings chosen were from the early part of the nineteenth century, such as Audubon would have glimpsed upon his arrival. Audubon may have been least interested in the formal garden, surrounded by a picket fence; but it was there, since no pretentious home would have been without it. The Garden Club of America donated an annual Founders Day fund for the restoration of this garden, the work being done by the New Orleans Garden Study Club. The Shreveport Iris Society made large plantings of the native Louisiana iris around the lake and the small ponds of the estate.

Many other interested organizations contributed. The National Society of the Colonial Dames of America in Louisiana assumed the task of furnishing the library. The Daughters of the American Revolution supplied appropriate furnishings for the dining room. The Audubon Garden Club of St. Francisville, the nearby town, planted the entrance drive with native shrubs and flowering trees. Thus, with other generous gifts besides these, Oakley was restored as it must have been when the naturalist arrived.

No doubt the artist was comfortable at Oakley. Many conveniences that we now regard as commonplace, were unknown then; but certainly Oakley had every obtainable luxury, and the food prepared in its kitchen, and then brought into the house from the separate building which housed it, must have been delicious. When the plantation house became deserted, only the chimney was left of this kitchen. But Mrs. Francis Crocker had a photograph of the original, and reconstruction was made around the chimney, using some of the virgin cypress trees from Chicot State Park for the woodwork, and bricks from the old abandoned jail at St. Francisville. At present there is room in the building for a loom and a souvenir gift shop.

Reference to weaving reminds me of something I saw here, or possibly in a similar gift shop in Louisiana. There were some cotton towels, white with brown stripes. I assumed that the brown part had been dyed. But I learned that it was made from a naturally brown type of cotton; in slave times, the clothing of the servants was woven of this material. In texture it was just as serviceable, but it was not the cotton sold in the market place.

Audubon, however, must have been more interested in the forest, the fields and the bayous, and in the Mississippi river banks. Many of the surrounding live oaks were hoary in 1821. I was told that foresters have estimated the age of some of these oaks at from 400 to 800 years. It sounded like a slight overestimate to me, comparing these trees to those whose planting date is known at Brookgreen Gardens in South Carolina (at the Allston plantation), but I shall not challenge the forester. Not far from the house is a surely patriarchal cedar, blasted forlorn by lightning or storm, yet still every year sprouting forth a new bough of green to shield its nakedness. Looking around at the forest in which Oakley nearly loses itself, you feel sure that this scene is not measurably different from that of 1821.

You wonder how Audubon got along in a teaching job that left him only half his time free for bird shooting and study? He accepted the position in sheer desperation; not that he felt teaching beneath his dignity, but his mind was centered upon his chef-d'oeuvre, his colossus of pictorial books, and he resented anything that interfered. I am indebted to Robert Cushman Murphy's sprightly monograph, purchased at the Oakley gift shop, for the feeling I have for this singular and somewhat feral genius. I judge, then, that he was not quite so happy with his employers as they were animated and informed by his presence. Not that there was unpleasantness, for though his teaching terminated after a few months in 1821, he returned to West Feliciana Parish later to join his wife Lucy, who was teaching there. But in the short space of the summer of 1821 Audubon painted thirty-two of his birds.

Certain it is that Oakley never had a visitor like this one, before or after. Murphy has told me: "Physically Audubon was not only handsome and well-formed; he was also agile, graceful, wiry, and tireless. He danced so well that he was a favored teacher among well-to-do gentry and their pampered daughters." He was an expert fencer and teacher of the foil. As the birds knew, he was a sure shot. He played the violin, the flute, and the flageolet, and played and taught them well. His personal habits were exemplary. Such a man could have been a social success; he could have broken many hearts. But he was always faithful to his Lucy, who for months at a time, while her husband was living precariously away from home, was shooing the wolf from the door. We can imagine Miss Pirrie occasionally glancing at her robust and handsome instructor and reminding herself: "He is already married."

Whether or not Audubon could have qualified as a dandy, he chose the rugged life. He boasted that he could walk any horse to death in twenty days; he could have done it, too, no doubt. Despite Audubon's French name, Murphy finds he was American to the core —even to an extreme. "His mildly juvenile boastfulness, his absorption with the wilderness, his buckskins and long hair. . . ." proclaimed the fact. He was as western as Mark Twain; and this reminds us that Mark once said of Chaucer that he was a good fellow but he couldn't spell. Audubon couldn't spell, either, and his grammar was at times alarming, but, like so many souls uninhibited by accuracy, he could write racily, and must have talked likewise.

And do not get the idea that this artist, who was rashly proposing and taking subscriptions for an elephantine book that made any printer raise eyebrows and shake head, was a guileless incompetent when it came to a necessary trade. He could have made money in a dozen different ways: but he had to pursue, with everything in his arsenal, his Great Idea. In West Feliciana Parish, for example, "numerous pupils desired lessons in music, French and drawing," he wrote. "The dancing speculation fetched two thousand dollars, and with this capital and my wife's savings, I was *now able to foresee a successful issue to my great ornithological work.*" The italics are mine. Money was important to the End.

Was he lacking in business ability? Hardly. With his partner,

Rozier, he once ran a flatboat down the Mississippi with a cargo of 300 barrels of whiskey, for which he had paid twenty-five cents a gallon. This was at a time when taxes were something somebody paid somewhere—a word of vague import. Audubon and Rozier found a ready market for their cargo at two dollars a gallon. Naïve artist fellow, eh?

(11)

BLACKWATER FALLS STATE PARK

WEST VIRGINIA

Four miles southwest of Davis, on State 32

OUR PIONEER FOREFATHERS, wresting homes and sustenance from the wilderness, speedily became adept in using whatever natural material lay close at hand. That, of course, was dictated by necessity. The logs were there for cabin walls, the mud for chinking, and certain trees could be neatly split for roofing shakes. Many tools could also be fashioned from the forest, which, with crops of foodstuffs in mind, was all too dense and overshadowing. In that part of the Dakotas where there were no trees, the sod itself supplied the dwelling. So attached to their primitive homes did many of those western people become that they lived in them by preference long after they could afford the more pretentious wood and brick. There was certainly a delight in using the material that lay ready for the arm: the muscles might ache, but nature was made to serve. There was the sense of immediate conquest.

All this is elementary: it was pioneering. What is not so easy to trace is the peculiar satisfaction that modern Americans, who have the products of the world at their beck, seem to take in viewing the relics of this rugged adaptation. This still active rejoicing in "making things do"—does it spring from the fact that we sense an eternal insecurity in our world and like to believe that if need should come we, too, could survive? Are we all, even cosseted by luxuries as we are, still rude economists under the skin?

There was a time, remember, when *economy* meant simply "home" husbandry, and there was no other.

Such thoughts occurred to me when I was housed in the luxurious lodge that has recently been built at this West Virginia state park, just near the brink of the impressive wooded canyon through which the Blackwater River takes its impetuous course. Not only the lodge, but twenty-five cottages, in pleasant woodland surroundings, offer modern accommodation to visitors. I didn't think it a provincial viewpoint when my companion, the Director of State Parks, said with quiet satisfaction: "Practically all the material that went into these buildings came from this vicinity." I felt that he was stating a kind of modern version of the pioneer adaptation to which I have just referred—that joy of putting nearby natural materials to work.

As to the woods in the buildings, I am not certain, but I suppose they are native to the state. Practically all the stone used for the walls and fireplaces and chimneys was taken from a quarry of Pocono sandstone only twenty miles away. The blocks around the parking lots are Pottsville sandstones and conglomerates. The red flagstones leading to the lodge came from the south end of Canaan Valley, the other side of the ridge. The massive stone steps leading to the lodge were quarried in nearby Thomas. One of them shows ripple marks that tell the story of the shifting sands of long ages ago, before they consolidated into rock.

Mortar sand from close at hand; crushed limestone also—here are the materials, here is the lodge. Everything is from the region. It has merely altered its location. It belongs. Since I am not a West Virginian, there was nothing parochial, certainly, in the pleasure it gave me to know this. I, too, am probably a primitive economist in spite of the gadgets by which I am possessed.

The water of the Blackwater River is not black. It is dark; but it is hard to say exactly what the color is. No doubt it depends upon the light in which you see it. One of the earliest visitors called it "amber color." Someone later described it as red, and added that even the fish that swim in it are colored by it. The strange part of it is that the other tributaries of the Cheat River, whose waters finally come into the Gulf of Mexico, are not at all so stained.

At first thought, since it is so horribly obvious that one is in a strip-mining coal region, with its barren spoil banks yearning for some vegetation to clothe them, one might conclude that the color of the water is due to pollution. But it is not so. The reason for the stain is much more interesting, because it reveals a chapter of natural history hardly to be suspected from the present scene. The Canaan Valley must have been for long ages covered with the densest growth of hemlock and spruce. Gradually a deep humus accumulated, the peaty rankness of which was impregnated with tannic acid. This causes a "blackness" similar to that of a Florida cypress swamp when you look down into its water; though here, as there, if you see a small quantity in a glass, it looks more like tea. The waters of some rivers in the marsh-forest parts of Minnesota and Wisconsin are of this shade.

The Blackwater River is only about thirty miles long, but in that distance it shows two distinct dispositions. Starting in the southwest end of the Canaan Valley and coursing on resistant rock, it jogs along in a leisurely way, with marshes and meadows on its sides. But suddenly it turns at a sharp right angle, to flow in almost exactly the opposite direction, and now it begins to gallop. In the famous gorge the drop becomes 136 feet to the mile. Hence the spectacular falls and the deep canyon. At the point where the visitor comes out from the lodge to the adjacent overlook, he is standing 525 feet above the bed of the river. Enormous quantities of fallen rock are in the borders of the stream below him, hardly visible from this viewpoint, but painfully apparent to an ardent fisherman who may be trying to make his way along the river course. The sheer jump of the river at the falls is about 63 feet.

About two miles of the canyon lie within Blackwater Falls State Park. Thus the park is divided into two parts, with a north and a south rim. The section on the north side is for day use; it has an artificially created lake, picnic grounds, and playgrounds for children. In the southern section is the lodge, the furnished-cabin area, and later on there will also be a campground.

Though the Canaan Valley is not within the park, this name somehow manages still to dominate the regional scene. "This is the land of Canaan!" exclaimed one of the first white men who ever looked down upon its primeval wilderness. Our forebears knew and quoted the Old Testament. And they probably pronounced the word *K'nane;* I found that pronunciation current in the neighborhood today.

What the pioneer looked upon was indeed a wilderness. "No axe had scarred the trees, which stood so thickly that their branches interlocked for miles, and some of the soil beneath had not been touched by the sun for ages. The trees seemed as unchangeable as the rocks among which they stood, and those that were six inches through looked as old as the giants that were six feet in diameter and one hundred and twenty feet tall."

What was not heavy forest had become, by a secret process that nature has not revealed to us yet, vast "brakes" or "slicks" of laurel, almost impenetrable except by the animals that abounded here. "Laurel" is of course a general term here for tangled growth which actually consists of several shrubs. And how did these thickets come to rule over so many acres? Lightning fires might open up this dense forest, but why did there not follow a growth of sun-loving tree growth, such as is commonly seen? Was the accumulation of humus overacid for that?

At any rate, the terrain seems to have been too difficult for the Indian as well as for the white man, for, though prehistoric man was certainly here, apparently the historic Indian was not found resident by the earliest colonists. The raiding of the Cheat River settlements was done by tribes that came in from the north and east.

Imagine what these "slicks" must have been! They were described as "so matted with the summers and storms of centuries that a hunter among them would walk on the tops, where the branches that heavy snows had bent and pressed together formed a rough gnarly floor several feet above the ground. Beneath the laurels, bears and panthers had broken tunnels through the thickets, and little streams wandered below, seen only through an occasional opening. . . . The water of these rivulets was nearly as cold as ice all summer, and the ice itself did not disappear before mid-June."

Not until 1865 did a hardy settler make his home in this general Blackwater area. Solomon Cosner blazed his way across the Allegheny Front, spotted a place where a forest fire had raged, and began to clear some land. He found the wild country full of cattle, horses, and other stock that had been run in by marauders during the Civil War. The store nearest his little farm was twenty-five miles away. In later years Cosner said that he and his sons had killed more than 500 bears, uncounted deer, two panthers, and a wolf, in their vicinity.

The bears and the deer are still found at Blackwater, though the panther has long since gone, as has the wolf. Many of the smaller mammals are to be seen, including the snowshoe rabbit, with his seasonal color variation.

Well, this is the wilderness that was! How few years, after our robust country really got in motion, attacking its natural resources with both vigor and new tools, it took to create a scene of wreckage! Remember that Solomon Cosner found a primeval wilderness in the year 1865—no evidence of settled occupation, merely a great shaggy hideout for stock rustlers. Some years before, "five adventurous gentlemen" had made an expedition into the "land of Canaan" and described it as a country flowing with wild animals and prodigious forests. They related that in one afternoon, when they fished three miles of the Blackwater above the falls, they caught nearly five hundred trout of six to ten inches. In 1885 the West Virginia Central and Pittsburgh Railway laid its rails into Davis (now a faded community near the state park). The forests began to fall.

Just a few years! In the 1930's and 1940's the area around Davis was described as "completely desolate." As early as 1911 practically all the magnificent white pine was gone. That was the richest "take." In the same period the vast quantities of tulip poplar, red spruce, hemlock, and oak had been greatly reduced. "You can see," says a bulletin of the West Virginia Geological and Economic Survey, "throughout the park remnants of the black peaty soil which covered the original forest floor in great thickness. Forest fires burned over the lumbered-off slash year after year, as the end of the extensive lumbering approached, and the area west and north of Davis was then one of the most desolate and despoiled imaginable. The soil as deep as twelve inches even now is full of the charcoal left by the fires." Taken together with the naked spoil banks of the strip mining that had accompanied the devastation, this was an outrage you might think nature would never, never forgive.

But evidently men are to be forgiven by the earth mother, on the ground that "they know not what they do." There has been an extraordinary recovery, considering the shambles. The CCC made plantings of spruce on Canaan Mountain, with most encouraging results. The Monongahela National Forest borders Blackwater Falls State Park in many places, and both these reserves of course support each other. There are a few little enclaves of virgin growth tucked away in places which were too hard to get to for the lumberman and which somehow failed to be burned. Otherwise the tree growth you see dates from about 1925, and the reforestation is surely remarkable.

Since most of the area around Blackwater Falls State Park lies at elevations of 3,000 to 4,000 feet above sea level, the conditions for skiing and other winter sports are likely to be nearly ideal. Snow cover is not only heavy, but the snow lies long. On the average, there are between seventy and a hundred inches of snow. The freak year of 1957-58 brought more than two hundred inches, which proved to be more than anyone wanted; but that winter was abnormal throughout the east.

While I was at Blackwater Falls I had an opportunity of witnessing the extraordinary bird flight that for the past five years or so has been a fascinating attraction for visitors at the lodge during the autumn months. Distinctly, I am not advertising this phenomenon, for I have no means of knowing how long it may continue. Bird behavior is not under state control.

Facing the entrance side of the lodge is a screen of evergreen trees. This new forest growth, less than thirty-five years old, is really only a thin belt, for behind it there is open space. At dusk, as I stood outside the lodge, the starlings began to arrive. The prodigious numbers reminded me of the bat flight at Carlsbad Caverns; and, against a leaden sky, one had the same notion that the black specks were grains of pepper being sprinkled out of the sky from a colossal shaker. The birds came in waves, and the rhythm of the arrival of separate flocks had something of a military precision. Into this thin belt of trees, with almost incredible swiftness, approaching the roosts at high speed and suddenly alightning as though the dormitory had a number for each bird—how many birds rested in those trees that night? A very rash person may estimate. I shall not.

Where do they come from? How did it happen that just a few years ago these flocks chose this spot for a perching place after the day's work? Why do they come only seasonally? Are they on their way, eventually, to Washington, which is not merely the nation's capital but also the capital of the starlings? I could find nobody in the park at the time who could answer my questions.

As I have said, this amazing bird flight, which continues for more than an hour in the twilight, is nothing to be confidently advertised. It may not continue to happen. The birds may change their venue. But if you *should* be at the Blackwater Falls Lodge . . . when it takes place do not miss it!

(III)

CATHEDRAL STATE PARK

WEST VIRGINIA

On U.S. 50, near Aurora

THE AUTHOR of the following statement is unknown to me. I found these words quoted in an excellent geological pamphlet on Blackwater Falls State Park and the surrounding region:

Old lumbermen still speak with a kind of awe of the volume of timber which left the Valley. A pretty good stand of hardwood timber in West Virginia may yield 15,000 board feet per acre. Exceptional ones may go to 20,000 or even above. In Michigan and Minnesota white pine stands are sometimes good for 40,000 board feet . . . well, some of the Canaan acres yielded 80,000 to 100,000 board feet. Remove your hats, visitors; this was once lumberman's holy ground.

Well, I have been a recent visitor to this part of West Virginia, and I did not remove my hat in joyous recollection of the multitudinous board feet that once grew here, but now do not. Much of this former lumberman's holy ground in the vicinity of the park resembles—was I about to use the word "desert"? That would be an insult to the true desert—the mysterious and beautiful land of scant rainfall with its marvels of adaptation and survival. There is hardly a word suited for the strange desolation of a countryside stripped of its forest cover, stripped of its topsoil, ages upon ages of humus accumulation savagely burned away. "Shambles" might be a suggestive word. This was the scene of land-butchery.

It is quite useless to despair of the kind of morality and mentality which led to this brutal use of natural resources. What is done is done. There is no going back—not in any length of time we can contemplate—to what was there. A slow healing process, maintained with intelligence, will bring bloom back to these sallow acres. Not the same bloom, but something enjoyable to look upon. It is being managed. If the conditions were similar to those on the moon, good land managers could probably do something even then.

Nor is it at all useful to wax sentimental about the passing of the mighty eastern forests which the white men first looked upon, and traversed and tamed as they pushed toward the setting sun, a greater freedom, and available places of settlement. These had to pass. They were bound to be chopped and utilized by a growing nation. Conservationists now know how to gather, and still have. That is some consolation. Still, it is not too extravagant to wish that a little more of that "lumberman's holy ground" had been less accessible, or that we had salvaged a few more samples of the forest wilderness like Cathedral State Park, in the neighboorhood of Aurora, West Virginia.

How many board feet of virgin hemlock and hardwoods there may be in this priceless preserve I do not know, nor do I care. The point is simply that the board feet are still there, standing vertical, drawing sap from the damp earth, tossing their heads against the sky. I wonder how many people of West Virginia have seen these precious woods and realized what they possess in these two hundred acres? I wonder, moreover, if West Virginians know how this forest came to be salvaged from a widespread wreckage?

As you might suspect, it was due to a single man. Call him a man of foresight, idealism, a lover of beauty, a stubborn man—anything you please—this wonderful example of primeval forest remains unmarred because he said to the lumberman: "No, my friend, not *this*. Not so long as I live; and I shall try to contrive its security even longer than that." There are similar instances of such preservation in other states. In Indiana it was John Lusk; and so that state possesses the virgin woods of Turkey Run.

Here, in Aurora, it was Branson Haas. His wife called him Brance. I am told that some called him "Uncle Billy." I trust this was with his permission. We gather that he was quite a man, one who did not refer to his hoe as "an agricultural implement." Lacking in the graces, maybe, but he could be trusted with the stewardship of something worth defending against picklocks. Indeed, because he showed himself a faithful steward, he came into ownership of a large farm of which this forest was a part. It had been the property of a wealthy Ohio man, who one day decided that he no longer cared to keep it. Branson Haas then operated it as a dairy farm.

I suppose Brance's neighbors, when they heard of the tempting offers for the board feet which he refused, must have been puzzled. A man who turns down a good offer for a growing tree merely because he prefers that it continue to grow where it sprouted is a subject for lifted eyebrows.

The state of West Virginia acquired this tract from Haas for much less than its actual worth. I mean, of course, so far as you can place a monetary value on something both magnificent and irreplaceable. Haas only made the reservation that he should be caretaker of the forest as long as he lived. So it was agreed: and could one imagine a better caretaker?

A virgin forest like this at Cathedral is almost beyond description, and the camera lens is balked by it. The reason is, probably, that your experience in these woods lies not so much in what you see as in what you feel. You can say that these hemlocks are giants in girth and height, and publish the dimensions. Interspersed are hardwood trees, oak, yellow birch, cherry, or whatever, whose bark as high as you can reach is so shaggy with age that it does not resemble the bark of a young tree of the same species. You may observe and tell hundreds of details, and still you fail to reveal the character of the forest as a whole.

One simply cannot know what the primeval forest is like without venturing into one. That such a forest is a bit frightening to urbanized man is no wonder. It is strong medicine for one who has lost both physical and spiritual affinity with the wild. I can imagine that some, though they might delight in the experience of walking a trail through it, and feel somehow ennobled by the contact, would emerge from its twilight-shade with as much sense of relief as they would greet daylight on leaving a cave. Yet they have been gazing at living history.

Francis Baily, the English astronomer who visited wild America in the early days of the eighteenth century, spoke of the "psychic influence" of the forest wilderness. And he was no softy, either. "It is a feeling of confinement, which begins to damp the spirits, from this complete exclusion of distant objects. To travel day after day, among trees of a hundred feet high, is oppressive to a degree which those cannot conceive who have not experienced it. . . ." Yet we get the impression that our voyageurs, trappers and mountainmen actually exulted in the freedom they found in just such wilderness.

However that may be, there is one feeling the visitor to Cathedral State Park will have. That is reverence. It *is* a cathedral; the name given it is no flamboyant one. The delightful walks within it are, in fact, aisles. It is, besides, an ancient cathedral, like Canterbury. It tells the story of a long-gone time. West Virginians may vacation here (and visitors from other states, too) and find a refreshment of mind and spirit not to be had in other places.

And—would you believe it? I was told that there is a feeling on the part of some people in the state that Cathedral should be "improved" a little; that there should be roadways in it, so that people could more readily inspect it from their automobiles. It is really difficult to know what to say to such people. An ironic retort, such as suggesting that they take their rollerskates to church, would be not merely rude but ineffective. Yet I doubt that a serious explanation—that you don't nick a segment from a perfect whole—would be understood either. But I'm sure there are plenty of conservationists in West Virginia who will defend the integrity of Cathedral.

(I V)

CHUCALISSA*

TENNESSEE

Off Highway 51, south of Memphis, on the Mississippi River

Who were these people who occupied the prehistoric Indian town that is being preserved so skillfully and effectively just a short distance from downtown Memphis? They lived there, presumably, about six hundred years—from about the year 1000 to 1600, a period long enough so that, whether by interior development or through contact with other peoples, there was a change even in the construction of their houses.

The different types of dwellings reconstructed here are well displayed to the visitor. There is also something that the public delights in—an archaeological development that may be seen *in progress.* For this is no frozen exhibit. Even when the museum is finally completed there will be constant changes aimed at revealing the lives of the southeastern Indian, as artifacts are brought to light.

The visitor to Chucalissa will probably meet at least one Choctaw Indian guide. Two amiable and intelligent members of this once-powerful Mississippi tribe contrive to bring a sense of reality to the area. If the visitor does not happen to see either of them, let him by all means obtain a copy of the brochure *Pasfalaya,* about this Indian town. The two guides whose pictures are shown therein are named L. D. John and Harry Martin. The names do not sound Indian—the Choctaw long ago despaired of correlating their own peculiar method of assigning names with that of the white man.

* This prehistoric Indian town is a 30-acre portion of T. O. Fuller State Park.

According to native custom, an infant was given a name connected with some natural phenomenon witnessed at the time of its birth. Later the men received a war title. The ancient Choctaw, we are told, were so averse to speaking their own names that only a third person would do it. A man's wife never called her husband by his name but referred to him as "my son's (or daughter's) father."

The guides at the Indian town are Choctaw, yes. But are they descendants of the folk who inhabited Chucalissa at the time, say, when De Soto and his followers were pushing their exploration to and along the Mississippi River? Probably not. More likely, but yet to be demonstrated, they are closely related to the Chickasaw. Or more closely still, perhaps to the Unica, who lived north of the Natchez people on the Yazoo. However, this makes little difference, for these regional Indian groups had more points of similarity than differences among them. The Pasfalaya (Long Hairs), for example, let their hair grow to full length instead of shaping it according to a pattern. The custom differentiated the Choctaw from the other tribes, to be sure; but it is of little import within a common civilization.

Of the Choctaw, John R. Swanton of the Smithsonian Institution commented: "They had less territory than any of their neighbors, but raised so much corn that they sent it to others in trade . . . their beliefs and customs were simple . . . they seldom left their country to fight, but when attacked defended themselves with dauntless bravery. In other words, the aboriginal Choctaw seemed to have enjoyed the enviable position of being 'just folks,' uncontaminated with the idea that they existed for the sake of a political, religious or military organization. . . . And apparently like the meek they were in the process of inheriting the earth because none of their neighbors could compete with them economically."

Naturally the coming of the white man put an end to all that. The Indians became pawns on a chessboard of European rivalries of which they had only the faintest comprehension.

Whether or not the present Choctaw guides at Chucalissa are directly related to the ancient ones who built the mounds and the earthworks, who made the baskets, pottery, beadwork, and featherwork revealed from the excavations—L. D. John and Harry Martin are certainly "in place." L. D. is the first Choctaw in many generations to set his hand to the art of pottery making. And we are told that when schoolchildren come to Chucalissa, they at once set up a cry: "We want Harry. . . ." For these young people, the guides surely bring the place to life.

These six-hundred-year occupants of Chucalissa had time to accumulate a big "public dump," which the archaeologist can delicately finger. But in the tunnel-like entrance into the exhibit area, which is actually a present-day cross section cut through an ancient earthwork, the visitor can read the story of a prodigious primitive effort in earth-moving. The fill that surrounds the central plaza—550 feet long on the inside arc of the plaza and 1,200 feet along the outside periphery—is estimated to contain 280,000 cubic feet. For the most part it was moved in basketsful, and delicate excavation has uncovered the weave pattern of these baskets where a laborer, looking at his wornout container, decided that he needed a new one and dumped the old one along with its contents.

On emerging from the entrance trench, we see the large open plaza that was the center of all communal activity. This was the tribal meeting ground, the ceremonial dance court, and the playfield where stickball and chunkey were played. The knack of turning out stickball rackets has not been forgotten by the present-day Choctaw, and the game is still played at the annual all-Choctaw fair, when the several tribes compete.

Stickball was played by most of the southeastern Indians; the northern ones played the lightning-fast, related game of lacrosse. Chunkey (chung-kee) was another ancient game. In this play, the flat-sided chunkey-stone was rolled down an alley about 200 feet long. The opposing players then threw sticks or spears in an effort to hit the stone. Incidentally, it was a highly favored gambling game, and as we know, these ancient folk loved to place a bet on the nose of horse or man.

The Frenchman Bossu has a good description of the stickball game as he saw it played during his early travels in this region. "The Choctaw," he wrote, are very active and nimble. They have a game similar to our racket game. . . . Neighboring villages invite one another . . . men and women gather in their finest costumes and pass the day singing and dancing. The day following is that on which the match is to take place. They agree upon a goal 60 paces distant and indicated by two large poles between which the ball must pass. . . . There are forty players on each side, each holding a racket two and a half feet long [actually each had two rackets] and a ball covered with deerskin. . . . it is a fine sight to observe the players with their bodies bare, painted in all sorts of colors, with a tiger tail fastened behind and feathers on their arms and heads, which flutter as they run. . . . The players never become angry."

Our French traveler goes on to describe another stickball feature which was so unusual that it may have been a custom restricted to the Choctaw. "After the players have finished, the women whose husbands have been defeated try to avenge their spouses. They play with a different kind of racket. They run against one another very swiftly and shove one another like the men, being equally naked."

At reconstructed Chucalissa there are poles indicating the court where the ancient game took place.

Only the more important persons lived on this basket-filled ridge surrounding the plazza. Several dwellings like those which housed the chief men of the village have been reconstructed. The mass of the population lived to the north, south, and east of the central area.

On the west side of the plaza is a burial mound which remains to be excavated. In the year 1541, when De Soto was in this vicinity, the channel of the Mississippi River was such that a fine view of the stream was to be had from the top of this mound. On the north side is the large Temple Mound on which the public buildings stood, and also the residence of the tribal chief. This point was the dominating feature of the village.

As has been said, Chucalissa (House Abandoned) is a continuous piece of archaeological work and study, not a finished one. Additional excavations of the main village area will be made during the summer months, when the visitor may see how archaeological finds are turned up by methods so painstaking that almost nothing is missed or spoiled.

The informative brochure *Pasfalaya* contains a statement made by Emmett York, chairman of the Choctaw Tribal Council of the Mississippi group. It is worth repeating: "We hope the American White People will always remember that we were once your friend, and still we are friend."

In this spot in west Tennessee, not too far from the place where the treaty of Dancing Rabbit Creek was signed, it is not out of place to consider the brutality with which the Indians of the region were torn from their homes and transported westward. Maybe it is just as well that the inhabitants of Chucalissa moved into the unknown of their own volition. The white man wanted the land and the Indian had to go; it was inevitable. I like the way old chief Apushmataha of the Choctaw sized up the situation.

Apushmataha was approached by Tecumseh, with his dream of Indian unity. But the shrewd Choctaw leader saw that it was too late. He persuaded his people not to indulge in illusions. At the same time, when Andrew Jackson painted an alluring picture of the "superior hunting grounds" in Oklahoma as a inducement for the Choctaw to move westward, this wise elder statesman said, with blistering bluntness: "Further lying is unnecessary. I have hunted in both places, and I know which is best."

(V)

CUMBERLAND FALLS STATE PARK

KENTUCKY

Eighteen miles southwest of Corbin, on Highway 90

ON A WALL of the lounge of the comfortable lodge at Cumberland Falls State Park there hangs a picture of the late T. Coleman duPont, a native of the Commonwealth of Kentucky. It is the figure of a competent, kindly, and understanding man. Coleman duPont was all of that. Below the picture appears the following rather mystifying inscription:

This photo of T. Coleman duPont, in recognition of his gift of Cumberland Falls to his native state of Kentucky, is hereby presented to the Commonwealth of Kentucky this 10th day of July, 1952, commemorating the 25th anniversary of the first round-trip by automobile to Cumberland Falls from the Corbin side of the river on July 10, 1927 by:

ROBERT A. BLAIR
TOM W. GALLAGHER
I. O. CHITWOOD
WADE H. CANDLER

I have said that the inscription is rather mystifying. I meant, of course, to the stranger. Nobody in Corbin, and perhaps few residents of the Commonwealth, would fail to get the point. But maybe the visitor from Rhode Island or Kansas, in driving into the park, has also been a bit surprised to see a sign that says he is upon the "Kiwanis Trail." This is unusual. Service clubs are admittedly useful

Charley Bowlegs Creek Cypress Swamp,
Highlands Hammock State Park, Florida

Fall Creek Falls in the summer, Fall Creek Falls State Park

Blackwater River courses through a wooded canyon,
Blackwater Falls State Park, West Virginia

Mount Mitchell, Mount Mitchell State Park, North Carolina. Viewed from Roan Mountain, Tennessee.

The prehistoric Indian village of Chucalissa, reconstructed on its original site; T. O. Fuller State Park, Tennessee

A regatta at Kentucky Lake State Park, Kentucky

"Biscuit Rocks," an erosional form in Hartsborne sandstone,
Petit Jean State Park, Arkansas

Girl Scouts tidy up before visiting the "Little Whitehouse" that F.D.R. loved, Franklin D. Roosevelt State Park, Georgia

The Needle's Eye, Petit Jean State Park

The Acadian House Museum, Longfellow–Evangeline State Park, Louisiana

The Gabriel Oak, Longfellow–Evangeline State Park

Fishing pier, Myrtle Beach State Park, South Carolina

Oakley Plantation, where Audubon, the great illustrator of American birds, gave painting lessons while creating his "elephant folio"; Audubon Memorial State Park, Louisiana

A scenic view of Myakka River State Park, Florida

A vista at Poinsett State Park, South Carolina

Cumberland Falls, Cumberland Falls State Park, Kentucky

organizations; they do many admirable things; yet I know of no other instance where one of these clubs has been so honored in a public reservation. With respect to DuPont, the reference is clear enough. It was his generosity that saved Cumberland Falls from extinction. But what had a "round trip by automobile" to do with it?

It is altogether a wonderful tale, this of the preservation of one of the loveliest waterfalls, in a charming setting, which can be visited in the United States. Without rattling the bones of a controversy that involved blood, sweat, tears, recriminations, and downright feuding, it may be remarked at once that Cumberland Falls was a *cause célèbre*. In the history of state parks, it is a classic victory, won against apparently hopeless odds by a valiant band of conservationists who did not have sense enough to know when they were beaten. The saving of the beauties of Dinosaur National Monument from destruction by dams has, in the national parks picture, something of the same tint. Yet, of the two performances, the preservation of Cumberland Falls was perhaps the greater feat, for the vast pressure of nationwide idealism that saved Dinosaur was lacking here. The ardent preservationist souls of Kentucky had to go it pretty much on their own, and one of them said wryly to me: "Every night we retired from the day's combat and licked our wounds."

The controversy dates back to the roaring twenties, when prosperity seemed endless, and only the blue heavens were the limit of the bigger and better in business. It was a time of mergers, and of "holding companies." Notably, electric power companies were gathered and stacked like playing cards. The famous Samuel Insull, in Chicago, was a name as electric as the current that flowed through the wires of his holding company. It was a time of expansion—without much consideration whether the development was worthwhile, or what it would cost.

The passion for progress crept up on Cumberland Falls. On Cumberland Falls, mind you, which had long been famous as one of the finest scenic sites of the eastern states! Here, surrounded by the Cumberland National Forest, was a potential state park of magnificent quality, on which the Kentucky State Park Commission had had its eye since the creation of that body in 1924. But the Cumberland Hydro-Electric Power Company held an option on 200 acres surrounding the falls and there were no funds available for purchase by the state, even if the corporation were willing to relinquish its option. In an advisory capacity the then young National Conference on State Parks came into the picture, and contributed nobly to the preservation of what was a cultural asset not merely of the commonwealth but of the nation.

Looking back on it, we see a bitter contest of the kind that conservationists know all too well. When T. Coleman duPont offered to purchase the area and donate it to the state, he walked into much the same difficult situation as John D. Rockefeller, Jr., encountered in his efforts to preserve Jackson Hole, Wyoming, for the people of the nation. In the language of such controversies, the side that wishes to preserve irreplaceable scenic and scientific localities is a stubborn barrier in the way of progress—the word being taken to imply that there is no kind of human advancement except that which is purely commercial. As the contest waxes and epithets are tossed like bricks, the conservationist is marked as not merely stubborn, but dangerous. DuPont did not escape vilification, though later there was expressed a decent shame about it.

The struggle was too long and too involved to be recounted here. Despite the fact that the power interests were well financed and at first had most of the newspapers of the state on their side, whereas the conservationists, with their one-dollar memberships in a "preservation association," were always poverty-stricken, Cumberland Falls was saved. Tom Wallace, the redoubtable editorial chief of the Louisville *Times*, wielding one of the journalistic world's most trenchant pens in the cause of the protection of natural beauty, was "a host in himself."

It turned out, also, that the falls cost the DuPont family more than the original offer of $230,000. And this story, too, is a cheering example of faith and understanding. For DuPont, although ready to contribute the $230,000 if the deal were consummated in his lifetime, was unwilling, in case of his prior death, to commit his estate. Since DuPont did, in fact, die before the Kentucky legislature could act, it became necessary to appeal to his widow, son, and daughter. The appeal was not in vain. To them this was a sacred obligation, and the sum required was forthcoming, even though it had grown to $400,000.

Ruminating in his entertaining Louisville *Times* column, long after Cumberland Falls State Park had become a beautiful establishment, Tom Wallace said: "I could not forget the days when Bob Blair, Wade Candler, Tom Gallagher [and 'Sonny' Chitwood*] . . . fought shoulder to shoulder, shield to shield, for Cumberland Falls when 'practical businessmen' in Corbin and in Louisville derided those who were attempting its salvage. . . ." With this statement we

* Chitwood's name has here been inserted, since it is quite obvious that its omission by Wallace was only a lapse of memory, which he would wish corrected.

are coming to the explanation of the "round trip by automobile" mentioned in the marker of the hotel in the park. Also to the reason that the highway is called "Kiwanis Trail."

Though it is now only about eighteen miles by road from Corbin, Kentucky, to Cumberland Falls, it was formerly seventy-six miles. When you visit this state park and note the nature of the terrain of this part of the Cumberland Plateau, you will see why this was so. Except on foot, to get from Corbin to the falls without going the long way around, it was necessary first to find a gap in a high ridge and second to bridge a deep gully that perhaps marked the place of a former water course, which has now dried. Dry or not, it was a formidable barrier.

"The Four Horsemen" of the Corbin Kiwanis Club, enthusiastically in favor of making Cumberland Falls a state park and knowing well the virtues of publicity, placed a sign: "We want a good road to Cumberland Falls" on an old Ford car, and spent eight hours getting down—they wonder now how they did it—to the old Moonbow Hotel, a famous hostelry accessible from the western side by ferry across the Cumberland just above the falls.

That was a beginning. Then these Kiwanis men put through an extraordinary project. They actually turned out a crew of volunteer workers and built a bridge across the gully that barred access to what is now the main part of the park. The crew included a local minister, one Carl Vogel. Imagine the audacity of it! The crew was by no means skilled, and the bridge had to support a vehicle. They felled more than 1,200 trees—oaks and tulip poplar and pines—and created a structure 268 feet long, thirty feet above the bottom of the gully. Not only was this bridge, built by volunteers, like the fat man who said "I can't climb much but I can shovel," a good one; but later, when it was replaced by a modern highway arch, the state engineers could find no better spot than the one the Kiwanis club had chosen.

This same crowd canvassed the countryside, soliciting one-dollar memberships for the Preservation Association. Any honors this Corbin crew have received are richly deserved. Particularly, may we never forget Tom Wallace, whose first editorial on the subject, "Save Cumberland Falls," appeared on July 27, 1925. Bob Blair has a framed copy of that issue of the Louisville newspaper hanging in his office in Corbin.

Now, what is it these courageous men saved for posterity? What is this Kentucky state park of which the natives are so justly proud?

Look first at the Cumberland Plateau and the region that surrounds Whitley County. The Kentucky part of the Plateau is often called the "eastern Kentucky coalfield." That puts its rocks, geologically, in the same time span as the Pennsylvania coal. All these rocks are sedimentary—sandstones, shales, conglomerates, coal seams. The conglomerates are very resistant to erosion, and so you see them as craggy pinnacles—knobs up to 1,300 feet—overlooking a terrain that, viewed from the top of one of them, appears as a series of flat-topped ridges, deeply cut by stream valleys.

The Cumberland River here follows a lazy and meditative course, with generally slow water, until it creates the big bulge—almost turning back upon itself—where the major part of the park now lies. About midway in this big bend the spectacular falls come tumbling no less than sixty-eight feet into a plunge pool below. In time of high water the tumble is some ten feet more. Since the river at this point has a width of 125 feet, the volume of water is great even at the slackest season.

Much has been made of the "moonbow" of Cumberland Falls, and it is indeed an uncommon phenomenon. Some say there is only one other like moonbow in the world—that of the Victoria Falls in Africa. I like those claims. They imply great enthusiasm. But whether or no, this moonbow is something worth traveling far to see. The plunge of the falls, on a bright moonlight night, causes a mist to rise from the basin below and float slowly down the gorge. If a breeze is blowing upstream the mist is lifted upward, giving the best effect.

Many a year people have come to the falls just to see this moonbow. So much has been said about it that an even more brilliant spectrum, a rainbow seen frequently in the morning at the foot of the waterfall, has been rather neglected. The full effect of this, too, depends on the amount of water, the light, and the direction of the wind. Likewise not enough known is the waterfall in a hanging valley about 600 yards downstream from the great falls, hidden in a narrow ravine, and a moderately arduous hike for the average visitor. I did not see Eagle Falls myself, but I saw it reflected in the radiant faces of a young Connecticut couple who, on a day of frosty, winy air, came back to DuPont Lodge and told me about their visit to it. Great are the joys of tramping these less accessible trails when one has the legs for it: and most people are perfectly able, if they will!

Hardly less impressive than the falls is the view up the Cumberland gorge as the visitor sees it from the patio in the rear of the lodge. It is really a deep cut, this gorge, and were it not for the fact that the sides are so beautifully clothed with forest growth, it would look precipitous. But as it is, it seems really velvety. Here is a recipe, from one who does not commonly offer medical services: if you feel distraught, not at peace with yourself and the world around you, sit for an hour or two on the patio of DuPont Lodge and look up that gently winding V-shaped valley of the Cumberland. There is restoration in it! Then reflect whether a dam across the Cumberland, to impound water for a purpose that might be better achieved somewhere else, would be a more valuable employment of this natural gift to man!

Cumberland Falls State Park is not, in extent, very large. But it does not pretend, either, to perform too many functions within its area. It is essentially a place to rest, to gain faith, to delight the eyes, to unkink sedentary legs—all those kinds of higher recreation (as I think)—and to amble along astride a good horse on the bridle path. Its original area has been extended, however, and most wisely, to include a tract of land on the opposite side of the river—where the very good second-growth trees were in danger of being stripped away to serve as mine props: and you can imagine what a blight that would have created, looking down upon it from the developed part of the park! This land was fortunately acquired in time, and part of it now serves as a picnic ground and parking area. Later, another part of it will make an excellent location for campers.

The lodge at Cumberland Falls State Park is open the year around. Some people would find the winter climate here too crisp for them. On the other hand, others do not need, and do not want, the tropics. I found one of the fine all-year-round cottages occupied all winter—and *every* winter—by a man who during the summer season operates a camp in the Adirondacks of New York. He says this is the best place he ever found to spend the winter months.

A good naturalist program at this park would be a rewarding investment. Nature has a fine story to tell here, but except for the specialist, it needs lively interpretation.

(VI)

DADE BATTLEFIELD STATE HISTORIC MEMORIAL

FLORIDA

One mile south of Bushnell, on U.S. 301

OSCEOLA, the famous Seminole Indian leader, was not present on the morning of December 28, 1835, when Major Dade marched his column of federal troops through a barren of grass, palmettos, and small pines in the direction of Fort King, now Ocala. Osceola had business of his own, arising from the fact that General Wiley Thompson, the Indian agent at Fort King, had humiliated him the year before. He had been carrying the seething recollection of the manacles on his wrists, and waiting for his opportunity.

The "massacre" of the Dade detachment had been completed by the Seminoles led by the three chiefs, Micanopy, Jumper, and Alligator, before Osceola arrived to tell his compatriots that his journey to Fort King had been successful. Wiley Thompson and a fellow officer had been ambushed and shot. At the Dade Battlefield, of the eight officers and one hundred men in the command, there were only three survivors. The Second Seminole War was on in earnest, and it proved to be one of the longest and most expensive federal adventures in the relocation of the American Indian.

The visitor who comes to this well-kept Florida state memorial and enters the excellent museum to learn the story will be reminded of a similar massacre which took place on the Little Big Horn in Montana when the cavalry under George Armstrong Custer were killed to the last man. The Custer Battlefield is now a national monument administered by the National Park Service, which means that it is regarded as having national significance. Surely the Dade Battlefield is equally worthy of state preservation. It tells the same sorry story, which, now that the nation is mature, we may blushingly offer in confession—of the bloodshed and havoc wrought by the white man's callous indifference to a solemn treaty, and the rapacity that deprived the Indian of his home lands.

Whether one considers what happened both at the Little Big Horn and near Wahoo Swamp in Florida massacres will depend, of course, on how one construes the word. In the sense that no quarter was given, both could certainly be defined as massacres. But they were not massacres in the sense that helpless people were involved, as was often the case in the bloody French and Indian wars in the northeast. They were military operations between two armed forces, and in both cases the losers were outfought or outgeneraled. If the Seminoles had lost their entire force near the Wahoo Swamp, and Major Dade had been the victor, we may wonder whether it would have gone down in our history as a massacre.

As it was, the Seminole chiefs, defiant of the order that they should leave their Florida homes and head for an unknown frontier west of the Mississippi, were taking a long chance in attacking Dade and his detachment. The federal troops had a six-pounder with them. Ineffective as the cannon might be physically, it carried psychological persuasion for Indians who had no such arms. Indeed, when this six-pounder was fired during the battle, many of the Seminoles "went over the hill" for a while.

It was a slip on the part of Major Dade that gave the Seminoles their chance. The pine barren looked sufficiently open so that the commander relaxed his vigilance. Instead of sending out the usual flankers, he ordered the whole force to plunge straight ahead, with Dade riding behind. It seemed impossible that Indians could be in ambush behind such feeble growths as young pines and palmettos. But they were there. The survivors of the battle estimated that there were from 400 to 1,000 of them. Chief Alligator said later that when they left the swamp that morning he counted 180 followers. As the Seminoles had a reputation for truthfulness, this may be taken as correct.

And that brings us back to Osceola, for the Dade Memorial somehow has its chief association with that remarkable Indian—a quarter-breed, some say—who, at a conference table with federal officers, had once drawn his knife and sunk it into the table before him, saying: "*That* is the only treaty I will ever make with the whites!"

Osceola's Seminole name may have been Asi-yaholo. In that case it would mean that, Indian fashion, he got his name from something that happened when the "blackdrink"—the ceremonial vomitive made from the berries of the yaupon shrub—was being passed around with a peculiar accompanying cry, "ya-ho-la!"

It became a famous name over the years. There are many who can remember standing up in school on reciting-day and spouting a poem called "The Seminole's Defiance":

Blaze, with your serried weapons!
I will not bend the knee!
The shackles ne'er again shall bind
The arm which now is free.

When it came time to get rid of Osceola the federal army resorted to a trick which made even the Seminole's enemies ashamed. In company with Wildcat and some other chiefs, he came into St. Augustine in October 1837, under a flag of truce. He and his companions were seized and made prisoners. He was shipped up to Fort Moultrie in South Carolina, where he died at the age of thirty-four. Later an inscription was placed on his grave:

Osceola—Patriot and Warrior
Died Jan. 30, 1838

The few remaining Seminoles have a private opinion, which they are likely to express publicly only in a murmur: "Estahadkee holowagus loxeeojus," which means, "White man no good, he lie too much." Insofar as it may refer to the white man's observation of treaty contracts made with the Indians, it would seem to be justified.

Osceola is said to have remarked to his jailers before he died: "The white folks had the newspapers; the Indians had no newspapers; the Indians had no fair showing." There seems to be something in that statement, too. It is well to have a newspaper or commentator on your side.

One thing the visitor will notice with surprise when he views the museum exhibit at Dade Battlefield. Among the fine exhibits created for the Florida parks by the Florida State Museum is a diorama showing the scene of the "massacre"—a barren of scrubby growth. Yet when you walk out of the museum, you are in a rather heavily wooded area, shaded by many old live oaks. It seems strange. The scene has altered much since 1835. But the diorama is historically accurate, as of course it should be.

(VII)

DOUTHAT STATE PARK

VIRGINIA

Nine miles east of Clifton Forge, off U.S. 6

Douthit; Douthitt; Douthet; Douthat—how our first families changed the spelling of their names! When I visited Douthat State Park, not far from Clifton Forge, I had, at the very outset, asked how the area got its designation. For reply, I received more than I asked for. The superintendent handed me a sheaf of single-spaced typewritten sheets, constituting an exhaustive genealogy lovingly put together by some member of the family. I assume that *Jonathan* is the man who, in an oblique way, has lent his name to this park. This Douthat had an early grant from the Crown, and the survey upon which ownership was established was known as the Douthat Survey.

The Douthats certainly got around, in Virginia. The genealogy told me that they were everywhere from tidewater to the mountains. Moreover, I had been informed that there was a family relationship between them and General Robert E. Lee; but the truth seemed to be that the Lees had owned some of the land around Clifton Forge, and thus came into the picture.

It was getting late in the year when I visited Douthat State Park. There is a disadvantage in this, if one is writing about parks. Part of our enjoyment of such areas is undoubtedly derived from the presence of others so happily partaking of this form of recreation; especially the shrill delight of children at each new discovery of nature's offerings.

Yet there is as surely an advantage in coming to a woodland park and tramping its trails after the crowds have gone. In November there are days when the air is better than Chian wine; when the waning sun, slanting in upon a sheltered exposure, reveals, unobscured by broadleaved trees, a hundred plants, even some with brave flowers, which have defied the seasonal warnings.

And on those quiet trails, the dry leaves crackling underfoot, you really have a chance to meditate, while you are filling your lungs with pure air. You are reminded of what Joseph Wood Krutch said, when writing of the Grand Canyon of the Colorado: "How long will it be before there is no quietness anywhere, no escape from the rumble and the crush, the clank and the screech which seem to be the inevitable accompaniment of technology? Whatever man does or produces, noise seems to be an unavoidable by-product. Perhaps he can, as he now believes, do anything. But he cannot do it quietly."

Here, today, on the Douthat trails, there is neither clank nor crash. If a jay suddenly sets forth a defiant yell, you laugh joyously at the shock it gives you; and if a squirrel sets up an admonishing chatter, telling you to go home where you belong, you incline to agree with him—but only in principle.

The leaves having mostly fallen from the broadleaved trees, save the oaks and younger beeches that resist the season's order, the evergreens now have their turn. The human colorist had better beware how he mingles his green and brown pigments, but nature does it with lovely results.

Some of the briary shrubs in the forest lose all their leaves; some save part of their leaves; and others maintain a cocky robustness by means of the brilliant varnish with which they are coated. Here and there late toadstools are heaving up the leaf cover; and some blooms appear on plants that should have gone to sleep weeks ago, but are sitting up like children reluctant to depart "while anything might still be going on."

Too few people know the woods at this delicious time of year—except the man with the gun. I have nothing against this man, if he is really a sportsman and is out even more for the zest of hiking the forest and pitting his skill against that of the usually wary wildlife. But better still, it would be for more folks to foot it along the trails to discover at firsthand the thousand small miracles of nature that can never be called out of a printed book, howsoever bravely and neatly phrased.

Did Jonathan Douthat, or whoever obtained this grant of land from the Crown, think such thoughts as these? Probably not. The struggle to "get ahead and even to keep alive in those early days of settlement made it too great a luxury to do or think other than what necessity directed. Now the pendulum has swung full to the other side. Now it is a price too calamitous for urbanized human beings to pay, if there be not these havens of recreative refuge provided by the nation, the states, and other units of government."

Some time in 1936 an article in the Richmond *Times-Dispatch,* written by Thomas R. Henry, noted that the state of Virginia had obtained a $5,000,000 park system for less than $100,000. The statement pointed to the fact that, in the preceding depression years, the federal government, through its alphabetical agencies, had been creating public recreation places where none had been but where there was a need and where the nature of the land was such that this seemed the wisest possible use of it.

Douthat State Park was one of those areas. The Virginia Park System had a formal opening on June 13, 1936, at Marion. This site was chosen because Hungry Mother State Park was individually dedicated on that day. William E. Carson, that staunch defender of the cause of state parks, was chairman of the Conservation Commission at this time. (On the Skyline Drive in Shenandoah National Park the visitor passes a well-deserved marker in memory of Virginia's devoted conservationist.)

The State Commissioner of Parks was evidently in favor of the region of the Douthat Survey from the beginning; but there was considerable rivalry to obtain the federal funds that would result from such a project, with its hundreds of CCC enrollees and its use of local labor. Several other areas were considered. The government requirements were challenging. And one of the determining factors was to be the local attitude. How much true enthusiasm was there in the vicinity? Not merely to have a federal project at work, but rather to have a sound understanding of what recreation places should be: the importance of the preservation of such natural areas for the generations to come. The government could furnish money: but it could not provide understanding.

This question was readily answered at Clifton Forge. Owners of the land of the old Douthat Survey, J. Martin Perry, A. C. Ford, A. H. Grimsley, W. Kent Ford, and Floyd King, donated their holdings, to the extent of 1,920 acres, for a starter. Later enough acreage was added by gift and purchase to bring the total to 4,980. Of these, 2,500 acres were within what was anciently known in western Virginia as "the Big Survey."

Once the federal authorities had approved this selection, it was not long before the Chesapeake and Ohio Railroad began bringing the CCC boys to Longdale. The cabins that were built during that period are still in remarkably good condition. Additional cabins have been constructed since. If you should go into the building now used as the residence of the superintendent and carefully note the woodwork—not merely of the building itself but of much of the furniture—you would realize that handcrafts were far from extinct in western Virginia when this work was accomplished. To its pioneer sturdiness these artisans added a touch of elegance.

Wilsons Creek was dammed to create sixty-six acres of lake. When I saw the pretty little sand beach on the edge of the lake, the nature of the sand struck a chord of memory. I said to the superintendent: "Why, this looks exactly like the beach sand down on the Atlantic shore." He laughed: "That's just what it is. That sand was brought up here from somewhere in the vicinity of Virginia Beach." Rather odd, isn't it? For some of this quartz sand originated here in the Alleghenies, and made the trip down the rivers to the sea. At least a few grains of it are back where they started from.

The ninety-two miles of hiking and horseback trails are so laid out as to supply access to every natural phase of the area, highland, and cove. I like the names of the trails: Blue Suck Trail, Tobacco House Ridge Trail, Middle Hollow, Salt Stump, Buck Lick, Brushy Hollow. "Blue Suck" may need interpretation for the outlander: a suck is a kind of whirlpool.

The forest cover at Douthat, though pleasing and well suited to recreation, is not outstanding. Whether the forests on the high parts of the area were ever of great size, nobody seemed to know. The nature of the soil in this region would suggest that the big virgin trees were in the coves. There was a period of lumbering here, but apparently nobody ever made enough out of it to pay for taking off all the original growth. "Prices were low," someone told me, "and a good deal of the wood was shipped to Europe."

Europe apparently didn't want beech. For along the coves there are still some magnificent specimens, unhurt except for the initials, hearts and arrows, and other memorials of the lovesick and the vain which have been carved upon them. The bark of the beech invites inscription. I saw one tree upon which was carved "Joe and Mae." Not very far away was another beech on which were the names "Joe and Pearl." The similarity of the letters led me to compare the two closely. I am convinced that it was the same Joe. I can't help thinking that Joe would have been wiser to have spaced his announcements farther apart.

I have mentioned before that locally there was genuine enthusiasm to have parts of the old Douthat and Big Surveys perpetuated as public land for recreation. There could hardly be stronger testimony of this than the fact that when the artificial lake was created by the damming of the creek an old family burial ground had to be removed so that the dam could be built on the only logical site. Now, moving the bones of one's forbears is a serious matter, perhaps in Virginia more than anywhere else. But one of the members of the families involved said, after long deliberation: "Mr. Ford asked me and my brother Ed would we consent to this. It's quite a thing to do, and you have to think a lot about it, but Ed and I give our consent, and we got the other folks to agree."

As I was leaving Douthat State Park, a few gunshots in rapid succession reminded me that the hunting season was still on. That, in turn, reminded me of what I had been told of Dusty, the little buck deer who, as a fawn, was adopted as a pet by one of the foresters and so came to the park when it was created. Everybody knew Dusty, who commonly disappeared for a few days and then "reported in" hurriedly when something gave him a fright. Dusty had all the bad habits of a wild animal that becomes too tame—such as eating cigarettes and candy bars and drinking carbonated thirst-quenchers—but he must have been a favorite among the visitors to Douthat. But one day Dusty didn't "report in"—and he has not been seen again.

When I heard the gunshots, I could well imagine what had happened to Dusty. For my companion was telling me, in quite a matter-of-fact way, the results of the first day's deer hunting in the vicinity (not in the park, of course). "Yes, sir," said my informant, "first day they shot six deer and four mules. A feller that got one of the mules, he says, when they asked him, 'Well, I knew it was an animal, because it moved.' "

There should be a good market for motionless mules.

(VIII)

FALL CREEK FALLS STATE PARK

TENNESSEE

On State 30, at Pikeville

IN THE definitive report made in 1934 by members of the National Park Service, after exhaustive studies of the qualifications of Fall Creek Falls State Park as a recreation demonstration area, the following conclusion was reached: "The Fall Creek Falls area would be an asset to any state park system."

Never was a verdict better justified. If for no other reason than that these 16,000 acres of wooded country are situated in the center of a triangle which has at its corners the three great population sites of Nashville, Knoxville, and Chattanooga, the future of this state park as a priceless possession of Tennessee is assured. For these cities, like all other urban places, are growing. Fall Creek Falls has two group camps now, one able to provide for 94 persons and the other for 144. No crystal ball is needed to discern that this is only a beginning.

This area was deeded to the state of Tennessee by the United States Department of the Interior in May 1944. It is an interesting fact that the competent and self-reliant superintendent who took over at the accession is still managing affairs there. It argues well for the man—but even better for the state. In the foreseeable future, human beings will continue to sow best where there is a good chance of being present at the reaping.

Boy Scouts, Girl Scouts, church groups—the young folks that in a few fleeting years are to be the voters and conservationists as well as the parents of other children who need the knowledge and pleasures of some sort of wilderness—what worthy planning went into such provision for them! In the dangerous and increasing estrangement between human being and nature, the children are in some respects better off than their elders, for they have had fewer years to become insulated by gadgetry—yet even they find it difficult in this modern world to adjust to primitive conditions that were once the natural environment of every boy and girl. I present an instance:

The superintendent and I were looking at the buildings of the group camps. I was being cheered by the realization that good craftsmanship still lives in these rural places, for we had been looking at the stone masonry that forms part of the structures. I remarked also upon the fine quality of the material. "Yes," he said, "I think it's a better stone even than the famous Crab Orchard sandstone—and it came right from within this park, too." Then he added, looking up at the light fixtures on the ceiling:

"Here's a funny thing. In the first days of our group camping, before the light wires were run in, we asked whether we should have electric lighting or kerosene lamps. I was surprised when the vote was almost all for kerosene. The children felt that it would be more like going back to primitive old times, in a forest like this. I couldn't help wondering how long they would be trimming lamp wicks and getting the odor of kerosene off their hands before they might change their minds."

"Well, I see they changed their minds."

"Yes, sir. I guess, after all, people can't live surrounded by luxury—I mean what our ancestors would have called luxury—and give it up all of a sudden. Yes, sir, they got tired of trimming sooty wicks. Don't know as I blame 'em."

Before I saw Fall Creek Falls State Park, I had unearthed from the National Park Service files the old RDA reports. How fortunate it was that in order to determine the eligibility of demonstration areas the Interior Department was able to call upon such highly skilled professional men in the scientific and technical fields! Geology, forestry, history, wildlife—all these were discussed dispassionately, though not without liveliness. There were no axes to grind, no political considerations to contend with. For these men there was only one important question: *What is here?* The answers would indicate whether the area was worthy of establishment.

Of human history, white-man history, there was not much of interest in this region. The Cumberland Plateau was settled rather late. James Roberson obtained a grant of small acreage in 1826. It is said that the famous Sam Houston owned a tract in what is now the nearby Bledsoe National Forest. In a period of lumbering, a few families moved in, and after the accessible timber was off, a handful remained to try farming on a marginal basis or one not even so promising as that. Frequent deliberate firing of the woods, in a misguided attempt to provide stock forage, fortunately did not reach certain sections of the "coves," where there are virgin yellow poplar, hemlock, oak, and hickory. There used to be fine chestnuts in these coves, too, before the blight came. One wonders whether, somewhere in our eastern forests, a few remaining specimens of this valuable species may not develop a resistance to the disease that will permit an immune generation to grow. This is certainly to be hoped.

A rather rare shrub, or small tree, is the big-leaved magnolia (Magnolia macrophylla). How widespread it is, I am not sure, but I know it is well named. I came at a season when its dry leaves had been shed and carpeted the ground. "Carpeted" is exactly what they did; the size of these leaves needs to be seen to be believed. Locally it is called a "cucumber tree," from a striking resemblance to the fruit.

Geologically speaking, this region is to a vast extent representative of the ancient time when shallow seas made a series of invasions of the land surface. Both at the bottom of the sea and in the flood plains, deposits of shells, sand, mud, and occasional swamp vegetation then became compacted and cemented into firm rock. Thus were formed the limestones and sandstones, the shales and conglomerates of today, with some seams and pockets of coal that have never been worth mining except on a gopher scale.

In later years the whole plateau was uplifted, with only a few minor invasions of the sea thereafter. For the visitor, the main point is that into this folded and faulted sedimentary rock "the drainage pattern has become deeply intrenched." Those are the words of the geologist. As *we* say it, it is bewildering to come suddenly to the edge of a gorge (as at Millikan's Overlook, for instance) that has certainly few rivals in wildness and ruggedness east of the Mississippi.

Decidedly, the gorge (with its tributary canyons) is the principal feature of this state park. The falls of Fall Creek, at the season when the water is highest, are unquestionably magnificent. The volume is not great, but the sheer drop is no less than 256 feet, and because of the small volume of water, compared, for instance, with the falls of the Cumberland in Kentucky, the effect is all the more spectacular—ribbonlike, lacy. It is a grave error, when announcing the tourist attractions here, to use such words as "a hundred feet higher than Niagara." True, it is a hundred feet higher—but the two are not to be compared, and a picture is created in the mind of the prospective visitor which cannot be realized. It is also an error not to make it perfectly clear that the wonderful experience (and the sight of these falls *is* magnificent) can be had only when the parent stream has enough water to tumble over the gorge.

The National Park Service investigators foresaw, in RDA days, that, unless this fact were stressed, there would always be disappointed visitors, some of them extremely vocal. At least partly for that reason, the suggestion was then made that the area should be named "Caney Creek Gorge" or something similar, so that the recurrence of the word "fall" would not magnify the expectations of the visitors. Whether there was any merit in this suggestion is not for me to say; but I certainly feel that this state park would still be scenically superior, and a superlative geological wonder, even if no water were there at all.

Yes; the falls, when at their height, are certainly something the visitor will never forget: but the whole picture of the deeply incised canyons is really the most remarkable attraction of the park. You wonder indeed how the comparatively little water that arises in this limited part of the watershed between the Cumberland and Tennessee Rivers could accomplish so tremendous a scouring task. The streams are not large—they are all known as "creeks." Yet Fall Creek, as we have noted, leaps over a caprock to plunge into a basin 256 feet below; Caney Creek has two waterfalls, one of 85 and the lower of 40 feet; Rockhouse Creek falls 125 feet, and Piney Creek 85 feet. All these, being small feeder streams, flow for a shorter time than Fall Creek.

This state park is large enough (and remote enough) to offer a well-balanced wildlife experience for the enjoyment of the visitor. In general, the plant and animal life is similar to that of the Great Smokies and the Blue Ridge at comparable elevations. That means, for instance, deer, foxes, an occasional bear, rabbits, squirrels, turkeys.

Where the wild turkey has been restored to its native haunts, I have been told by many state park men, it proves to be almost a number-one attraction for the children who visit. Even the deer may take second place. That is logical. Deer are often seen by these young folks in zoolike conditions, fenced in, yes, but always evidently wild creatures. But the turkey in captivity, wild or not, seems to be just another domestic bird awaiting Thanksgiving time. See them in the forest of a state park, and what a difference! "The wild turkey symbolizes the primeval wilderness as the white settlers first found it," wrote John Stuart Martin.

This noble fowl, so essentially American, was found in southern swamps and northern forests. The Pilgrims, coming to establish Plymouth colony in 1620, rejoiced in their plentiful numbers. Turkeys were pitilessly hunted; yet that was not the major reason that they were almost extinct by 1920. They simply declined with the gradual disappearance of the kind of forest growth that alone could sustain them.

As the superintendent of Fall Creek Falls and I were driving along one of the roads in the park, a hen turkey crossed in front of us with that "going somewhere" straight-line flight so characteristic of this wild bird. We stopped and watched her alight in the midst of a band of no less than twenty. Even wild, the turkey seems to be unafraid of people so long as they remain in an automobile. This fine flock looked at us curiously and then proceeded to cruise for mast in their methodical way. Many a state park, in a region where conditions permit, has successfully been stocked with wild turkeys. The spadework of the Pennsylvania wildlife people in the delicate job of breeding this bird to a truly wild form has resulted in similar successes in other states.

The Tennessee state park folder says of this area that "organized hunts for deer, turkey, grouse, squirrel, quail, rabbit, raccoon and opossum are conducted annually by the State Game and Fish Commission." Hunting wild animals is one thing, and preserving them as part of a precious wild scene to be enjoyed in its wholeness is another. Surplus wildlife may exist, but can the concepts of hunting and preservation exist together? What are state parks for, primarily?

Since we are on the theme of nature, here is something I saw at Fall Creek Falls that set me to wondering why wild creatures sometimes do certain things that have no apparent purpose. In the early days of the park a wooden water tank was installed near a campground. It was a very good tank, too—didn't leak a drop. That is, it didn't until a few years ago, when it became an object of interest to bluejays. In a few days of feverish activity, they riddled it, starting above the water level. The wood of the tank had been treated against decay; it couldn't have had an attractive flavor. There could hardly have been any insect life in the wood; it was regularly painted. We know that California jays sometimes riddle a telephone pole with holes; but they use them to tuck acorns in, for storage purposes. The Fall Creek jays put nothing in, took nothing out. The superintendent said to me: "I wish some of your nature friends would tell me why the birds picked on this poor tank of mine." Can any reader guess the reason?

(IX)

FRANKLIN D. ROOSEVELT STATE PARK

GEORGIA

Near Pine Mountain, on U.S. 27 and off Georgia 85

ABRUPTLY RISING to a height of 1,500 feet from the gently rolling lands of middle Georgia, Pine Mountain is both an interesting geological curiosity and a cool oasis in summer for the surrounding population. Perhaps this elevation is the southernmost remnant of the Appalachian chain, but it is entirely unlike knobby outliers like Lookout and Kennesaw above Atlanta. This rocky fold stretches for many miles in a general easterly and westerly direction, and at the eastern end is deeply slashed by the six-mile gorge of the Flint River, whose waters have formed the famous cove, four hundred feet below the topping cliffs above. This is scenic country which Georgians have for many years traveled far to enjoy.

It is historic country, too. This part of Georgia was originally included in the territory ceded to the United States by the famous Indian Springs treaty of 1825. In nearby Columbus there is a monument near the spot where General James Oglethorpe, leader of Georgia Colony, had almost a hundred years before secured peace with the chieftains of the Creeks. Oglethorpe was looking westward to determine what his charter had included in the delightfully vague wording: "from the Atlantic Ocean to the South Seas."

On the north side of Pine Mountain, the town of Hood was once a hopeful mushroom. Its gold mine, so far as is known, never made anyone rich, and may have been one of those feverish prospects that resulted from the finding of actual pay-dirt at Dahlonega, where originated the often-quoted saying: "There's gold in them thar hills."

Kings Gap, on an old Indian trail, lay at the base of the mountain on the southern side and was a post office on the stagecoach mail route between Columbus and Newman. An envelope with the cancellation "Kings Gap" upon it would be an important find for a collector today.

Above Kings Gap was a spur of the long mountain known as Dowdell's Knob. From this spot the view is really magnificent. The scene stretches out on three sides, across the rolling farmlands cut into geometrical pattern, interspersed with patches of woodland, and finally ending in a soothing haze where vision ceases and pleasant imagination begins. Beyond that horizon is the deep South, the Gulf of Mexico, indeed, the "South Seas" of Oglethorpe's fanciful charter.

No, this view is not merely magnificent; it heals the frayed soul of one who has emerged from the conflict of the market place. The spirit finds renewal here. And this is not mere rhetoric. Ask anyone who has looked upon the loveliness unrolled below Dowdell's Knob. You cannot now ask the Indians, who for centuries regarded it as almost a sacred place, even though for them it was also a very practical signalling tower. You cannot ask Franklin D. Roosevelt, either, though we know that of all places on the friendly mountain this was his favorite. We shall see later in this chapter how the Roosevelt personality overflowed upon this Pine Mountain and its surrounding plains and made the whole county almost a symbol of his will to overcome physical misfortune, and the peace and neighborliness he discovered during his valiant struggle.

Roosevelt experienced a spiritual satisfaction in the crags of Dowdell's Knob which had been demonstrated in a strange manner by one of the Dowdell brothers. These two migrants from Virginia, in 1828, were the first permanent settlers in the region. They were Lewis and James, but I have not been able to discover which of the two it was who from his nearby plantation led his slaves up the mountain to these rocks every clement Sunday, gathered them where they could face the expanse of field and wood below, and preached them a sermon under the bright sky. The content of the sermons has not been recorded. It may be that a favorite was the parable of the good steward. At any rate, he is said to have been a just and kindly owner, at a time when few questioned the morality of human bondage.

Here Roosevelt first brought a picnic lunch to his favorite spot of quiet contemplation; then afterwards he had built, upon a projecting point, a cook-out fireplace for the roasting of wieners. The stone fireplace is still there, as in his picnicking day, but it is no longer used, being maintained as an unpretentious memorial.

The visitor to the 5,063-acre Franklin D. Roosevelt State Park, if he comes in from the Hamilton and Chipley side, finds a sign at the entrance: "Pine Mountain State Park." That was the name of the reserve until recently. Indeed, he will no longer find any such town as Chipley, for this place (population in 1950 was 817) decided that the profits of tourism should not be ignored, and therefore that the place had better be called Pine Mountain.

The change was not to the taste of one resident with whom I discussed it. "You live in Washington?" he challenged me. I admitted that I sometimes had residence there. "Well, how'd you like to have the name of Washington changed to Cherry Blossom? Bring more visitors in, I reckon." Sentiment for old ways, old names, dies hard in some people.

The first several miles of the road that ascends into the park climbs along a knife edge, going eastward, with such a sharp slope on both sides that, before the leaves come fully on the trees, the plains below can be seen clearly through the lean forest growth. The dogwood and the redbud thrive mightily in just this part-shade, and their bloom precedes the foliage of the blackjack and other oaks that with loblolly and longleaf pine makes up the cover of this tenuous soil. But a little after the ivory bracts of the dogwood have fallen, there comes a profusion of color upon the native shrubs, the laurel, rhododendron, and especially the flame azalea. ("We used to call it *honeysuckle* when I was a boy," an old man told me when I stopped to talk with him. The local names for flowers are oddly at variance.) The small green fruit of the maypop, a passion flower, is often used by the country women hereabout for making jelly.

Poor, sadly abused countryside this was, when it was chosen as a recreation demonstration area* during the depression. Not more than

* During a period of several years beginning in 1934, as part of the Federal Land Program, the National Park Service acquired and developed forty-six recreation demonstration projects in twenty-four states, with a total of approximately 400,000 acres, for the purpose of demonstrating how marginal and submarginal lands could be retired from agriculture and better used for park and conservation purposes. A number of these areas were added to existing areas administered by this Service or established as new units of the National Park System. Most of the areas, embracing a total of about 200,000 acres, were conveyed to the states for administration as units of the state park systems with the condition that they be used exclusively for park and conservation purposes.

300 acres of what was set aside as parkland was adapted to farming; and years of cutting and burning, cutting and burning had left little in the shrunken soil for the growth of even a natural cover.

It was in 1934 that a Civilian Conservation Corps camp was established on the top of Pine Mountain. But the supply of water there was scant, however copious it was at the base of the ridge, and the camp was moved down to the little town of Warm Springs. The Roosevelt Inn (formerly "The Tavern"), the stone cottages for overnight guests, and the fine overlook patio were built during this make-work period, as were also the cabins on Lake Delano and the camping facilities for organized groups, where 150 young folks can be accommodated, with staff quarters, infirmary, and mess halls. The scenic highway that follows the mountain crest from U.S. 27 into Warm Springs, along an ancient Indian trail, was directly the result of Franklin Roosevelt's enthusiasm for a region with which his name was to become so indelibly associated.

In the field of physical recreation this Georgia state park has an unusual kind of nearby competition, if that is the word for it. It might, on the other hand, be regarded as supplemental recreation. Just below the town of Pine Mountain, and partly draped upon a shoulder of that imposing ridge, are the Ida Cason Callaway Gardens, established by the philanthropist Cason J. Callaway in memory of his mother "as a sanctuary for native plants and wild flowers of the Appalachians."

The Gardens have nominal admission fees, but the development is nonprofit and, in the words of the donor: "I'm trying to fix it so that anybody who wants to see something beautiful can find it here." A superlative domain of 2,500 acres, this garden includes a lake with a five-mile shoreline and offers fishing and golf, wildflower trails, swimming, water skiing, a sightseeing trolley line, and even a "Cleopatra's barge" trip for those whose hiking ability no longer matches their desire for adventure in a bright world of natural beauty.

But if "competition" should happen to be the right word for the gardens, it does not apply in respect to Warm Springs, the little town at the base of the mountain which has become world-known as the seat of the Warm Springs Foundation for the treatment of infantile paralysis. It is hardly believable that a visitor could come to Franklin D. Roosevelt State Park without making the pilgrimage to the "Little White House" and the amazing community, dedicated to human service, which has resulted from the visit in the autumn of 1924 of a man who was stricken with poliomyelitis in the prime of his life.

What has been done, and what is being done, at Warm Springs in the treatment of infantile paralysis is an epic story that could naturally receive only a passing reference in a chapter like this. In a world of conflict and insecurity, the mere knowledge that such a center of highly skilled benevolence can exist and flower is a solid rock to stand upon. But, as we have seen, there is hardly a corner in the whole region that is not in some way a reminder of the man who arrived, with brave hopefulness, at the old Meriwether Inn in "Bullochville" to try the warm waters that the Creek Indians, generations before, had believed to have healing powers.

The springs had no magical powers then or now; perhaps the Indian tribes, holding them as sanctuarial ground, knew their quality for what it was—a path toward alleviation, and in a place of peacefulness, where nature could restore the spirit. The geologists tell us that the rain which falls upon Pine Mountain descends nearly 4,000 feet to a vast pocket of rock, where it is somehow warmed and returned to the surface at the base of the mountain.

It was not alone the good that he found in bathing and swimming in these waters that brought the Hyde Park visitor back again and again. He learned to love the region, and the region responded to that affection. Late in 1931, Roosevelt started building a home at Warm Springs which was completed the following spring. It was modest. The total cost, if you can believe it, was $8738.14; and this included landscaping.

In May 1932 Roosevelt held a big housewarming for his friends and neighbors in his new home. An old memorandum gave the cost of this party as $31.07, and the items were carefully set down, including a crate of lemons at five dollars.

These details may seem unimportant. They are not so. From first to last, the modest scale of living enjoyed by the man and the President at Warm Springs was the secret of his delight there, as well as the reason for the charming intimacy with his neighbors. He was one of them. Once Roosevelt said to a friend: "I am *somebody* down here." Readily we can guess what he meant. To be president of a great nation was indeed imposing, but it could not equal the affection that shone in the eyes and rested in the hand grasp of those who loved him as a friend and good neighbor. That was being "somebody," and he deeply sensed it.

The proud owner of the Little White House, built for less than

$9,000, was a man not unaccustomed to luxury and the refinements of living. He had come from what used to be called "the upper class." But when he had his house built at Warm Springs, it was just such a home, with a lived-in appearance, as a native of moderate means would have had. There was no electric refrigerator—just a plain icebox; and the old-fashioned ice cream freezer was the kind you fill with ice and rocksalt and laboriously grind with a handle.

Roosevelt was unquestionably one of the shrewdest and most successful men of politics in modern times. Yet the thoughtful visitor to this affecting memorial will have the feeling that here, at Warm Springs, Roosevelt deliberately separated himself, so far as he could, from the political scene. The residents of the area were getting up a local barbecue to observe the homecoming of Governor Roosevelt just after his election in New York State. "I want to meet the people of the county," he told a Warm Springs man over the telephone. "I want to shake hands and know them. I do not want any politics mentioned. I want the sheriff on the platform with two guns, and the first one that mentions politics—bang!" He had established a refuge to which he could flee from his own talent.

A marker on the Pine Mountain drive notes that in the early days of Roosevelt's visits to Meriwether County he observed that no great effort was being made to reforest the cut-over and burned-over areas which held no promise for farming operations. On his own farm and wooded land on Pine Mountain, as a demonstration of what might be done in erosion control and the redemption of starved acres, he set out 5,000 longleaf yellow pines in 1929 and 1930. The plantation was doing very well until the advent of a tornado in 1954, which destroyed about half the stand. Those which escaped looked very thrifty when I saw them.

Typical, too, of Roosevelt's desire to help the neighboring people by showing them the proper use of land was his purchase and operation of 1,750 acres of Pine Mountain. A hundred and fifty acres were under cultivation and six hundred more were fenced for cattle. Otis Moore, we learn from Joyce Ruth Stevens's charming little book *Hi-Ya Neighbor*, was the farm manager. One day he suggested to the owner that they plant a little cotton to help pay the operating expenses. Roosevelt shook his head in decided negative. "Otis," he said, "we have something more to demonstrate than just running a ranch here. By our example, others will see that cotton is not a necessary crop in the South. . . . No, we'll grow no cotton."

Here, then, at Franklin D. Roosevelt State Park, is an unusual situation. At one side is a delightful nonprofit recreation development replete with facilities that the state park could hardly hope to match. On the other side is Warm Springs and the Roosevelt Farm, the Little White House, and the great center of therapy conducted by the Foundation.

It seems not impossible that some day these units, all possessing high quality of their kind, may be pooled to create one of the most significant state reserves in the country, call it by the name of state park or by any other. In such a case, what began as Pine Mountain State Park, that is to say, the rugged wooded terrain itself, might revert to what it once was, a place of trail and wildlife where nature took its way with little intrusion by man.

(X)

GULF STATE PARK

ALABAMA

On Highway 182, east of Gulf Shores

IF WEST FLORIDA had fingered a little farther to the west, and if Louisiana had pushed its boundary a little farther eastward, the two states of Mississippi and Alabama would have been securely landlocked. As it is, from the Pearl River to the Perdido, along the Gulf Coast, is a distance that the motorist, without pressing, can travel in a morning. And what a strip of sparkling coastline it is! From Pass Christian to Pascagoula, in Mississippi, many years ago, people of ample means built fine houses upon this desirable strip. Jefferson Davis had a mansion near present-day Biloxi. Woodrow Wilson, when President, had a "winter White House" here, I recall.

Alabama's partnership in the Gulf Coast is less well known. At Moss Point the main highway swings northerly toward Mobile and then continues inland to Pensacola, Florida. Many tourists do indeed drop down to the beautiful Bellingrath Gardens, but they are still not near the Gulf. A few may go to Dauphin Island, on the west side of Mobile Bay—that thirsty tongue which laps up the yellow waters of the Tombigbee, the Black Warrior, the Alabama, and other streams which once were the roadways into upper Alabama, and are still navigable for craft of light draught. Of the Baldwin County side, little has been known until recent years.

Yet, for me, the visit to Gulf State Park and the southern end of Baldwin County was in the nature of a homecoming. For I could remember the black night, in a torrential rainstorm, when the little ferry brought me across from Mobile to Fairhope and unloaded me on a shaky pier, leaving me to transfer my drenched luggage into a wheezing motor train that ran from the dock up to the little town.

This was Fairhope—the idealistic venture of the soap manufacturer Joseph Fels, who was a devoted follower of the single-tax theories of Henry George, and sought to establish to the world that such a community could prosper. In a real sense, Fairhope was "out of this world." It was hard to get to; and once there, nobody could make a living out of the soil, which would produce long-leaf yellow pine and sedge grass abundantly, and little else. That was before agricultural chemistry found a way to release the ample plant food which was always there, awaiting magic. Now, in driving down the county toward the salt sea, one can see the change. Where there were only piny-woods cattle and pigs wresting a meager subsistence there are now fertile fields, fat cattle, dairies, orchards of pecans. There may have been a few cottages at Gulf Shores. It was not an easy place to reach over dirt roads, and I have forgotten how much of the Gulf coast we Fairhopers ever saw.

I do applaud the unusual modesty of the little advertising folder before me, entitled "Go Gulf on Alabama's Coast." It says: "We make no claim to having a tropical climate during the fall, winter and early spring, but we *do* have a temperate climate." That, in park literature, is an understatement. It is better than that. You will not be uncomfortable at any time, in the average winter, at this point on the Gulf of Mexico. This state park has its "season," of course, which snaps shut like a woodchuck trap on Labor Day—mainly because children must go back to school, though the finest days are just arriving, here as in so many other places. But Gulf State Park is actually open for enjoyment the year around, and in the first days of March, when I occupied a cottage there, there were plenty of people doing the same, including several wanderers from out of state.

On the Gulf front, to be sure, the wind was rather sharp, and it was good to seek the shelter of a great dune. But on the lakeside part of the park, and especially along the charming winding road that leads from the entrance down to Cotton Bayou and then around to the shore, the chokecherries were in full greenish-white bloom and the magnolia buds were swollen to the bursting point. Wherever there was grass, it was green and lush. The dewberries and blackberries gave promise of a fine crop to raid later for the breakfast table. Here you were unaware that the March wind was gnawing at the shoreline dunes, trying to build and to destroy at the same time. A very moderate amount of artificial heat is needed indoors. Yes; a temperate climate, this. In Mobile the azaleas were spendthrifts of gorgeous color.

In the evening, just after sunset, the twilight on the lake was opalescent. It seemed impossible, looking out from the trees over this expanse of fresh water, that just beyond the sandspit on the other side a salt tide was ebbing. For this soothing park has, by nature and by adroit development, two entirely different aspects which can be enjoyed one above the other, or, if one likes, by turns. On the beach side in the summer season, when upstate folks come down to feel the Gulf breezes, I suppose there it is the usual bustle, the usual crowd. However, there is also the northerly side of the larger of three lakes, for those who wish some quiet relaxation.

These lakes were once lagoons. The Alabama Conservation Department, in order to accommodate fresh-water fishermen, performed an ingenious renovation task a few years ago. Unique, so far as I know, was the scope of the project: salt-water bodies were turned into fresh-water ones, the fish were killed, and the lakes restocked. I don't know why anybody should be so fickle, but if you so wish, you may, within a hundred yards or so, fish alternately in Gulf water and in fresh water. Tidal gates were constructed to allow for the outflow of fresh water after heavy rains and to exclude the salt tidal advance.

On the land side of the lakes there is an interval of wet land, with a vast variety of vegetation. The zones of animal life here are measured, as in the great Everglades, on a scale of inches, rather than thousands of feet as in the mountainous West. This kind of place is the joy of the ecologist, even if he must cut his way into it with a machete. No lack of plant food here for the great variety of broad-leaved evergreens and the pines and junipers, the palmettos and strangling vines. The deer that were introduced here some years ago (of course they were native, but had been wiped out by gunners) are on the increase. I saw none, but their "runs" across the roads indicate that they are becoming plentiful. The raccoons, those garbage-can bandits with black masks, were certainly in evidence. I don't know whether it is these fellows, or skunks, which do the rough plowing on the roadsides in a search for grubs. They do not put back their divots; thus behaving like unsocial golfers.

Big enough—nearly five thousand acres—to present an adequate picture both of shore and of backland, Gulf State Park has unusually fine public accommodations. The bathhouse cares for 2,000 people, and on the lake side there are twenty-one comfortable cottages, some of them duplex. Of picnic space there is plenty, and the many barbecue pits remind us that we are in a section of the country where "barbecue" means just what it says—succulent meat that has the aroma of woodsmoke. Whoever has not tasted the true product of the barbecue expert has missed the joy that Charles Lamb described as being the lot of the Chinaman who accidentally stumbled upon roast pig.

Gulf State Park is twenty-seven miles long, according to the printed literature. But you must not think that as much of the Gulf Coast as that is included. Would that the state of Alabama owned so much of the precious silver strand and lovely dunes! The figure of 27 miles is explained by the fact that the Dixie Graves Highway, mainly an inland road but with occasional good vistas of the blue Gulf, connects the true park area with Fort Morgan (likewise a state park) on the very tip of the long spit which ends at the entrance to Mobile Bay. To be sure, this is a very fine road to travel. But the highway strip should be at least twice as wide as it is, for the intrusions are already in view.

Every visitor to Gulf State Park will go to Fort Morgan. This is historic ground of more than ordinary significance in the history of our land. Because the Civil War is nearest to us in point of time, we think of this fort chiefly as being, with Fort Gaines on Dauphin Island across the channel, a stalwart guardian of the "soft underbelly" of the besieged Confederacy—the entrance to Mobile harbor and to the strategic rivers above. It was that, indeed. Not until August of 1864 did Admiral Farragut succeed in cracking its defense with an assault by land and sea. But hundreds of years before the Civil War the importance of this spot had been seen by adventurers from Europe. In 1559 the Spaniards established the first permanent colony in the region and are said to have built a small fort of sand and logs, locally known as Fort Serof.

In 1699 the French under Bienville took over. Mobile Point became the harbor for the commerce of the region, since Mobile Bay was too shallow then to permit the larger vessels to navigate upriver. Then came the period of chessboard swapping in the chancelleries of Europe—France cedes to England, England gives back to Spain, and Spain, under pressure, retires in favor of the new United States. But this has been a strategic point, no matter what flag was flying.

On the site of the British Fort Bowyer the infant republic built Fort Morgan in 1840. It was a beautiful piece of craftsmanship, following a design patterned after the Michelangelo five-point-star of the Italian engineers. If the brickwork was really the product of slave labor, it was remarkable for that time or any time. Fort Pulaski, near Savannah, shows the same artisan delight; it was probably a strong conviction on the part of the designers of the long chain of defenses on our coastline that a fort should not be merely a thing of utility, but should have grace as well. This fort was named for Daniel Morgan, the Revolutionary leader who made the British so uncomfortable, and Daniel could not have wished for a finer memorial. Time, and the slap-happy constructions incident to reactivation in days of stress, have tarnished the original beauty of this structure, but have not altogether obliterated it. Indeed, when we recall the terrific beating the fort took from Farragut, we realize how well preserved it is.

Mobile Point lays claim to a much older occupation than that of the Spanish. If you love a dash of persuasive mystery in your historical cuisine, this will be your dish. More than three hundred years before Columbus sailed for the Indies, there was a Prince of Wales, Madoc. Robert Southey, the English poet, wrote a long poem about this prince and his famous voyage "toward the setting sun." Madoc sailed on and on, through storm and hazard, till:

> I looked
> And saw a bird slow sailing overhead;
> His long white pinions by the sunbeam edged
> As though with burnished silver. . . . Never yet
> Heard I so sweet a music as his cry. . . .
> We left the ship
> And cleft with rapid oars the shallow wave,
> And stood triumphant on another world.

And what was this other world? Some people, including Hatchett Chandler, believe that Prince Madoc's rapid oars cleft the shallow waters of Mobile Bay—nay, further, that he came ashore right where Fort Morgan stands. The year was 1170.

I mention Hatchett Chandler, because when I knocked at the door of the building marked "Office" at Fort Morgan, Chandler emerged—a most agreeable, communicative, and intelligent gentleman, with a sly sense of humor lurking in the corner of his eye. He is a sort of guardian-spirit of Fort Morgan. He has written a considerable series of "Little Gems from Fort Morgan," of which the story of Prince Madoc is Number 23.

I asked Chandler whether he believed that Prince Madoc landed here. His eyes twinkled as he replied: "You'll see, after you read my pamphlet." But I do not see. Chandler is a deep man, with, as I have said, a somewhat roguish eye. He is inclined to challenge me, and other skeptics, to prove that Prince Madoc did *not* land here at Mobile Point, in 1170. He evokes analogy. In 1620, the astronomer Kepler announced his famous "harmonic law." Good authority said that Kepler was all wrong. In 1895 Professor Barnard at the Lick Observatory "picked up Ceres and measured her diameter—only 485 miles—as Kepler had predicted 275 years before." This proves that scoffers can be wrong, and that Madoc *could* have stepped ashore where Fort Morgan stands.

I liked Chandler, and I like the Madoc story. I am going to believe it, because I am going to assume that the twinkle in the local historian's eye was caused by the bright sunlight. And, anyway, Virginia Cavalier Chapter of the Daughters of the Revolution has a fine tablet near the fort entrance "in memory of Prince Madoc, a Welsh explorer who landed on the shores of Mobile Bay . . . and who left behind, with the Indians, the Welsh language."

Do not miss Fort Morgan, and do not miss Hatchett Chandler. Mr. Chandler will show, also, that Isabella de Soto spent several months here, awaiting the return of her Hernando. Then go back to your quiet cottage at Gulf State Park and consider the powers of analogy.

(XI)

HIGHLANDS HAMMOCK STATE PARK

FLORIDA

Six miles west of Sebring, off U.S. 98

It may be, as the dictionary suggests, that what is known on the land surface of Florida as a "hammock" is just another spelling of the better-known word "hummock." But the similarity may be accidental; and perhaps those are right who think that the Florida hammock was named for a Seminole Indian word of like pronunciation. At any rate, these strange little "islands" of rich soil, which left to their own ways become nearly tropical jungles, constitute one of the most fascinating of all our American wildernesses. Cleared of their dense growths, these were the garden spots of the Seminoles. When, during the long war with the white men, the Indians were driven from such lush cornlands, they faced lean times.

The observant Florida tourist knows, even if he has not thought of it in scientific terms, that the zones of differing vegetable and animal life here involve an elevation of feet, sometimes even inches. As you ascend from the bottom of the Grand Canyon to the North Rim, you pass through as many zones of life as though you had traveled northward more than a thousand miles. But such changes are no less remarkable in Florida. To the student these changes are most impressive. Driving in a region which at first glance seems absolutely level, you will note the constant shift in the type of scenery you pass through. Of course, the great community of living things which you do not see changes also.

A short distance west of Sebring the state of Florida is preserving, as a truly great example of its material inheritance, one of these fascinating hammocks, together with a cypress swamp. Once known as Hooker Hammock, now as Highlands Hammock, this delightful and meaningful combination of jungles and cypress swamp has been judged by good authorities as being of national park caliber.

Florida has been particularly fortunate in its acquisition of areas suitable for a state park system. Most of them were donated by individuals of humanity and imagination who wanted the future generations to delight in them. Some areas were bought at nominal prices. Only one was paid for at nearly full market value.

Highlands Hammock was mainly the gift of the Roeblings—John A. and Margaret Shippen Roebling of New Jersey. The Roeblings were developing a large estate near Lake Placid, Florida. As they flew over Hooker Hammock in a plane, it seemed to them a perfect wildlife refuge, if nothing more than that. The comment of Mrs. Roebling to her sister should be remembered: "People have taken most of the state of Florida for their playground. I want to save a bit of it for the birds." That is just what the generosity of the Roeblings made possible.

The hammock, with its adjoining cypress swamp, proved to be much more than a wildlife refuge. As a promotional group the Highlands Hammock Association was formed, there being many county citizens who wanted to help. During the years 1930 to 1936 the Roeblings donated about $400,000 for lands and major protective developments, sending their civil engineer Alexander Blair to take charge of the work. The initial acquisition consisted of 2,500 acres; since then the boundaries have been extended until now there are 3,800 acres. So many state parks are continuously adding acreage that the figures given here must be accepted as the latest available when these chapters were being written. More important, of course, is the fact that a park intended to protect and perpetuate a true picture of the organic community life natural to the region must be of sufficient size.

In 1934 the National Park Service assigned a Civilian Conservation Corps camp to develop a botanical garden and arboretum on lands east of the hammock area. With foot-trail and shelter construction, picnic grounds and similar facilities for public use, this development led to the acceptance of the area by Florida as a state park.

To Highlands Hammock each year come thousands of visitors—

including many from other parts of the state—who have never before seen a hammock jungle nor come to grips with a cypress swamp. It is an adventure into a strange world. Not for nothing do the students of ecology find especially informing their studies in swamps and bogs. Don't be alarmed at this word "ecology." It is simply scientific shorthand, to describe the studies of living forms in their community, or *home* environment. Perhaps in the swamp these relationships may be most clearly observed.

To the urban eye, a cypress swamp looks forbidding. "It gives me a creepy feeling," a northern visitor was heard to say. Certainly, if you look down into the black water from the admirable catwalk that gives you a wonderful circuit of this swamp, it looks abysmal, fathomless. The water may, at that very spot, be only a few inches deep, but it is nearly opaque, so charged is it with tannin and organic matter. However, if you dipped up a glassful and held it to the light, it would look like fairly strong tea. And you cannot be sure, unless your eyes are accustomed to such a scene, whether the object in the water not far from you is a log or an alligator. Logs and alligators give excellent impersonations of each other.

The water of Little Charley Bowlegs Creek, which takes its way through the swamp, seems hardly to move. Sometimes the silence, if you are alone in this wilderness, makes a dull noise in your eardrums. And then suddenly a woodpecker hammers a tree. . . .

Charley Bowlegs Creek is a name with a fine homely smack, isn't it? It is one of those chummy appellations like that of the mountain in Great Smoky Mountains National Park called "Charley's Bunion." Sensitive souls think these names vulgar, and would wish to call the places something banal, but fortunately they don't have their way. A long-ago president of Amherst College wanted to change the name of a small peak locally known as Bull Hill, to Mount Taurus. All he got from his neighbors on that proposal was a sour look.

Charley Bowlegs seems to have been an Englishman with a mildly piratical viewpoint, who had joined the Indians and gone native. Charley never could have imagined, when a creek was named for him, that this creek would give in later years so much pleasure to so many. The catwalk, taking off from near the wild orange grove on the hammock, traverses several hundred feet of the swamp, crosses Little Charley Bowlegs, and returns to another point on the hammock. At intervals on the wooden trail there are turnouts for those who wish to live a while with the scene, without impeding traffic. It is worth taking plenty of time.

The present catwalk, a device for enjoying a remarkable experience—of invading a swamp with dry feet—began, it seems, as merely a bridge built by Alexander Blair and one of his men, Tom Paige, so that they could get to the other side of the swamp without making a long trip around. Visitors who came to see the early development found the bridge alluring; thus naturally it became a part of the interpretation program when the park was finally established.

Nowhere can be found a better illustration of how a keen resident naturalist, deeply in love with the surroundings, is able to add to the "take home" pleasure and stimulation of the visitor. Here in Highlands Hammock State Park, as indeed in any such national or state preserve, the visitor is free to take his joy in any admissible way. If you wish merely to lounge or picnic, you can do that. But to experience the intimate contact with the wild requires the help of the trained eye and ear of the naturalist; and with a fast-growing interest in nature study, among both children and adults, such service is eagerly sought.

Here, at a small charge, twice a day except on Mondays, the visitor can make a trip in a sightseeing trailer drawn by a jeep, accompanied by the naturalist. For an hour or more, he can follow a scenic drive through the hammock proper, through pines, scrub, and the south-boundary marshland, where there is almost certain to be an opportunity to see alligators, turtles, herons, egrets, bittern, ibis, anhingas, and the many other native dwellers. Deer, too, of course. But, if you wish to have the wonderful sight of ten thousand wading birds returning to their rookery near the Country Road Bridge to roost for the night, you must get there about sunset and wait a while. It is something never to be forgotten.

The average person, in the wilderness, actually sees very little. The trained eye sees much. And, with the help of the naturalist, the visitor begins to sharpen his own powers of observation. One day, for example, the guide stopped at a point where the cabbage palms were twisted and leaning at drunken angles, in their effort to reach the sunlight. The naturalist asked: "Do you notice anything interesting here?" Promptly a man in the group replied: "Yes, I see them—two owls in that tree." Sure enough, there were two owls above them. That wasn't at all the lesson the guide had intended. But merely being along with a trained observer had brightened one pair of eyes.

That strange and brilliant red lichen, growing in the dark jungle; the "knees" of the cypress, the purpose of which in tree economy has never yet been acceptably explained; the glossiness of the feathers of the American egret, which, once you have noticed, enables you to identify that bird with certainty; the gossamer golden webs of a jungle spider that in a favorable season light the spaces with shining torches—are these little things? In themselves, perhaps yes; but they add to our understanding and appreciation. They enrich a holiday.

It may be that the alligators attract an undue amount of attention. These leftovers from a geologic period when the saurians of enormous size ruled part of what is now the United States have a sure fascination for those who have never seen them in their natural home. There is a local belief that the eyes of a male alligator shine red at night, whereas those of a female shine green. If that is so, asks our naturalist-guide dryly, why is that baby alligator over there riding on Red-eyes's back? The truth is probably that at night, when you shine a flashlight on the reptile, the eyes look different depending on the angle of reflection.

Our naturalist tells us of the strange things that may happen when she is taking a night ride with visitors. "An armadillo running ahead of us decided to hide himself in a hastily made hole right in the rut where our jeep wheels had to go. No chance of taking the sightseeing trailer around him; the road is too narrow. Now, you know an armadillo when he goes down in a hole to hide takes a deep breath and puffs himself up so that you can't pull him out of the hole. But, just a short time before, I had read that if you grabbed him by the tail and with your other hand tickled his belly, he would let out his breath and you could pull him out. I tried it, and it worked! Just one of the novelties of the day's round."

Over the picnic area, in the spring months, the swallow-tailed kites may be flying low. You can see, by day, wading birds gobbling up their prey in the lowlands almost anywhere you look. Along the ditches, as you pass, turtles give you a quick glance and splash into the water. The raccoons, little prowlers in a black mask, rattle the garbage cans at night, and sometimes when you take off the cover, you find an opossum asleep inside. There are otters—you may not see them, but they are here. The armadillo is shy, too; but campers hear him grunting at night like a pig.

No; the treebeard, or Spanish moss, is *not* a parasite. One of the good things about being with a naturalist is that you can forget a lot of folklore that just isn't so. The mistletoe is a parasite, but this moss that festoons everything is neither a moss nor a parasite. It gets its living out of the air, and does very well on a telephone wire, if it can't find an unrented tree. No; there are no poisonous snakes in

Florida which climb trees. Indeed, your chances of being struck by any venomous snake hereabouts are about the same as danger from lightning; maybe less.

And so it goes, in this hammock-swamp world that has been preserved for future generations, to enjoy and to comprehend, and to feel kinship with.

In summer, Highlands Hammock State Park is much used for organized camping by boy scouts and 4-H groups, mainly from Miami, Fort Lauderdale, and Tampa.

(XII)

KENTUCKY LAKE STATE PARK

KENTUCKY

Fifteen miles northwest of Murray, off U.S. 68 on Highway 94

From its well-chosen site well above the level of Kentucky Lake, the guests of Kenlake Hotel look out over a placid body of water which covers what was once the hill-and-dale borders of the Tennessee River. Somewhere out there, this river of history used to flow, quietly enough at some seasons, a raging flood at others. Just where was it, one wonders. Presumably about midway between the shores we see below—but it is all incorporated now in one of the world's largest manmade bodies of water.

Millions of visitors to Kentucky Lake State Park, even though they have come primarily for fishing or other recreative sports, cannot fail to carry away memorable scenes of today and yesteryear. This Tennessee, for example, was one of the vulnerable spots in the bastions of the Confederacy when, a century ago, the civil war was being waged. Who first thought, in the early days of the war, of placing a naval group on the Tennessee and Cumberland rivers, where they poured their waters into the Ohio, for the purpose of wrecking the Confederacy's lines of communication? Probably many military men had the idea from the outset, since this was logically the defensive weakness of the South.

There was no thought at the moment of the battle of Shiloh. Halleck's troops were merely on a mission to Albert Sidney Johnston's rail communications. It was when the Federals found that the Confederate forces were concentrated at Corinth, Mississippi, that the whole complexion of the invasion suddenly changed. Yes, decidedly this Tennessee River, now enwrapped for 184 miles of its lower length in a vast basin of slack water—which forms a lake with 2,300 miles of wooded shoreline—is a river which has seen great action.

And in all ways what a river this Tennessee is, even as changed by the operations of the Tennessee Valley Authority! The headwaters of the feeding streams in the southern Appalachians are not far from the Atlantic seashore, yet they travel by this meandering route till they enter the Mississippi delta at the Gulf of Mexico. Notice, too, how the river sweeps down into Alabama, then back into Tennessee, and finally through Kentucky.

Since 1933, TVA has built or acquired a total of twenty-five major dams in the Tennessee Valley area, nine of these dams being on the Tennessee River itself and the remaining ones on tributary streams. Kentucky Dam, which created the great lake we are now describing, is the "spigot" in the TVA flood-regulation operations, with the largest storage capacity of any of the reservoirs. We are told—a challenging fact to the imagination!—that in this Kentucky Lake, in times of extreme flood, there could be stored as much water as would cover the surface area of Massachusetts to a depth of one foot.

Naturally, the complex of dams is intended to help protect several millions of acres of land in the lower Ohio and Mississippi valleys. But this Kentucky reservoir also forms the connecting link of an Ohio-Mississippi-Tennessee waterway that makes it possible, the year around, for vessels of nine-foot draft to ascend to Knoxville—a distance of 650 miles from the confluence of waters at Paducah.

The dams in this stretch of navigable water are equipped with locks to raise or lower boats moving on the river. Or is it a river any more? Each dam along its course is built at the proper height to form a reservoir which extends the navigation channel at least eleven feet deep to the next upriver dam, the uppermost dam, Ft. Loudoun, extending the channel to Knoxville. So in effect the Tennessee is for the greater part a chain of lakes now, rather than a river.

Though the basic purposes of TVA were flood control, power, and unimpeded navigation, there has emerged from the colossal undertaking a byproduct of reservoir recreation of such scope as would have been beyond the wildest dream of the recreationist of half a century ago. Thirteen state parks, totaling 19,600 acres, are located on these artificial lakes—three in Kentucky, seven in Tennessee, two in Alabama, one in Mississippi. Sixty-odd county and municipal parks are found on the shorelines of these lakes. Great Smoky Mountains National Park borders the north shore of Fontana Lake. National forest lands fringe many reservoirs above Chattanooga. Fish and wildlife agencies and state conservation departments administer 200,000 acres of land and water.

This seems a long prologue to the story of Kentucky Lake State Park. But since this book will have room for only one of the state parks that derive from the TVA operations, it is only proper to present the background against which all of them were developed.

About every recreative outdoor facility you could name is found at this state park, and, with a few exceptions, all are free to the visitor. There are a few special services, which the commonwealth, properly enough, does not operate. Horse and pony livery, a miniature train with a real locomotive, a few things of that sort. This is ideal country for horseback riding. Unfortunately, this amiable sport, a fine exercise, is in danger of disappearing from our roster of recreation. The carriage roads that John D. Rockefeller, Jr., with so much loving imagination built on Mount Desert Island in Maine are not being used for the purpose. The cost of maintaining a good string of horses has soared almost beyond the purses of the many people who would like to hire them. Liability insurance, for one thing, is more than most liverymen can afford, on top of the other rising costs. When I was at Kentucky Lake the concessioner there did not know whether he could carry on. What a pity! For this exhilarating outdoor activity is the one that dyspeptic Thomas Carlyle often said provided the only relief for his digestive troubles—and this says nothing of the sheer joy of cantering or ambling along a velvet bridle path on a brisk morning when the sun and air renew the depths of the spirit. The automobile, with all its patent usefulness, will never be more than a poor second to Dobbin.

But fishing! Here we come to the great drawing power of Kentucky Lake. On the grounds, not far uphill from the boat dock, you will see a small building, well constructed but with no exterior signs to suggest its function. You will ask, as did I: "What is that building for?" It is the fish-cleaning house. Get that? A *special* building for the cleaning of the bass, or crappie, or bream, or sauger, or whatever the visitor snatches out of the lake. Maybe similar facilities exist in other state parks; I have never seen one. Good wives who have had their fishermen spouses clean fish in the house will rejoice that here at Kentucky Lake a special facility for the purpose is provided.

A fish-cleaning house, admittedly, may be no great matter in itself. But it surely emphasizes the fact that the world—that part of it which can get here—comes mainly to catch fish, and, as a corollary, *does* catch fish. You may have heard the expression "a fisherman's paradise" so many times that you are inclined to sniff and discount it. But this lake, with the other mainstream reservoirs of TVA, really and truly furnishes wet game in plenty.

Talk with the manager of the boat dock operated by the park authority. He is the fisherman's fisherman. His little moored piscine empire, at the lakeside below the hotel, is the classic bazaar of the fishing world. Formed from two old ferryboats welded together, one section is a general store, a snack bar, a bait emporium, a department store of every accessory that fish have ever had for lure. The other section, in the slack winter season, is lined with outboards being repaired, reconditioned, or stored. All is shipshape. It is deliberately planned to so fascinate our Izaak Waltons with the gadgets of their pastime that they will hang around there, forgetting that they really came to get a boat and fish.

And they do come: and from long distances! There is an airport just outside the park, a small one where private planes can land. The day I was at the park, a Minnesota manufacturer, on his way to visit friends in Mississippi, landed at the airport for "a few hours of fishing." He actually started the outboard motor less than half an hour after touching the airport strip.

I asked the boat-dock manager what kinds of catfish were caught here. I confess, a catfish to me is a catfish—just a catfish. Maybe I had heard of channel cats and blues. But this fisherman's fisherman reeled off a list of varieties of catfish which sounded like an ichthyologist's textbook. The late David Starr Jordan of Stanford University could have done no better. He also told me of a catfish caught in the churning waters of the river below the Kentucky dam, which weighed 100 pounds. Who am I to doubt?

Fishing, by the way, is unrestricted on the Kentucky waters of this lake the year around—even commercial fishing. The above-mentioned boat dock, operated by the park authority, is just one of 108 docks situated on the Kentucky and Tennessee shores of this great lake. There are, in addition, many privately used boathouses built and maintained under lease from the park authority, at a reasonable monthly rental charge.

In 1951 the commonwealth built a comfortable modern hotel in Kentucky Lake State Park, at a cost of $600,000, with a generous number of vacation cottages, pleasantly located among the trees, and equipped with complete up-to-date facilities. The visitor pays a charge for accommodations somewhat in excess of the prices at privately operated resorts of the neighborhood; it is the policy not to enter into competition, at least in this matter of direct pricing, with private enterprises.

Every year, spring and autumn, sailboat regattas are held at Kentucky Lake State Park. Just as there are rough campers and soft campers, pier-fishermen and surfcasters, gun toters and camera-and-binocular hunters in the world of wildlife—just so you find outboard speed enthusiasts on one hand, and on the other, the fellows who scorn gasoline power and love the noiseless filling of the sails. For such, there is at this park not only ample room, but also the comradeship of the enthusiast who operates, mostly for the love of it, this sailboat concession. This man was an executive in a great corporation. When he retired, he traveled for a while, looking for the ideal place to pursue his favorite sport and also to provide the opportunity for others to do so. Here, he says, he found it.

The summer before my visit to the park, a ghost appeared out of the historic past of river navigation, providing vast interest and excitement for the visitors. It was the old *Delta Queen*, long a famous traveler on the Ohio and the Mississippi. Uplake it steamed, and dropped anchor not far from the state boat dock. It had come from Cincinnati and Louisville, by way of Paducah and then into the Tennessee. Entering the navigation lock at Kentucky Dam, it had been lifted at one hoist to the lake level above: no mean river lock, that! When the passengers swarmed ashore, it seemed that river travel had come back again. All that was needed was Mark Twain at the wheel.

(XIII)

LONGFELLOW-EVANGELINE STATE PARK

LOUISIANA

At St. Martinsville, on Highway 31, seven miles east of U.S. 90

GABRIEL *truly is near thee, for not far away to the southward,*
On the banks of the Teche, are the towns of St. Maur and St. Martin. . . .
Beautiful is the land, with its prairies and forests of fruit trees;
Under the feet a garden of flowers, and the bluest of heavens
Bending above, and resting its dome on the walls of the forest.
Those who dwell there have named it the Eden of Louisiana.

IN THE DAYS when the literary galaxy of Boston was styling itself only half jokingly "the Hub of the Universe" there was a Harvard student named Edward Simon. He was a native of St. Martinsville, Louisiana, and the story of the six thousand French colonists of Nova Scotia who went into exile rather than to forsake their Catholic faith and swear allegiance to the British Crown was a touching drama he had heard from childhood. For many of these expatriate people of Acadia had settled in that beautiful countryside of which St. Martinsville was the market town.

Simon one day related the historic tale to someone who then suggested to Nathaniel Hawthorne that he use it in his writings. He did not, but the tale finally came to the attention of Henry Wadsworth Longfellow, in a roundabout way, and was put into verse. Thus emerged *Evangeline,* over which, as Katherine Tynan has suggested, more honest tears of sympathy have been shed than over any other writing.

Right up to the present day the tragic love story of Evangeline and Gabriel retains its power to stir the heart. The names Evangeline and Gabriel were inventions of the poet, but it was a very real Emmeline Labiche who came to St. Martinsville three years after her Louis Arceneaux. When Emmeline's barge touched at the landing on Bayou Teche, Louis was among those who were there to meet it. And under the great live oak which still flings shading branches over a great space at the creek bank, Louis was forced to stammer a bitter revelation—he was already married. The trunk with her long-treasured wedding gown was gathered up, to go with Emmeline to the Widow Borda; but Emmeline was not there long. Her grave can be seen in the old Attakapas Cemetery, a small part of which has been preserved near the Catholic church.

Nearby, is another tomb, with the worn inscription: "Jne. Aspasie Bienvenue Espouse de Pre. Olivier Deveron. . . . Femme respectable et tendre mere." (Woman worthy of esteem, and tender mother.) What finer tribute could anyone be paid?

The slow-flowing creeks that find their way through the coastal plain of Louisiana to the Gulf of Mexico are called bayous. One of these is the Bayou Teche, along which the descendants of the Acadian exiles still live and farm. These are the Cajuns, about whom many a novel has been written. The words "bayou" and "teche" sound decidedly French, but, in truth, both words are of Indian origin. When the first settlers arrived in the region, about 1775, the wilderness was occupied by the Attakapas tribe, which was not only hostile to the white man but greatly feared by its red neighbors, since its diet did not exclude occasional human flesh. France established a military post here for the protection of the settlers.

As to the word "teche," it seems to refer to the unusually serpentine course of the bayou. According to legend, there was a snake—not just a very large snake, but a snake of really heroic proportions—which was making its way southward from somewhere up in the highlands. It did very well on its journey until it got to the soil of the coastal plain, which was slithery after a rain. And it had been raining. The snake slipped and slipped in the gumbo. All its efforts got it no farther. Its squirming merely had the effect of boring down into the soil. When the snake gave up, there was a deep, twisting trench which, filled with water, became Bayou Teche.

Bayou Teche borders Longfellow-Evangeline State Park on one

of its sides. The park is not large—about 157 acres—but what there is of it is sheer loveliness. As you enter it from the highway, it has much the same aspect as the "parks" of England which were for centuries the pride of the aristocracy. But as you go toward the bayou the woods become denser, and the picnic ground is found in a spot that must be a fine refuge on a hot summer day. The oaks and pecans are nothing less than magnificent, in a region where these trees attain great size and age. From the building that houses the museum you look toward the Gabriel Oak, larger and probably older than the Evangeline Oak down in the town. It is surely a superb specimen.

Some of these venerable oaks (does the name signify a different species?) have the singular habit of drooping their lower branches to the ground, as though in lassitude, saying: "Too heavy! I just can't hold it up any longer." Then, having gained a second wind, the branch begins to grow upward again.

The museum is in a small three-story cottage that was built in 1765 on a land grant owned by the Chevalier d'Auterive, commander of the Attakapas Poste in the service of His Majesty. Hand-hewn cypress, fastened with wooden pegs, went into the construction of this perfect example of early Acadian architecture. The house is furnished as it would have been in Acadian times; also reconstructed is the outdoor *cuisine,* with its "whistler's walk," by which the food went to the people of the house. The *magazine,* or storehouse, is likewise a facsimile. The bricks used then were sun-dried and deteriorated easily unless they were kept covered with plaster.

On the porch of the museum house is an object which belongs to a later period but which is a remarkable example of the superior handcraft produced by necessity in the more or less isolated plantations. This is a hand-carved cotton compress, with screw pin, the wood taken from the heart of some enormous curly oak. The modern machinist looks at this contraption with amazement, for though the whole machine was crude, the threading of screw and matrix, to be of any value, must have been done with perfect precision. How the settlers adapted to their needs whatever was readily at hand! What could be more efficient for the purpose than this rudimentary tool standing beside the fireplace—a besom fashioned from a stick and corn husks? And you feel sure that this partly-rotted *bateau,* recovered from the bayou—a cypress log hollowed out by chipping and burning—brought many a passenger and many a small cargo up the Teche.

Again the visitor is reminded of the fact that New France is all around him, when he stops before the arts-and-crafts shop to read the sign: "Centre de Métiers Acadiens: Métiers et Cadeaux." The Louisiana State University, through its extension service, developed this project to perpetuate the art of weaving, palmetto work, basketry, and other similar crafts. The craft house is a faithful reproduction of the simpler homes built by the Acadians on their arrival in the Teche country two hundred years ago. A mud chimney outside saved floor space. From the little porch, a flight of stairs led up to the attic, where was the *garçonnière*, or room for the boys. Rich or poor, all Acadian boys had their own quarters.

And life for these Acadian exiles, getting a fresh start in an unfamiliar land, was hard. An echo of their austerity can be heard in the familiar parting words to a newly married couple, even today: "*Adieu les mariés, couche-couche et caillé!*" Or, literally, "so long, honeymooners, *couche-couche* and clabber!" Clabber is of course curdled milk, and *couche-couche*, a cereal of corn meal eaten with milk or black coffee. This farewell is a rustic reminder that though it may be cake and wine on this your wedding day, you must expect to get back to a simple diet tomorrow.

Quite properly, the Longfellow-Evangeline State Park is a memorial to that remnant of the Acadian exiles who finally gained a haven after their heartbreaking buffeting among strangers—cast ashore empty-handed in a dozen ports along the Atlantic seaboard, homesick, hungry, with only the bitter memory of their burned homes at Grand-Pré on the Basin of Minas. But twice fortunate is the memorial state park with a charm of larger scope. And this is the luck of Longfellow-Evangeline.

Without trying—and succeeding because it does *not* try—St. Martinsville is a town of infinite allure. You sit in Hebert's restaurant and sip, from a small cup, a coffee that truly fulfills Talleyrand's demand that it be "as black as the devil." This is not the chicory coffee favored in other parts of Louisiana. This bean was blackened like a Moor in the roasting. All around you, in soft tones, the French language is being spoken—not one kind of French, but several, if you know something of the language and your ear is attuned to the nuances. This restaurant is not contrived for tourists. The townsfolk eat here.

Across the street is the church, with the figure of St. Martin of

Tours in front. The church was completed in 1832, but within the structure is incorporated the original chapel of the time when the settlement was Poste des Attakapas. The beautiful post office, also within your view, is said to be the only federal building converted from a private residence. This lovely structure was the luxurious home of Eugene Duchamp de Chastagnier, who came here from Martinique and duplicated the sugar plantation home he had had there.

True, St. Martinsville and its surroundings are all French, but there are several kinds of French here. Eldest (and justly proud) are the descendants of the military and governing circle of early Attakapas times. Next in time come the Acadians, sturdy peasant folk whose industry and pluck developed the Teche country. A third wave came from France at the end of the eighteenth century—aristocratic refugees who were fortunate enough to get themselves and some portable belongings out of the revolutionary terror just ahead of the tumbril and the guillotine. When they arrived they thought it only a temporary harbor, where they would await the restoration of king and court. But the beautiful Teche land won their hearts and most of them remained.

With the advent of the aristocrats, the businesslike military post became a "*petit* Paris." "The barons, marquises and counts," we are told by our historian, "tried to maintain on the banks of the Teche bayou the same extravagant, stylized formality of the social life they had hitherto enjoyed in Europe. . . . They gave '*fêtes champêtres*' costing fortunes, great balls where the minuet was danced," the ladies wearing the court gowns they had saved from the wreckage. There was even a French opera company in this "*petit* Paris."

About a mile and a half from the town's center is Oak and Pine Alley. In 1820 Charles Durand arrived from France, a man of great means, something of an eccentric, or as the French said, *un original.* Instead of planting the usual *allée* of trees at the entranceway to his estate, he had his slaves contrive a cross of oaks and pines. Part of the body of the cross is still there; originally it was three miles in length and extended from the house to the wharf on the bayou. "But the stately beauty of the moss-draped oaks and pines was not ornate enough to serve as a driveway for the bridal party of M. Durand's two daughters. For them he provided something like golden spider webs." In St. Martinsville folks still will tell you of this extraordinary event. Spiders were brought from nearby Lake Catahoula, and when they had spun their webs in the oaks and pines, slaves dusted them with gold. One doubts that the wedding guests called out "*Adieu . . . couche-couche et caillé*" on this Lucullan occasion.

The amazing and glittering history of St. Martinsville blends perfectly with the Acadian memorial. If you are fortunate enough to talk with M. André Olivier, at his museum at the foot of the Teche Bridge, you will get the full color of a town that is like no other. M. Olivier is the *doyen* of the historical department of the Teche; he is the one-man chamber of commerce. He is a descendant of Hughes Charles Honoré Olivier de Vesin on the one side, and of Acadians on the other. Gentleman, raconteur, historian, curator—almost, one would say, *procureur-général* of culture in this little corner of France, Monsieur is not ashamed to be a tradesman, too. I love him better for that. And also for keeping alive that old Louisiana custom of giving *lagniappe*—which I had thought had utterly vanished with the advent of the cash register and the chain stores.

(XIV)

MOUNT MITCHELL STATE PARK

NORTH CAROLINA

Thirty-three miles northeast of Asheville, off Blue Ridge Parkway

> . . . THERE IS *no caprice or mistake in tests derived from the vegetable world; manners may make the man, but the sun alone modifies the plant: man may be fused down by social appliances into one uniform mass, but the rude elements are not to be civilized, nor can nature be made cosmopolitan —which heaven forfend!*
>
> Richard Ford, *Gatherings from Spain* (1846)

IN THE YEAR 1784 a party of five men—all good naturalists—climbed the mountain in New Hampshire which is known as Mount Washington. Two of the hikers were prominent Congregational divines, Dr. Jeremy Belknap and Dr. Manasseh Cutler. Dr. Cutler "guessed" that this craggy peak was about 9,000 feet in height, which estimate, being almost 3,000 feet in error, was perhaps the wildest guess ever made by a mountain-climbing clergyman. We may be sure, however, that the New Hampshire peak was named for the beloved George Washington in the belief that it was the highest mountain in what was then known of the United States.

Nor was the supremacy of Mount Washington questioned for many years after it was named. That was just as well as far as Dr. Jeremy and Dr. Manasseh were concerned. If they had known that there was, in the Blue Ridge of North Carolina, a mountain almost 400 feet higher than Agiochook (which was the Indian name of the one they climbed) they would have been surprised indeed. And had they known that Mount Mitchell is one of a group of five within a short radius, every one of which is much higher than Washington, they might have fallen into premature decay. But here, carefully measured, not by guess but with modern measuring devices, are the heights of the peaks within Mount Mitchell State Park: Mitchell, 6,684; Craig, 6,645; Balsam Cone, 6,611; Cattail Peak, 6,583; Big Tom, 6,558. Mount Washington tops at 6,288 feet.

What a charming youthfulness is involved in this search for and proclamation of the superlative! The biggest, the highest, smallest, heaviest, softest . . . or the *first.* What a mundane triumph it is, that *first!* Yet, juvenile and unimportant as it seems to the philosopher, this striving and competitive spirit perhaps shares of the essence—the will to know—which has brought humans far along the trail of progress. And we must not think that the men of highest talent have not entertained the feeling. Did not the accomplished French botanist, André Michaux, leap for joy and sing the *Marseillaise* when he reached the top of Grandfather Mountain, being blissfully certain that it was the highest point in the Appalachian chain? Grandfather, "carved in rock and plumed with ferns," had, "in the furrows of his face, worn by the lapse of time, clinging and creeping, the most beautiful flowers and vines," wrote Michaux. Then, as now, Grandfather is magnificent. But Michaux sang on the wrong peak.

The visitor to Mount Mitchell State Park is able to say that he has stood upon the highest point of land east of the South Dakota Black Hills. He can attain this glory quite inexpensively, too, for the famous Blue Ridge Parkway will take him to the junction of another excellent road which leads almost to the top of the mountain. At the end of the road, he has a choice of several trails—rugged or gentle, as he pleases.

Much more exciting to my mind is the incomparable adventure these Southern Appalachians offer in the field of natural history. For these sleek, hazy, billowy ranges—hills beyond hills as far as the eye can follow—are truly the display window of botany, a floral and woodland wealth that has no counterpart in our country, having resulted from a geological history sharply unlike that of the Appalachians of the north.

True, these mountain plants spread, as distinctive types, as far as Canada and Florida—but here an unequaled concentration may be seen. There are almost as many species of native trees here as there are in all of Europe. At various zones of the delectable mountains, more than 1,300 kinds of trees, shrubs, and herbs exist. Of mosses alone, there are more than three hundred; and of funguses, eighteen hundred.

How markedly different is this scene from that of the northern end of the Appalachian chain! The great ice sheet of Pleistocene times did not come close to these ancient mountains, though the attendant cold molded their way of life. There was no scouring and tearing and creasing such as New England underwent. There are no streams of boulders such as were strewn along the bulldozed sides of the northern hills, as the ice finally retreated. There are mountains with bald tops—very difficult to explain, by the way—but the baldness is simply an absence of forest growth, not of smaller plant life. This is not the stark baldness of the northern summits of rock where only lichens and some subarctic plant life live a furtive existence. Down here, there is no timber line.

What seems incredible at a glance is that the plant life of Mount Mitchell State Park is that of Canada rather than that of the lower regions of the Carolinas. You who come from the far north to visit this cheerful scene will feel quite at home atop Mount Mitchell. For what are you surrounded by? A forest of almost pure spruce and fir balsam; and the few deciduous trees are just those you have left behind you in higher latitudes. Yellow birch, the canoebirch, the moose maple, and the sugar maple. And some hemlock, too, which is probably the tree the folks of the southern mountains refer to as the "spruce pine."

Also rather pleasing is the distinction these remote mountaineers make when they call the fir tree the "she-balsam" and the spruce the "he-balsam." The big blisters of the fir tree, full of the puckery liquid resin of cough cures and thin-section mineralogical mounts, can be "milked," whereas the spruce, though having other merits, like all males, has not that special attribute.

Here in this park you have before you a living example of the fact that altitude may produce similar plant life just as latitude may; and, with this spur to the imagination, you realize why a mountain top straddling the very equator may have its head in perpetual snow.

"Some folks, like myself," says a naturalist, "find the north woods at times monotonous; in undiluted quantity they are stern, and finally almost suffocating. In the Southern Appalachians where, dark and gleaming, red spruce and balsam fir crown only the loftiest peaks, their rarity, their aloofness . . . all make them a goal worth the climb that will certainly set you to breathing quick and deep in the thin aromatic atmosphere." I don't know that the word "monotonous" is apt, but in general I know how this naturalist feels—the

Canadian tree life found on the upper part of Mount Mitchell, which constitutes the state park, is in pleasing esthetic contrast to the trees you see at all lower elevations of the Blue Ridge.

The great glaciation, however, presented New England with an asset that these southern mountains lack. The deep gouges in the landscape made by the weight and power of the mile-high ice, which later became thousands of ponds and lakes, have no counterpart in the Blue Ridge and the Smokies. But, then, Mitchell's summit is not an "outpost of the Arctic," as a skillful writer has justly termed the summit of Mount Washington. Plenty of snow there in midwinter, of course, and cold; but no ferocity such as makes Mount Washington a phenomemon and a threat to unwary hikers even in late spring and early autumn.

Donald Culross Peattie, a lover of these mountains, noting the fact that here is a forest "which has its wild flowers not only at the foot of its trees, but in the tips of them," says: "As an instance of this I recollect gazing down once, in July, from the slopes of Mount Mitchell at the coves of the Craggies . . . as far as eye could see, tossing with the creamy blooms of the chestnut [alas, alas, the chestnut!] which in those days was king of the cove hardwoods. There were so many, the chestnuts, and each crown bore such a myriad of long shining catkins, that as the wind threshed those woods the whole sea of waving leaves seemed breaking into whitecaps."

In such a truly equable climate, upon a residual soil wealthy with the accumulated humus of countless years, the "original" forest growth in these southern mountains was magnificent, as we can see from the virgin sections that still remain, largely through preservation within Great Smoky Mountains National Park. Before the blight, there were chestnuts eleven feet in diameter; and there is today a mountain laurel six and a half feet through at the stem! And these great boles must be considered in light of the fact that forest trees, densely packed, tend to great height rather than girth.

Yet, by the turn of the century, though hauling was not easy in this region, the white man's need of wood was already beginning to tell upon a seemingly inexhaustible supply. First, the cabinet woods —walnut, cherry, magnolia—then construction material; then, what have you. "The mills did not bother, once, with logs less than twenty inches thick. In a *decade*, they were glad to get logs [only] twenty-four inches at the stump end."

In 1915, when Locke Craig was governor of the state of North Carolina, the upper part of Mount Mitchell, somewhat more than 1,200 acres, was set aside as a state park. It was one of the first preservations of its kind in the south; perhaps it *was* the first. The governor, gifted with the foresight that characterizes conservationists, fortunately had a responsive legislature; the Act passed that year is so crisply, adequately worded that it is worthy of reproduction here:

Whereas the summit of Mount Mitchell in Yancey County is the greatest altitude east of the Rocky Mountains, and whereas the headwaters of many of the important streams of the State are at or near the said summit, and the forest is being cleared, which tends to damage and injure the streams flowing through the said State from the mountains to the Atlantic Ocean; and whereas it is deemed desirable that this beautiful and elevated spot shall be acquired and permanently dedicated as a State park for the use of the people of the entire State seeking health and recreation; and whereas, unless the said land is acquired by the State at this time, the cost of acquiring it at a later date will be greatly increased and the watercourses may be damaged, and the beauty of the scenery destroyed by removing the growth therefrom, and irreparable damage accrue; now, therefore . . .

"The cost of acquiring it at a later date . . ." If only more states, and if only the federal government itself, had realized in 1915 the truth that lay in those words, what vandalism of irreplaceable assets, what obnoxious inholdings, what miles of tawdry summer shacks along a precious seashore would have been avoided!

A commission reported favorably on Mitchell's crest, and it was acquired for $20,000. Thus began North Carolina's venture into state parks, which now preserve fine specimens of the natural scene from the mountains to the sea. Incidentally, North Carolina is one of those states which believes that the educational value of her preserves is not fully exploited without nature study and guidance at the hands of competent naturalists. So, besides a good park museum atop Mount Mitchell, there is a naturalist on duty in June, July, and August. Near to the summit are paved parking areas, picnic shelters and tables, campgrounds, a restaurant, and a recreation lodge. The foot trails are exceptionally well planned.

The visitor to this state park will not leave its beauties and its satisfactions without learning something of the tragic fate of the man for whom the mountain is named—Dr. Elisha Mitchell. The grave of this devoted man, for forty years a professor at the University of North Carolina at Chapel Hill, is just where it should be, on the mountain top where over the years he had so painstakingly sought to determine the altitude with perfect accuracy. Dr. Mitchell, with such instruments as he could then use, did not arrive at the exact figure, but his final measurement was only twelve feet in error, which was doing nobly.

He was a Connecticut Yankee by birth, this clergyman turned college professor, and was graduated from Yale. First a mathematics teacher at Chapel Hill, he later turned to his true interests, chemistry, mineralogy, and geology.

In the summer of 1835, Dr. Mitchell was told by André Michaux that the highest peak in the eastern United States was certainly in the Carolina Appalachians. Off went Mitchell to the Black Mountains, and measured, as best he could, what he thought to be the highest point of a notable group. He expressed so much confidence about it that a geography and atlas of 1839 stated flatly that Mount Mitchell was the highest east of the Rockies.

Then began a strange, not altogether explicable, dispute—a mild but sad professional feud—between Dr. Mitchell and Senator Thomas Lanier Clingman, for whom the highest point in the national park of the Smokies is named. Perhaps the feuding was mostly on the part of the senator, who was a man of "intrepidity, prodigious conceit, stupendous aspirations, immense claims, more than common ability and much curiosity," as has been said by a North Carolina writer. Clingman stated that *he* was the first to measure the highest Black Mountain peak. But he went further and averred that Dr. Mitchell *did not* measure it, a statement which was uncomplimentary, to say the least.

About the middle of June 1857, Elisha Mitchell, who actually had no way of proving that he had measured the highest Yancey County peak in 1835, 1838, or even in 1844, set up his camp at the foot of the Black Mountains, accompanied by his son, a daughter, and a servant. After two weeks of measurements at lower levels, he had reached an altitude of about 6,000 feet. Then he quit work on a Saturday afternoon and told his son that he was going to visit two former guides, Big Tom Wilson and William Riddle, on the other side of the mountain. He would be back Monday at noon.

Monday came, but not the doctor. Nor the next day, nor the next. Then, becoming worried, the son went to Big Tom's place. Big Tom recalled that in 1844 he had guided Dr. Mitchell up the mountain, and suggested that perhaps the professor had taken that same route down this time. The fact was, he had. But this time, perhaps in the darkness or dim twilight, he had fallen to his death from a cliff to a rocky pool many feet below. Mitchell Falls, as the spot is now called, lies about a mile from the summit of the mountain.

(X V)

MYAKKA RIVER STATE PARK

FLORIDA

Seventeen miles east of Sarasota, on Florida 72

A "VISITING FIREMAN"—in this case a National Park Service man—asked one of the rangers at Myakka River State Park: "What are your troubles here?" He was talking shop—the bus man on holiday. The answer was: "Poachers."

In a way, that answer really tells a lot about this magnificent state park. To have poacher trouble, there must be something worthwhile poaching, there must be enough to pay for risk. And here is a park that answers the dream of the naturalist-conservationist—a park big enough to permit the natural community ebb and flow of organic life; or, in the words of a policy statement adopted by the National Conference on State Parks, "characterized by spaciousness and a sense of freedom from outside influences . . . selected for its intrinsic values."

As to poaching, one feels that in Florida, as in other places, it constitutes a threat, or kind of vandalism, which will grow less menacing with the passing years. The poacher will more and more succumb to tavern brawls, or expire from an excess of moonshine whisky. It may be that the day will come when a few venerable poachers are preserved for much the same reason we wish to save the whooping crane: we desire that *no* species become extinct.

Before entering the gates of this remarkable state park, which preserves for posterity the inherent wonders of a great flood plain in our semitropics, it is only just to pay tribute to the excellent road signs on the highways that lead to Florida state parks—at least to those I have visited. Unobtrusive but legible, and spaced at intervals that will cheer the visitor from other states, who when traveling in a sparsely settled countryside is constantly wondering whether he may not have passed his objective without realizing it; these signs seem neither too many nor too few. The tourist has himself to blame if he can't find Florida's state parks.

Somehow I was reminded of a day when in my own state I came to a crossroads with five different ways one could proceed, and not a glimmer of a directional sign. True, they were not main roads; but they were the kind that people like myself love to travel because they are not highways, but lead through untamed scenery. I went back a quarter mile to a farmhouse to get directions. Then I committed an indiscretion. I said, a little peevishly: "I should think the town would put up some signs on that crossroads."

For that, I got a look that pitied and chided my imbecility. The farmer said: "I been living here man and boy for sixty year, and I ain't got lost yit."

Now, as to Myakka. I knew before I came that this park would be superlative, because I knew how it had come into being. I had heard about A. B. Edwards of Sarasota (the city about seventeen miles west) and his friends and associates who loved this picturesque region, who had hunted in it, camped in it, and knew it like their own back yards. A friend of mine, an early enthusiast for Myakka River, has told me:

"There wasn't any association, as I remember it. Just Mr. Edwards and a loyal group who yearned to save this wild broadness of the flood plains. I can't remember a single time they ever met in a hotel at luncheon or dinner and just 'talked' about it. They used to go out to what is now the park, build a campfire under the big live oaks at the Upper Lake, and 'live' their enthusiasm, after getting loaded with gopher stew, big slabs of fried yams, corn bread and palmetto honey, with a pot of coffee on the coals. . . ."

At this point, I interrupted my friend. "Pardon me, Ray: did I understand you to say *gopher* stew? You don't really mean they ate *gophers?*"

"Why, certainly. Do you mean to say *you* never ate gopher stew? Where have you been all these years?"

It was a slight misunderstanding. My idea of a gopher came from a part of the country where a gopher is a pouched rat (*Geomys bursarius*). I didn't know that a certain kind of tortoise in Florida was also called a gopher. The president of a Saint Augustine bank told me afterward that gopher stew was what the Olympians ate and misbranded ambrosia. Pardon my ignorance, friends. I'll try it on my next visit.

This broad valley of the Myakka has been compared to the African veldt. What aptness there is in such a comparison is not for me to say, not having been in the veldt. What is at once obvious to the visitor is that this land is distinctly different from any other in Florida; and this singularity is being preserved with integrity in the management of the area.

When the first master plan was drawn, it was designated that Myakka was to be a wilderness sanctuary except for two small "use areas" connected by several miles of road through the palm and oak forest bordering the flood plain of the river. This plan has been faithfully kept, so that an effective bird and animal sanctuary exists while full opportunity is given the visitor to sense the wilderness. All along the road one can see the nature of the surroundings. You know what the country is like without invading and disturbing it.

A band of turkeys came into the foreground, feeding boldly, while I was driving along. I had seen wild turkey flocks before; but somehow I had never before been so impressed with the nobility of this Western-hemisphere fowl. They fitted so perfectly into that wild picture! With some amusement I recalled the feelings of the inimitable Ben Franklin, who thought the turkey, rather than the eagle, should be adopted as the representative of our nation. Ben was a little rough on the eagle, I agree; yet there was some truth in what he said. "He is a bird of bad moral character . . . you may have seen him perched on some dead tree, too lazy to fish for himself . . . like those among men who live by sharping and robbing, he is generally poor and very often lousy . . . the turkey is in comparison a much more respectable bird."

At any rate, the turkey belongs here; the Indians of old must have delighted in his flesh. And is the name Myakka a variant of the Timucuan word *myaca,* which means "large"? It might be. On early Florida maps there was an Indian mission of that name on the Saint John.

The Myakka River State Park is one of the greatest natural wildlife sanctuaries in this country. With its 28,000 acres, it is big enough to be an unimpaired, free-working community. Deer and turkey, squirrel and coon can roam at will. The enormous flocks of wading birds, however, are the jewels of the region. It has been estimated that thirty thousand of them roost in one central rookery at the north end of Upper Myakka Lake. What Margaret Shippen Roebling said of Hooker Hammock—"let's save something of Florida for the birds"—finds fulfillment here.

The truth is, that ardent conservationists came to the rescue of the many species of wading birds none too soon. Even now, in Florida, which materially has mushroomed so phenomenally, it is touch-and-go with the egrets and the wood ibis, for example. The *Florida Naturalist* reports, as this is being written, that these two species are "at a crisis in their history," due to drainage operations, drought and disastrous storms, and an ever-present threat of real-estate developers who eye the northeast corner of Everglades National Park.

Though there are such great numbers of wading birds here, the visitor must not get the idea that he can see them at any time he chooses. Those who come to the park primarily to see or study the birds would do well to make inquiry of the superintendent before their visit, for these water fowl have seasonal habits. It is like seeing a mountain goat at Glacier. Part of the thrill, if you *do* see some, is due to the fact that nobody can guarantee that you *will.*

Fish, however, are always abundant in these lakes and in the river—bass, bream, perch, and catfish—and I can testify that it was a happy day for the fisherman as I watched at the dam on the Upper Lake.

The park has five rustic cabins, built of palmetto and live-oak logs. "They are not city accommodations, but take you back to the days of our ancestors," says the literature from the Florida Park Service. Indeed, anyone who would regard these excellent cabins as uncomfortable would do better to remain at home. Each has a huge open fireplace, an electric stove, a refrigerator, and a hot-water heater. Our ancestors were happy with just the fireplace.

My understanding is that at present the park authorities have no intention of increasing cabin accommodations. None of the parks is very far from cities or towns amply supplied with accommodations. "We cater to campers," the director told me. No admission fee is charged in the Florida state parks, but there is usually a parking fee. This fee, it is felt, offers better control and results in less vandalism and other misbehavior. Outboard motors are permitted only upon the lake.

(XVI)

MYRTLE BEACH STATE PARK

SOUTH CAROLINA

Three miles south of Myrtle Beach, on U.S. 17

THUMBING THROUGH Beatrice Ward Nelson's *State Recreation,* printed in 1928, I came upon the following statement: "South Carolina is without state parks. No organized movement for the creation of such areas has been considered, although there exists the feeling among some of the public-spirited citizens of the state that a system of state parks would be valuable. . . ."

In less than thirty years—much less—that "feeling among the public-spirited citizens" must have become an eagerness and a stout resolution, for today South Carolina has a well-balanced system of state parks, admirably selected, well managed, and offering not merely physical recreation but the opportunity to realize the natural and human history of a commonwealth rich in both. South Carolina is one of those fortunate states which has its head in the mountains and its toes in the ocean. From Table Rock State Park in the Appalachians to Hunting Island, the semitropical barrier island southeast of Beaufort, "the young, the old, the rich, the poor, the mother of a family, the laborer, the farmer, the college professor—all have a state park within approximately fifty miles of home." So reads the publicity, and the map supports the claim.

This chapter, however, is rather unusual, for as I write I am visiting Myrtle Beach State Park. I shall attempt a brief description of this superb area, with the full knowledge that by the time my words are in print the park may have become wholly untenable for man. Overhead, and at no great distance overhead either, the tremendous super sabre jets, the F-100's, roar. Curiously enough, they do not seem to affect in the slightest the chatty group of cedar waxwings grouped together in their social manner in a nearby yaupon. Perhaps the birds long ago concluded that this is a cumbersome, expensive, and rather dangerous way of flying, and really not worth their notice. But as to human beings within the park, there is no such complacency. The civilian, though he may applaud any and all agencies of military defense in the abstract, does not relish the idea of being so readily imposed upon, especially when he is on vacation and seeking relaxation.

The planes, rising from the airstrip—if they rise quickly enough—take a course on the way out to sea almost directly over the 740-foot fishing pier which constitutes one of the chief attractions of the park. About a year before this was written, one of the jets, failing to achieve elevation fast enough, took away a large part of the fishing pier, and four unfortunate fishermen died. A week before my visit to Myrtle Beach State Park, another jet crashed between two houses just beside the fishing pier, on privately owned property. Miraculously, no lives were lost; even the pilot escaped with minor injuries. More recently, three of the great jets, flying low over the pier on take-off, were lost within an hour—although no physical damage was done to the park structures. But the occupants of the fishing pier have bad moments when the jets pass overhead. I can testify personally to the feeling that my scalp has been lifted; and I think I shall do my surf fishing about twenty miles farther south.

At the moment, the situation is unpromising. The military (who, the park superintendent told me, are personally very courteous) feel that the state park unfortunately is in the way. Nor is there much point in asking why this particular spot was chosen for the air field in the beginning. The Atlantic coastline is long and has some stretches of wholly undeveloped land, as well suited to flying over as the precious patches of wide, gleaming white beach for which the ideal use is human recreation. Not long after the airbase was built, part of the fine forest within the park had to be chopped away as it was a hazard to the jets in their take-off. This is the only bleak and uninteresting part of the park today. There are stumps, shrubs, and coarse grasses now where the migrating birds used to revel in the sheltering shade of a junglelike growth.

Indeed, here at Myrtle Beach you have the finest possible example of the findings of the survey group sent out by the National Park Service to explore possibilities for public ownership of good beaches on the Atlantic and Gulf shores. The survey and the widely circulated brochure *Our Vanishing Shoreline* did not include the Myrtle Beach strip for two reasons. First, miles of the choicest coastline had already been privately developed beyond any financial possibility of acquisition for public ownership. Second, there was already a state park in this area, with a frontage of more than a mile and visited by more than 400,000 persons a year. And it was seemingly secure. Conservationists, always combating encroachments and alert to threats, will be disturbed but not surprised at what is happening here.

Let us look back at what this "silver strand" was only a few years ago.

Older citizens of the Carolina tidewater country can recall the time when there was "nothing there." Private development began with the extraordinary vision and financial courage of a corporation by the name of Myrtle Beach Farms, Inc. This group knew that with a rapidly expanding population, larger incomes, and greater leisure time, the superb Myrtle Beach front—as fine as any shoreline in America—would eventually be enormously profitable.

The developer demonstrated a keen intelligence in setting aside an area for public use near what was to be the center of the city. (Part of this park, I observed, has already been invaded for the construction of a school.) A generous section of the corporate holdings was donated for a state park. At first the park land straddled U.S. Highway 17, but an exchange of land eventually consolidated the park property all on the ocean side of the highway and lengthened the beach strip to somewhat more than a mile. Although this was not the first South Carolina park to be set up—Cheraw was acquired in 1934—the first park visitor in this state entered the gate at Myrtle Beach in 1935.

At the time the park was donated to the state there was a CCC camp across the highway, and the buildings, including the five cabins fronting on the ocean, date from that period. With only five cabins, and thousands of families eager to occupy them for the one-week limit during the season, the park authorities have been obliged to resort to a carefully conducted "drawing" each year. However, the jet planes may cool off the widespread desire to occupy these fine cabins. A family that had stayed in one during my visit left in the morning with taut faces. "We thought the roof was being sucked right off the house," said papa. "We were planning to stay four days. I reckon one will be enough."

One look at Myrtle Beach State Park as it was. Yes, actually as it is, except for the destruction of the patch of woodland before mentioned. Not a large area—312 acres—yet it is a classic example of beach, dune, littoral forest, with everything for the playful and the thoughtful. The gently sloping beach is one of the widest and safest. Among the pines, cedars, and oaks, with a shrub understory of flowering and berried plants, there are winding pathways for the nature-walker and the bird-watcher. Wherever the sun sheds enough of its warmth and light, the ground is carpeted, especially in the spring, which comes early to this low country, with violets, lilies, and many other blooms. Even at the height of the season, the beach is commodious enough so that nobody feels cramped or jostled. The fishing from the staunchly built pier is excellent at certain times in the year; and it is never without some reward.

(X V I I)

PETIT JEAN STATE PARK

ARKANSAS

Fifteen miles southwest of Morrilton, on State 154

THE NAME of this state park arouses curiosity. Who was Petit Jean, or "Little John"? What did he ever do that earned him the right to have named for him a flat-topped mesa fourteen miles long and something less than five miles in width, rising eight hundred feet above the Arkansas River?

In Arkansas, of course, French names are not at all unusual. Fourche L'Anguille, Fourche la Fave, La Grue, Terre Rouge, Casse-tête, La Grange, Des Arc, Encore à Fabre—the state is sprinkled generously with reminders that the voyageurs of New France roamed the country even before their flag flew above the government house at Nouvelle-Orléans. But Petit Jean, what of this fellow?

If you like romances of the sort that once made the mid-Victorian maiden swoon with visions of a fairy prince: Petit Jean was really a stunning Parisienne whose lover set forth for the New World, telling her that when he returned to France they would be married. So she shipped on the same ship as a cabin boy, calling herself Jean Somebody-or-other. Would you believe it, neither her fiancé nor the rugged sailors recognized her in her disguise, which seems to suggest that, at that period, a large majority of France's population had poor eyesight.

There is a more believable legend to the effect that a certain Jean La Gaze, wealthy and aristocratic, fled from France just ahead of the butcheries of the Revolution and came to New Orleans, where he outfitted a small vessel and ascended the Mississippi into the Arkansas River. He picked a spot on the south brow of this mountain for a home. Misfortunes came—the death of his wife and daughter—then finally his young son, *Petit Jean*, died. Jean La Gaze lost his mind and wandered in the forest, playing upon his beloved flute. Imaginative settlers of later times would frighten one another by saying that they had heard the flute strains of ghostly John.

Or maybe Petit Jean, somewhat undersized for his age and stiff black beard, was just another beaver trapper on the tributaries of the Arkansas. It might be as simple as that.

Dr. T. W. Hardison of Morrilton was inclined to believe the story of Jean La Gaze. If he did so, we shall go along with the doctor, for he was the superior and devoted man who, more than anyone else, made it possible to preserve this extraordinary outlier of the Ozarkian uplift, which rises abruptly from the valley floor. From 1909 until his death a few years ago, Dr. Hardison faithfully cared for the medical needs of the neighboring mountain folk. His life and that of his wife were closely a part of the mountain called Petit Jean. The spirit with which he gazed upon his surroundings may be readily guessed from a few words of his own:

"Twenty years ago a man stood on the brow of the Mountain, looked up and down into the valley at the abandoned fields growing up in broom sedge and sassafras, at the dilapidated farm homes that dotted the picture, and said, 'What is this desolate country good for?'

"The same day another man stood on the same spot and looked down at the same valley and the same homes . . . and said, 'What a beautiful place in which to live . . . What opportunity!'

"Facts are not changed by individual points of view, but it is true that the man who saw nothing but ugliness in the landscape will never find happiness or contentment here; and the other, who saw opportunity in the neglected fields at his feet, who saw beauty and felt inspiration, will find in this environment all that is needed for contented living.

"If he has faith in the rational and orderly processes of what Thoreau called 'the mind of the universe' he will enjoy the calm assurance that through the turbulence and struggles of life, there is an Intelligence that gives purpose to everything in nature, including our own lives."

This was the caliber of the country doctor who longed to preserve, safe from lumbering and other despoliation, the genius of the mountain. In 1923, the third meeting of the National Conference on State Parks was held in Turkey Run State Park in Indiana. Dr. Hardison was there, and his interest was heightened and his resolve encouraged by this meeting with other fervent conservationists. He began to stir interest.

Early surges of enthusiasm tend to be somewhat excessive—and there was feverish thought of a Petit Jean National Park. It was not quite of that wide significance: but everyone who saw it knew that it would qualify as an outstanding state park. The prospective donors of land, chagrined that the word "national" would not be used, withdrew their offers—all save the owners of one eighty-acre tract. So Petit Jean started with that, and without money for maintenance. Now more than four thousand acres are included in the park. Of this, the Fort Smith Lumber Company gave more than a thousand acres, a section that added to the reserve the Seven Hollows locality—a series of parallel ravines of great charm and interest.

One geologist has compared Petit Jean Mountain, as to its general topographic effect, with the famous Mesa Verde in southwest Colorado. Certainly the area by strict definition is a park rather than a recreation area, because of its scientific—that is to say, mainly its geological—interest. It is a haven of refuge in the warm months, with its elevation and its cover of forest. The growth of trees, mainly pine and oak, with some hickory, is not distinguished, and in this lean soil it is hard to believe that there was ever any heavier cover. But what there is is sufficient to provide shade and to make up the pleasant landscape that belongs to a rocky terrain.

So far in the development of the park the merely recreation aspects have been emphasized. There is an excellent lodge—named for Stephen Mather, first director of the National Park Service; there are also a number of overnight cabins. The lodge perches almost on the edge of a rugged promontory that beetles over the steep-sided canyon of Cedar Creek. Hardison Hall, a dormitory that can accommodate 150 persons for group camping or meetings, is in great demand during the summer months.

A canyon of this proportion seems out of place on a mesa of such limited dimension as Petit Jean; but the Arkansas and its tributaries were probably deeply intrenched before the geological uplifting of the region took place, and the shale-sandstone Atoka formation, underlying the resistant so-called Hartsborne sandstone, is rather easily eroded. Hence the cliffing and the shelter caves, Cedar Falls, and the vast amount of boulder material seen at the foot of the slopes. In a word, this rock arrangement has given the mountain its form and shape.

"The rocks in this part of Arkansas are all of Pennsylvanian or Coal Measures age." I am quoting the geologist. "The Hartsborne standstone contains fossils, especially fragments of tree trunks, limbs, and leaves. These fossils are of the kinds that are very common in

Pennsylvania rocks throughout the world, and occur in many places in Arkansas and Oklahoma. They represent the plant life of that age, and are the remains of fernlike or rushlike trees that then flourished. These are the plants that have gone to make up much of the coal found in many parts of the world."

Some peculiar fossils, about the size and shape of a pecan nut, have also been found in the sandstone. They probably represent bud-like appendages that grew on the ends of the limbs of certain trees.

Petit Jean State Park is within easy reach of Little Rock, Pine Bluff, and Hot Springs, to mention only three population centers, with thousands of school children who would delight in a firsthand contact with the story of nature provided in a good seasonal naturalist program. Petit Jean and its rock history, are attractive subjects, ready to come alive through the efforts of a good interpreter.

Consider, for instance, the great variety and the strangeness of the erosional forms seen in the exposed sandstone in the park. One area in the rock, which has weathered along joint planes, reminds one of a herd, if herd is the word, of great Galápagos tortoises moving out of the open and disappearing in a grove of trees. Locally these and similar, larger formations are called turtlebacks, though one apt description refers to them as "biscuit" rocks—and they do indeed, from a little distance, resemble a giant display of this product fresh from the oven.

And the view from the rim of Petit Jean is most impressive. The big Arkansas River meanders below, taking its course through a great fertile plain, so different from the hardscrabble, rocky, sometime sterile spot on which the visitor stands. In places the drop from the rim is practically sheer, and an occasional hawk or vulture may be seen skirting the rock a hundred feet below one's feet, patiently searching every crevice and undercutting of this natural fortress.

The late Dr. Hardison, who was curious about anything that pertained to his beloved mountain, was always seeking reliable information and lore concerning Indian occupancy and interest in this Petit Jean mesa. Of course, it was Indian country, generally speaking, and the shelter caves showed use—but did the red man have any special attitude toward this dissected height of sandstone rock? Dr. Hardison's inquiries unearthed at least one mystery story—hearsay, to be sure, but still not smacking of invention.

A family named Mitchell had come from Georgia about 1835, and settled on Rose Creek. The few Indians they encountered at that time were migrants, who usually camped at the foot of Petit Jean Mountain. On the side of the mountain was a petroglyph, or what was supposed to be one, which had come to be known as "the gun barrel." It was "carved deep in a boulder, to perfect dimensions."

About 1908 the Mitchells, who still lived here, saw the Indians for the last time. They came in the largest caravan the family had ever seen—ten hacks or spring wagons drawn by ponies wearing brilliantly decorated harness with buckles of silver. Hitherto, when the Indians visited the mountain, they had been seen making observations from the rock of the gun-barrel petroglyph, and then spending some days in a search of the nearby mountainside for something: never finding the object of their hunt, apparently.

On this last visit, the Indians as usual went to the gun-barrel rock and oriented themselves. But this time they also asked questions of the Mitchells. Could the Mitchells remember a giant white oak that once stood at the foot of the mountain? Or could they recall just where there was once a group of trees that stood in the middle of a field?

About a week after the Indians made this final visit, they left camp during the night. The campfire ashes were still warm in the morning, but no trace of the visitors. There had been a full moon that night. Daylight revealed that the visitors had dug a hole in the field not far from the creek—a hole "big enough to hold one of the spring wagons."

Neat, eh? What had been buried in that field, if anything? Did the "gun-barrel" rock carving point to whatever had been buried, or did it happen to be a point in a triangulation that included some trees long since gone? The assumption would be that the red men found whatever they had long been seeking. What was it?

Petit Jean State Park does not occupy the whole mountain. It has an interesting neighbor, and one that guarantees a fine buffer protection for the park itself. This is Winrock Farm, owned by Winthrop Rockefeller. Here one of the five sons of John D. Rockefeller, Jr., has established a ranch of one thousand acres on the mesa, with five hundred more acres in the valley below, where Santa Gertrudis cattle—the famous Brahman-Shorthorn cross originated on the King Ranch in Texas—are being raised, and many valuable experiments made in the selection of feed grasses. Knowing that both his name and his hobby would attract visitors, Rockefeller has built a generous show barn and reception center where the public may learn of the valuable work being done, without interfering with the ranch operations.

(XVIII)

POINSETT STATE PARK

SOUTH CAROLINA

Eighteen miles southwest of Sumter, on Highway 261

YOU MAY never have heard of the Fall Line, if you happen to live in one of those states where such a geological landmark does not exist. To the South Carolinian, the Fall Line is the realest possible thing. It determines whether he is up-country or low-country.

Even a visitor from one of the central states, though the words "Fall Line" mean nothing to him, has been conscious when driving his automobile down from the Blue Ridge, across the Piedmont plateau, through the sandhills and then on to the sea, that at a certain point the landscape becomes not just different, but markedly different. Abruptly he has reached the place where the rivers no longer *fall*, where the streams cease to hurry along with their load of reddish-yellow mud and begin to laze, with dark tannic stain, wider and clearer. The Fall Line!

The plant life informs the traveler of the sudden change. Not now the scrubby oaks, turkey and willow and blackjack, but a dense tangle that stays almost evergreen the year through, surmounted by great live and laurel oaks, magnolias, gums—and in the swamps the gaunt bald cypress. On certain open pine flats the white honeysuckle, at the touch of spring, perfumes the soft air. The jessamine? Ah, that is everywhere! Festoons of Spanish moss—not truly a moss, but an air plant, which oddly enough belongs to the same family as the pineapple—may be seen everywhere, draping not only the trees but the telephone wires along the highway.

The geologist makes no wonder of the Fall Line that bisects South

Carolina between the border of North Carolina and Aiken County. He sees this as a former shore of the Atlantic Ocean at an ancient day after the present Appalachians were heaved up. Many a time afterward the sea invaded and retreated, laying down deposits that mingled with the waste from the highland sediments. But the Fall Line remains a distinctive separation point down to the present day.

Except for a few slight, sandy elevations, you expect this coastal plain to be flat. And so it is, except in one notable spot. Here nature, a deft magician with perhaps a quiet satisfaction in taking impossible rabbits out of hats, has provided a complete and delightful surprise. The High Hills of the Santee! From time out of mind this long narrow ridge that parallels the Wateree River for almost forty miles, rising sharply out of swampy terrain, has been called by this name. To imply that this unexpected refuge is a thing of beauty because it looms out of ugly surroundings would of course be contrary to fact. The lower lands are of an integrity and beauty no less than those of the hills. But to the prosperous planters of the early part of the eighteenth century this was a haven, with fertile soil, and they built themselves many a stately mansion there.

Here were clear streams and dashing waterfalls. It was a blooming colorful world when the dogwood and the plum, the azalea and the redbud, and above all the mountain laurel, paint the woodland. And what a providential haven it must have seemed in the days of the Revolution, to General Nathanael Greene and his worn-out men, when he made a summer camp here overlooking the streaming wide swamp of the Wateree.

At this point the reader may well ask: "Why do you call them the High Hills of the *Santee* if they adjoin the lowland marshes of the *Wateree*?" A look at the map will give the answer. Just near here the Congaree and the Wateree join to form the great Santee. The latter is the name for one of the three great drainage systems of the state.

Here, then, is a natural classroom where the budding naturalist—the school-age visitor—can go, in a few steps, from one life zone to another which is almost alien to the first. For every schoolchild who visits a state park—a state park that really qualifies as such—*is* a potential naturalist. Not necessarily because he is going to become professional, of course. But here love and understanding of nature are at your fingertips, undiluted by transfer in the printed word, or even in the photograph.

In these High Hills was laid down, fifty million years ago, a great bedding of shell life, at a period when sea temperature and other conditions must have been extemely favorable to the mollusk. Composed of sand and mud and lime carbonate, this hard rock is known as "coquina." In the construction of the bathhouse, the entrance portals, chimneys, and foundations at Poinsett State Park, this tough stone has been effectively used. High Hills "coquina" is unlike the rock of the same origin which is found in St. Augustine, Florida, and of which the Castillo de San Marcos there was built. Here, where Poinsett State Park is situated, ground waters circulating since the Eocene Age have changed the original lime of the shells to chalcedony so that the tough brown rock is actually composed of fossils, still preserving the delicate markings of the original.

Poinsett State Park—accent on the final syllable, Poin-sett′—was named in honor of one of South Carolina's most brilliant sons, Joel Roberts Poinsett. It seems rather odd that this man who was such a great figure in his day—natural scientist, statesman, military expert, architect, engineer, landscape gardener, canal enterpriser, and road builder—should be known to the public today almost exclusively as the man who brought from Mexico to his home plantation the poinsettia—the winter-flowering plant whose involucral leaves (often mistaken for the bloom) are such a brilliant scarlet.

Let us not exaggerate the achievements of Joel Poinsett. But he had an extraordinary range of interests and abilities. Almost any trip you may take in South Carolina will cross a trail of Poinsett's manifold works. Descended from the Huguenot stock that settled in the colony and made fortunes, Poinsett at the age of twenty-four was wealthy by inheritance and fancy-free. His father had intended him for the law, toward which the youth had a positive aversion. He wanted to be a soldier—and perhaps as a compromise chose medicine. Actually, though, his early years were spent in travel—Europe, Asia, and Latin America. A natural linguist, speaking several languages with understanding and fluency, he was the ideal American to send to Latin America in the days when our relations with those countries were almost nonexistent.

Thus Poinsett became the first accredited agent of a foreign government in Chile in 1812, and since at this time Great Britain's agents were bound to make things difficult for any representative of our Republic, Joel had a rough time of it. Besides, as a diplomatic agent of that period, he had a distinct flaw, the penalty for what was a supreme personal virtue. His passion for freedom—at home or anywhere—was such that he was known as the "flaming angel of democracy." He carried his ideal into his own personal life, for he deplored slave labor; partly indeed because he thought it ultimately destructive of good economy.

President Monroe sent Poinsett to Mexico as our first minister to that country. But the Mexican government wanted no "flaming evangels" and Poinsett was courteously asked to go home. President Van Buren made him secretary of war; that cabinet position has certainly never been occupied by anyone of more generous cultural endowment.

Poinsett's fervent attachment to the union led him to support President Jackson when the nullification battle was waged. It was not a popular stand in low-country South Carolina, but the people below the Fall Line could always recognize and forgive outstanding sincerity when they met it, as witness the case of Judge Petigru in Charleston, who never hauled down his union colors. "Everybody in South Carolina has seceded except Petigru," it was said in 1861. But the Judge never lost the esteem of those who knew him best.

Poinsett's greatest contributions were in the field of the natural sciences. In Washington he was an intellectual leader; first president of the National Institute for the Promotion of Science, an organization that was the forerunner of the Smithsonian Institution. To that Institution, Poinsett left valuable manuscript material, as he did also to the American Philosophical Society and the Pennsylvania Historical Society.

Joel Poinsett was buried at Stateburg, near which the state park is located. The grave is in the churchyard opposite the Church of the Holy Cross, which looks like an old parish edifice in England. So, near the state park that so fittingly graces his memory, Joel Robert Poinsett finally encamped, as did General Greene, upon what Washington Irving called "these breezy, health-giving hills" of the Santee.

There are five cabins in the park, also picnic areas, a trailer camp with electric and water connections, a lodge, a barbecue pit, and a lake with bathhouse. Many wooded trails lead the visitor to the quiet nooks.

It should not be forgotten that this section was also the home of "the Gamecock"—General Thomas Sumter. After the fall of Charles Town to the British in 1780, Sumter organized, with "Swamp Fox" Marion and Pickens, the forces that throttled Ferguson's Tories at Kings Mountain and so contributed to the surrender of Cornwallis at Yorktown.

(XIX)

STATE HOUSE — ANNAPOLIS

MARYLAND

On State Circle, in Annapolis

IT WAS the month of November 1783. Cornwallis had surrendered at Yorktown. The British were preparing to quit the city of New York. Everywhere in the colonies the patriots were jubilant. There were bonfires and much booming of cannon, though many thoughtful people, including some who had sacrificed to win independence, wondered whether a voluntary confederation of states would prove successful.

General George Washington was in New York, impatient to return to his Virginia home and to the properties that had deteriorated during his long absence as commander in chief. Not a penny had he taken for his services, and perhaps thinking mostly of the bitter dissensions of which he had been the victim, he remarked that he "would not take fifty thousand pounds to go through the experience again." Now he took leave of his officers at a little tavern called Fraunce's. The scene enacted there was deeply affecting, and shows us a Washington far different from the rather stern and immobile man depicted by the artists.

In the tavern were gathered only three of the twenty-nine major generals that Congress had commissioned—Henry Knox, von Steuben, and McDougall. Of the rest, seven had resigned, six had died, one was a traitor. Also present were a brigadier, a colonel, a senior dragoon. The moment was tense. Washington filled a glass with wine; the others followed his example. "With a heart full of love and gratitude," said the Commander, half choked with emotion,

"I now take leave of you. . . . I cannot come to each of you, but I shall feel obliged if each of you will come and take me by the hand."

A moment of confused uncertainty followed. Then Henry Knox stepped forward and held out his hand. But Washington, with tears in his eyes, could not let it rest with a mere grip. He threw his arms around this faithful and able associate and kissed him. That done, the rest were also embraced, from von Steuben to the youngest officer. Washington walked quickly across the room to the tavern door, waved a hand, and made his way across the street between a file of soldiers.

Now, with a stop at Philadelphia which could not be avoided, the great Commander was soon on his way to Annapolis, Maryland. Why to Annapolis? Because Congress was assembling there, in this charming little city at the mouth of the Severn, and it was before a lean and austere gathering of representatives that the general was to surrender his commission.

Another act, and a rather strange one, in the drama was to be enacted in the State House at Annapolis—in the very edifice which you may visit today. Not only that, but you may stand at the threshold of the very room where George Washington, reading from a paper that shook in his trembling hands, faced a group of men of very different temper from the officers he had embraced at Fraunce's Tavern.

The stop in Philadelphia, on the way to Annapolis, had consisted of a wearying round of festivities, of eager and adoring greetings, of wild public enthusiasm. Indeed, in Annapolis, the people of the city neglected no opportunity to show their love for, and their pride in, their commander. But here in the chamber of the State House there was manifest coolness; no intentional disrespect, but no tenderness. Thomas Mifflin of Pennsylvania was presiding at the session, and Mifflin was no friend of General Washington. He had been suspected of involvement in the ugly Conway Cabal, a plot to replace Washington as head of the armies. There was no definite proof of it, but both the commander in chief and Mifflin knew where each stood.

"Sir," said Mifflin, "the United States in Congress assembled are prepared to receive your communications." The general arose and stood before his chair. He had never been a ready speaker. He disliked loquacity and had warned his young friends against what he called a tendency to "babble." He was not made more at ease by the fact that when he bowed courteously to the assembly the bow was not returned. The congressmen were wearing their hats; they did condescend to remove them for a moment, but then clapped them on again.

If they wished to disconcert Washington, they succeeded admirably. The general stumbled awkwardly through his "communication." He was laying down his commission as commander and retiring to civilian life. In that brief declaration there was a great deal that did not appear on the surface. It had been suggested—and not wholly by unwise heads—that a democratic government would fail, and that Washington should be king. Such an eventuality would have violated every principle for which this Virginia gentleman had sacrificed; nevertheless, it had been widely discussed. Thomas Jefferson afterwards wrote that he was "satisfied that General Washington had not a wish to perpetuate his authority; but he who supposes it was practicable, had he wished, knows nothing of the spirit of America."

Perhaps Jefferson was right as to public sentiment; at any rate, this implied ambition could explain the surly reception given to Washington by the Congress. The experience with the British Crown's soldiery, over these terrible years, had evoked a hatred of military force. Besides, among these representatives of the states there were jealousies and suspicions, and no doubt an over-all fear that a confederation could not succeed; and out of their doubts it was easy to imply to George Washington that, after all, he was no superman, and that, even if he were, supermen would not be tolerated in the young nation.

Mifflin's reply, which he read with a distinct absence of warmth, was dignified. It applauded Washington's leadership and his "constant respect for civil authority"—a phrase that perhaps best showed how the wind blew. The reply was the work of several hands. Jefferson may have had the largest part in it. So, out of this Annapolis State House—still standing, still housing a legislature—George Washington emerged into the relaxation of a civil life that was to be his for only a short period before new duties were thrust upon him.

This State House of Annapolis has seen many other important events under its roof. The Jefferson Treaty Plan of 1784 was put forward here; and in the same year the Continental Congress ratified the treaty of Paris in which Britain finally recognized the independence of the colonies. In 1786 the Annapolis Convention, the first move toward the framing of our Constitution, met here. In all, this stately building has had more than 180 years of continuous legislative service, a record for which there is no parallel in this country. Only one other pre-Revolution state house survives; the building on Beacon Hill in Boston.

This state house was the third to be built upon the same site in Annapolis. Of the first not much is known, save that in 1697 it was described as ready for use, "a capacious and convenient edifice" of brick. It was destroyed by fire in 1704. Into that first capitol had been moved the records, "in good strong bags, secured with cordage and hides, and well-packed," which had been the fruit of the first legislative sittings at St. Mary's City. St. Mary's suffered a fate like that of Jamestown, when the capitol of Virginia was moved to Williamsburg. The first settlement became almost deserted in favor of the bright little seaport on the Severn.

About the second state house—or Stadt-House, as it was called for many years—we know that the residents became slack in its upkeep, and that Thomas Jefferson in 1766 snorted that the building looked as though it were "built in the year One." Indeed, there must have been an Annapolis epoch in which the townfolk were too busy with progress to pay great attention to beauty, for Jonas Green, the public printer, circulated a broadside in 1731, a quite villainous bit of doggerel, of which this is a sample:

> To try the cause, then fully bent
> Up to Annapolis I went,
> A city situate on a plain
> Where scarce a house will keep out rain.

The printer, being chided for this municipal treason, explained that the verse referred to a much earlier period in the town's history. But did it?

Whether Jefferson's scorn took effect or not, the General Assembly cast their votes for a new structure. A group of "superintendents" was appointed to replace the second capitol with a fine one—and a graceful building it proved to be. You might suspect that a committee of "superintendents" would come up with something like the culinary product of too many cooks. Not in this instance! Who designed the building? Several architects of the time have been mentioned, but it may well have been entirely the work of a builder named Charles Wallace. The *Maryland Gazette* of April 2, 1772, printed this item:

> On Saturday last March 28 about twelve o'clock, his Excellency the Governor, attended by a Number of the principal Gentlemen of this City,

was pleased to lay the First Stone of the Foundation of the Stadt House; on which occasion a cold Collation was provided for the Company, and after a few loyal and constitutional Toasts had circulated, the Gentlemen retired, the Workmen giving Three Cheers on their Departure.

His Excellency the governor was not present when the building was completed. He had trodden the homeward trail of all colonial governors for the Crown. Just when the state house was finally ready for legislative occupancy is not known, but there is record of a violent storm (West Indian hurricane?) in 1775, which tore up "a great quantity of the copper" on the roof, and "the market-house was blown down."

Certainly, at the time Charles Wallace built this state house, style had come to Annapolis. William Buckland was foremost among the "Georgians" who gave the town an elegance that still graces it today. For Annapolis had steadily grown and prospered since the day in 1650 when Thomas Todd set up a boat yard on the bank of Spa Creek. It was a notable port on the "tobacco coast," with a multitude of coastwise sloops going and coming from its safe harbor, and luxury goods being unloaded from ships from the West Indies and from European ports. Naturally, inns and taverns had sprung up near the water front. In one of these taverns George Washington and his brother Lawrence planned their trip to Barbados in 1751.

Prosperity; leisure; cultivation of the arts and amenities—these were here in Annapolis as everywhere. During the Revolution a Frenchman spoke of the city as "a very inconsiderable town [he meant as to population, thinking of Paris, perhaps] standing at the mouth of the Severn where it falls into the bay, of the few buildings it contains at least three-fourths may be styled elegant and grand. . . ."

From this same writer one gets a view of the softness that inevitably came to the colonial ports when they prospered. The puritan fathers of Boston had railed against these weaknesses of the flesh, and in vain. "Female luxury," our French visitor continues, "here exceeds what is known in the provinces of France. A French hairdresser is a man of importance amongst them, and it is said, a certain dame hires one of that craft at one thousand crowns a year." Finally our traveler looks at the State House. "It is a very beautiful building. I think it is the most so of any I have seen in America."

Old Annapolis has marvelously succeeded in escaping demolition from the push of contemporary urban development. If you will stand at the State House Circle, looking toward the harbor down one of the streets that radiate like spokes in a wheel, and if you let yourself into the spirit of the time, it will not be difficult to reconstruct the scene of that pleasant haven which Thomas Jefferson found "finer than Williamsburg, even though the *gardens* might be inferior to those of the Virginia city."

Much has been lost, but much remains, especially in the harbor district of Annapolis. It is good to know that an ardent and effective group of people in the city, who call themselves Historic Annapolis, Inc., are making excellent progress in their efforts to preserve the charm of the city. Careful and extensive research is being done, and much valuable information is being disclosed. But most important perhaps, the feeling locally is that Annapolis cannot afford to disregard the tangible remainders of the past which luckily she still possesses.

The old State House is lovely, and would be worthy of enshrinement if it were merely the place where George Washington rendered up his military commission. The Old Treasury Building, in the State Circle, is one of the oldest public buildings in the nation. The Flag Room in the State House contains what is probably the only existing American flag made in accordance with the Congressional Act of June 1777. The Governor's Reception Room, with its fine paintings, and its original silver doorknobs, will remind you that in the builders' time a public building was not merely a place of stark utility, but was in somewise an intimate "home away from home." And beyond all these attractions is Annapolis itself.

(XX)

WILLIAM B. UMSTEAD STATE PARK

NORTH CAROLINA

On U.S. 70, midway between Raleigh and Durham, in Wake County

A PLEASANT HIKE through the pure pine stands that now cover what were once ploughed fields in this part of Wake County, North Carolina, will quickly reveal the tragic story of what happens when man is concerned wholly with what he can wring from the soil, and not at all with what the soil demands from him.

These are agreeable resinous woods, here in William B. Umstead State Park. On an autumn day such as I had for my visit, cloudless and with the tonic of a stimulating westerly breeze, it was good to be afoot. But the former gullies, now being held firmly by the roots of the trees, make a rolling journey of what was once a flat plateau. And if you brush aside with your shoe the accumulation of fragrant needles, you see a floor decorated with quartz pebbles. The story jumps at you. A substantial topsoil in the beginning; then marginal; then submarginal; the fertility washed down into Crabtree Creek, and into the Neuse, and into Pamlico Sound: the farmer has let the soil wash down, and he is himself therefore "washed up."

I recalled that Colonel William Byrd, the salty Virginian diarist who ran the boundary line between his state and North Carolina in the early part of the eighteenth century, had made some libelous comments about his southern neighbors.

"Surely," he wrote, "there is no place in the World where the inhabitants live with less Labour than in North Carolina . . . where Plenty and a Warm Sun confirm them in their Disposition to Laziness for their whole Lives." One need not take this statement too seriously. The colonel wrote from wrath: he had made a number of appointments with the Carolina Commissioners, and these gentlemen had delayed. Besides, Byrd dispensed his acid judgments without partiality. He could be as cruelly ironical about the people of his own colony.

At any rate, it is not exactly laziness that impoverishes the soil. It is misplaced and ignorant human activity. Nature contrives to do very well if let alone.

As early as 1774 there were land grants in the section of the Piedmont country which is now Wake County. On a virgin soil derived from granite and gneissic rock and enriched with deep humus, the early settlers did very well. They raised tobacco, cotton, corn, wheat, and other small grain, potatoes, sorghum, and hay. The land was then, as the agronomists would say, "suited to agricultural use." In 1930, however, the land was "unsuited to agricultural use." Was it suitable for *anything,* in 1930? Yes; but we shall see later what that was.

Bad cultivation, sharecropping, merchant-credit farming, and then, after the Civil War, that greatest curse of all, one-crop production. These led to this end: in 1930 you could wander through these Piedmont lands and see abandoned houses and stark chimneys where houses had been, and where families had been reared. You might have seen a certain 10,000-acre tract on which only forty-six families remained. Ten of these, by professional report, were apparently "making a living," though certainly not a very secure living. Twenty-two families existed "without obvious outside help"! There were fourteen on relief. Many were without farm animals. In a last-ditch effort for survival "the people are obtaining income by stripping the last vestiges of timber from the area." It was a dark period, but there was a market for fuel wood in nearby Durham and Raleigh, and so down came the trees that were holding the remainder of the soil against erosion.

These quite hopeless acres became a demonstration project of the recreation potential of submarginal lands. In view of the enormous increase in population since that time, and of the consequent need for recreation facilities for bulging and expanding cities, the choice was a peculiarly happy one. Raleigh is rapidly extending to the westward; nearby Durham flourishes; and here is a forest area, now about 3,900 acres, within a short distance of those centers. Originally called Crabtree Creek Recreation Demonstration Area, because it lies in the watershed of that stream, it was later named, as a state park, for Governor William B. Umstead, who died in the middle of a four-year term. Governor Umstead had been notably interested in parks and in general conservation ideals. His home was in Durham.

Was this not a wise use of land? The people on these exhausted acres, brave though they might be, did not have a chance to lead dignified lives. The eroded, stripped fields have already been covered with thrifty pines, mostly shortleaf, but you may still see the furrow slices clearly where a plough wasted its time in those last years. There are sections of mixed pine and hardwood, and a large area wholly of broadleafed trees, predominantly oak, but with magnificent towering tulip-poplars in the lower parts of this rolling, fairly rugged terrain.

The depression, though it left bruises, had its brighter side. Many social advances were made which would otherwise have waited long for realization. Park lands were acquired which the rising prices incident to a renewed prosperity would have prohibited. The great National Park System itself was a beneficiary of that time of economic stress. The development of the Crabtree Creek area for public enjoyment, for physical and moral well-being, was one of many such happy issues. This wise use of the land having become a fact, the next question was where to go next. What was to be the nature of the development?

In William B. Umstead State Park the basic consideration "what shall we best do *here*, regardless of what might be advisable somewhere else," seems to have been well followed. North Carolina happens to be one of the fortunate states with one of its boundaries on the ocean and the other in the high mountains. The climate of the Piedmont region is far from intolerable in midsummer, but it is only natural that the vacationing residents resort to the shore or the mountains. Thus, for the most part, William B. Umstead is a spring and winter park. It could greatly increase its "summer business" if it changed the tenor of its present management.

At present this park has three complete group camps on the shore of a manmade twenty-one-acre lake. When the youth groups are there in the three summer months, there is naturally no opportunity for fishing on this lake, and since that is the time of year that fishermen from the nearby cities would like to drop a line, it is planned to create another lake above the present one, for boating and fishing. The benefits that derive from these group-camping activities are so vital as to need no comment. Many organizations are represented among the happy youngsters who learn here at first hand so many of the ways of nature which might seem dull when they come out of books.

Picnicking is available, of course. The nature of the forest litter and of the soil make these spots clean and inviting—if thoughtful users keep them that way. The hardwood section of the park is a sort of wilderness area—not quite a sanctuary, but bordering upon it—with a trail that closely follows its boundary line. This is only one of the several good hiking trails. Tent and trailer campgrounds, with individual campsites and modern washhouse facilities, complete the development.

The William B. Umstead State Park presents an unusual opportunity for the refinement of recreation. Without depreciating the many desirable physical relaxations offered by such a preserve, I feel that North Carolina here, and in four of its other parks, has realized that education can be fun; that there is a great challenge to any state to preserve and *tell* its natural and human history to its people. Especially to the youngsters, who are going to be the parents and voters of other generations; and above all, to tell that history in the best possible way—through actual contact under the guidance of a skilled interpreter.

If "education" is a word you shy away from, saying: "I just want to relax. I don't want to be told or to learn anything," just forget that I have used the word. Call the shot your own way. But an increasing number of adults who, to please their children perhaps, take a walk under the guidance of a good naturalist are discovering that *this* is as satisfying a form of recreation as they have ever known.

Modern man, unless specially trained, *sees* very little during his infrequent contacts with the wilder natural world. Children see more, feel more, smell and taste more keenly, but even they, urbanized as most of them have come to be, need a discreet introduction to the ways of plant and animal, in the guise of an expert who loves his field. The trained naturalist is the answer. He can readily transmit his knowledge and enthusiasm to the counselors who lead the youthful groups—for these counselors, too, can be very much ignorant of nature.

The aim is not so much the learning of facts as a re-association, a discovery of kinship with nature, so that, in the words of the lovely sign Roberts Mann wrote for the Cook County Forest Preserve, you accept an invitation "to walk, as folks have walked for generations, and be friendly with my trees, my flowers, and my wild creatures."

Consider what the schoolchild of North Carolina can see in this forest park, when his imagination is led to reconstruct the past. The forests of North Carolina contain today more kinds of trees than grow in the whole of Europe. There was a time when these Piedmont lands, now relatively free of woody growth, were tracts of deep shade, in which the wood bison and the wolf and the elk roamed.

The Moravians, when they came to these parts, saw flights of passenger pigeons which surpassed belief, and mention was made that in a single roosting place, 1,200 were easily killed in a few minutes. There were deer and wild turkeys; the streams were dammed by beaver. These animals and many birds disappeared, some of them never to return.

The wild turkey has been brought back and thrives; can you imagine the excitement of the youngsters in camp here when a big hen suddenly flurries across the road before their eyes, with her frightened maternal squawk? For a moment the place is transformed: it has become the land of Boone and the pioneers. The beaver have returned, too, and have taken well to their new home. You may see here and there one of the big muscular stems of the river grape swinging loose from a tree, where a beaver has neatly chiseled it from the butt, the inner bark of it being much to his taste.

For those who like to think in terms of the practical (just as though joyous understanding of nature were not practical!) it is suggested that North Carolina children—many of them future good farmers, we hope—can also see here the results of unwise treatment of the land. A little museum to be erected some day can display, in the very heart of the fact itself, the agricultural ruin that eventually brought this park into being.

PART 4

THE MIDWEST

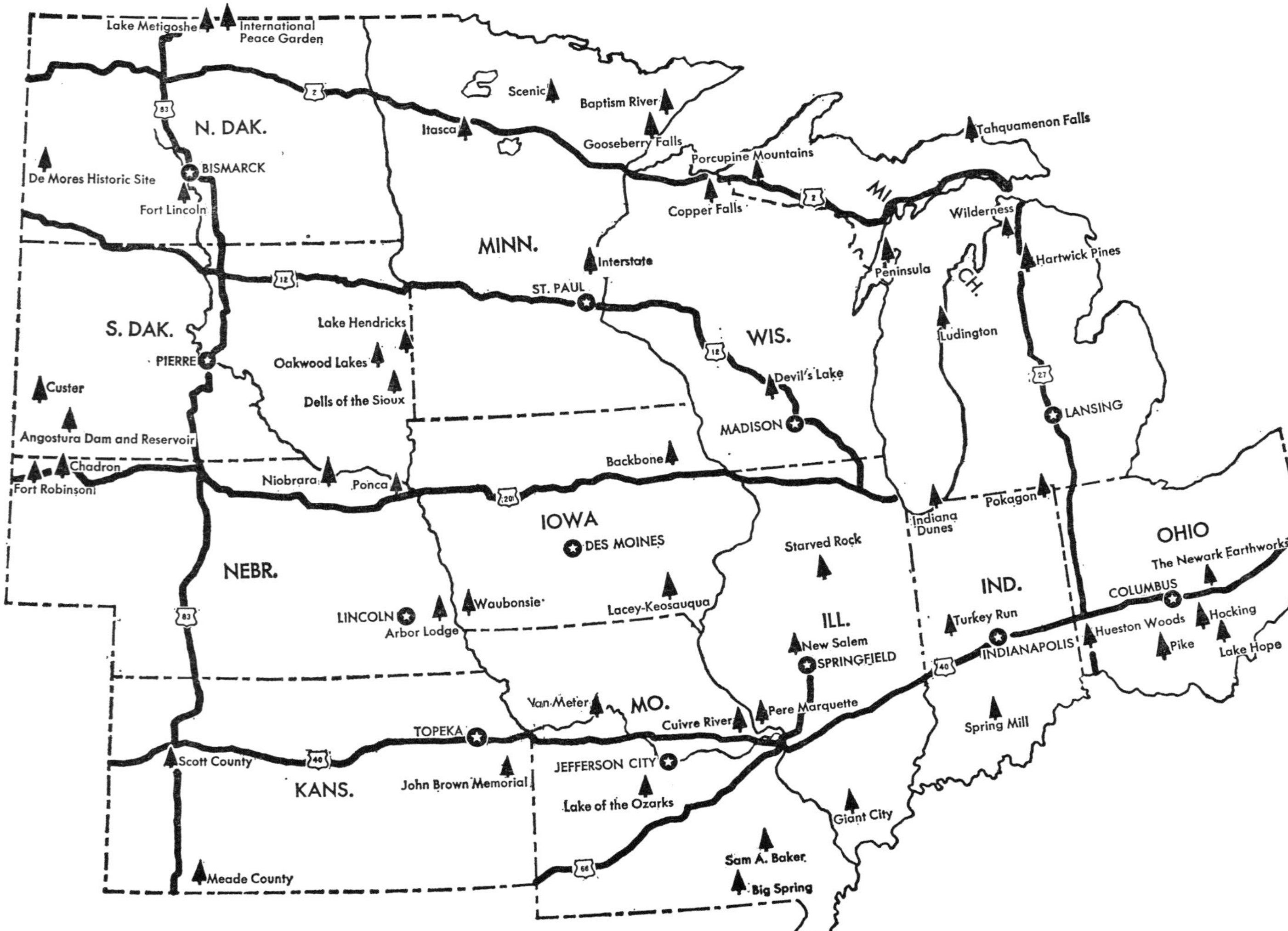
Lake Metigoshe
International Peace Garden
N. DAK.
BISMARCK
De Mores Historic Site
Fort Lincoln
Scenic
Baptism River
Itasca
Gooseberry Falls
Tahquamenon Falls
Porcupine Mountains
Copper Falls
MI
Wilderness
MINN.
Interstate
Peninsula
Hartwick Pines
CH.
ST. PAUL
S. DAK.
Lake Hendricks
WIS.
Ludington
PIERRE
Oakwood Lakes
Devil's Lake
Custer
Dells of the Sioux
LANSING
MADISON
Angostura Dam and Reservoir
Chadron
Backbone
Fort Robinson
Niobrara
Ponca
Pokagon
Indiana Dunes
IOWA
DES MOINES
Starved Rock
OHIO
The Newark Earthworks
NEBR.
IND.
COLUMBUS
Waubonsie
Lacey-Keosauqua
Hocking
LINCOLN
ILL.
Turkey Run
Hueston Woods
Arbor Lodge
New Salem
INDIANAPOLIS
Pike
Lake Hope
SPRINGFIELD
Van Meter
MO.
Pere Marquette
Cuivre River
Spring Mill
TOPEKA
JEFFERSON CITY
Scott County
KANS.
John Brown Memorial
Lake of the Ozarks
Giant City
Sam A. Baker
Meade County
Big Spring
83
2
12
201
27
40
66

(I)

BACKBONE STATE PARK

IOWA

Four miles southwest of Strawberry Point, off Highway 3 on State 410

EVEN BEFORE the inauguration of the National Conference on State Parks, the state of Iowa had begun to take an adult view of its cultural resources. Its leading conservationists seem to have realized that there were eligible spots of state significance that should be as lovingly preserved as any of national significance. And this was perhaps only to be expected of a political unit which contained such figures as Major John F. Lacey, Louis Pammel, and Thomas MacBride, to mention only three.

Congressman Lacey, as Chairman of the House Committee on Public Lands, had successfully promoted Mesa Verde as a national park. He was one of the first to stress the importance of setting aside the petrified forest of northern Arizona, and he lived long enough to see it declared a national monument. He urged the protection of the fine Bandelier archaeological ruins of New Mexico before they could be despoiled, but when these finally came into the National Park System, the valiant champion of the birds and the bison and the memorials of prehistoric culture was no longer present among us with his insistent voice. For one of the great achievements of conservation, the Act for the Preservation of American Antiquities, voted in 1906, we are indebted to Lacey.

What determination and vigor! Lacey always meant what he said, and there is a bit of local history that indicates how his declarations were implicitly accepted. Not far from New Sharon is a little place named Lacey. Here the major had deeded some land for railroad purposes, with the provision that if the railroad station were ever closed the gift should be considered null and void. The building caught fire and burned, whereupon the railway people swiftly moved a boxcar to the scene and tickets were sold as usual. There was no dalliance in dealing with the major.

On the map of Iowa highways you read this brief statement: "In all the park areas the natural flora and fauna are encouraged, and every effort is made to keep the larger portion of them in a natural state. In monument areas preservation and restoration work is being done in an effort to hold and perpetuate the State's historical background." This is the fact, and as a concise declaration of purpose it could hardly be improved.

Backbone State Park was Iowa's first venture into the field. No one would say that it is a place of national significance. But no one would question that here Iowa is preserving a precious segment of its inheritance. The greater part of the state—marvelous agricultural land, among the richest to be found in the world—is flat. But in the northeastern corner the land rises abruptly from the Mississippi River, and here the tributaries of the great stream wind through rocky ravines and wooded valleys. True, it was not in the vicinity of the Backbone that Marquette, after landing from his canoe on the west bank, "observed signs of human feet on a prairie trail." Remember, he said that "we silently followed the narrow path and after walking about two leagues we discovered a village on the bank of a river. Then we approached so near that we could hear the savages talking. . . . I asked them who they were. They replied that they were Illinois; and as a token of peace they offered us their pipes to smoke." Then come, in Marquette's relation, some pathetic words, in view of subsequent Indian history. "The chief thanked us for 'making the earth bright with our visit.' " A lovely metaphor of welcome! The white man, alas! brought murky skies in later years.

This visit did not take place in Backbone, but it is in this northeast corner that the limestone of the Silurian Sea now shows its mass—that dolomitic limestone produced in days when shell creatures multiplied abundantly. Their fossil remains are found through sixty feet of rock which was once sediment on the floor of the ocean.

The Backbone region is a strangely carved island rising from the gentle roll of the Iowa prairie. West of Dubuque, it lies almost in the center of Richland Township of Delaware County. The Maquoketa River here makes a strange loop. It bends back upon itself to the north for half a mile or so, then turns so sharply to the southeast again that at one point a good stone slinger could stand in the river and land a missile in water flowing in exactly the opposite direction. The Backbone proper is a narrow ridge lying within this loop. In older days, when folks felt closer to that fallen angel, it was called "the Devil's Backbone." But just *Backbone* seems to cover it.

Above the twisting Maquoketa the cliffs rise, sometimes sheer, a hundred feet or more. The weathering of this rock has created strange shapes—castles and battlements, slender columns, flying buttresses, odd representative figures of the sort that visitors like to contemplate and name. Just as Hamlet pointed out cloud forms to Polonius and made him see in them camels and weasels. "Or like a whale?" "Ay, very like a whale."

So altogether different from the Iowa of the tall corn and the well-nourished porker! No wonder it gives the people of the state—and visitors from elsewhere, too—a certain thrill of adventure in the wild. For it is, indeed, a pocket edition of wild country, and it still has stands of trees that were growing when the first white men came. Louis Pammel counted the rings of two white pine stumps that began their life during the Revolutionary War. A white oak was there when Stephen Long was cruising through that country. There was one pine of almost four feet in diameter which could be traced back to the time when this domain was part of New France. Pammel wrote in 1919, when this state park was about to be acquired: "The Indians protected these trees and why should we not do the same?" Of the ancient glorious trees at least two hundred are preserved. Considering what has happened to much of our natural scene, this is probably exceptional for a vulnerable midwest forest growth.

E. M. Carr, an editor and lawyer, was one of those who lent a voice and heart to the creation of Backbone State Park. He told about an elderly gentleman living near Independence who came every year to camp for some weeks in the valley on the west side of the Backbone and to drink the water from one of the springs nearby. This man said that the water renewed his health each year. Editor Carr's comment on this was interesting and suggestive of a fundamental truth about such places of refuge for ailing folk of any age. He said: "It is quite probable that the environment contributed more than the spring water. The Backbone is surrounded by primeval forest where the thousand voices of nature soothe the senses and help to restore overtaxed nerves. At night this man was lulled to sleep by the whisperings of the pine trees, and in the morning he doubtless forgot his cares and infirmities while watching the long high ridge curve its dark green back into the rising sun." So was a human need for wilderness seen by an Iowa editor in 1919. What shall we say of today's imperative?

When Backbone State Park was dedicated in October 1919, it included 1,300 acres. Later additions have brought in over 100 acres, so that now the Backbone is the central feature of what the geologist Samuel Calvin described as "a modestly picturesque" scene. Come to think of it, probably the maximum sense of restfulness will be found in that "modestly picturesque" region rather than in the neighborhod of the grandly spectacular. If anyone wants rugged trails which constitute a good introduction to the hazards of Alpine climbing, they are here. Yet the crest of the Backbone can also be attained by the ambler.

As Calvin suggested in his study of the area, it poses many challenging geological problems. During the glacial period, when at long intervals the northern ice was invading and receding, there was a fourth advance, called the Iowan, which apparently did not surmount the Backbone. Had it done so, surely the spiry towers and other carven features now seen would have been plucked and toppled. Thus the region is a fragment of what is called "driftless area" such as is found on a great and puzzling scale in Wisconsin. "If it can only be *let alone*," said this writer wistfully at the time when the creation of such a state park was in the stage of hope, "it will remain a source of purest pleasure . . . if avarice does not transform its forest land into pastures, or does not attempt to 'improve' it as a profitable summer resort."

It *was* "let alone," fortunately for the people of Iowa, and in the sense those words were employed. There are, in the park, an artificial lake, a large auditorium, cabins, shelters, and all the other facilities associated with physical recreation; but the wild aspects have been sedulously preserved, and the visitor may have (as in Rock Creek Park in Washington, D.C.) the gently thrilling experience of fording the Maquoketa four times, going back, as it were, to pioneer days. A concrete flooring under the stream will make it a safe venture for the tenderfoot, provided he does not rush into it at full speed. Put her in low gear and *ease* through.

A state fish hatchery lies within the park boundary, and just outside is a Conservation Department pine forest, where hunting with bow and arrow is permitted. As the number of hunters is limited, and as most people get nothing more with bow and arrow than a sore thumb, the danger to the deer is minimal.

(11)

BIG SPRING STATE PARK

MISSOURI

Four miles south of Van Buren, on State 103

THE FIRST DEED of land in the creation of this outstanding park was passed to the state of Missouri in October 1924. It must have been about two years before that Governor Hyde, skiffing down the Current River from Van Buren in one of those "john-boats" peculiar to the Ozarks streams, gazed upon a phenomenon of the first order and decided then and there that it should be no private holding for commercial exploitation, but rather the property of all the people of the commonwealth.

Here, at the foot of a rocky cliff on the tough limestone known as dolomite, amid boulders tumbled by erosion, there gushes an enormous volume of water, offering a spectacle that has no rival in any other state. Whether it is in fact our "biggest" spring may depend somewhat upon the technique of measurement. The total flow of the Silver Springs *group* near Ocala, Florida, is certainly much greater. The average flow of Big Spring and that of the *upper pool* of Silver Springs are just about the same. Why quibble? Both represent extreme examples of their kind. The maximum amount of water poured from Big Spring a day is estimated at more than 840,000,000 gallons. The water geologist can make something of that statement, but the average person cannot visualize such quantities. So it is better to put it this way: the average daily flow from this spring in the past twenty years has been more than enough to supply the needs of the whole city of St. Louis.

That is, after all, not the chief point of astonishment. This Ozarkian region of the Salem Plateau is classic for the great number and the volume of its springs. Before me is a map made by the Missouri Geological Survey, showing the location of 159 springs in the state. (Curiously enough, four of them are called Big Spring, and eight of them are named Blue Spring. The country folk ran short of names, like the parents of eighteen children.)

It was the *nature* of this mammoth gush that so enthralled me that I sat for ten minutes on a boulder, possibly with my mouth half open in shameful vapidity and just *stared*. Many a spring tends to "boil" as it emerges from the ground. But this monster acts like a giant suddenly set free from a containment that has put him in a frenzy. If you have ever seen your fire department attach a hose to a hydrant and then turn on the water, and watched the first burst come from the nozzle, you will have some notion of the fury of Big Spring. There is here a touch of the human fever to be free, after a long period of enchainment. Students of spring behavior ascribe this surge to some restricted channel or orifice lying beneath the dolomite rock.

The tremendous outpouring creates a broad river of clear cold water which, incidentally, will ensure the fisherman in the lower river a catch of the small-mouth bass that would not otherwise be found there. Crystal clear and cold—oh, very cold—the water from Big Spring creates what they call "Spring Branch," flowing a thousand feet or so to join with the Current River.

The visitor does not readily forget the trip he took in a john-boat from a point just below the bridge across Spring Branch, down to the Current River and beyond the junction of the two streams; great sycamores and other trees throwing shadows across the waterway, fishermen on the banks, quick glimpses of happy campers behind a screen of undergrowth—a fine sylvan prospect!

The john-boat of course is equipped with a motor, and perhaps it needs to be; for I forgot to ask the young concessioner who operated it whether the brisk turns were intended to give me an added thrill or whether they were meant to get the boat over shallow places on which a rower might strand. Just once he shut off the power and let her drift, so that in the clear water we could see very eligible fish—and plenty of them—waiting for the fisherman's lure.

The occurrence of so many and such great springs in the Ozark region has been the subject of much study and careful measurement; yet mystery surrounds the matter still. One cannot imagine anyone looking at Big Spring, the daddy of them all, without asking himself the question: Where is this water coming from? And next: Why is it in so much of a hurry? This is a region of many rivers. Can it be that part of their flow sinks into the ground through porous bedding and follows some subterranean channel till it finds an outlet like this one in Big Spring State Park? There was once a theory that much of this water has its origin in places of higher altitude, in surrounding states, or in the Rocky Mountains, or even in the Great Lakes. But that notion has long since been discarded. As to a source in the Great Lakes, this theory seems easy to disprove: many of the Ozarkian outlets are *higher* than these lakes.

Engineers have sampled the Current River, along which many of the largest springs are situated. They have found no important decrease in the river flow, such as would account for the great outpouring of the springs. Perhaps the explanation lies in the fact that this is all what the geologists call "karst" country—that is, a country of caverns, solution valleys, sinks, natural bridges, and like formations. Sinks, it should be explained, are caused by the collapse of the roof of a cavern which has been dissolved to such thinness that it can no longer bear its own weight. The pool area near the outlet of the spring in Round Spring State Park (not far from Big Spring) contains examples of this type of cavern. Suggestive, too, is the fact that from the base of the cliff where Big Spring brawls out of the unknown a number of "flow-tubes" are visible above. Water once poured out of these, in days when the Current River had not deepened its valley to the present point.

All this sounds rather technical. After all, "the spring's the thing." But most of the visitors at one time or another seek to know the explanation of what they see. During the summer season there is a naturalist in the park. He gives talks and shows slides in the amphitheater behind the museum; he leads guided hikes through the woodland, and on the whole conducts a program of rewarding interpretation.

Indeed, the whole Ozark region is open to interpretation, both for the visitor from another state and for the Missourian from some other locality. Geologically, historically, and in terms of social behavior, these hills are as fascinating as the southern Appalachians in the East.

Start with the rather teasing word "Ozark." It's an unusual name; it originated in the French *aux arcs,* phonetically identical with the present word. *Aux arcs* means "at the place where you find the bows," and this refers to the kind of bow used by the Indians to project arrows. The French, coming into what is now Arkansas, which was inhabited by the Quapaw tribe, called these people "ark-ansaws," and the fact of being with them was "aux ark-ansaws."

My companionable and intelligent guide, when I visited the Big Spring, as well as Alley Spring State Park and Round Spring State Park—all interesting areas, though the latter two are small—is himself an Ozarkian, from a cheerful little city named Saint James. In this city, by the way, there is a fine recreation park donated by a local family and beautifully maintained.

My trip from St. Louis down to Big Spring State Park showed me a landscape such as I had never seen anywhere else in the nation. From the time we entered state route 21 till we were near Ironton—much more than a hundred miles, as I recall the distance—the excellent highway led us through an almost unbroken green forest, predominantly oak of several species. Not primeval forest; certainly far from that. But the trees were of good size, and little cutting was observable from the highway. If one has the time and the desire to drive on a cheerful road on a summer's day, this is without doubt one of the most delightful. What the highway bypasses in the long distance I know not; but I should imagine not many population centers. For the rest, a few crossroad post offices or general stores—and that is about all.

We fell to discussing the Ozark people—evidently a folk much like the south-Appalachian dwellers. I asked: "How do they get a living in these hills?"—knowing well that the original forests were long ago brutually eliminated and that the land is not very productive in general. "A man has to be born in the Ozarks to know how to get a living here," was the reply: and what a succinct revelation these words contain! They suggest a remote little world where you expect little but you *do* know how to contrive that much; where you make do; where you eke out; where you can get only a little of this and a little of that, but putting everything together you maintain an existence that is satisfactory. A stranger to the region would starve to death pretty promptly were he not helped to find his way by these kindly, stubborn inhabitants.

Stubborn? Oh, yes. The Ozarkian cannot easily be pressured to change his ways. It puts his hackles up. He has been burning the woods for generations, thinking you get good pasturage that way. Tell him directly he can't do it and he tells you where to go. But there are other ways of approach; my guide said to me jubilantly: "We've got that burning licked." The way to effect a change in this rural thinking seems to be to prove to *one man's* satisfaction that burning the forest produces neither good forage nor good timber. Then you let your convert work upon his neighbors.

The 5,800 or more acres of Big Spring State Park are well wooded, but rare is the conifer in all that cover. Yet the superintendent who was "born and raised" in the vicinity tells me that when he was a boy all was short-leaf pine as far as one could see, save for the usual broad-leaved trees of the river margins. It is hard to imagine such a thing. What a change of ecology in the eastern Ozark region this suggests! The woods that give grateful shade to the fourteen housekeeping cabins are composed mainly of oaks, hickories, and the like.

These capacious cabins date back to CCC days, and they are still in remarkably good condition, considering the lapse of years. Who was the forgotten landscape artist who spaced these cabins so judiciously that no occupant feels elbowed and yet the most timid, when night comes on, have sense of neighborship?

There is a stand of the first-growth pines, happily preserved, not far from the town of Eminence. These may be viewed from the highway. Plantings of pine are being made on the national forest lands, and one sees thrifty young conifer volunteers in spots along the road. Perhaps some day may see the hills again wooded with what the lumberman sacked in times of seeming plenty.

The Missouri state park system, which for many years plodded along under frankly political guidance, has entered a period of great promise. The awakening of interest among the Missourians in their history and prehistory has already been mentioned. Beyond that is a mounting feeling that the recreation needs of the state's populous centers must be provided for. In many cases, as in Van Meter State Park, plans for physical recreation facilities can be combined with archaeological preservation and demonstration without prejudice to either. This arrangement might be true also at Boonslick, in Howard County, where there are four salt springs and one salt well. Salt was made here by the sons of Daniel Boone in 1807 or a few years later. In the year 1837 we find that salt making was profitable, salt being sold at one cent a bushel of 50 pounds. One cent! Ah, but the penny of 1837 was a mighty coin!

Better days for the Missouri park system—not denying that under the political spoils system good and loyal park managers do sometimes get preferment—began when the legislature set up a six-man bi-partisan State Park Board, with the Board chairmanship alternating annually between the two major political parties. A state park fund was provided for fifteen years in the State Constitution of 1945 and, in 1959, was extended by the voters until 1972.

"Those who know the beauty of the Current–Eleven Point country of southeast Missouri, and have seen its clear, spring-fed rivers winding among quiet hills have long cherished the hope that these streams would remain unchanged." Thus reads the foreword of "A Proposal: Ozark Rivers National Monument." The area, if it comes into being, will be in the National Park System. The Missouri state legislature indicated its support of this general objective by requesting Congress in early 1959 to enact legislation "so that these great scenic and recreational values would be perpetually protected from destruction by man-made encroachments." The National Park Service has made a study of the plan and the region and has published a report.

The proposed area would consist of about 113,000 acres, located along some 190 miles of the Current, Jacks Fork, and Eleven Point Rivers. The state parks, however, including that of Big Spring, would not be affected by the plan, except that in all probability the two areas, in neighborly operation, would find mutual profit.

(III)

CHADRON STATE PARK

NEBRASKA

Nine miles south of Chadron, on U.S. 385

ROGER TORY PETERSON describes the greeting of the western meadow lark, as it comes through the open windows of the automobile on the wings of the clear morning air, as "bubbly and flutelike." That is perfect. The liquid notes have something of surprise, something of challenge, something of an independent spirit which says that the driver of the car may have the surfaced road at his own pleasure, but he had better keep off the grassland border. Perhaps it was its nonconformist quality which led the people of Nebraska to nominate the meadow lark as the state bird.

Of course, this western meadow lark is not the exclusive possession of Nebraska. The state, however, has done well to honor him. It is hard to believe that a note so penetrating, so invasive, could be also so lovely. A certain tenderfoot tourist, whose driving experience had heretofore been restricted to the eastern seaboard where the big manufacturing cities were twelve miles apart, confided to me, when we were chatting in a Chadron motel, that the meadow larks actually frightened him. He had come down from Miles City, Montana, to Belle Fourche, clipping a small triangle from Wyoming, and then by way of Rapid City to this northwest corner of Nebraska.

"No," I said, consolingly, "I don't think you were frightened by the meadow larks. I think the birds just reminded you that you were already frightened. You drove a good many miles without seeing a town; not even an occupied house. You began to wonder why anybody had taken the trouble to build such a good highway through *nothing*. You kept your eye on your gasoline gauge and asked yourself whether, if your ignition failed, your bleached bones would be found two years later in this vast expanse. And just as you had concluded that you were alone in this hilly wilderness, you saw another car coming toward you as you were approaching a narrow bridge."

He gave me a sharp look, as though he had encountered a spiritualist. "That's absolutely the truth," he said. "How did you know?"

"Experience," I replied. "Long experience. It's a sure bet that the only car within twenty miles of you is going to reach the narrow bridge exactly when you do. It is Kismet. Nobody knows the answer.

"I am not a mind reader. As I say, it is experience painting this picture. Your road map indicated certain places on your highway that you assumed to be towns. You were disconcerted when you discovered that they were either mirages or places where the ranchers came in to get their mail. You did not know, however, that you were in a country where a motorist in trouble is never passed by. There is always someone, sooner or later, who will come and help you. People out here are 'neighbors' and heaven knows they have learned that the hard way. This is still pioneer country.

"The deserted houses you saw along your road were those of pioneers who had more courage than capital, and thus could not meet two successive grasshopper years; also those who did not realize that you cannot make a crop country out of land that nature intended for grazing animals.* Nature is stubborn about that; also unforgiving. The deserted farmhouses, with their eyeless windows, made you feel utterly forlorn, homesick, lost, and all but hopeless."

"Right you are," said my eastern motorist. "And was I glad to see Tchadron!"

"It is good to be in *Shadron*," I went on, "for that is the way it is pronounced, though I don't know how our folks here happened to make Chadron out of Chardon, which was the name of the French-Indian squaw-man who lived and trapped here in the time of the fur trade. Now that you are here, you will want to do two things that will add to your understanding of the history of the country and give you something to remember next winter when you

* Mari Sandoz, in *Old Jules*, quotes a bitter piece of rhyming carved into the door of a deserted house on those dry lands that rebelled against the plow:

30 miles to water
20 miles to wood
10 miles to hell
And I gone there for good.

The Octagon, one of the ancient preservations comprising The Newark Earthworks, Ohio

Porcupine Mountains State Park escarpment overlooking Lake of the Clouds, Michigan

A restored blockhouse at Fort Lincoln, out of which General Custer and his troops rode to their deaths at the Little Big Horn; Fort Lincoln State Park, North Dakota

Restored ceremonial earth lodge, Fort Lincoln State Park

A herd of bison in Custer State Park, South Dakota

The Needles, Custer State Park

Starved Rock, upon which a French fortress once stood;
Starved Rock State Park, Illinois

Covered bridge over the narrows of Sugar Creek,
Turkey Run State Park, Indiana

One of the buildings in the reconstruction of Lincoln's New Salem, New Salem State Park, Illinois

Rutledge-Camron Saw and Grist Mill, New Salem State Park

The Hope Furnace, one of the relics preserved from the heyday of the village of Hope in mid-nineteenth century when it was known as "a bustling little Pittsburgh"; Lake Hope State Park, Ohio

Devil's Lake, Devil's Lake State Park, Wisconsin

HERE 1475 FT
ABOVE
THE OCEAN
THE MIGHTY
MISSISSIPPI
BEGINS
TO FLOW
ON ITS
WINDING WAY
2552 MILES
TO THE
GULF
OF MEXICO

Sign in Itasca State Park, Minnesota, marking the origin of the Mississippi River

Drifting sands, Indiana Dunes State Park, Indiana

In Big Spring State Park, Missouri

Missouri Headwaters State Monument, Montana, marks the starting point of the Missouri River

are home in your suburban town. One is to go out about six miles and visit Chadron State Park; and the other is to learn something about this corner of Nebraska, which is historic ground, packed with the romance of our great western expansion.

"This little city you are in, for instance, was platted for settlement in 1885. While the eager crowd, hungry for a bit of land that would make their fortunes, were waiting for the word to move in, they lived out here at a place called O'Linn, about six miles west. O'Linn is just a memory now, but on that plain the Sioux and the Cheyennes used to have their famous sun dance, during which aspiring young braves, besides undergoing tortures of several other kinds, were forced to gaze at the full sun with open eyes; and why they didn't all become stone blind is as much a mystery as their secret rites.

"And here, too, is the site of Red Cloud's camp. You will see, from the nature of the ground between Chadron Creek and the sandstone ridge that the place was well chosen. About two miles up the creek were the camps of Swift Bear and Red Leaf. The Fifth Cavalry and the North brothers' Pawnee scouts surprised the Indians here and forced them to surrender, with the loss of all their ponies. This was in the fall of 1876, and it brought the big 'Sioux war' nearer its inevitable end."

"I want to know more about these things," said my tourist acquaintance. "I think I'll stick around here a while." I hope he did; for I was not exaggerating. This mountainous corner of Nebraska has seen great events; and the town of Chadron itself was one of the famous gun-popping frontier towns when Dawes County cowpokes rode in from the cattle country to shoot up the groggeries and dance halls.

The excellent hiking and nature trails of Chadron State Park reveal a rugged terrain that astounds the outlander who remembers that his school geography stated that Nebraska is a "plains state." Certainly that is true, but what such a visitor has forgotten is that there are low plains and high plains. He is here in elevated country. In Chadron State Park he can reach as high as 4,350 feet above sea level. Farther south and west, in Banner County on the border of Wyoming, there is a point that touches 5,430 feet, considerably higher than Denver, the mile-high city.

These deeply dissected formations, with their towering buttes and dark ravines, constitute what is known as the Pine Ridge country of West Nebraska. Sometimes local people like to refer to them as "the little Black Hills." There is indeed a slight resemblance; that vanishes, however, on closer acquaintance. No granite here which mushroomed into overlying sedimentary rocks, but indurated sands, the washings from the Rockies as they slowly rose in the Cenozoic era. It was during this "recent" (only 70 million years ago, perhaps) period that the Alps and the Himalayas thrust up from the sea floor —much of the landscape of today was then formed.

There was no hurry. The sands accumulated, later to harden into rock of varying resistance to the weather, and the hiker among the bluffs of Chadron State Park observes layers of rock of different appearance. The changing rate of the Rocky Mountains uplift did that—the accumulation of sediments was fast or slow as erosional streams gnawed avidly or gently. Later, when this Pine Ridge region was itself uplifted, the upper beds of rock took their turn in the never-ending tearing-down process. Water and winds have worked to create a topography which offers satisfaction both to the lazy trail ambler and the cliff-climber. The Ponderosa pine dominates the ground cover, but ash and elm and boxelder and hackberry, and even birch in shady hollows, give pleasant variety to the scene.

The hackberry, by the way, is a living tree with a link to the far-gone geologic past. You can find the tree flourishing today in many places in Nebraska; yet as a fossil it is associated with the remarkable Ginkgo Petrified Forest State Park in the state of Washington.

Chadron State Park came into existence in 1921. At that time it was exactly township size. From time to time the public property has been increased, until now there are 1,500 acres in the preserve. Considering its importance both scenically and historically, it seems that this is little enough. The opportunity available here to teach, in the most effective way, both the natural and the human history of a great state, is evident even on a brief visit. Something is being done toward that end; much more could be done with a vigorous interpretation program. Near the group-camp buildings, which have a capacity of 250 persons and are in active demand in the summer season, there is an outdoor amphitheater in a cheerful forested setting—an ideal place, when the fire is glowing, to tell the story of a region and its people, past and present.

Grasses are not thought of as scenic. Yet not the least important part of the old-time Nebraska—the Nebraska of the plains Indian and before him a more primitive resident—which is preserved here are the communities of buffalo grass, blue gramma, big bluestem (the dominant prairie growth), and the other lowly herbs that grow in this kind of land. Besides the meadow lark, the horned lark and the lark bunting and the lark sparrow chose these grassy domains as their nesting grounds; and they still do. The Merriams turkey was here, too, and though it was exterminated, it has been reintroduced.

Did prehistoric man live here? For many years the plains area—and most of Nebraska, therefore—was considered by archaeologists to be barren ground. Subsequent discoveries of great importance changed that view. Not far from Scottsbluff, which is now in an irrigated section, on top of an isolated mesa known as Signal Butte, a Smithsonian expedition excavated three distinct levels of human occupation, separated by layers of wind-carried soil.

No reason, then, to suppose that the ancient ones did not know this clear, sparkling Chadron Creek—now stocked with rainbow and brown trout for the fisherman.

(I V)

CUSTER STATE PARK

SOUTH DAKOTA

Five miles east of Custer, on U.S. 16A

THAT WAS a grand flash of insight on the part of Ralph Waldo Emerson to remark that "all institutions are but the lengthened shadow of one man." In the brilliant history of the National Park Service, now nearing its fiftieth anniversary, the shadow of Steve Mather is undimmed.

Of course, even the most inspired leader can do nothing alone. There must be, with him and behind him, a solid phalanx of workers and believers, full in faith. But the vision of the "one man"—and Emerson did not intend to exclude the other sex when he used the word "man"—his driving force, his personality, his stubbornness in pursuit of the idea—these after all are what result in the "institution."

In South Dakota, the existence of the great Custer State Park—72,000 acres in the heart of the famous Black Hills—represents the lengthened shadow of Peter Norbeck. This able son of a Swedish immigrant to our developing west, who became governor of the state and later one of its senators at Washington, was ever a stalwart friend of the National Park Service. He loved nature and its every manifestation, forest and plain, wildlife and geological wonder. Against formidable opposition he, with John Kendrick of Wyoming, brought into being Grand Teton National Park, so ardently desired by Stephen Mather, though the victory came just after the first director had retired from the Service he was instrumental in creating.

In the United States Senate, the voice of Peter Norbeck could always be counted on when the conservation of natural beauty was at stake; moreover, though many of his colleagues disagreed with what they regarded as his undigested notions of political economy, they held him in affection, as was demonstrated in 1930 when, in its last hours of session, Congress authorized a memorial to Stephen Mather, just deceased. Robert Shankland describes the unusual and amusing event in his delightful book *Steve Mather and the National Parks.* Congressman Louis Cramton of Michigan, another great wheelhorse, managed the bill for the memorial in the House. Nobody expected it to have a chance in the hectic hours of a dying session. "What Norbeck had done was to buttonhole all the public lands committeemen he could find . . . divert probable objectors into the ante-rooms, and clear the bill by unanimous consent." Cramton, also highly regarded for his steadfast adherence to his ideals, was able to get results in the House. Only legislators who have the confidence and affection of their fellows can do this.

It was natural for Peter Norbeck to regard as his greatest achievement the creation and development of Custer State Park. Up to Norbeck's second term as governor, this area was a game preserve, which had been founded in 1913, when the federal government sanctioned its separation from the Harney National Forest. The state park, when it was created in 1919, had been constituted in a rather unusual way. It consisted of 40,000 acres of "lieu" lands, which had been acquired from the Forest Service in exchange for scattered school sections and Indian lands. A fraction of the whole derived from private holdings; the rest came out of the Harney National Forest. At the outset, then, the park had more than 61,000 acres, and later additions have increased its size, making it one of the ten largest state parks in the nation.

When that wonderful scenic highway was being built—the one that leads the tourist through switchback and tunnel among the amazing needles that show the granite core of the Black Hills worn down into spires by the countless ages of weathering—Peter Norbeck was never long absent. He had tramped over every square mile of this Black Hills country. Now, when he saw some vista that was especially dazzling, he would say to the highway engineers: "Run the road here." "Oh, Senator, that's impossible. You see—" Peter never saw. He just said: "Well, run the road there, anyway." A resolute Scandinavian, deeply in love with scenery, was Peter. And they usually found that the road *could* go where the Senator indicated. It was expensive. But it was truly a paying investment, as every tourist to the Black Hills knows.

Perhaps the outstanding quality of Custer State Park is that it is an integral part of the region—the Black Hills of South Dakota—in which it is located. No visitor to the park could omit a tour of this region—on one side is historic ground, on the other a geologic phenomenon. It is likewise incredible that a tourist in the Black Hills region could fail to visit Custer State Park. The buffalo that graze in this park—as they do also in Wind Cave National Park nearby—belong there by sovereign right. They are all that is left, a vivid and picturesque memory, if you will, of the enormous herds that once governed the economy of the plains Indian. Custer contains about 750 of the animals, an adequate number so that they may do well. The deer and elk, wild turkeys, mountain sheep, and goats are all a natural part of the scene.

The Sylvan Lake Hotel, facing Harney Peak from the granite cliff of which it seems to be an integral part, and the park museum, both constructed of uncut boulders with the lichens still clinging to them, fittingly proclaim that they are no alien devices of office architects, but are the very Black Hills themselves. In the museum the pictorial record deals exclusively with the Hills—the early expeditions of the army into the Sioux domain, the geology and the forestry—all of which are skillfully explained in the exhibits.

And what are these famous Black Hills of South Dakota? Are they a "preview," or a forerunner, of the Rocky Mountains behind them? Not at all. On the contrary, we are told, they were there long before the present Rockies, or the Alps, or the Caucasus, or the Pyrenees came into existence. They were already being worn down by erosion when the site of the Himalayas was a marshy plain. A great granite dome, or batholith, slowly thrust up beneath a cover of more ancient strata, shouldering it aside as a humble mushroom might do with the woodland earth on a sunny morning after the first ground freeze of late autumn. You will see in these hills that the layers of once horizontal rock run evenly in concentric rings around the central dome—easily detected by the colors or by the mineral crystals shining from the matrix.

This is one of the most heavily mineralized spots in the country. In some respects—notably, the occurrence of rare minerals—it resembles the region of the pegmatites in New Hampshire and Maine—but here everything is on a colossal scale. Lithium minerals, beryls, feldspars, manganese, and bentonite—and emeralds, rubies, and sapphires—if you can find them. And—gold!

There was gold in the Black Hills. There still is. The Homestake Mines at Lead have given up more than a half billion dollars' worth of gold, and they are still producing. But those who visit Custer

State Park and the Black Hills with a feeling for the stirring frontier history of the region will not be thinking of the Homestake and its hoards, but of the military expedition of 1874 led by George Armstrong Custer—a thousand soldiers, and two gold miners—which Robert J. Casey, in his racy book about the Black Hills, has sardonically termed a "great mission of friendship into the Sioux Never-Never Land."

The ostensible purpose of the Custer expedition was to "obtain the most information in regard to the character of the country and the possible routes of communication through it." For this military purpose, the presence of professional gold miners would hardly seem necessary. Besides, Gouverneur Kemble Warren—the same Warren who took and held Little Roundtop at Gettysburg and saved the day for the Union army—had made a fairly adequate map of the region almost twenty years before.

It was a gay, shining show of soldiery that Custer led into Never-Never Land. He could not have imagined that the two gold miners, successful in their quest, were pointing the finger precisely toward his own tragic death on the Little Bighorn only two years later.

"August 2. Command still in camp. There is much talk of gold and industrious search for it is in the making. I saw in General Custer's tent what the miner said he had obtained during the day. The miners expressed themselves quite confident. . . ." Thus reported Colonel William Ludlow, engineer officer of the expedition.

At Fort Laramie, in 1868, a solemn contract had been made with the Sioux and Cheyenne Indians, providing a great area exclusively for their use and sustenance. White men were to be rigidly excluded from this area, which included the Black Hills. There is no reason to believe that when this agreement was made the federal government acted in other than good faith. The good faith of the Indians, in respect to treaties, had never been in question from the time of Massasoit and the Pilgrims of Plymouth.

But, just as Indian chiefs could not always control their young and eager braves, so the government in Washington could not always resist the pressure of avid fortune seekers. Custer's gold miners, you understand, did not discover gold in the Black Hills. For many years it had been known to be there. The Sioux and the Cheyenne were merely alerted then that the white man was going to break his promise again—that the only thing solemn about the solemn contract of Fort Laramie was that it would be repudiated with a solemn countenance.

Ah, had the concluding words of Engineer Ludlow's report been heeded! "The Indians have no country farther west to which they can migrate, and only the Saskatchewan country north of the United States boundary, which is still the home of the buffalo, offers a possible home. It is probable that the best use for the Black Hills for the next fifty years would be as a permanent reservation. . . ."

Coming over the Needles Highway, at the foot of a ravine, the visitor has before him what seems to be a natural jewel set in a matrix of rugged rock—Sylvan Lake! Actually, the little gem was manmade, the result of a prosaic purpose many years ago: turning the wheels for a sawmill. Here were milled the boards that went into the original Sylvan Lake Hotel, which was destroyed by fire in 1936. It is from the campground at the south end of Sylvan that the visitor sets off for the climb to Harney Peak, the highest elevation in the United States east of the Rockies. From its top, looking eastward, a granite wall is seen, and it is upon the other side of this ridge that Gutzon Borglum chiseled the impressive heads of Washington, Jefferson, Lincoln, and Theodore Roosevelt which constitute the Mount Rushmore National Memorial. The scale of this greatest rock sculpture since the days of the Asian potentates may be gauged from the fact that the heads are proportionate to men 465 feet tall, and that a man could stand erect in the eye of Jefferson.

The Borglum undertaking, viewed askance by many conservationists—purists, maybe—who felt that this assault upon the virginity of nature's own face partook somewhat of the insensate human pride which was punished by the gods in the ancient Greek tragic drama, has become one of the great chapters of Black Hills history. And many a conservationist doubter, standing with the crowds in the national memorial as they look up in hushed silence at these figures of the builders of the nation, is ready to concede that he may have been wrong and that the daring exhibition of combined engineering and artistry has justified itself.

At least this sight convinced President Calvin Coolidge, outwardly one of the least emotional of men. For when the funds for the sculpture were exhausted in 1928, Coolidge urged Congress to appropriate another quarter million for the completion of the work.

Calvin and Grace Coolidge, the Vermonters, came to the Black Hills in 1927 and made of the State Game Lodge a "summer White House." This is one of the never-to-be-forgotten wonders of Custer and the Black Hills. Nobody expected the supposedly dour Coolidge to accept the invitation to holiday in the Black Hills—but he came. It was viewed as a long chance that Coolidge would enjoy it if he did come—and he liked every minute of his stay. The crudest of Chamber of Commerce methods were employed—even to damming off a section of creek and filling it with hungry fish—and nobody yet knows whether the laconic and uncommunicative Coolidge was fooled or not. The chances are that he was not, and that he felt the special pleasure of the sage who knows, and keeps to himself, something which the "smart feller" thinks his prospective victim does not know.

Anyway, the Coolidges reveled in their visit to the Black Hills and to Custer State Park. What used to be Squaw Creek is now Grace Coolidge Creek; and from the top of Harney you see, to the south, a peak with a tower on it where a fire guard scans the surrounding country to detect the first wisps of smoke that might mean trouble. That peak is Mount Coolidge.

(V)

DEVIL'S LAKE STATE PARK

WISCONSIN

Three miles south of Baraboo, on State 123

FOURTH of July weekend! Has every family within three hundred miles of Devil's Lake decided to camp in this park over the holidays? It begins to look that way. There are already fourteen hundred tents and trailers inside, and fifty at the entrance clamoring for admittance. And still they come.

Wall tents, bell tents, A-tents, fly tents, pup tents, tents and more tents. There are swagger trailers, homemade trailers, station wagons with bulging sides, station wagons with bedrolls, and just station wagons.

"Is there room for us?" "Maybe. It's crowded, but you may find a vacant space." By driving your tent stakes across the ropes of a neighbor, with apologies for the intrusion, you can edge in. If you don't mind togetherness, you can have plenty of it now. At least half the campers are from out of state. So are at least half the visitors to Devil's Lake State Park throughout the season. The total number of visitors, for the year, will be well over one and one half million. Is that a record? For a state park of this type and size—about 2,500 acres—it would seem so. Of course, New York's Jones Beach, on the edge of the greatest population center of the nation, receives far more; but you don't camp there.

If you want to see for yourself how Americans have boosted the camp equipment business to phenomenal proportions, you can do so at Devil's Lake, Wisconsin. You begin to wonder how the property can take such a hoofing and survive. Only by expert management, such as is clearly demonstrated here, can an impossible situation be avoided. The officials at the park, when I visited it, were unexcited; all was in astonishingly good order; nobody was turned away; what happened was just what was expected. But what a clean-up-job! The park manager shook his head when I asked him what the projected new highway from Chicago would do to him. He just shook his head. No answer was expected or needed.

This "urban explosion" everyone talks about has come about so abruptly! Who in Wisconsin, for example, back in the early days of the century when far-seeing folks invited John Nolen of Boston to visit the state and recommend a few areas of park caliber—who could possibly have envisaged invasions of this kind?

Nolen was a good judge of the possibilities. He recommended four areas primarily. Of these Devil's Lake was foremost. The others were Wyalusing, Peninsula, and the Dells (or Dalles). Actually, Interstate was the first park to be opened, in 1900.

Before anything could be done about the Dells, they were out of the question. Private enterprise and cottage development had moved into that most attractive and significant region on the edge of the "driftless area" connected with the last stage of the ice age, to an extent that made acquisition merely a sighful might-have-been. Devil's Lake and the Dells offer a good lesson in preservation. Compare the exploitation of the Dells and the development of the park. In spite of overuse in a few spots, the park preserves the natural beauty and the geologic wonders of the area with affectionate integrity.

Just as the noble Palisades of the Hudson were being blasted away before the gifts and idealism of a little group of preservers put an end to the destruction, so Devil's Lake was under threat of quarrying when it was established in 1911, after the purchase of the major part of the land. In this case, it was the quartzite cliffs that were being demolished. You would not readily think of any commercial use for quartzite, save for road material perhaps; yet this rock, the product of the loose sand brought into an inland sea from the north a billion years ago, was found to be valuable, in selected pickings, for fine grinding and use in making a highly resistant fire brick.

It cost $175,000 of public money to move the quarrying operations to another location—a real bargain when you consider that the beauty and meaning of Devil's Lake State Park is inherent in these magnificient quartzite bluffs, where different degrees of weathering have produced so many colorful scenic effects, surrounding and overlooking a gemlike lake at their foot.

After the First World War a windfall of 800 acres that had been declared surplus by the federal defense authorities was added to the park.

When John Nolen recommended Devil's Lake for preservation, he probably had in mind not merely the physical charms of the region, but also the scientific qualities that make it an outstanding area of study for the children of Wisconsin and for guests seeking to know nature's ways. With excellent reasons, the University of Madison sends classes here for firsthand geological and biological study. The University of Chicago used to have a regular summer-session camp here; Northwestern University has sent many a field party.

As you approach the park from the south, about halfway from Madison you see what appears to be a sleek line of hills, with one sharp indentation. This apparent smoothness is illusory. The Baraboo Range has been pitilessly dissected by those bulldozers of nature—infinitely slow time, stream erosion, weathering—which make the old thought of *everlasting hills* a misconception. What you see here, in fact, is all that remains of a mountain mass that was once as rugged and probably as high as the present-day Rockies—which in geological reckoning are but children of yesterday. In this respect, one is reminded of the Arbuckle Mountains of Oklahoma.

The quartzite rocks that were folded into this uplift were the cemented sands of river burdens that came down from the north into an ancient sea. And this great mass went the way of all uplifts, the very height of which is certain to produce fast-flowing, devastating rivers. The present city of Baraboo, which takes an active and sometimes embarrassingly ardent interest in the state park, is in a lowland between two modest ranges that remain from the unimaginably ancient alpine heights.

And this city of Baraboo has its attractions, too. No place that has been the winter quarters of one of America's great circuses—that of the Ringling Brothers—could fail to inspire nostalgia in a lover of the sawdust. For the circus was one of our folkways—as charming a leisure-time pursuit as ever picked a yokel pocket. And the elephants! Except for the circus, our rural people would have known them only by picture. The big warehouselike building where Ringling's elephants used to spend the winter months amusing themselves in the ways of elephants, is still there.

All of which might seem to be drifting from our subject, but it isn't. For, if you drive over a strip of park road on the south side of the lake, along the edge of a scree of quartzite blocks that frost and sun have pried from the cliffs above and sent tumbling toward the waterside—along this stretch of road you are just where the Ringling elephants toiled. This bit of road was built with elephant labor, lent by one of the Ringling brothers who had a special interest in the park. I suppose some of the circus help lent a hand, too. Perhaps it is merely coincidence that just above this road, reached by a foot-trail on the east bluff, is a rock that looks to some imaginative people quite like an elephant, and nearby it is Elephant Cave.

One more thought from a lover of elephants before we return to geology. The sign of health in a working elephant—such as those who toil in the teak yards of Burma—is said by their mahouts to be that their ears flap and their tails switch and their trunks keep moving. I enjoy the mental picture of the elephants in Devil's Lake State Park, moving quartzite blocks—ears flapping, tails switching, trunks swaying, keeping in prime physical shape with such a worthy labor.

In the picnic shelter house at the south end of the Lake are four dioramas made and placed there by the University of Wisconsin. They are unusually good, uncluttered, readily comprehended without benefit of geologic skill. The first in order shows the east bluff of the present park at the Paleozoic period, when much of North America was covered by water. The bluffs were then being submerged under a burden of incoming sands. The second diorama shows the process by which an ancient river, having cut through the Paleozoic sediments, created the gap—that dent in the hills you saw when coming from the south. The gorge is today 300 feet lower than the level of Devil's Lake.

There followed the coming of the ice sheets, flowing from the north in a series of advances. That same ice invasion was a mile thick over most of New England, but here in Wisconsin was much smaller. Moving into the Baraboo Range, on its last advance, the glacial ice was split when it came to the east bluff. One lobe flowed into the narrow valley to the south, the other invaded north of the lake as far as the present golf clubhouse. So the two lobes of ice came into the gorge from north and south till they were less than two miles apart. There they stagnated, and as they melted they left walls of glacial till—boulder and sands—known as moraines. Into this basin the meltwater came and remained, creating the present lake. Just to the west lies a "driftless area," which the ice sheet did not reach. Wisconsin, of course, is notably a superb location in which the work of the ice age can be observed.

Devil's Lake. Why is an evil spirit the patron of this lovely bowl of blue water? The Indians named it, but they left no written explanation of their reasons for doing so. Maybe they sought to propitiate the dark spirits that lay at the bottom of this "bottomless" pit. For local tradition here, as in so many other places, firmly insisted that Devil's Lake was bottomless. Actually, the deepest spot today is fifty-six feet.

For those who come to Devil's Lake State Park for other than frolicking, the many fine trails lead to delightful field exhibits of exceptional types of "margin" floral life. This spot, just on the dividing line between northern and southern species of plants, reveals the river birch along the lake shore, large white pines on the rocky slopes, and a cover of oak on the bluff tops. My copy of Devil's Lake *Nature Trail Guide*, a self-guiding leaflet with lively references corresponding to numbered stakes, is a model of literature of its sort.

Unfortunately, in an area where a million and a half persons vacation annually, the naturalist must indeed be a philosopher, for even if the percentage of vandals were infinitely small, they would be enough to do enormous damage. So it is here; the patient naturalist bows to the fact and wonders just when it will be otherwise.

At Devil's Lake there are prehistoric mounds, too—birds, many bears, lynx, linear walls, indeed about all the fanciful effigies that art or devotion impelled the mound-building aborigines to create. The Baraboo region is exceptionally rich in these relics. Probably the Man Mound, not within the park itself but not far distant, is the most famous of them. The forms of deer, eagles, and turtles can be explained as emblems of the clans into which the tribes were divided; but what of this Man, which was originally 214 feet long and had a shoulder width of 48 feet? That is, it did before some farmer who preferred a corn crop to prehistory, plowed off the lower part of Man's legs.

Those who think of state parks as something more than romping grounds—important as mere physical recreations certainly are—will not forget Parfrey's Glen. True, this scenic and scientific spot, about five miles east of Devil's Lake, is not exactly a part of the park itself. The State Board for the Preservation of Scientific Areas set aside its 168 acres for preservation, with only the most rudimentary development, including a small picnic ground. During his fruitful years as professor at the University of Wisconsin, Dr. Norman C. Fassett constantly resorted to the Glen for botanical research, and there is a plaque to his memory at the entrance.

Here can be seen, in the deeply recessed rocky gorges, where pre-Cambrian streams wore through the tough quartzites and conglomerates, some of the original Wisconsin forest, magnificent pine and oak spared simply because the lumberman looked at the rugged surroundings and decided that it would cost too much to get the logs out.

Parfrey's Glen is not much visited; which is as it should be. There is too much of scientific importance here to risk vandalism. It is true that young couples from Baraboo, with a restricted and nocturnal interest in biology, come here, but they do the place no harm. The cult of Astarte never had any following among the Vandals of old time.

(VI)

FORT LINCOLN STATE PARK

NORTH DAKOTA

Five miles south of Mandan, on a county road

THE TOURIST INDUSTRY was not started day before yesterday. Almost from the time our ancestors got well settled on the eastern seaboard they began scouting the fringes of the wilderness, journeying "for to see and for to admire"—the White Hills of New Hampshire, the Falls of Niagara, the Natural Bridge of Virginia. In mid-nineteenth century Henry Thoreau told his friends in Concord that the whole world was right in that town. They doubted it—and traveled. Emerson warned his neighbors that they would find nothing in Europe that they did not carry with them. They thanked him kindly for the advice—and bought a ship ticket.

The Dakota cavalry post called Fort Abraham Lincoln had not long been established under the command of Lieutenant Colonel George A. Custer, in 1873, when the curious began to swarm out from the east to sample the frontier. The Northern Pacific Railroad had reached Bismarck, and the engineers were surveying for a practicable route to the Yellowstone and beyond to Puget Sound. If any such railroad were to justify itself, settlers must be moved into the new lands; thus, there would be traffic for the railroad.

The new line already offered inexpensive passenger rates. The bona fide emigrants may have accumulated slowly, but not so what Custer's wife called the "excursionists." She noted that the fort was inundated with them. They crossed the Missouri to the fort, "caring nothing about Dakota's agricultural opportunities," but apparently wishing to achieve the distinction of meeting a military celebrity, which George Armstrong Custer certainly was.

Custer was not exactly a wallflower when it came to publicity, but the tourists began to annoy him. According to Elizabeth Custer, a couple of persistent spinsters from Brooklyn refused to leave the fort without greeting the commander, thus forcing the officer into hiding for several hours in an unroofed hencoop, where he nearly got sunstroke. At least they returned home able to say that they had seen Custer's pet animals, a badger, a prairie dog, and a wild turkey.

The first fort at this point on the west bank of the Missouri was McKeen, an infantry post. It has been said that a hardened athlete, on foot and given enough time, can run down the swiftest of horses, because of his greater endurance. Whether this was a consideration when the infantry post was set up we cannot know, but soon a cavalry post was added. The two forts, joined by a short military road, were designated as "the Fort Abraham Lincoln Reservation."

North Dakota, through the agency of its first-class historical society, has preserved a remarkable cluster of memorials, not only of its own settlement and growth, but also of the people who occupied the plains before the white man arrived. Bitter and sudden may be the North Dakota blizzard, and blistering the sunbaking of the summer, but like all people who have valorously survived primitive hazards, these folk have an ardent love of their soil and a determination that their past shall continue to live. Of all North Dakota's historic preserves, which number more than forty, one may safely say that Fort Lincoln is the foremost.

It was at Fort Lincoln that the flamboyant reconnaissance of the Black Hills was organized, ostensibly to map the area (though that had already been as competently done as was need) but actually, as was well known to Custer and his men, to take a look at the prospects for gold, reported by earlier adventurers to be found there.*

The pressure to open up the Black Hills to gold seekers did not originate in military circles. Many of the top army men, including Custer himself, had at least mild sympathies with the plight of the hard-pressed redskins and were by no means proud of being obliged to make a display of force in favor of the repudiation of contracts.

But it was Custer and his brave men who had to pay the penalty. For, one tragic day, out from Fort Lincoln went a long column headed for Montana, destined to crowd the gathering tribesmen back upon their dwindling reservations. A brave sight indeed it was —cavalry, artillery, and infantry, pack mules and ponies laden with

* We have discovered a rich and beautiful country. . . . We have discovered gold without a doubt, and probably other valuable metals . . ."—Letter from Custer to his wife, August 2, 1874, from camp near Harney's Peak.

supplies, 1,700 animals in all, 1,200 soldiers, civilians, and scouts, and a line of wagons with forage that, as Elizabeth Custer saw them, "seemed to stretch out interminably." The band at the fort played "The Girl I Left Behind Me." Mrs. Custer learned on the fifth of July, 1876, that only the horse Comanche, of all Custer's command on the bluffs above the Little Big Horn, was still alive.

For many years the Custer massacre was to be a vivid historical event in the minds of young Americans, even those whose knowledge of Gettysburg and Shiloh were dim. Of course, Chiefs Gall, Crow King, Sitting Bull, and Crazy Horse never spoke of a "massacre." They regarded it as a military operation, a successful one.

The last garrison to occupy Fort Lincoln moved out in 1891. The buildings had already begun to deteriorate. There was no longer any need for the post. Still, the structures were there and no great repairs would have been required for historical preservation if an extraordinary looting spree had not taken place. Beginning with a foray here and there, the neighboring settlers in 1894 moved in for desirable building material. When they finished, only three buildings were left intact. The house of General Custer was gone. About $1,000 worth of lumber was all a government appraiser could find there in 1895. It seems spendthrift carelessness on the part of settlers to have left so much! "About all that remained were a few stones and bricks marking the foundations of the buildings which a few years before graced one of the outstanding military posts in the Northwest."

Fortunately the work programs of the CCC and WPA made possible the reconstruction of enough buildings at Fort Lincoln, including the McKeen Blockhouse, to convey an idea of frontier military life. A fine museum, of native granite and timber, houses a brilliant amplification of what the visitor sees in the reconstruction. To the original grant of seventy-five acres made by the federal government to the State Historical Society, the whimsical Missouri, in one of its channel changes, added considerably more, with the result that this is now a park of good size for picnics and simple recreation.

But the interest of Fort Lincoln does not rest in the restored military post. Even more interesting to many a visitor, and especially to those who come from outside the state, is the restoration of the old Mandan Indian village within the park boundaries. As early as 1750 the Mandans were established in nine villages, all but two on the west side of the Missouri River. When Lewis and Clark wintered here during their exploration of the northwest, the Mandans were still a numerous and prosperous nation, but Slant Village, seen within this park, had already been destroyed, probably deliberately by the Mandans themselves, as archaeological investigation suggests. "Slant" was just what the word indicates—a village built on sloping ground.

We know how friendly and helpful these settled Mandans, who lived in well-built, dome-shaped, earth lodges, were when the whites first came among them. If afterward they lost some of their ardor for white neighbors, it was only natural. As one of their chiefs tells it: "In my young days there were no white men, and we knew no wants. . . . The white people came; they brought with them some good, but they brought smallpox and they brought evil liquors; the Indians since diminish and they are no longer happy." The chief might have mentioned other results of contact with whites, which were not parlor conversation in Queen Victoria's time. At any rate, this excellent Indian nation which some say once numbered enough to muster 15,000 warriors—shrewd traders, good economists, peaceful except when the Sioux and Assiniboin tried to levy on them—dwindled from the ravages of booze and disease to the point where they practically ceased to exist.

The Mandan earth lodge, though it may have originated in the lower Mississippi Valley, was as well suited to the physical features of Dakota—"making do with whatever is at hand"—as the sod houses that the white settler occupied in the early days, a few of which can still be seen in the state. Maximilian, the Prince of Wied, who came among the Mandans in the course of his rugged travels, described these lodges as being usually thirty or forty feet in diameter, except where used for ceremonial purposes, and from ten to twenty feet in height. "The huts are of circular form, slightly vaulted, having a sort of portico entrance . . . in the center of the roof is a square opening for the smoke to find vent, over which is a circular sort of screen made of twigs, as a protection against wind and rain. . . ." And perhaps also to resist an inrush of mosquitoes, who were described by Mrs. Custer in her *Boots and Saddles* as being murderous in her fort days.

The Mandan women did most of the work in the construction of the earth lodges. It would be easy to jest that this was characteristic. But among the Mandans it may have been for other reasons that the women had become the house planners and constructors. In fact, it was long-accepted custom that the erection of the house was a function solely reserved for the woman of each family. Thus, some years ago, "when the time came for laying out the ground plan of the earth-lodge on the Capitol grounds at Bismarck, two women from Fort Berthold, Mrs. Holding Eagle (Scattered Corn, daughter of Move Slowly) and Mrs. Sitting Crow, were secured to preside at the essential rites and ceremonies accompanying this important tribal performance."

All the restored lodges at Fort Lincoln are open to the public, and one of them has been furnished with such equipment as was used by a typical Mandan family. They had—among other kinds—*canopied* beds! An odd luxury, the visitor may think, as he gets in this fine park a clear picture of the life and culture of the prosperous and happy people who once dwelled here.

The Mandans, too, though they do not have a historical society and are now so few in number, still treasure their past. When the restoration of Slant Village was in progress, they enthusiastically lent "their invaluable assistance."

(VII)

HOCKING STATE PARK

OHIO

Twelve miles southwest of Logan, off Highway 374

In the oil and gas fields, to the east of Hocking State Park, the drillers talk of a certain "Big Injun sand," which they strike some hundreds of feet below their rig. Oil drillers have a language of their own, usually based upon a shrewd knowledge of geological facts or local history. In this case, they are probably making humorous reference to a cliff on the Licking River east of Newark, where the Indians once painted a big black hand pointing toward a ridge on which excellent flint for arrowheads and spearpoints could be found. The geologists have chosen, since this cliff exposes an interesting type of rock, to call the formation the "Black Hand" sandstone.

The casual visitor may ask what difference it makes what geologists, in their shorthand language, call any particular kind of rock. The visitor has come to look, to admire, to rest, to picnic, or merely to find a cool valley where on a blistering day he can get away from the heat—has he not? Yes, admittedly, with only one reservation. Despite the fact that the ordinary visitor has not come with the primary purpose of receiving a short course in geology, he cannot visit a park like Hocking without being curious. The chipmunk does not fatigue his brain wondering what makes the sap ascend the oak tree. The fact that it may bear acorns satisfies him. But the endless curiosity—about why, and when, and how, and what—is the spark that has brought man to the point where he is.

No intelligent adult, and no lively child, can visit this extraordinary area without asking himself, or somebody else, how these scenic wonders came to be. What happened, to create all this? Nature did it, yes; but why here, rather than somewhere else in Ohio? And under what circumstances?

There is one brief—and reasonably accurate—answer to such questions: *Black Hand sandstone.* Acted upon in many ways, under many conditions, through the countless centuries of geologic time: of course. But still, it was only the kind of sandstone called Black Hand which could result in the strange and beautiful effects seen in the six units of the park. And though this is all part of the same general romance of natural history, the amazing thing about these six separate areas is that each one has a perfectly clear character and quality of its own. You cannot content yourself, after a visit to Old Man's Cave, by saying: "I know what Hocking State Park is like, now." Indeed, your life isn't long enough to know what it is *all* like, for in this rugged domain there are places that you will never reach. But when you have gone in turn from Old Man's Cave to Ash Cave, and to Rock House, and to Cedar Falls, and to Conkle's Hollow, and finally to Cantwell's Cliffs—only then can you confidently claim to know what Hocking State Park is like—and how the puzzling Black Hand sandstone behaves.

If this Black Hand rock, in some parts of the park more than two hundred feet thick, had all been of the same character, or composition, the picture would have been entirely different. But this rock is divided into three distinct zones. The upper zone is firmly cemented and stoutly resists weathering. The lowest zone is similar, but you will probably see it only at the lower falls at Old Man's Cave. The middle zone, on the contrary, is readily susceptible to weathering and erosion. Throughout the park can be seen big and little instances of the results of this zonal difference in the sandstone.

This difference accounts for what are called the "caves." They are not true caves, though none the less spectacular for that. They are really "rock shelters," similar to the many that housed the prehistoric people of our Southwest. For that matter, there can be little doubt that these "caves" of Hocking were used by generations of historic Indians. Otherwise, why would there have been found in Ash Cave such quantities of ashes, the result of years of campfires? As late as 1890 the pile of ashes was three feet deep, a hundred feet long, and thirty feet wide. A good many primeval forest trees went into the making of such an accumulation!

The approach to Ash Cave leads to a surprise. You have been coming through a narrow gorge, densely covered with many kinds of hardwoods and hemlocks and pines—and suddenly you emerge from the forest in full face of the great overhang, the largest overhanging ledge among the Hocking Park units. It is a big horseshoe with an arc of 700 feet and nearly a hundred feet high. As usual in Hocking, a little cataract comes pouring down into a pool at the foot. This stream is a small one, save at times of heavy rainfall, but even so, the spray from the plunge of the water eats constantly at the softer zone of the sandstone, "sapping" like a military engineer of the old days. Still, one wonders if there must not have been, in times past, much greater flows of water from above, to create the undercutting now seen.

The Ohio Federation of Women's Clubs voted Old Man's Cave as the outstanding beauty spot of the state. Certainly it is the most popular of the six associated areas. Is it the provocative name? It *is* beautiful, no question of that; but other eyes might choose elsewhere. For my own part, I found that Cedar Falls pleased me best. It gave me that little tug at the heart that cannot be explained or justified; it just *is*. Let us take cheerful thought that there is some special attraction for everyone. Admission is free: you take your choice.

It is probably true that Old Man's Cave is the most extensive example of what the forces of erosion can do when a softer layer underlies the more resistant rock. If you start at the upper end of the gorge and go down over the easy trail, you see Old Man's Creek cascading over the harder rock, terminating in the high Upper Falls. Here the undercut ledges are clearly the result of older streams of water, finally deepening the bed to its present level.

Numerous potholes tell the story of swirling rock material that gradually bored down into the sandstone. In the north wall of the gorge, high above the stream, is the great overhang where, the story goes, a fugitive from West Virginia, after the Civil War, lived as a hermit for many years. It was an ideal place for a hermit then. In these days he would be somewhat annoyed by the thousands of visitors who come every year to clamber among the boulders and cool themselves in the dense shade, where remnants of the ice-age plants are still growing out of reach of the sunlight.

Rock House, unlike the cavelike shelters of the overhangs, is a true cavern, though still not like the caves that are found in limestone formations. At the head of a valley, a sheer cliff of the Black Hand rises from the bed of the stream. Here is a natural wonder that the casual visitor finds difficult to understand. What produced this house? Certainly not the same forces that acted to create Old Man's Cave. It is a tunnellike passageway through the cliff, open at both ends and two hundred feet long, with windows topped by Gothic-like arches and supporting columns between. Geologists tell us that the cavern resulted from the "jointing" of the rock; but what force actually excavated this great room? Apparently it was not done by water. What, then? The explanation that weathering was responsible, breaking down the rock into grains of sand that were removed by wind in the course of a million years, sounds fantastic, but the experts assure us that it is true.

Rock House has been a tourist attraction for more than a century. As early as 1835 "a 16-room hotel, complete with ballroom and livery stable," standing where the park shelter is today, housed many an important person. There was even a United States post office in the hotel.

Less welcome guests have made use of Rock House over the ensuing years. It was an ideal hideout for highway robbers, horse thieves, and other fugitives, and also for the elusive bootlegger who flourished in the days of prohibition.

Cantwell Cliffs is the most northerly of the Hocking State Park units. Here the erosion of Buck Run has produced another kind of scenic phenomenon. It is a showy example of the manner in which the undermining in this kind of rock creates one escarpment after another, as the resistant cap rock collapses when the middle zone is eaten away. The trail here winds its way through narrow passages among huge blocks of fallen, "slumped" rock. One of these narrow passages is called "Fat Woman's Squeeze." It isn't clear why the sex distinction was made. According to life insurance actuaries, overweight is impartially distributed. Maybe some plump lady actually got stuck, though in truth the place is not quite as narrow as it looks.

Between Rock House and Old Man's Cave is Conkle's Hollow. This is real, almost untouched wilderness. The trail up the gorge is for those who like a rugged challenge. The gorge is probably the deepest in Ohio. Hemlocks, birches, and other hardwoods screen out the sunlight. Near the upper end of the hollow the cliffs are almost vertical, while at the back end of the gorge a series of waterfalls cascade into a small plunge pool.

On the west wall of the chasm is a large block of sandstone on which is carved:

W. J. Conkle 1797
A. O. Cow . . . 1898

The later inscription, made by a Mr. Something Cow, is unimportant, despite what Mr. Cow may have imagined; but the Conkle inscription, dimmed by the years, records what is probably a relic of the first exploration by a white man in this area.

Downstream from the Lower Falls of the area of the Old Man's Cave is another gorge, wider and deeper than the first, called the Lower Gorge. If you were to follow the trail through this, it would lead you to Queer Creek and so on to Cedar Falls, and you would then be halfway between the two caves of Ash, and the Old Man.

In order to preserve the unspoiled beauty of Cedar Falls, the Ohio Division of Parks has provided only the bare necessities for visitors. I hope it may always be so; for this is as charming a spot as can be found anywhere. It is not only the falls themselves weaving lacy ribbons along two grooves in the rock face to the pool below; the forest growth, with great sleek beaches—and what is lovelier than the delicate bark of this tree, even when old?—rearing their heads far above the fern-covered glen, gives the impression of a happy island saved from the march of enterprise.

Here at Cedar Falls there is quiet; there is restoration for a tired mind or body. Is it not exciting, like the tumbling chasm that brings the major number of visitors to the cave of the hermit. Easy of access, perhaps it is the ideal area in the park for—what shall I say? the *mature?*

Ohio has done well to preserve these choice areas, and also the considerable surrounding state forests. The region, of course, was well known many years ago and was popular for picnic gatherings despite the poor means of access. Beginning with the acquisition of a block of land that included the Old Man's Cave region, the state has widened its holdings since 1924 to include many thousands of acres of forest, and the cluster of park units here described. The alluring qualities of these parks are demonstrated by the fact that, though most of the usual facilities for physical recreation are missing, they draw an increased number of visitors year after year.

(VIII)

INDIANA DUNES STATE PARK

INDIANA

Ten miles west of Michigan City, on State 49

AT THE ENTRANCE to Indiana Dunes State Park is a huge glacial boulder. There is no label on it to tell where it was torn from a cliff or where it was locally stranded. At first glance, it might seem out of place here among these hills of sand, ancient woods, and swamps. But, however remotely, its story is that of the major forces that created both the dunes and the great Lake Michigan whose waves have put the sand ashore. The Dunes are just another and later chapter in the book of a mysterious cold spell we call the ice age.

Over the tollhouse, at this entrance to the park, is an inscription that causes many a visitor to ponder. Perhaps it is rather cryptic to most, though there are many who, on reflection, see the thrilling scientific truth that lies behind the poet's expression. It is a quotation from Francis Thompson:

> All things by immortal power, near or far,
> Hiddenly to each other linkéd are,
> Thou canst not stir a flower
> Without troubling of a star.

Of course this quotation could be justly used in any national or state park, or indeed any place where nature is given elbow-room. But if this inscription was put at the Dunes by Colonel Richard Lieber, as I suspect it was, he chose a place where it has a special significance. Nowhere more easily than among sand dunes is the delicate balance of the organic and inorganic world observed. The "balance of nature," we commonly call it; but we must not look upon this as a frozen equipoise. Quite the contrary.

Here at Indiana Dunes we see the stark struggle for transitory victory at every stage of change, constant change. The tree and shrub bend before the storm of drifting sand; they are overcome and buried deep; they lie there for years, to reappear as white skeletons when a new series of storms has torn the cover from their tomb; so it goes endlessly. On a day when that north or northwest wind blows down the long sleeve of the lake, the visitor will find a little newly made dune on the paved walks near the pavilion. It is a very tiny dune, this at his feet. Multiply it by the years, by the centuries, by unrealized lapses of time; set the grasses and shrubs and trees upon their task of tying down these hills of sand—succeeding here, failing there, creating a forest here only to lose it at some other point—and you have in miniature the story that explains these two thousand acres on which so many millions of people now joyously make holiday.

"Thou canst not stir a flower. . . ." No; nor can you know just which grain of sand, in which gale that comes down the lake, will set at work forces resulting in strange changes in duneland. But "a star" has been "troubled."

One writer about the dunes mentions that the topography of a certain part was so changed in two weeks' time as hardly to be recognized. Another observer speaks of young trees three feet high being completely buried within six hours. Yet the casual visitor sees that a balance is maintained, and probably will be till some far off time when this particular struggle is ended and a new kind of balancing begins.

When John Tipton, in 1821, was surveying this strip of dune country to set a boundary line between Indiana and Illinois, a big crescent of sand hills and wooded ridges extended from above Michigan City well into what is now the Chicago district. The dunes that once stood around Gary, and from there into the second-largest city in the United States, have been of course long since scooped away to make place for factories.

Even when John Tipton saw the dunes in their pristine natural elegance, he didn't care for what he saw. In those days agricultural land was desired above all things, and what use were small mountains of beach sand, with intervening marshy spots that looked as though they would defy drainage? His report was that these lands "can never admit of settlement nor never will be of much service to our state."

No blame to surveyor John. Within his knowledge and reasonable assumption, he was right. The amazing industrial development which was to make these waste lands of incalculable value as an escape from civilization was something nobody could vision. Men were then applying their brawn and skills to abolishing the wilderness. The time has arrived when men look anxiously around them to preserve the last vestiges of that all but vanished wild.

Three miles of perfect white sand beach invite the many millions of urban dwellers to come out from the umbrella cover of huddlement and acrid smoke, of jangled nerves and fevered competition in the market place, to enjoy the healing effect of what is perhaps the most rudimentary human contact with nature: the touch of sand and water on the body, the basking in full sunlight to the music of splashing waves, the swimming, the idling in a boat with rod in hand, the filling of lungs with unpolluted air. Some would have us believe that man evolved from a creature that came out of the sea. Certainly he loves to go back to the water, whether it be sea, lake, or pond.

The quarter million people who come every year to Indiana Dunes State Park are mostly interested in a day in the sun and in contact with lake water. It would be merely the echo of wistfulness to suggest that more than a minority (an always increasing minority, however) will make use of the park's other qualities.

These other qualities are transcendent, and are being stoutly preserved. On this state park, mind you, except for access ways, there are no roads on which to speed and so see nothing whatever. This is a park with a magnificent beach, and you can get to it easily. But for those who seek to come closer to nature, there are just trails, cleverly planned trails which, when followed with leisurely enjoyment, open up the Book of the Duneland. When you have made the tour afoot, you have gained an understanding that cannot come to you by hearsay.

You will, by following such trails, see the creation of the dune country from first step to last; or rather, I should say, from a beginning to a climax, since what appears to be a dune in its finished and permanent stage, clad with an old growth of black oak and other girthy trees, may be only a step in another, longer cycle of change. You will have seen first the unbound, shifting sand of the shoreline, prey to every puff of wind; above that, the grasses taking advantage of a quiet nook to bind the wanderer before he becomes a giant; and you will see high dunes where the giant has long ago been handcuffed and pegged down.

But he is not a dead giant, and he sleeps with one eye always open for opportunity. His sly watchfulness was proved by the great blowout on Mount Tom. Something happened here to undo all the patient work of the vegetation. Most probably a wilder wind than usual opened up a spot no bigger than your fist at first. And now see how the once-wooded dune has taken up residence somewhere beyond! He has gone traveling, and nobody can say, by looking at him, where in the struggle he can be made to rest. He is a "live" dune they say. Truth is, he was never dead. Just awaiting the moment.

You who fancy yourself good at quizzes, try this one. Under what unusual circumstances did the growing dunes lie quiet long enough for grasses and roots to tie them down? Why didn't they move inland and farther inland till they were out of the reach of the northerly wind? In the formation of these wonderful dunes were involved more than slight changes of climatic and weather conditions, without a doubt. The dunes were long in the making. They have seen the level of Lake Michigan at several stages higher than where you now dabble your toes in the water's margin.

This superb preserve is administered on principles that are occasionally, and sometimes with a lifted eyebrow, known as "purist." When a tree falls on the wooded dunes, it remains where it lies, harbor for insect life, the latter in turn food for birds, the carbonaceous matter finally going back into the soil. Naturally, if the fallen tree is an obstruction, or the dead tree a menace to visitors, it is removed. But whatever one may think in general of this philosophy of management, in this particular place it is not merely fitting but imperative.

Of all topography, dune country is perhaps the most delicate. All one has to do, to realize that the surface must be austerely let alone, is to view the moving dunes of Death Valley, the gypsum dunes of White Sands National Monument, or those of the country west of Yuma. Unbind these Indiana dunes, and though it might not happen right away, they might eventually be pushing against the house foundations in Chesterton, even Valparaiso. Have a good look at what is already happening where the big Mount Tom blowout is moving down the slope upon the group-camp cabins which in the season are occupied by the Girl Scouts of Whiting!

Here and there among the tangled underbrush are faint remains of habitation where some optimist once tried to "farm it," and there are traces of long-forgotten roadways, now starting from nowhere and leading nowhere.

Look, indeed, at the biggest blowout itself. Once merely a disturbed handful of sand, it is now a huge amphitheatre in which stand or lie the gaunt remains of large trees, stripped bare, the projections of the limbs sharpened to thorny points by sand blast. They have been given an uncheerful resurrection. Viewing this stark crater, I was reminded of the gentleman who pointed out some Florida dunes to me, on the ocean front, with the remark: "We could easily recover the valuable ilmenite (titanium sand ore) from those. It wouldn't do the slightest harm, because we would put all the quartz sand right back again." All I could say to that remark was: "You say *we* would. Have you consulted with the winds and tides?" My gentleman had, apparently, never heard of Humpty-Dumpty, and the efforts of the King's horses and men to restore an original shape.

During the summer season the park maintains a naturalist to give tours and slide talks and to answer the questions about duneland which arise in the minds of inquiring persons. As everywhere, it is probably the younger folk who profit most by these excursions. They are getting at first hand, on the spot, an acquaintance with a most unusual animal and vegetable life, one that could arise and continue to exist under no other conditions. For each of them it is a revelation that, though Indiana is a political unit, in the natural world there is not one Indiana but many. Should they come from other states, this understanding goes home with them.

For example: you would not expect to find cactus here—but there are the spiny plants with their creamy blossoms. You would not look here for the noble white pine, but here are ancient trees of that species, a leftover from a period when the forest association was of a different nature. The patch of tiger lilies may mark the spot where once a squatter had a cabin. The marshes, so rankly growing with cattail and other vegetation that they are a forbidding jungle, are but a few feet away from the oaks and maples and tulip-poplars that shun wet feet. And though the bear and deer and wolf and wildcat that once roamed these woods have long since sought new lands, there are still plenty of the smaller animals. One enthusiastic botanist has called duneland "a great floral region of the United States."

This is historic ground, too. Not only was it visited in the days when the French explorers were seeking easy routes by which to consolidate an empire in the new world; it was later to become part of the conquest of the English-speaking pioneers moving westward; and one day it was to be surrounded by a rich region of smoking industrial chimneys. Before that, all this dune country was crisscrossed by well-worn Indian trails.

We have come to think of the pre-Columbian red man as a rather static dweller. But we are gradually learning that these early folks were tourists also. There is no reasonable doubt that many of the curious western Indians crossed the country to have a look at "the water over which the sun rises"—the Atlantic. They visited, attended "conventions" of a sort, traded, and even traveled far to make a hostile sally. The Iroquois of central New York, those alert inventors of confederation, were familiar with the western country as far as the Black Hills of Dakota, and it is recorded that a body of their braves trudged all the way to the lands of the Wisconsin Foxes, to avenge some insult. If this is so, their natural course would have taken them through the Indiana dunes.

Frances Howe, a granddaughter of the Joseph Bailly whose homestead was only a few miles west of the present Dunes State Park, has left an account of the old Indian trail that ran past the house, "a deep wide rut made by centuries of pacing feet." She tells of the passage of Menominees, Winnebagos, Foxes, Sacs, and Sioux who one day sallied eastward along the dunes, brilliant in paint and war bonnets, going to attend some great council near Detroit. The tourist camp where you may pitch your tent or place your trailer, not far from the Waverly Beach Road, was a favorite camping spot of the Indians, who knew a good creekside, well-drained location when they saw it.

It is always difficult, and sometimes unfair, to try to fix the early efforts that have resulted in the preservation of a state park like this one on Lake Michigan. Who first suggested that the place should be set aside for public ownership and enjoyment? Usually many persons and groups experience the enthusiasm for a long time; suddenly it begins to crystallize; a definite "movement" is on its way. Certainly the Prairie Club of Chicago early took a strong stand toward the preservation of these dunes. In 1916 the Daughters of the American Revolution in Gary began to campaign for a park, and a National Dunes Association was incorporated. Senator Taggart of Indiana once tried to have the federal government make a national park or monument of the dunes, and though Stephen Mather seems to have been convinced of their significance, nothing came of the proposal: World War I intervened.

Meanwhile, industrialization was fast moving in. At a legislative session in 1923, Mrs. Frank J. Sheehan, as chairman of the Dunes Park Committee of the Indian Federation of Women's Clubs, pointed out that where a few years before there were fifteen miles of dunelands, only six miles were left, and those were in danger of becoming tawdry resorts, or of being destroyed for commercial purposes.

Richard Lieber, that farsighted and doughty carrier of the gospel of worthy state parks, was director of the Indiana Department of Conservation. Indiana Dunes was only one of the projects on which he was ardently working, but it was surely one that was near his heart. The colonel was a man not easily discouraged. Of course, this could be said of all the conservationists who have buzzed and buzzed like relentless gadflies till "something got done." If any of them had known really what discouragement was, there would have been few parks, national, state, or any other.

Colonel Lieber, in 1925, got Governor Jackson to come and see for himself the wonderful cultural asset of the state which was endangered by procrastination. The governor was convinced that no further time should be lost, and the park got underway. Judge Elbert Gary, president of the United States Steel Corporation, answered an appeal for funds with a check for $135,000 and a total contribution of $250,000. He sensed, with his keen intelligence, what such a park would later mean for employees of his great corporation. Besides a tax levy for the purchase of the lands, there were other fine donations that made the park possible.

And so, here it now is—Indiana Dunes State Park, which offers in such an uncomplicated way, without frills and without features that could only detract from its quality and purpose, the two essentials of a fine restoring experience close to nature and a stimulating educational experience for those who so elect.

(IX)

ITASCA STATE PARK

MINNESOTA

Twenty-one miles north of Park Rapids,
a short distance west of U.S. 71

HERE, 1,475 FEET ABOVE THE OCEAN, THE MIGHTY MISSISSIPPI BEGINS TO FLOW ON ITS WINDING WAY 2,552 MILES TO THE GULF OF MEXICO.

TERSE AND SUFFICIENT, this marker in Itasca State Park stands at a spot where a stream of cold water emerges from one of the thousands of glacial pools that reflect the blue of Minnesota's sky. The outlet is hardly more than ten feet wide. Behind it, in late summer, the ripening tops of wild rice are bending before the breeze. You cannot see the whole historic lake from this location. Shaped, as someone has described it, like a deformed wishbone, its arms flail out vaguely westerly, easterly, and to the north. And it is from this north segment that the Mississippi starts upon a course that will end only in that colossal delta of silt, far below New Orleans.

Across the neck where the infant Mississippi leaves the lake is a causey of cobbles. A bevy of younger children are scrambling back and forth across the slippery stones, risking a thudding fall that will prove whether heads are harder than rocks. The small fry probably do not care whether this is the Father of Waters they chill their feet in. But on the sandy bank of the little stream you see a line of shoes and socks that belong to older folk.

It seems a bit like the footgear of devotional Mahometans outside their mosque—for on the faces of these men and women, barefoot, wading in the stream, there is an intense and satisfied expression. They are here for a purpose. They can say, all the rest of their lives (and at least half of them are from other states): "I have walked in the Mississippi at its source." An elderly woman parts the overhanging alder branches as she returns, skirt held high, from farther down river. Her face is serious, and triumphant. She has come a thousand miles to do this. Can anyone doubt that this is truly a great experience?

Is this, in geographic fact, the headwater of the Mississippi? There has been quibbling about the statement. Some would say that there are streams—at least four of them—that flow into Itasca from low and soggy ground in the surrounding basin, and that any one of these might be called the source. For my part, I accept this spot as the birthplace of one of the world's greatest rivers. For the other brooks enter the lake, and become a part of it; and a lake is not yet a river. Joseph N. Nicollet, the French mathematician, astronomer, and explorer of our midwest, put it well: "Itasca Lake, concentrating these minor streams *and sending them out as one*, is the true head of the Father of Waters." Therewith, for me, the discussion is closed.

So Henry R. Schoolcraft was right. This extraordinary man, ethnologist and student of the North American Indian, husband of a Chippewa lass, federal agent for Indian affairs in our then northwest, led an expedition in 1830 to attempt to determine the true source of the Mississippi. Chief Ozawindib (Yellow Head) told Schoolcraft of a body of water called by his people Omushkoz, and translated into French by fur hunters and voyageurs as Lac la Biche.

By Omushkoz the Ojibway people meant "the lake of the female elk." *Biche* is the doe of the European red deer; and sure enough, the lake appears on Beltrami's map as *Doe* Lake. Beltrami, the Venetian exile-explorer, never saw it, but got the name from his guides. Just south of Itasca, within the park, is another and smaller body of water now called Elk Lake. Whence the name, and when? If you like to solve puzzles, you may decide to go to Itasca to find the answer. You will probably become so enmeshed in the manifold beauties of the park that you will forget your reason for coming. That will be just as well, too.

Schoolcraft finally reached Omushkoz. He wrote to a fellow scientist in 1832: "We made a portage of six miles, with our canoes, into La Biche, or Itasca, which is the true source of this celebrated stream [the Mississippi] being at the same time its most western and northern head."

But now here is Schoolcraft calling this fountain lake *Itasca.* What does he mean by that? Itasca does not mean lady elk in any Indian tongue. The explanation is that Henry Schoolcraft invented the name. "La Biche" did not satisfy him; it might apply to any northwest lake of the period, then or now. He wanted a name that would establish the importance of the water, as being the birthplace of the Mississippi. So, being something of a Latinist, though no Cicero, he put together the two Latin words *veritas* and *caput,* and he had it: Itas-ca, or as the Romans would not have said it, "The True Head." The True Head of the Mississippi.

I am somehow reminded of what Chief Ten-ei-ya of the Yosemite Indians said when some ardent white men told him they had named a local lake in his honor. He gave them a freezing look and replied: "The lake already has a name. We call it Py-we-ack." Oh, well, never mind. After all, Itasca is a pleasant-sounding name and comes more trippingly to our national tongue than Omushkoz.

At preachers' Grove, within Itasca State Park, the visitor will face a marker with the laconic inscription:

IT TOOK 200 YEARS TO GROW THIS TIMBER.
FIRE CAN DESTROY IT IN TWO DAYS.

Two hundred years in relation to some of these virginal forest giants of Itasca is even an understatement. To the visitor who has never come into intimate, arm's-length touch with such ancients of the northern woods, the first few hundred yards along the roadway after passing the park entrance will be a revelation. The approach is simply magnificent. The great trees at Preachers' Grove, at Peace Pipe Springs, and along this entranceway, in the opinion of an outstanding forestry expert, "probably got their start after a fire in the year 1714." One red, or Norway, pine showed fire scars in its 227 annual rings.

It is true, of course, that the primeval forest renewed itself as a result of lightning fires, or fires that were deliberately set, for one purpose or another, by the aboriginal people who roamed within them. Itasca presents, under the scrutiny of the forester, the best possible example of this process. The dates of the burnings are as clearly revealed as though they had been recorded in a diary.

"The major portion of the Itasca red pine grew up after the fires of 1803 and 1811. Along the trail to La Salle Springs are trees that owe their origin to a series of burns that took place about 1772. The 75-year-old jack pines can be traced to a fire of 1865." (This was computed some years back, of course.) It furnishes us with some insight into the processes of nature. But this, very definitely, does not mean that the state parks of today, with their trees of patriarchal age, can be consigned to the accident of a tossed lighted cigarette.

With its great size—over 32,000 acres—and its location in a countryside such as this, Itasca State Park is also an ideal proving-ground for the management of wildlife. Managed it has to be, since any disturbance of purely natural conditions starts a chain reaction whereof, over the short turn, nobody can know the result. What was the wildlife before the white man set foot here? There were elk, there were bears, there were moose and deer, there were wolves—predators to keep the populations down, with lean years that kept the predators themselves on a starvation diet. It is curious that some of the earliest white adventurers described game as being so scarce that they could not live off the land—though, as to that, some sarcastic commentator has retorted that the hunters were probably just poor gunners.

Certainly, in the early days, this was beaver country; yet, by 1901, this animal was reported to be almost extinct. So Canada sent four beavers from its Algonquin Park in Ontario to the state of Minnesota. In little more than fifteen years, a count showed 127 beaver houses, occupied by more than 630 animals. They were outrunning any possible food supply from within their cruising ranges. But nature took its course, and so within a few more years it was again difficult to find a colony. At the present time, the beavers are on the increase again, and the visitor may see their houses and dams, and in the quiet of the evening observe them playing or toiling at Chambers Creek.

Another experiment was the reintroduction of elk—a fine animal that truly "belonged." Fourteen of them were captured in Jackson Hole, Wyoming, and set free in Itasca. "In these days," Victor Cahalane of the New York State Museum told some enthusiasts who planned to introduce these animals into northern New Hampshire, "elk can be an expensive and annoying luxury." So it proved in Minnesota. They had to be fenced, and at first some died as a result of running into the fence. The wolves killed some. The remainder "domesticated," and when they multiplied too rapidly, they were turned loose in northern Minnesota and there ate up the farmers' hay and straw.

The rapid increase of deer is a problem of many other state parks. Too many deer means that pine isn't reproduced. Yet visitors to parks love to see deer, want to caress them and feed them lollipops. The deer's heels may be as dangerous as a butcher knife, but its face is angelic, and a wilderness park without deer would be like an omelet without eggs. So there is the management problem again.

Itasca, almost an ideal wilderness park, intends to give visitors that glimpse of wildlife which is all they can expect to have (at least as concerns the larger animals), yet keep its forest renewing. Of the small animals—the squirrels and raccoons and porcupines—there is no lack, of course. Observations in New York parks have shown the porcupine to be nearly the favorite animal of the tourist. Yet, the porcupine is a very devil among the saplings, and there is almost everywhere in forest country a price on his rather stupid head. I say stupid, but maybe his natural defense—an animal chevaux-de-frise—has made him reckless of human might and cunning.

Ah, the imposing giants of the long-ago forest of Minnesota! Again and again, the visitor comes back to them for delight and woodland solace. In the partly cleared space where stands the fine lodge, the modern cabins, the cafeteria, and the gift shop, there remain some giants with boles which have the catfaces of wild fires that failed to kill. The wounds have healed through the unguents that the great physician, nature, happily provides when conditions are right. Notable as is this park as a preserver of the source of the Great River, possibly its crowning glory, after all, is in its trees.

The trails are a delight. The Lind Saddle Trail makes a circuit that passes within sight of twenty-eight lakes and ponds—sometimes in virgin growth, sometimes in the cutover lands; for, of course, J. V. Brower and the stalwart conservationists of the early days of this century were fortunate to be able to save what they did from the ax and saw of lumbermen who sat in the comfortable saddle of those exploiting times. It was not easy.

J. V. Brower, it appears, was a man of iron determination. He was a scholar; wrote books that proved him an able historian; and was altogether a rugged personality—lawyer, seaman, legislator, and archaeologist. When the park was established by law in 1891, we may be sure it was with no hearty assistance from the lumber interests. Those who opposed the state park bill were able to have stipulated that whoever became commissioner, and did the spade work, would pay his own expenses and receive only a pittance for a brief period, followed by nothing at all. "At this time," says John Dobie in his book about the park, "there was not a single acre of state park land, nor a cent of money in its fund. It was truly a park on paper only." For a long and doubtful period, the park passed into the hands of the lumbermen and their political friends. But, as Brower said: "These men cannot undo, cancel, or abandon the cause of the park; they can only delay its completion."

Minnesota has come a long way since those times. Nature made it a superb region for state parks with both delightful physical recreation and cultural meaning. The development of these havens, which in a few years will be beyond price, is admirably balanced. Fine as Itasca is, we are not forgetting, for instance, the way the state is safeguarding from commercial intrenchment its strip of magnificent coast on the north shore of Lake Superior. Here, with the invaluable help of C. R. Magney, an ex-justice of the Minnesota Supreme Court, the state is adding one after another of small but fine areas: Baptism River, Temperance River, Ray Berglund, Caribou Falls—and this does not include them all.

This rockbound coast, from Duluth to the Canadian border at Grand Portage, is little known to most Americans. Would that every mile of it were park! That, of course, is not now possible, but the wisdom of the state, moved by the dogged persistence of such men as Judge Magney, is making part of the dream a reality.

(X)

LAKE HOPE STATE PARK

OHIO

Fifteen miles northeast of McArthur, north of U.S. 50, off State 278

THE GREAT SEAL of the state of Ohio pictures the rising sun over several conical mountains, with sheaves of wheat in the foreground. One who comes into the state from the west, being familiar with the design on the seal, might naturally say: "I see the sun and the wheat sheaves; but where are the mountains? The artist must have been thinking of some other region."

No; there is no mistake. The traveler merely has not yet come far enough east. At Chilicothe, the high knobs appear. Indeed, after ascending the scarcely noticeable Mississippi escarpment, you are upon that Allegheny Plateau which extends across southeastern Ohio into Pennsylvania, West Virginia, and New York.

Lake Hope State Park, a charming and restful wooded refuge within the Zaleski State Forest, nestles in that same Allegheny Plateau. The Lake, of course, is manmade. The Resettlement Administration, co-operating with the State Division of Forestry, dammed Big Sandy Run in the northeastern corner of Vinton County, and created 120 acres of recreation water surface which, seen at any point except at the dam itself, gives the impression of a perfectly natural setting.

If you seek a place to relax, to be free of the din and the jostle, perhaps to meditate a little on your place in this baffling world, here it is. For, although the whole extent of the park is less than two thousand acres, you will not be disturbed from your dreams by a motorboat. You can paddle, you can row, you can put up a sail, but you can't annoy other vacationers with mechanical contraptions, and they won't annoy you with such.

There may be several thousand people at the park; if you like to watch happy children dousing in the water or digging their toes into the sand (and most of us do), you will see plenty of them here; if you want to creep away somewhere and feel alone, there are many opportunities in both park and forest. Hundreds of picnic tables are available, and sleeping cabins, and housekeeping cabins. The charming lodge, built of the famous Berea sandstone, supplies good meals; and there is a naturalist, throughout the summer season, to provide a natural history program of hikes, tours, and evening programs. Ohio is one of the states which makes full use of discoveries in the field of parks and recreation. One of these is that the more fish you catch in these waters, the more fish there are to catch. Hence, Ohio has "liberalized" fishing. Another is that many, many people *want* the service of trained naturalists, and find it vital to full enjoyment.

Lake Hope is the only place where I have seen a naturalist bitten twice on the same day by the same snake. A black racer, one of our valuable and nonvenomous snakes, came out of the oak woods near the lodge and started across the parking lot. The naturalist happened to be coming out of the lodge at the moment. Here was a specimen that could be used in the evening talk about snakes! So the naturalist, with his nylon collecting bag, started after the black snake. There wasn't time to get a forked stick, with which to pin down the snake's neck. Result: a lacerated finger. And the snake wasn't to be blamed: he was going about his business and was the victim of an assault. That evening in the lodge, a crowd gathered around to hear about snakes and to see this one. The naturalist reached into his bag—and promptly got bitten again! Was he disconcerted? Not in the least. "I'm glad to have had this experience," he said, with a grin. "I was never bitten before." The snake went back into the woods next morning, having preserved his self-respect.

On the way to Lake Hope I saw a flaming red wildflower that was new to me. Knowing that there was a resident naturalist, I intended to ask him what this flower was. I didn't have to. On entering the lodge, I saw a table in the lobby covered with labeled, fresh wildflower specimens. My flower was among them.

Make no mistake: people are becoming more and more interested in the natural world around them. The skilled naturalist in a state park fills an urgent need.

To an outlander like myself, the Lake Hope–Zaleski region offered a fascinating bit of topography and geology, as well as the human story that inevitably goes along. This, for example, is not rich farming country: in a few pockets, kitchen gardens flourish, but nothing extensive. Yet, in the westward push of crowding America, people moved into this region, feverishly gophering here and there, searching for something materially worthwhile. What they found around the present Lake Hope Park is explained best by a brief glance at the geological story.

About 200,000,000 years ago—we won't mind a year or two plus or minus—this region was part of a vast lowland, so near sea level that slight uplifts or subsidences made enormous differences. In such unstable conditions were laid down, successively, coal measures, limestones, layers of flint, layers of clay, some shales, and much sandstone.

The prehistoric and mysterious people we call the Moundbuilders were here, and they, too, searched for material of some worth. In the Zaleski black flint they soon knew they had a prize; never were better arrow and spear points made than from this rock. They could not only use this flint, they could trade it; and so Zaleski black-flint artifacts have been found far away from the source. This particular flint outcrops northwest of the lake near state route 328.

The importance of another kind of flint found not far from the park was discovered by the white man. "Vanport" flint, though inferior for arrow points, and so not thus used by the Indians, proved to be the perfect millstone for the grinding of grains. It was similar to the famous buhrstone of France, and as early as 1814, at least fifty families in McArthur were quarrying the rock and fashioning millstones. A pair of seven-foot stones sold for $500. Marketed as "Raccoon Millstones," such buhrs were famous for half a century.

The little fenced cemetery on the hill where a woodland trail leads to a lookout over the valley of Raccoon Creek is a quiet reminder of the old settlement called Hope, from which Lake Hope gets its name. Any deceased hamlet with a name like *Hope* conveys to the visitor a pathetic commentary upon the vanity of human wishes. Hope was a busy place in the fifties of the last century—"a bustling little Pittsburgh," some enthusiast called it. The cemetery, surrounded by a young forest that is almost exclusively composed of several varieties of oak, has its own story to tell: a tale that explains much of what one sees in this region of sharply defined hill and valley.

To the settlers it must have seemed that they had stumbled into vast riches. Here was coal; here was iron; here was limestone; here were thousands of acres of primeval forest that could be used for charcoal; here even was an eight-foot stratum of wonderful clay with which to line a furnace. And it was no ordinary clay, this. But nobody would have guessed at the time that of all the deposits of that Pennsylvania geologic period the clay would finally prove to be the most valuable.

The Hanging Rock Iron district that extended from this county of Vinton into Kentucky was long famous. A Parisian banker, Peter Zaleski, was financial agent for a group of Polish exiles in France. Looking toward the new world for a field of investment, Monsieur Zaleski bought a large tract of land and laid out the town of Zaleski. The forest in which Lake Hope State Park lies is also named for this enterpriser who, as it happened, never crossed the ocean to look at his investment, though a pretentious house was built for him here.

Just north of the entrance road of the park you will see what remains of the Hope, or Big Sandy Furnace. Except for the stones around the hearth where the iron was drawn off, the sandstone-block furnace is still in good condition. However, unless the caved blocks are somehow replaced, the whole structure will come down within a few years. It is too well worth preserving for that! Anywhere in the vicinity of the furnace one may pick up bits of a glassy slag, mostly brown, but sometimes among these is a lovely translucent amethyst, the waste of the old smeltings.

But the visions of colossal wealth were after all illusory: this coal and iron field looked sufficient, but Hope did not realize that there were bigger coal seams, better coal, richer iron deposits, which would before long make this an unprofitable operation. The Civil War gave the business a temporary boost, but at the end of that boom, during which in 1864 iron went to $80 a ton, the Hanging Rock District was through. Besides, the "limitless" supply of virgin forest for conversion into charcoal was practically exhausted. Looking back on it, the development of coke for smelting was a lifesaver for many a fine stand of timber. Charcoal was one of the best, but all things considered one of the most wasteful, sources of heat. It took 325 acres of forest to supply one furnace like Hope with fuel.

When you look across Raccoon Creek Valley at the hillside opposite Lake Hope, you see a great yellow scar on the landscape. It is not beautiful and one wishes it could be screened off from what is otherwise a charming prospect. This is a strip-mining operation where the famous Hope fire clay is obtained. The middle part of the clay seam, of light gray color, makes a product that will withstand very high temperatures.

That brings us naturally to a comment upon strip mining in general. It was, and is, certainly, a logical way of tapping a resource that it would not otherwise be commercially possible to obtain. But from the viewpoint of the lover of natural scenery the result is horrible. In southern Indiana I have seen it at what I hope is its worst. Perhaps the reason one does not feel this flaying of the earth's skin in southeast Ohio quite so deeply is the hill-valley topography. But the desolate spoil banks one sees on every hand in the approach to Lake Hope make one thrice-happy to take refuge within the park.

Sometimes the old strippings, when they have a good mixture of lime in them, gradually recover with a volunteer growth of sweet clover and locust. Some of the mining companies, to do them justice, have made hearty efforts to return the desert to forest or pasture. But where the limestone is missing in the spoil banks, and especially where the overburden is full of sulphur-bearing coal fragments, we shall be much older before seeing nature supply a green garment for this nakedness.

Fishing is good in the 120-acre lake. Bass of good size have been taken, and there are plenty of crappies, bluegills, and catfish. Squirrels, grouse, and raccoons are abundant; and deer, sensing the protection available within the park boundaries, are moving in. There should later be a restoration of wild turkeys, the noblest of the fowl. Ohio once had them in profusion. From the nearby Waterloo Game Preserve, operated by the Ohio Division of Wildlife, pen-raised birds will be released in many suitable areas in the southern part of the state.

(XI)

LUDINGTON STATE PARK

MICHIGAN

Eight and a half miles north of Ludington, on State 116

ONLY A FEW MILES from this exceptionally fine refuge of beach, dune, and forest loveliness, and down on the water front of the city of Ludington, there is a boulder marking the "first grave" of the devout and heroic missionary priest, Père Jacques Marquette. He was, to be sure, one of many such fathers who toiled and suffered to bring the cross to the children of the wilderness. But we have good reason to know that this young Jesuit was measurably successful in his sacrifices. The words "first grave" tell us that, after his interment here on the east shore of Lake Michigan, a group of his Chippewa converts came and removed, reverently, the mortal remains of their *bon père* to the mission he had founded at Saint Ignace, on the straits of Mackinac.

Father Marquette, his frail but tenacious body finally worn out at the age of thirty-eight from ceaseless voyagings on lake and river—one trip of discovery, you remember, with Louis Joliet, on the Mississippi—had, beyond his religious zeal, something of the naturalist's power of observation. After reading his journal, you may wish that he had described this strip of dune-clad Michigan coastline, as he saw it in the years between 1669 and 1675. For, be very sure, he appraised its natural qualities with a keen perception. His description of the harvesting of the "wild rice" by the Menomonees (the French called both the Indians and the plant "wild oats," *folavoines*) could not be bettered.

This wild grain of the north country of the lakes is, to be sure, neither rice nor oats, but an entirely different plant, a first-cousin of a plant found in Asia. But the good father found that it looked like "the wild oats that grow up in our French wheatfields . . . only twice as long as our oats." He found it a welcome food "when reduced to meal by pounding, and mixed with grease: almost as palatable as rice would be, without seasoning."

It is likely that Marquette left the lakeside and footed it over the Indian trails that followed the highest ridges along the back dunes, which were then covered with hardwoods and pines—especially white pines—which grew with a luxuriance such as we shall never see again. As in Maine, in Thoreau's time these noble pines were slaughtered with reckless avarice. Not every last one, fortunately. There are protected stands within the state parks which afford a notion of what the early woodsmen and travelers saw. In the more than 3,700 acres of Ludington State Park there are twenty-five miles of well-marked foot trails, laid out in CCC days and graveled; and these trails, following the high ridges mainly, give the hiker a glimpse of varied scenery he will long remember. Along these seductive trails are shelters and comfort stations, and guiding maps are available.

More than three miles of sand beach on Lake Michigan, four miles more of shoreline on Lake Hamlin, a good fishing body of water that empties into the larger lake through the swift-flowing Big Sable River, and additional water frontage on the river itself, make a total of ten miles of shore. The Michigan front can be cold, windy, and riotous, even in summer. Groins all along the beach dispute the sway of the gales which over countless centuries produced the great heaps of sand that the winds seemed just as anxious to tear down as to build. In other words, a most excellent natural recreation beach.

There is good reason for the existence of Big Point Sable Lighthouse at the place where it sits—within, but not part of—the park. This is one of the most important points on Lake Michigan to the shipping trade, for here, on the narrowest part of the lake the great ore-freighters must turn this jutting headland, facing a strong current that would like nothing better than to set them ashore. Someone has told me that in one storm alone forty boats were sunk here. If that sounds like too many, we know that six sailing vessels went down near the Point in a single gale in the days when lumbering was a feverish industry; and as a result the federal government erected the lighthouse.

It is interesting that, besides the great waves the winds can hurl upon this strip of lake coast, there are changes in the water level itself. You wonder how, indeed, the level of such a great body of water as Michigan could vary much from one month to another. The variation, to be sure, is not great in terms of footage, but only a slight change can become a danger to man's plans along this shore. I do not know of any study of water level which has been made here, but records of the Corps of Engineers for Lake Huron show a high of more than 583 in 1886, and a low of more than 577 feet in 1926. At any rate, the rise in water level, joined to the effect of gale winds, contributes to the creation of the dunes.

Who is not susceptible to the lure of dunes—to their clean, sunbathed nudity as they drift to and fro on the ocean or lake front, or achieve a cover of grasses when they are just in process of being tied down, or finally acquire a forest growth as they grow aged and sedentary? Have you ever been along the dunes on a winter day, when the winds were blowing a biting blast, and found, in a little dune ravine, a place where you could snuggle and enjoy the pleasant, sparkling temperature of late September?

Of course, these sand dunes of Ludington State Park are by no means the only examples of such aeolian formations on the state's shorelines. In ranges and groups, they appear from the state line on the south to the Straits of Mackinac, and there are notable deposits along the north shore of the Keweenaw Peninsula; but certainly these near Ludington are among the best. In *A Guide to the Wolverine State* they are described as "whimsically shifting, barren, and somber." Whimsical and barren the most recently formed sand heaps may be, but *somber?* I doubt that the visitors will find them so.

In the shadows of such dunes, the more thoughtful of Ludington's guests may get a little vision of the processes that have, over the millions of years, made sandstones of just such giant heaps; rocks whose consolidated toughness still displays the action of the wind which formed them—easily distinguishable from the sandstones that were laid down on the shore of a shallow sea. When more millions of years have passed, the geologists of the distant future—if that future can afford the luxury of geologists, or if those scientific men have not transferred their interests to the other planets—may examine the sandstone rocks of this region and say: "Ah, this was once the location of great dunes, probably upon the lee shore of a great lake that ceased to exist when the land sank and allowed the ocean to come in, as it had done many a period before. . . ."

It was on a mid-August day that I visited Ludington State Park, along with a portion of the 400,000 day-visitors that come here annually. It was wonderful weather; the trails were enthusiastically sought; the campgrounds, containing space for 250 tents, were full. The sun was still high in the sky, and the ranger at the gate was saying, with genuine regret: "Sorry; every spot is taken." The rangers themselves have been campers, many times with their families, and they do not like to turn folks away, especially when there are tired children peering hopefully from the car windows.

It is forty miles to the next nearest state park, and there is no assurance that this one will not also be full. There are some other parks, public and private, in the general area—in those the chances may be just as slim. The nation is becoming more and more camping-minded. The question for the administrators of state parks is: shall the campers already settled be comfortable, or shall an added number of campers be admitted for whom no adequate facilities are provided? There has been some thought of creating a one-night-only camping space for those who cannot be given regular space: at least in order to let a tired family who may have come a long distance have a rest before they move on. But generous as this idea is, it implies more personnel, more facilities: in the end it does not solve the problem. The truth is that the popular state parks, whose delights become widely known, need more and more campgrounds; this calls for more money (not easy to come by, the park people will have you know) and greater care so that the natural endowments of the area will not be sacrificed by the expansion of facilities.

And camping is one of those elusive, whimsical pleasures anyway. At the campground nearest the beach on Lake Michigan a few days of chill winds and murky leaden skies will empty many a space (though the folks on the Lake Hamlin side are usually more comfortable). A camper sulking in his dripping tent is a morose sort of Arab . . . but that is the way of it . . . and weather will continue to be irresponsible. During my visit, at least, the camper's life was a rewarding one at this most ingratiating state park.

The water in Hamlin Lake is held at constant level by a dam that intercepts the Big Sable River. But the present dam is the second one at this spot. Almost a century ago the great lumber boom reached the vicinity of Ludington, and the big logs of virgin timber were floated down to a mill in what was named the village of Hamlin. The site of the village is within the state park, and a lively inscription tells how, in 1888, this dam suddenly burst, sweeping the mill, forty houses, and more than a million board feet of logs and dressed lumber out into the greater lake below.

The lumber from the sawmill used to be hauled on a mule tramway to long piers that extended into Lake Michigan, whence it was taken down to ports along the southern end, to do its part in the building of homes in the West. But that disaster was the finish of Hamlin, which had been named, they say, in honor of Hannibal Hamlin of Maine, Vice-President of the United States when Abraham Lincoln was President. I am quoting local tradition as to this; out of curiosity I looked into a biography of Hannibal Hamlin written by his grandson, and found nothing to indicate that he was ever in Michigan, or connected with the lumber business. This may have been just a fancy to honor the Vice-President, who was then a stalwart in the ranks of the rising tide of Abolitionists.

Moreover, it is said that at the second inauguration of Mr. Lincoln the White House was decorated with white-pine boughs from Hamlin Village on the Big Sable River. Certainly, no American tree could better suggest beauty, woodland fragrance, and utility.

It is a cheering thought that at Ludington State Park so many people—approaching half a million a year—find their pleasure with no resort to the artifical amusements available on the suburban arc of any large city. The park is dedicated to the interests of the hiker, the children with shovel and pail, the fisherman who doesn't take himself too seriously, the snowshoer and skier in winter, even the groups that come in to enjoy a touch of nature in the season when the leaves are off the trees, the snow crunches underfoot, and the Canada geese (maybe a hundred or more of them) are honking their thanks for a little feeding. This is a far world from the one I saw in August when I was there, but one that has its own rewards. In years of heavy snowfall, the winter visitors are many.

The Ludington Outdoor Center, always booked solidly from April until after Labor Day, is a distinctive feature of the park. It consists of a group of buildings in a secluded setting, well removed from the general park activities. Into this area you "*pack* your blankets and other personal equipment," on the foot trail over Hamlin Dam, unless you find it more convenient to put them in a boat and row across the lake. A large barrackslike building provides dormitory facilities for fifty campers at a time. The dining room is of good size and has a stone fireplace, and the rustic tables and benches can be moved around to suit one's purposes. All the buildings have electricity, and down-wood is plentiful enough in the vicinity to supply the fireplace and keep the barracks cosy. So, if you belong to that exclusive fraternity that "wants to get away from it all," this outdoor center is for you.

In a little pamphlet about the state parks of Michigan, published by the Department of Conservation, I find an arresting paragraph, well worth repeating:

> The quest for beauty is widespread, and has a bearing on the recreational industry. It is a prime factor in the choice of vacation sites and routes of tourist travel. It plays a part in many forms of recreation. Many hunters and fishermen get more enjoyment from the scenes about them than from the game and fish they take. Among the natural resources some materials are exhaustible and some features could be seriously impaired by destroying their natural beauty. *But the enjoyment of beauty, in itself, takes nothing from the scene.*

The thought has been expressed many times, in many ways, but I have not found it in better terms than this. It is what might be called, without wrenching the language, "the common sense of esthetics," as applied to the concept and management of state parks.

(XII)

THE NEWARK EARTHWORKS*

OHIO

At Newark, on State 16 and State 79

REVERENTLY, as was surely befitting, I have just finished reading a truly epochal book. Printed in 1848, it was the first publication of the Smithsonian Institution. Two years before this date, Congress had accepted the trust of James Smithson, the Englishman who left his property to the United States for "the increase and diffusion of knowledge among men."

The annual income from this noble bequest was at that time $30,950, and the Regents, of whom the President was ex officio the presiding officer, had after great deliberation resolved to divide the sum into two equal parts, one to be devoted to original research and publications, the other to the gradual formation of a library, a museum, and a gallery of art. When you visit the present buildings of the Smithsonian—rich to bewilderment—recall this humble beginning!

This fine quarto, which I obtained from my state library, bears the presentation autograph of Joseph Henry, Secretary of the Smithsonian Institution—that remarkable man whose discoveries in the field of electricity rivalled those of Faraday, and whose heroic-size statue is patted by the droves of school children who come to the state museum at Albany, New York. Once I asked a skillful woman interpreter there why none of her little visitors could pass that statue

* The Newark Earthworks, a general title, includes three state memorials: Mound Builders, Octagon Mound, and Wright Earthworks.

without patting it. "Oh," she replied, "because it is *so big*." Well, Joseph Henry, the man, was likewise big.

The Smithsonian's first publishing venture was *Ancient Monuments of the Mississippi Valley* by E. G. Squier and E. H. Davis, two pioneer archaeologists who surveyed and excavated among the numerous remains of the work of the people we commonly call "mound builders." Because these dimly realized aboriginal folk were much more than mere builders of mounds, Squier and Davis preferred to denote the mysterious relics as "ancient monuments of human labor and skill." Much devoted digging and study has since revealed facts that these two pioneers could not have known; but, to this day, the story is still cloudy.

The alert Ohio Historical Society administers, besides other preservations, fifteen of the finest sites where the mound builders created their strange earthworks, where they buried their dead chieftains together with artifacts which reveal consummate artistic talent and are evidence that these people traveled far and wide, Compared to their social structure, that of the historic Indians was anarchic and rude.

Of these Ohio sites Fort Ancient, seven miles east of Lebanon; the seventy-foot-high Miamisburg Mound; and the finest and largest, Serpent Effigy near Locust Grove, are nationally famous. At Newark, not far east of Columbus, may be seen the parallel walls, the great circular earthworks, and the Octagon. Since progress has cruelly moved in upon what was once a colossal production, the visitor must put the jigsaw pieces together; he can rest in the shade of the fine trees, on the greenest of swards within the monument, and wonder what sort of activity really went on in that long distant time.

Ah, if we could see these Newark Earthworks as Squier and Davis saw them in the first part of the century! Habituated as these men were, at Newark they exclaimed with surprise and respect. "Here," they wrote, "covered with gigantic trees of a primitive forest, the work presents a truly grand and impressive appearance, and in entering the ancient avenue for the first time, the visitor does not fail to experience a sensation of awe such as he might feel in passing the portals of an Egyptian temple or in gazing upon the silent ruins of Petra of the desert." They added: 'These works are so complicated that it is impossible to give anything like a comprehensive description of them."

Very sketchily, the following is what is meant by "the Newark Earthworks":

Between the south fork of the Licking River and Raccoon Creek, the original work covered an area more than two miles square (according to Squier and Davis, though the printed folder says "two square miles," which is very different). There were three grand divisions, connected by parallel walls and earth risings of a minor character. The parallel walls were not high, but vestiges of them can be traced for many miles beyond this center of activity. Indeed, if you drive on some of the streets on the west side of the city of Newark, you will see vestigial mound heaps in some of surburbia's back yards.

First, there is the octagon earthworks, enclosing fifty acres, joined by parallel walls to a circular embankment of twenty acres. A separate area consists of the great circle earthworks, with the eagle effigy mound at its center. Finally, a quarter of a mile east of the great circle is the Wright Earthworks State Memorial, now a small section of a former large square enclosure that was a feature of the whole great achievement of the builders.

In view of the present state of the remains, an attempt at a written description of what the visitor will see at Newark would have feeble results. Fortunately, Squier and Davis, with Charles Whittlesey of Cleveland, made a most exact plan when they were there, and a study of this map, reproduced in the Historical Society's folder, will be rewarding. For, as was sure to happen, the erosive features of "civilization" have obliterated much.

Perhaps, since such intrusions as a fair grounds, amusement devices, and a race track successfully operate here—not to mention the Ohio Canal that was thrust through before Squier and Davis limned the works—the wonder is that so much of the original is in existence. When you stroll in the charming meadows and under the wonderful old beeches, you feel rather thankful that so many trees were spared.

Timothy Flint, an early observer of the mounds, made the interesting comment that "the most dense ancient population existed in precisely the places where the most crowded future population will exist in ages to come." So much the worse, then, for the monuments the ancients left behind them.

As to the Octagon (it was, as built, not perfectly octagonal, but substantially so), it is now golf links. This sounds like a profanation; actually, the Historical Society has a serviceable arrangement with the golf club by which the grounds are well and devotedly maintained. And you may be sure that these mound-building aborigines were no strangers to games of stick and ball as well as of the favorite and widespread chungkey.

Squier and Davis were shrewd enough, in their time and with their resources, not to set an arbitrary date for the construction of these mounds and works. They were reasonably sure that they represented the work of a mainly agricultural people. Their chief reason for figuring the passage of time "in centuries" was the mature forest of slow-growing trees which had encroached upon the scene. "The forests covering these works correspond in all respects with the surrounding forests; the same varieties of trees are found, and they have a like primitive aspect." And a speaker before the Historical Society, years ago, concluded his address with the words: "Of what immense age, then, must be the works referred to, covered as they are by at least the second growth, after the primitive forest state was regained?"

Squier and Davis found an oak tree, twenty-three feet in circumference, growing on an embankment.

Modern archaeology can greatly reconstruct the story of these notable earthworks. They are representative of what is called, to distinguish it from the manifestations of historic Indians (or perhaps, more properly, the Indians of *our* historical acquaintance), the Hopewell culture. The Hopewells, in tools, weapons, and ornaments, were the elite of the tribes of the eastern United States. They traded far and wide for materials, from Florida to north of Lake Superior. Barter included obsidian from the Rockies and mica from the Carolinas. They had highly specialized craftsmen and artists who produced many art objects that could not be improved upon by us. Using the stems of plants and the barks of trees, and presumably on a simple loom (though none has been found), they carried out extensive weaving. We now assume that they flourished about 750 years ago.

The Ohio Historical Society, incorporated in 1885, administers nearly sixty state memorials. Fifteen of these are archaeological sites, twenty are historic sites and monuments, fourteen are historic houses; and there are eight museums, two reproductions, and five areas preserved because of exceptional natural history phenomena. The operation of these areas by the Society, as entirely distinct from that of Ohio's scenic and recreation parks, is so different from the operation of such areas in other states as to require a brief explanation. True, other states differentiate, in administration, between the two classes. Here, however, we have the unique situation of management by an institution which acts as an official state agency and at the same time maintains its own integrity. This arrangement has been so successful that other states have investigated it, and the Society has prepared a paper explaining fully the Ohio concept.

The Society, in respect of the administration of state memorials, is a governmental agency insofar as the governor appoints six persons to serve on its board of trustees, and the state makes appropriations for the support of the areas. But in fact the Society suggests desirable appointees, and its autonomy is so definitely recognized that it is in a position to accept or decline newly proposed memorials when they are adjudged not worthy or when there are unworthy restrictions. Such confidence, that the Society might do a better job than the usual state agency, was illustrated as far back as 1902, when the General Assembly appropriated funds for the centennial anniversary of the admission of Ohio into the union, and placed the management of the entire celebration in their hands.

It is probably not safe to assume that this arrangement, which in Ohio has been so successful, could be readily adopted in other states. The Society itself realizes that it arrived on the field at just the right time; that its general performance and acquisitions could not be duplicated today. Still, some of the younger states, that are just getting started in the business of preservation, may study the Ohio experience to great advantage.

The Ohio Historical Society is venerable in years, but it adapts itself well to modern methods of presentation and interpretation. Its main museum at Columbus is nationally known for its research and collections on prehistoric people—the Gravel Kame, Adena, Hopewell, Fort Ancient. The natural history collections are extensive, and the library is outstanding. In 1961, more than 2,500,000 persons visited the state memorials.

The Society has one of the largest leaflet programs of all historical agencies in the country, and they are splendidly prepared and produced. Since 1955, when the teaching of state history became mandatory in Ohio schools, the requests for leaflets by teachers and pupils "have staggered the Society's officers," says a report. In 1957 about 400,000 were distributed.

In recent years the Society has gone into the field of pictorical publication. Filmstrips have been prepared for use in the schools: *Ohio Past and Present; The Ohio Canals; How a State Law is Made in Ohio*. The Society's radio program, *Once Upon a Time in Ohio*, is directed to children in grades four through eight, and reaches a widening audience every year.

(XIII)

NEW SALEM STATE PARK

ILLINOIS

Nineteen miles northwest of Springfield, on Highway 97

Abraham Lincoln, aged twenty-two, came into New Salem "like a piece of floating driftwood." Those were his own words. It was an apt simile, for the flatboat that he was piloting down the Sangamon River on the way to New Orleans stranded upon the dam of the Rutledge and Camron saw-and-grist mill at this spot. He came ashore and looked at the little "town," just under three years old and typical of the restless, venturesome real estate speculations that were mushrooming in the country's new West. Here the young Lincoln stayed for six years. Here he swung a hearty ax, clerked in a general store, enlisted for the Black Hawk Indian skirmish, went bankrupt, was appointed postmaster, and entered politics.

And what a pushing, enterprising, fortune-seeking period it was, surely! Rutledge, a South Carolinian, and Camron from Georgia, looking at the booming wilderness with discerning and hopeful eyes, find a little plateau overlooking the Sangamon Valley. This is the place! This location on the bluff will be a good spot for homes, and a mill here will attract settlers looking for house lots. A commodious tavern will supply an air of distinction. The development offers a desirable homesite for $10; a humorously small amount of money as we see it today, but not at that time.

New Salem, the place is named. The people begin to filter in. By 1831, when Lincoln and his step-brother and cousin came ashore, it already seemed a flourishing venture. There were fond aspirations of making it the county seat. But a nearby settlement called Petersburg had the edge, and little by little New Salem faded from sight, like so many other similar ventures. However, in 1831 it had looked promising. Lincoln thought so, and so did his employer on the flatboat trip, one Denton Offut. Offut decided that a retail store would do well here, and he had already marked young Lincoln as a reliable assistant.

It is probably true of all great men that, as they perform their deeds and become involved in affairs of import, their reality as human beings fades in the eyes of the average man. To the man reading about the classical period of Greece, for example, Socrates will inevitably be more akin to us than any of the political and military heroes described by Plutarch. The humble statue maker, henpecked by his wife, buttonholing cobblers and tinkers on the street corner and making them answer his shrewd questions, and finally rendering an account of himself at a trial for his life—this man is such a one as ourselves.

It may be that Lincoln is one of the few great figures that have not so gone out of our orbit of kinship, because he always retained an essential humility and a homely human approach, always kept a delightful sense of humor and a feel for the comic. During the terrible years of 1861-65, he told some of the best stories heard by anyone, just as he had told them in New Salem, Illinois, three decades before. Speaking for myself, my visit to New Salem State Park awakened in me an intimate sympathy with Abraham Lincoln, a sense that now at last I understood the man, a feeling I had never quite had before.

The Lincoln of the beautiful memorial in Washington is grand, indeed—but I could never see myself reflected in that heroic figure. But the Lincoln of the statue—ax in one hand and a book in the other—in New Salem State Park is a Lincoln that could have been myself. I mean, very simply, that I, too, in those formative years, tossed about like a cork, wanting to be something or somebody, unsure what I sought, wasting time pleasurably, failing at this and that, achieving small successes that had no import—somewhat like the Lincoln of the New Salem hamlet on the bluffs above the Sangamon. Of course, if it were merely *myself*, this personal reference would be impertinent. But there are millions who will feel as I do; I know I am on safe ground in speaking for them. *They* will find something of themselves when they walk the streets of this adroitly reconstructed village, which is at once the scene of Lincoln's young manhood, and also a precious picture of a pioneering era in which America faced West.

The superintendent at New Salem said to me: "We have curiously little vandalism in this park—not even scribbling on the walls and that sort of thing. I suppose it may be because of a certain reverence for Lincoln's memory in the minds of all kinds of people." Yes; that certainly has something to do with it. If the place were *merely* a historical reconstruction of a town, perhaps it might be altogether different. But I feel that something prompts even chronic offenders to decline to vandalize their own persons. For all this is, as I have said, something of themselves.

For many years after the close of the Civil War, it was natural that the growth of the Lincoln story would be focused upon the patient, generous Lincoln of the tragic struggle. The Emancipator, here and abroad, was the dominant figure. It is true that those who had known the young Lincoln of New Salem and Springfield days rushed into lecture and print with a welter of anecdotes and claims of personal relations, all tending to magnify the importance of the narrator and to emphasize the fact that "I knew him when." Thus originated the tale of the love affair with Ann Rutledge, which, in the hands of cool-blooded historians, has been exploded. It was natural enough; and the tellers of tales about Lincoln were not so much fibbers as enthusiasts who had peddled their wares so long that they had come to believe them perfectly truthful.

What was needed, however, was exactly what has been achieved in New Salem State Park—the introduction of today's mobile Americans into the little three-dimension world in which young Lincoln lived during those six formative years. To do this, the village itself had to be re-created, cabin for cabin, shop for shop, as it looked when the young man came ashore from his stranded flatboat. It is, then, frankly a reproduction, but one done with such skill that at least one visitor—the only one for whom this writer can absolutely vouch—was swept back a century and a half as he walked the streets. At the entrance to the village a pair of oxen, drawing a Conestoga wagon, might have swayed along with the unconcerned diligence of their kind; in "skid row," down at the farther end, roisterers and rollickers might have been drinking hard liquor in Clary's "grocery." In my mind's eye they all came to life unfailingly.

By the way, we are reminded, when we speak of Clary's "grocery," how words change their meaning over the years. During a political contest, an opponent of Lincoln's charged sneeringly that at New Salem "this man" had "run a grocery." Lincoln replied in his usual unruffled but positive manner that he had done no such thing. What was so disgraceful about running a "grocery"? In Lincoln's

New Salem a *grocery* was a saloon; a place where whisky was sold by the glassful. Lincoln, indeed, when he was partner in a general store, sold hard liquors for "off" consumption. Every general store did so. Not only that, but practically everyone drank whisky. It was the sovereign remedy for fatigue, loneliness, and whatever ailed you. Berry, Lincoln's partner in the unfortunate business enterprise that left the young man neck-deep in debt, made huge inroads upon the firm's whisky stock. As we know, young Lincoln was himself singularly temperate.

Down at the end of the village at Clary's, you can easily guess what a rough and ready gang patronized the "grocery." Bad men, really bad men, were probably few in the settlement, but the grogshop had an unsavory name. The boozers were mischievous, idle-minded, and could be vindictive, and it was fortunate for Lincoln, as joint storekeeper, that even the worst of the rough set admired his decent and friendly behavior. The Clary Grove boys had broken the windows of Reuben Radfords' establishment and sent him looking for a milder neighborhood. It was his store which Lincoln and Berry operated.

The visitor's pleasant walk through New Salem reveals thirteen cabins, the tavern, and ten shops, besides a school where church services were held. One of these buildings happens to be the very one Lincoln knew. This is the Onstot Cooper Shop. Henry Onstot, in 1834, while he was running the Rutledge Tavern, built this shop and the following year erected a house just to the west of it. What restless people these were! The history of the little town for these few hectic years almost gives forth the sound of the buzzing of bees. A year here or there, and then suddenly off to greener pastures.

It was with Onstot's son Isaac that, according to legend, young Lincoln studied at night by the light of a fire of Cooper's shavings. A few years after Lincoln left town, this building was moved to Petersburg. In 1922 it came back to New Salem and, stripped of the "fancying up" it had acquired, was placed on its original site.

Not a single cabin, not a single shop, not a square yard of this Sangamon bluff hamlet, is without its sense of the presence of young Lincoln—of him whose education had been "by littles," but whose ambition, though vague and wavering, was to "amount to something." And here are such pioneer ventures as Samuel Hill's carding mill and wool house, into which Lincoln must have looked with naïve wonder at the ingenuity of the machine, which got its power from the treading oxen. Samuel advertised: "The machines are nearly new and in first-rate order, and I do not hesitate to say, the best work will be done. Bring in your wool. . . ."

All the cabins and shops are furnished with the articles in use in the days of the booming village. Some, in fact, are unquestionably the very ones that saw service when Lincoln was there. In the doctors' offices are the surgical instruments, the mortars and pestles and books. There are the same old cord beds that tired or intoxicated citizens slept upon, and flax shuttles and candle molds and corn-meal chests; and you see behind one of the cabins a typical ash receiver into which water was poured to make lye. When you pass behind the high mound of earth that separates the parking lot from the early nineteenth century, you are not merely with Abraham Lincoln, but with the roving, eager settlers of his pioneer day and acquaintance.

Back in 1917 the Old Salem Lincoln League was formed in Petersburg to insure that this memory of Illinois and of Lincoln should not die. William Randolph Hearst, the publisher, had given a talk in Petersburg in 1906, at the Old Salem Chautauqua, which was in its day a lyceum center second only to the one in western New York. Hearst became so interested in the village site that he bought it and transferred it in trust to the Chautauqua Association. With his consent it was given to the state of Illinois, to become a state park. In 1931, the legislature appropriated funds to begin the reconstruction that one now sees. Naturally, this state park is one of wide national interest. Automobiles from every state in the union are frequently seen in the parking place.

There is a country road, not hard-surfaced, which goes into Springfield. When this was but a horse and buggy highway, Lincoln used to walk it, and nowadays you may see Boy Scouts, and men and women too, tramping this same road reverently, straggling along with tired feet on a hot and dusty day, but happily returning to their homes with the memory that where Lincoln trudged, they too have followed.

Another excellent feature may some day be added in New Salem State Park. Those who have read the wise and delightful *A Sand County Almanac*, written by the great conservationist Aldo Leopold, may remember a nostalgic description of his:

> I am sitting in a 60-mile-an-hour bus sailing over a highway laid out for horse and buggy . . . in the narrow thread of sod between the shaved banks and the toppling fences grow the relics of what was once Illinois: the prairie.
>
> Here are the lupines, lespedezas or baptistas that originally pumped nitrogen out of the prairie air and into the black loamy acres. A cemetery flashes by, its borders alight with prairie puccoons. There are no puccoons

elsewhere . . . Through an open window I hear the heart-stirring whistle of an upland plover; time was when his forbears followed the buffalo as they trudged shoulder-deep through an illimitable garden of forgotten blooms . . .

Well, some day, when the means are provided to collect some of these almost extinct and forgotten prairie plants and grasses—victims of an intense agricultural industry—a plot of them may be planted at New Salem. It will be most fitting, for they are part of that prairie that greeted the eyes of the first-coming white men—and of Lincoln. It will be a refuge for them; and it will seem as worthy of reproduction as the red haws and wild plums and osage oranges, and all the other native shrubs and trees that have been planted along the streets of New Salem; or as the herb gardens that you now sniff, before seeing them, outside the cabins of the two doctors who labored here.

(XIV)

PORCUPINE MOUNTAINS STATE PARK

MICHIGAN

On State 107 along Lake Superior, twenty miles west of Ontonagon

A GROUP of Chippewa Indians, heading with a good catch of whitefish toward the range of mountains that parallels the southerly shore of Lake Superior, laid by their paddles and coasted pleasantly along, gazing up at the green wooded heights above them. They were a little to the westward of the place where the squaw had lost her bowl—*On-ta-na-gon* it had been humorously named by this Algonquian tribe that ruled what is now the Upper Peninsula of Michigan. Whether the bowl had been mislaid, or had been lifted by some sister squaw with deft fingers, long ago became an academic inquiry. On-ta-na-gon, "I-have-lost-my-bowl," still retains its primitive name.

Suddenly one of the Chippewas pointed at the skyline. "Look!" he said to his companions, "there's Kaug!" Kaug was the Indian word for the porcupine. And sure enough, the outline formed by the profile of the mountains, as seen from this point of the lake, looked like that "crouching" animal.

Later came the French adventurers into this wilderness of the north; the *coureurs de bois*, the *voyageurs*, the missionary priests seeking to recover pagan souls. These Frenchmen were at ease with the natives. They married the pretty, dusky girls; shared pot luck with the warriors; strove to understand them; and if the policy of the French government had always been as ingratiating as that of its pioneers, North America might now have French as its official tongue. For, as that brutally frank Virginian, Colonel William Byrd, wrote in his diary: "After all, a sprightly lover is the most prevailing missionary that can be sent among these, or any other infidels."

The Frenchmen lost no time in learning Chippewa words. Pointing at a porcupine, for instance, they would ask: "What call you that beast?" "That," would reply the Indians, "we name *Kaug*. And what name have *you* for Kaug?" "We call him *porc-épic*." *Porc-épic*, which is to say, a pig with spines; and with some of my rural neighbors Kaug is even now a "quill-pig." And *porc-épic* easily becomes porcupine—thus these mountains are called today.

Before driving to the gate of the Porcupine Mountains State Park, which easily ranks with the best parks in the nation, the visitor might do well to orient himself in respect to the Upper Peninsula in which it lies. This northern section of Michigan, stretching westward from Sault Sainte Marie, where the waters of Lake Superior cascade into the lower level of Lake Ontario, has remained a vague and romantic bit of geography over the years, despite the furious attack upon its mineral and forest resources in boom days. Sault Sainte Marie is the third oldest surviving community in the United States, dating from 1618, yet the statesman Henry Clay described it as "the remotest settlement in the country, if not in the moon!" Had he known of the wilderness that lay between the Sault and the Porcupine Mountains, he might have mentioned the planet Mars, instead of the moon.

The great five-mile bridge across the Straits of Mackinac has, within a few years, made a galvanic change. Not that hunters of deer and bear have not for years regarded this as great sporting country, and overcome all impediments to get there. But the local population has often wondered whether they belong in Michigan or somewhere else; and indeed the possibility of becoming a separate state has been discussed. It is about the same distance from the Michigan capital, Lansing, to the Porcupine Mountains, as it is to New York City. The Milwaukee and Duluth newspapers formerly beat those of Detroit into the peninsula.

Remote or not, this Upper Peninsula has seen its own wild days. Until the year 1940, almost a third of all the copper produced in the United States had come from the deposits of this region. But that statement does not tell the story. In the mineralization of this Lake Superior shore, and of that wilderness Isle Royale which is now a national park, nature indulged in an uncommon process on the grand scale. Native, or mass, copper (that is, copper metal in a practically pure state) exists in other parts of the country, and of the world. But here the nuggets were of simply incredible size.

Congress took notice of this copper mining, and the attendant hysteria that sent fortune hunters swarming into the Upper Peninsula in the early eighteen forties. It commissioned the famous Boston geologist, Charles T. Jackson, to make an official survey of the Keweenaw and lands westward. Jackson was no dabbler in mineralogy, but what he found here made him almost lyric. He visited a mine where men were cutting up, with sledge and chisels, a mass of the metal weighing eighty-three tons; masses of from eight to thirty tons were common. The practically pure state of the nuggets was distressing. With the only cutting methods available, it cost seven dollars a square foot of surface (one-side measurement) to get them into transportable form. No wonder the news of these giant masses, plus the coincident existence of silver in pure state, inflamed the minds of the get-rich-quick citizens of the country.

But more romantic still, it became certain now that these copper masses, often appearing on the surface of exposed rocks, had been the source of the tools and ornaments of the prehistoric men who built the mounds in Ohio and other locations, they in turn being perhaps descendants of others who had lived in the continent soon after the last retreat of the Pleistocene ice sheet. The finding of ancient shafts, stone tools, and charcoal made it plain that thousands of years ago a primitive people had found a rude way to extract the handsome metal and that they had traded it far and wide. Many a museum contains bracelets and gorgets and implements excavated by archaeologists, the source of which was certainly the Superior masses.

This was wild country when the first white miners were chiseling monumental nuggets. They were lulled to sleep by the howling of timber wolves. Indeed, wolves have never been absent from this northland. You may not see them, but they are still getting an honest living, sometimes within the park. There are probably not enough of them to keep the deer population down to the point where it would balance the browse. If you want wildlife in your holiday experience, you will find it in the Porcupines. Black bear, bobcats, plenty of beaver, red foxes and otter, coyotes and opossum (the last two not wanted, but that doesn't disturb them a bit), occasionally some moose, sometimes a few elk (the descendents of a planted herd) and marten. The marten had been almost exterminated, but have resumed their life here.

But there are no wolverines. Yet, Michigan is the Wolverine State. Competent mammalogists say there *never* were any wolverines here, at least in historic times. How then did the state come by the nickname? The explanations are farfetched. I remember once, in West Texas, meeting and chatting with an Iowa farmer at a motel, and his telling me that the day before he had seen a "wolverine." I replied that I had thought there weren't any in Texas. "Oh, yes, a lot of them," was the reply. He then informed me that a wolverine was "a small wolf." What he had seen was a coyote! I offer this as a possibility.

Of the savage obliteration of the primeval forest in Michigan, beginning with the white pine, it is useless to say much here. The dirge has been sufficiently chanted. It is not that these resources were not required for the needs of a fast-growing country. Quite properly they were there to be used. But then, pioneer development always partakes of the nature of looting—the devil take the hindmost. Anyway, the logging, first on the easier valley and flatland locations, then into the mountain areas, had in 1950, according to the well-informed Knox Jamison, reached the point where "several large companies are now operating on the last stand south of the park, and the end is in sight. In a few years now [the few years have already come] the park will be completely surrounded by a slash area which will write finis to the logging in the Porcupines."

How fortunate that Michigan, in 1943, had a governor and a legislature with the vision to insure the preservation of the remaining primeval woods of the Porcupine Mountains and the lower reaches of the Presque Isle River! A million dollars was appropriated to purchase the Porcupines region. By condemnation, trading, and some donations, additional land was acquired; and there are now more than 58,000 acres in the park—one conceived and operated on the highest principles, except for the hunting of animals, which is permitted.

To say merely that this state park is a place of beauty is to sell it short. It has outstanding significance, for on land of such historic and scientific import a thoughtful visitor may spend months. Only three small inholdings are left, one of them occupied by a pair of aged old-timers who are going to be permitted (as they should be) to live out their lives in their cabin. The rest is public recreation ground that does not require amusement devices.

If there were only space here to give even a moderate description of the geology of the Superior region of which the Porcupines are a sample! A long period of volcanic activity sent immense flows of lava over the site of present Lake Superior. Later, a great fault caused the part east of the present peninsula axis to sink, and the other part to rise. The highest point of this elevated part is the Porcupines. Government Peak, a favorite hike for the active, is 2,023 feet above sea level, the highest point in the northern tier of states between the Adirondacks and the Black Hills of South Dakota. And this trail is only one of a total of ninety miles of well-marked park adventures into the wild.

Between two great rolling ridges of the volcanic trap lie two beautiful lakes, one called Mirror, and the other the historic Carp Lake, from which flows a river that dives underground for a distance and then reappears. The best place for an enchanting view of the great hollow between the two highest ridges can be reached by a short footpath, and the visitor can drive right up to the beginning of the path and park his car there. This is a fine bit of planning, which allows the older folks to get close to the top of the scenic escarpment, yet involves no violation of the integrity of the overlook ground. Everything seemed to me wisely and imaginatively arranged: plenty of room in the use areas and no infringement on the natural features.

I have spoken of Carp Lake. I see by the park folder that it has been renamed "Lake of the Clouds." For myself, I beg permission to go on calling it by its historic name, one with a good homy and fishy sound.

In this park of quilly Kaug there are, naturally, cut-over and gaunt sections. The state came into the picture too late to save all that was primeval. But what remains of the virgin growth, conifer and hardwood, is so majestic as to bring a lump to the throat. What rock maples! Can you imagine a stand of these sugar trees, which the Chippewa used to tap for their confectionery, *ninety-five per cent pure?* Yet there are such stands. And the glorious white birch is everywhere. No wonder that the Finns and Scandinavians, birch-tree people, settled in and fell in love with this north woods. Incidentally, how fortunate it is that, driving along the long stretches of highway lined with these birches, as one comes westward on the peninsula, one is unaware of the burned and slashed forty-miles that lie behind on either side.

As one approaches the Porcupines from east or west, one sees a quick multiplication of motels, restaurants, and other caterers to the tourist. It would be natural to exclaim: "These people must have a pretty short season. Bet they have to make it fast!" But that isn't the fact. The summer season is short, yes. But then come the hunters, and later, in unbelievable numbers (considering the remoteness of the Peninsula), the winter-sports enthusiasts. Porcupine Mountains State Park offers delightful skiing and snowshoeing, and sportsmen make the trip, sometimes in special trains, from as far away as Chicago. A hundred inches of snowfall is about normal, annually, for this region.

In 1954 the Michigan Conservation Commission announced a policy for its state parks, that "these resources shall not be exploited at the expense of recreational values, though efficient management may dictate the sale, exchange or lease of parts of them . . ." Within three years after that pronouncement, and less than fifteen years after the legislative creation of the Porcupine Mountains State Park, a real threat arose. It was complicated by two facts: first, the state, though in possession of the park's surface land, owned only 38 per cent of the mineral rights; and second, the economy of the counties of the Upper Peninsula had been progressively disintegrating.

The unemployment and loss of population was serious. It was only natural, therefore, that, when a subsidiary of one of the great copper corporations came to the Commission with a proposal to lease part of the park and contiguous lands beneath Lake Superior for possible copper production, the announcement was greeted with enthusiasm in the Upper Peninsula. The proposal was conditional, however. If the company found copper in paying quantities, then it would mine commercially. There was not the slightest certainty that they would ever operate; but if they ever did, it would be in the far future. These uncertainties sufficed to develop a bitter antagonism between the commercial and the conservation groups. The worst danger was not in the possible mining operation in 933 acres of the state park. It would come from the erection of a smelter, presumably near the virgin trees of the Porcupines. Anyone who has looked at Butte, Montana, or Ducktown, Tennessee, can envisage what that would mean.

The prospective invasion, which would set a precedent for the ruin of this exceptionally fine state park, collapsed. The proposal for a lease was rejected. The fact that the conservation groups of the Lower Peninsula rallied effectively (and they had effective support all over the country, too) to protect the Porcupines has left some bitterness in the northern section.

Yet undoubtedly the future prosperity of the Upper Peninsula lies in the development of its outstanding recreation resources. A report by the Tourist and Resort Service of Michigan State University points out that "money values cannot be placed on wilderness. Recreation and refreshment afforded by solitude and grandeur of the Porcupine Mountains can only be measured by spiritual enrichment of those who visit there. *Nevertheless,* the economic aspects constitute important data for planning and administering such an outstanding scenic area."

Mining and lumbering in this region long ago passed the point of diminishing returns. It is a strange instance of a changed world that "solitude and grandeur" and the maintenance of unspoiled wilderness to attract the millions who need these spiritual joys, has proved the better *commercial* investment.

(X V)

STARVED ROCK STATE PARK

ILLINOIS

One mile south of Utica, on State 178, or five and a half miles southeast of LaSalle, on State 71

If you are interested in the history of the great struggle among England, France, and Spain for the possession of the North American continent—out of which contest finally emerged our own Republic of States—Starved Rock offers a dramatic and satisfying chapter of that epic story. The visitor, climbing the sandstone bastion and resting on its summit, looks down not merely upon fertile Plum Island and the broad Illinois River, and the modern deep waterway dam which affords safe passage to traffic from the Great Lakes to the Gulf—he looks much farther than that. His imagination will go back over the years to the day when Samuel de Champlain bet his money on the wrong horse.

In the earliest days of the seventeenth century, Champlain had led a force of Algonquin Indians, with some of his own soldiers, who carried long tubes which emitted smoke and spouted leaden balls that could kill at long distance, against the redoubtable Iroquois of the Mohawk Valley. The Iroquois, hardened warriors though they were, took to their heels in the face of this magic weapon. Thus they were humiliated in the very presence of an Indian nation that they had long held in contempt. But if ever there was a Pyrrhic victory, this was it. The Iroquois never forgave the French, and they never forgot that shame. To suggest that this was the main factor in the final outcome, the supremacy of the English, would be to overstate. But it was a considerable weight in the balance. The echo was to be heard later at the base of Starved Rock, now a modern state park where 60,000 people come on a single week-end day to picnic, camp, hike the trails, and otherwise partake of natural beauty, strange geological features, and rich history.

"Starved Rock." It is a strange name, for certainly the rock itself was not undernourished. The legends have it that, perhaps more than once, Indian combatants were pursued to this easily defended rock fortress and, refusing to come down and surrender, chose to die of starvation there. That some such thing happened is entirely likely. But over the years, in the telling, the facts acquire a heavily decorated mantle. As our local historian warns us, "the old Indian Chief Shick-Shack was 104 years old when he told the tale to a boy nine years old, who waited forty years to record it."

Really this part of the story of Starved Rock is of little importance. Let us say that Shick-Shack remembered well. In that case a band of Miami, Kickapoo, and Pottawattomi Indians did drive some Illini Indians to the top of the Rock, and either they starved there or they came down to be tomahawked. What is important is that the Iroquois Indians, mindful of their humiliation by Champlain, never relented for a day in their determination to prevent the French from conquering the country west of the Allegheny Mountains. The redskin siege at Starved Rock was merely an incident in that overall purpose. The Iroquois, allied with the English, not only boldly took the warpath into Illinois, but they had Indian friends and allies active wherever the French established a fort.

The Illini, or Illinois, Indians had been a numerous and powerful people when Father Marquette and Louis Jolliet, returning from their exploration of the upper Mississippi, stopped at the big native village on the north bank of the Illinois River just above Starved Rock. In 1675 Marquette founded the Mission of the Immaculate Conception in this village—the last missionary effort of the good father, who died the following spring.

Then came La Salle—René Robert Cavelier, Sieur de La Salle—and his faithful lieutenant Henri Tonti, the man with the iron hand. No figurative iron hand was this. It was actually metal, to replace a hand lost in warfare. To a shrewd, indefatigable, and ambitious statesman like La Salle, the importance of the Illinois River in the plan for French supremacy was evident. Empowered by a patent from King Louis, he claimed the western regions for France, and foresaw a seat of government here, rather than at far-off Quebec.

La Salle felt that his settlements were too far south properly to repel advances below the Great Lakes. What is now called Starved Rock, with its surrounding country of abundance, looked like a perfect center for his operations. Besides, after his great service to the Crown, he had a right to a little personal profit, and he saw a feudal state of his own at this choice spot. In 1683 he built Fort St. Louis on what he called "Le Rocher"—pretty certainly the imposing sandstone Gibraltar of the present park.

This fort looked down upon Indian villages with a considerable population, and a friendly one when their suspicions were not aroused. Tonti and his soldiers—mostly a sad rabble, by the way—felled great trees of the virgin forest and made palisades on the exposed side. "Below it was the ancient village of the Kaskaskias," says the chronicle, "who abandoned it since the raid three years ago by the Iroquois." The place seemed truly impregnable if well garrisoned. "It is accessible only on one side . . . this side is barred by a palisade of white oak stakes . . . flanked by three redoubts of square beams . . . at the top of the palisade a kind of chevaux-de-frise, the points of which are tipped to prevent scaling."

A valiant fort indeed! Under its protection the pro-French Indians could again reap their harvests unmolested by the Iroquois. Even taciturn Henri Tonti admitted that the region was delightful. "A great plain adorned with trees and abounding in strange fruits; buffalo and deer plentiful; game fish and birds abounding."

Fort St. Louis, a diorama of which attracted much attention when shown at the Illinois State Fair a few years ago, never had to be defended in the way La Salle conjectured. The real struggle took place elsewhere, particularly among the European diplomats. After the beginning of the nineteenth century, the abandoned fort, rapidly decaying, housed stray travelers and traders.

The veteran soldier, Daniel Hitt, who bought "the Rock" and surrounding acreage from the federal government in the homesteading period, seems to have had a shrewd vision that the public of later days would regard the locality as a sort of birthplace of the state. Hitt was tireless in surveying, mapping, digging for relics, and collecting artifacts, and when he finally sold his property to a Chicago man in 1890, it was clear from the correspondence that a "resort development" was in view. The price, $14,000 for the Rock and a hundred acres of land, would hardly have been justified on any other basis.

"For a very short time," we are told, "the area centering around the Rock was the site of a boom to make it 'the Gibraltar of the

West,' a resort to which all Americans would flock. It was used as a picnic spot for many years, and at one time there was a dance floor on the summit. Later a hotel company developed the site as a scenic area."

A place of such natural beauty and historic significance was not overlooked by conservation-minded people of the state. Even at the time when Daniel Hitt sold the property, a movement had begun to secure it and preserve it in a dignified way for the people. The legislature finally authorized the purchase of Starved Rock and 280 acres of land in 1911, and since that time many additions have brought the total to more than 1,500 acres, with three miles of frontage on the south side of the Illinois River. The fine Mathiessen estate, with its generous woodland and attractive dells, was acquired by the state in 1944. Though it does not immediately adjoin Starved Rock park, it may, I suppose, be considered an integral part of it, and is a most valuable public asset for the years to come.

The three miles of frontage on the south side of the Illinois supply an effective example of the importance of naturalist guide service in a state park of rich geological and botanical resources. In Starved Rock State Park there are many magnificent trails, over which, to be sure, the visitor can make his unguided way if he chooses. But a skilled interpreter, with a trained power of observation, can endow these trail trips with special charm and meaning. To begin with, the nature of the river bluffs, with their entering canyons, needs some explanation. Why all these deep ravines, cutting deeply through the sandstone rock and resembling from the air a long series of ribs attached to a backbone, but without a sign of a similar arrangement on the opposite side of the river? You may have come suddenly upon these exposed sandstone rocks from a terrain of agricultural land without a suggestion of the towering promontories within the park.

The outcropping of this sandstone formation, known as the "St. Peter," is unusual in Illinois, though it underlies most of the state. But just at that point there was a great upfolding of the earth's surface, and it was along this wrinkle that the mighty glacial streams of a departing ice sheet found alternate layers of resistant and less resistant rock in which to carve their channels. Deeper and deeper they bored down, generally creating precipitous sides, till finally their outlets were on a level with the great river.

Since the St. Peter sandstone is rather porous in composition, it has been able to support fine forest growth. The park is full of magnificent trees, white and black oaks, walnuts, hickories, hornbeams—a wide variety of broad-leaved species interspersed with cedars and white pines. Since the white pine does not normally occur south of this location, the naturalist will suggest to his party that peculiar conditions in this postglacial region have created a little "island" for their survival from an ancient forest cover. The deep canyons, of course, are full of plant life that depends upon cool and shaded sheltering, altogether different from that of the nearby prairie.

Someone of excellent taste was responsible for the names of these canyons. How cheering it is to find that these names commemorate the historical pageant of earlier days! St. Louis Canyon; another named for Iron-Hand Tonti; one for La Salle; another for Hennepin; and still others for the Indian tribes that knew them so well, and made among them the very trails your feet travel on today. Kickapoo, Kaskaskia, Fox. Yes, and one for that unfortunate "conspirator" Pontiac, who awoke a little too late to the menace of the white man: even Pontiac has not been forgotten. The canyon of greatest size, the one with the widest valley, is very properly called Illinois.

By contrast, you meet the Devil several times within the park. Our forbears, apparently, never quite expelled this important person from their imaginations. So you have Devil's Nose, Devil's Bathtub, Devil's Paintbox. Very well; let us give these a leering eye and signal Satan to advance and give us the countersign. But—Lovers' Leap! That one is hard to take. I look forward to a visit to some park of geologic curiosities where the passion of love has not been expressed by a leap off a cliff. For I simply cannot believe that this tender testimony of despair was ever quite so common as our naming would indicate; especially among the Indian population.

Looking down from the bluffs upon the river is a remarkable experience; the visitor can also—in the long summer season—have the pleasure of seeing the bluffs from the river. Boat trips are made up to the Waterway Dam and Locks, and then, after a short walk, may be continued upstream on the other side.

Perhaps the most spectacular rock formation within the park is the great shelter overhang known as Council Cave. This was really a meeting place where Indian tribal deliberations took place. It is not, of course, a true cave, but merely a gouge in the side of the sandstone cliff where erosive forces worked on less resistant rock at the base.

The councils here, it is said, were invariably attended by a few carefully chosen women of the tribe, selected for their high discretion and their good memories. They were the recorders of the proceedings, not taking down notes in shorthand, but committing the speeches to their memories for future reference.

Though it seems almost certain that such a rock shelter would have been used by the prehistoric people of the region, the archaeological research that has been done here failed to produce much, if any, evidence of such occupation, and the excavations reached a considerable depth. It is possible that severe floods at some time washed out such evidence.

This is rich Indian country. Two village sites have been found within the park, as well as a few mounds, which have been excavated and studied. Two miles away, near Utica, the river plain is dotted with the mounds of an ancient people. One small cave within the park contained a pre-Columbian burial.

Spring and fall, a great and joyous flapping of wings takes place along the river valley. The Illinois is a notable flyway for migrating game birds, as well as for such visitors as the cormorants who roost in the bordering trees. Teal, mallards, bluebills, and canvasbacks, and frequently Canada geese pay their respects each year to the rich feed offered.

The larger animals that the early settlers found—the abundance that astonished Henri Tonti—have long since vanished, but the smaller creatures that prove so alluring to "city folks" are here still in plenty—the opossum, raccoon, fox, squirrel, and rabbit. The bird watcher will never be disappointed in Starved Rock State Park. It may be that he will see the bald eagle. For my part, I shall be well pleased to watch the little fellow with the tropical plumage—no songster, but a rare delight to the eye—the indigo bunting. A glimpse of him is warranted to chase away all gloom.

(XVI)

TURKEY RUN STATE PARK

INDIANA

Two and a half miles north of Marshall, on State 47

As THIS is being written, I am looking at a picture of John Lusk, once of Parke County in Indiana. His face reminds me of a thin-lipped, square-jawed man I once saw seated on the porch of a country store in a northern New York village. With great deliberateness he whittled contemplatively on a stick of soft white pine. Something prompted me to ask a bystander who this citizen was. After giving me the name, my informant said: "A mighty good man, too, if you don't *mad* him." I looked again, and decided that it was good advice.

Judging from this picture of John Lusk, he too was a good man, but not one to be madded. The eyes, peering out from busy eyebrows, suggest that this man went about his own affairs in his own way, willing to let the rest of the world do the same: a man not to be safely exasperated. He was never married. He did not even need the companionship of a dog. He was content with his few books and old family records. The picture shows him seated outside his house beside an anvil. The anvil looks mellow compared to John.

Yet this hermit, or semihermit, of whom many quaint yarns are told, was the man who made it possible for the state of Indiana to possess one of the last and finest stands of that rich primeval forest which, in this section of the country, went down before the march of eager settlers who had corn and wheat in mind. For years and years John Lusk, owner of hardwoods and conifers that watered the eyes of the lumbermen, shook his head. Some other trees, not his.

The handsomer the price offered, the more steely the refusal. The timber cutters might just as successfully have been dealing with John's anvil.

Why? What was behind this stout resolution to preserve the primeval trees? Who knows? Some said it was just plain cussedness, a cynical delight in saying no. It may have been a filial tribute arising; this was the forest of his father, Captain Salmon Lusk, who came with his young wife to the banks of Sugar Creek in 1826 and built their home in a beautiful wilderness. It was known that the garments of John's mother hung for forty years in a closet of the big brick house, treasured and undisturbed. Perhaps he felt that these were his mother's trees, too. Or John may have just loved the virgin forest, instead of placing his affections elsewhere. It might be as simple as that.

But there stood the trees until John Lusk died. They were (and by good fortune they *are*) magnificent. If, as I am, you happen to be susceptible to the charms of the beech tree, here are some of the loveliest you will ever see. The tulip-poplars, with not a branch for seventy-five feet, have the undeviating erectness of an engineered monument. There is a wild cherry in this state park that foresters say is the finest they have ever seen. The sycamores along the stream beds, the black walnuts of astonishing girth, the lacy-foliaged hemlocks that unexpectedly occur at the brink of the creek canyons, and the maples that gave their sugar to the Indians centuries ago—Pungosecone, "the water of many sugar trees," they called Sugar Creek—rise from a lush floor of ferns and grasses, mosses and lichens. No wonder that most people come to this park to walk the trails! Long before the state came into possession, it had been a favorite resort, and the people who came to enjoy its quiet shade and beauty were welcomed by John Lusk—if they behaved themselves.

But John Lusk finally had to leave his anvil. Then there was an estate to settle. There was to be an auction. The date was May 18, 1916.

The state-park enthusiasts of Indiana had long had their hopeful eyes on this land. Richard Lieber, as director of the Department of Conservation, was arousing interest in a number of desirable areas, and this one was to him a must. Juliet V. Strauss of Rockville (*The Country Contributor*) was to this prospective state park what Mrs. Frank Sheehan was to the park at Indiana Dunes. A commission had been appointed to make arrangements for the purchase of the property, but the state appropriated nothing toward the purpose, and the results of appeals for popular subscription were mainly best wishes.

So, with the Lusk sale coming on, the prospects for public ownership were dim. But a new commission, headed by Colonel Lieber, found newspaper support, which led to the creation of some real enthusiasm. As a result, the commission was able to attend the auction with $20,000 in its purse. Since an appraisal of $18,000 had been made, this sum appeared to be sufficient.

However, some of the Lusk heirs, with a private park in mind, had decided to get into the bidding. And a lumber corporation, with marvelous hardwood veneering material in mind, was not to be thwarted. When the bids reached $30,200, the state commissioners turned sadly away, and the lumber company had John Lusk's trees. But the drama of the auction saved the day for the conservationists. The public now became excited. After some prodding, the legislature appropriated enough money so that, with what had been donated by generous citizens, there was about $40,000 with which to pay off the lumber company. For that sum, then, the people of Indiana acquired Turkey Run. What a bargain it was, when one considers what would have to be paid for it today! This was a case of the state being late, but not *too* late.

As always, in writing of these affairs, we can mention only a few of the stalwart souls who labored and contributed toward the humane enterprise; in this instance, Colonel Lieber, Arthur C. Newby, Mrs. Strauss, Dr. Frank B. Wynn are a few of the leading spirits. What of the many unsung heroes and heroines of the campaign? Even if they get no blazon, they can visit Turkey Run State Park and say, with honest pride: "I, too—I helped preserve John Lusk's woods."

When Sugar Creek is at low water, it is an innocent-looking stream. But it can be a riotous torrent during the spring floods, and likewise on the occasion of heavy cloudbursts that sometimes occur upstream in summer when there is only a drizzle in the lower reaches. At such time there may be a sudden wall of water four feet high roaring down the canyon, and a rise of an inch an hour till a total of twenty-two feet is not uncommon. A fine fishing stream, then, and ordinarily a safe one, but good judgment is needed by the visitor.

It was on the bank of the Narrows, where now the creek is crossed by a modern highway bridge not far from the fine old covered wooden one, that Captain Lusk, father of John, built his mill.

When the floods came, he was able to float good-sized flatboats and send them down to New Orleans with his flour and other farm products. He built a new home of brick on the high ground above the mill; this property has now become part of Turkey Run State Park. I saw some white pines around it which reminded me of similar trees that are found in this part of the country. The white pine, though it flourishes in these farm dooryards, does not grow here naturally today. How did these trees get here? The explanation offered is amusing, and seems to be well authenticated. Amusing—and a little touched with sentiment, too, for it shows that our pioneering folks liked a dab of the exotic around them, if indeed some of them had not a nostalgic yearning for trees they had known in their former abodes.

Somewhere in this part of Indiana there was a settler who made excellent whisky. Every year, at the coming of summer, he loaded up a wagon with his beverage and drove up to Michigan. After peddling his product, and spending a pleasant vacation fishing up north, the distiller came back home with a load of white-pine saplings, which found a ready market. A state forester not long ago counted the rings of one of these pines, and the age of the tree agreed perfectly with the date ascribed to the two-way commerce of the whisky peddler.

Sugar Creek itself, like all such streams in this part of Indiana, has carved its way down through the sandstones that were deposited in the geologic times when a great shallow sea covered the region. The coming of the glacial ice, much later, poured drift material, boulders, clay, and sand into the old valleys, choking them up and forcing the floods of the melting ice to find new ways of seeking the sea. To bore down through the loose drift material was easy for such new streams; and, once established, the swift waters ate readily into the sandstones below. These rocks were of varying hardness, the toughest of them being nearest the top; therefore, many of the side canyons, deep, fern-clad, cold, and with precipitous walls, are actually wider at the bottom than at the top. Turkey Run, Rocky Hollow, Bear Hollow, Gypsy Gulch—all these little side canyons are reached by convenient and generally easy trails, and lead the visitor into an association of plant and animal life which is far different from that of the plateau above.

One of the most striking pictures is only a few steps from the comfortable lodge and cabins that overflow with fortunate guests during the warmer months, though accommodations are available throughout the year. At Sunset Point—aptly named because at a certain time of the year the sun seems to be going down into the waters of Sugar Creek—we stand at the point where Turkey Run enters the larger chasm. The name "Turkey Run," of course, dates back to the days when great flocks of these truly American fowl found a perfect night shelter in the overhanging rocks at the base of the gulch. One legend has it that the early hunters used to *drive* the birds into the Run. It does not seem likely. They were probably there by choice.

On the way to the verge at Sunset Point, the visitor must not fail to spend a little time with the Gay Log Cabin. He will not find many like it. It was not originally at this spot, but that is unimportant. Richard Lieber stumbled upon the cabin by accident one day in 1917 when he got off the road he had planned to travel. At very small cost, it was dismantled lovingly and set up in the park.

Daniel Gay, long before the Civil War, built this cabin with only a helping hand in setting up the huge squared logs. An ax, an adze, a drawknife, and a frow—and Daniel's muscle. Such logs! Can you envision trees that would enable this man to get out timbers of tulip-poplar thirty feet long, almost three feet in width, and six inches thick? All the doors, window casings, and the great mantel are of black walnut; hewn oak logs support the flooring. The boards in the doors are fastened to the crosspieces with wooden pins and the doors are hung on wooden hinges and fastened with a wooden latch. Housed in this cabin is a collection of pioneer farming and household tools and utensils of the period.

The little church, too, was brought into the park from another location, but it fits as perfectly as does the Gay cabin. Rude as it is, lighted only by such devices as existed when it was originally "raised," it offers those who attend the services held there during the season something of the simplicity of devotion that can only be had where "a few are gathered together." A friend of mine, a most religious man, complained to me that "the modern church is too well-lighted for meditation." He meant during services, of course. He would enjoy this little meeting house, I feel sure.

We may guess that Turkey Run State Park was the favorite of Indiana's great park man, Colonel Lieber. His ashes rest there, in a little commemorative rock-garden niche, shadowed by giant trees. Lieber was an outspoken man, not notably patient with fools or—as he saw it—despoilers of natural wonders and beauties. If he didn't write it, he surely would have agreed with the bitter frankness of expression employed in an early park booklet with regard to people who had been carving their initials in the sandstone of Bear Hollow:

> No more will ghouls mar this sacred place with their tools that destroy the beauty which God in His goodness has seen fit to give to the people of Indiana . . . the one who said that 'fools' names and faces are often seen in public places must have had in mind just such a place as this. . . .

Indiana, in truth, has been a fortunate state in the park world, both in the type of men and women who did the spade work in the acquisition of fine areas, and in the subsequent faithful and understanding management. And this is strange. For it has all come about in a state where the politicians have not shown any willingness to protect the park personnel from the poised threat of the spoils system.

From the 288 acres comprised in the first purchase, Turkey Run State Park by later additions has grown to about 1,500 acres. Not an acre too much, for though some of it is cut-over land, nature restores the forest growth readily in this region, and this will be one of the major parks where the future citizens can come to realize what their ancestors found when the westward trek was on.

On the Lusk Homestead the Nature Study Club of Indiana has placed a tablet which reads:

TO THE MEMORY OF JOHN LUSK,
WHO SAVED THE
TREES OF TURKEY RUN.

Well deserved, if ever a tribute was!

(X V I I)

VAN METER STATE PARK

MISSOURI

Fourteen miles northwest of Marshall, on State 122

SAM IRWIN, a farmer in this delightful area where in the future there will be ample resources for both physical and mental recreation, joined us as we looked at some of the fruits of a significant archaeological enterprise. Upon one of the heights of land along the Missouri River, created from wind-blown topsoil of the glacial period, is an excavation jointly sponsored by the Missouri State Park Board and the University of Missouri.

A skilled archaeologist like Robert T. Bray, who is director of this research center within Van Meter State Park, is naturally wary of the eager but ignorant volunteers who love to plunge their blundering shovels into just such a site as this. I never visit the scene of a scientific excavation without recalling what an old-time expert, Jesse Nusbaum, told me of the wealthy "collector" somewhere in the Rocky Mountain states who for fifteen years blithely vandalized precious prehistoric sites. Then, when he finally turned over his trophies to a museum—unlabeled, unrelated, often lacking even a notation of the region from which they had been excavated—they proved to be of little archaeological value.

This farmer, Sam Irwin, is different. Unpresuming, anxious to add to a store of knowledge that makes him a "happy amateur," he has acquired a remarkable knowledge of the history of the Indians who lived in this part of the state; and he offered an apt comment now and then which helped to round out the picture our group of visitors was aiming to construct. In this day of ample leisure time, it should be the ideal of our national, state, and other parks to create just such interest in knowledge.

And do many people like the sort of thing that is being offered at this archaeological demonstration? In one month 3,200 visitors signed the register—and consider how many people do not sign such registers. Remember, too, that no swimming is available, or boating, and certainly no "amusements." The visitor can camp here, and the master plan for the area envisions the creation of a little lake and also the provision of sufficient opportunities for quiet relaxation. But at this time practically all the visitors come to see a prehistoric site in process of scientific and professionally directed excavation.

Curiosity? Of course. How else do we arrive at the point where it becomes fun to know? Would these same visitors be as interested in studying labeled exhibits of artifacts in a well-ordered museum as they are in watching the archaeological students from the university take relics from the ground? Of course there is a dramatic quality to this work-in-progress: the expectation of seeing the excavator, working with the delicate fingers of a watchmaker, bring up something of interest and value from the earth cover.

Yet, the visitors do not overlook the rude little exhibit that is housed in an old chicken coop. One phase of interest leads easily into a further interest. Missourians have within the past decade developed an increased interest in their historical background. A notable instance is the city of Marshall, not far from Van Meter State Park—but it may be found also in many a town and small city in the state.

The visitor to Van Meter is handed a single sheet of information, provided by courtesy of the Missouri Archaeological Society of Columbia. This leaf is a model of concise statement; it bears the impress of a first-class interpreter. Since no adaptation of it could make it more to the purpose, it may as well be quoted:

"You are walking over the ground where, 230 years ago, stood a bustling Indian town of the Missouri Indians after whom our state and the great Missouri River were named.

"In or near this large town took place some of the first meetings between the French explorers and the Missouri Indians. The first European fort on the Missouri River, Fort Orleans, was built on the river bank not far from this spot. The exact location of Fort Orleans has not yet been discovered.

"Today, students enrolled in the regular archeological field classes of the University find brass, glass and copper ornaments—proof of this early contact—as they excavate and study the varied remains of the Missouri Indian.

"Nearby and preserved in the park area are campsites of early hunters dating back thousands of years ago. The 'Old Fort' lies on a hilltop to the west. It is thought to be a ceremonial earthwork of the Hopewellian Indians who lived in the area from the time of Christ to about 500 A.D. Mounds are other evidences of the long continued use of the 'pinnacles' by the Indians. It is planned to investigate and interpret all these things in the future.

"As you tour the area, your questions 'How does an archeologist work?' and 'What does he find?' will be answered, at least in part. Talking with the students and archeologists and reading publications available through the Missouri Archaeological Society will help to answer your further questions."

Looking at a map of the state of Missouri, one sees that from near Waverly on the west to Boonville on the east the Missouri River makes a great bend. To be sure, this vagrant stream makes many minor bends within the big one; but the wide sweep was so noticeable to the early cartographers that they all recorded it in their mapping.

Rather to the western side of this big bend occur a number of the high ridges locally known as "pinnacles," which, as we have seen, are great dunes of a finely pulverized silt or sand known to geologists as loess. Loess has two important properties: when well watered, it produces vegetation generously; and when eroded, it cuts down almost vertically. Those who have traveled the Natchez Trace Parkway of the National Park System will remember some of the sunken roads toward Natchez where the top of the loess dune is a score of feet above the head of the traveler on the road.

It was upon this pinnacle that from about the years 1690 to 1750 the historic Missouri Indians made their home. They were a peace-loving Siouan tribe. They could fight if they had to, but they were hardly a match for the roving and belligerent Sacks and Foxes, two Algonquian raiding nations that had pooled their resources in a fairly close federation. These, coming out of what is now Michigan, Wisconsin, and Minnesota, made it important that the Missouris choose a site not only of good farming land within good prairie hunting ground, as well as close to the big river, but also upon a defensible height of land. Here it was—an admirable home.

There were deer, elk, and bison nearby. The excavation has already revealed the range of the food supplies of the little colony. The soil was highly productive, except in time of drought. There were springs of excellent water just down the slope from the top of the ridge. The drainage was perfect for the maintenance of good health. But what do we see now as we stand on this ridge and look around? Were these copses of big trees there when the Indians occupied the site? Surely not. One of the advantages of the location—that of commanding an unbroken view of the surrounding country—would then have been sacrificed. It is certain that this forest has come in upon the loess mounds because the later white occupants of the region plowed the ground for crops.

The diarists of the Lewis and Clark expedition seem to have located a Missouri Indian village on the north side of the great river. This may have been an error, or it is of course possible that the Missouris did have temporary quarters there. But it is clear that the site on the south side was more suitable for resistance against the raiders from the east.

After 1750, these people found the Van Meter site no longer tenable. They may have been weakened by some infectious disease contracted from the French or other traders. At any rate, they moved upstream about ten miles to another site, where, archaeological work has revealed, their trading for "civilized" materials greatly increased. Even so, their relentless enemies finally drove them out of the region entirely.

They moved into Kansas and Nebraska, first as tolerated guests and later merging with the local tribe, thus losing their identity among the Otos, likewise a Siouan people. This historical fact is evident from the resemblances of Missouri work found in sites of the Otos farther west. As to the Fort Orleans of the trading period, our leaflet tells us that "its location has not yet been discovered." Perhaps, since we know that it was situated on the margin of the river, it never will be. As was the case of Fort Caroline, on the St. Johns River in Florida, the whimsical stream may have changed its course and washed everything away.

Perhaps much of the allurement the many visitors to the excavation site have found derives from the businesslike presentation of part of the finds. It is as though Bray and his associates were saying to the public: "Don't expect a finished museum here. It is not the time, and we have not the necessary structures. A deserted chicken house will have to serve to display the complete skeleton we have exhumed, which has been jacketed with plaster to keep it intact;

also some reproductions of the coiled pottery work (showing how the utensils were made and decorated with incised designs on the lips and upper sides). Over there, in a rude showcase, you can see a few of the artifacts we have found, including a really choice specimen of the paired stones that were used to straighten arrow shafts. This one, of a grooved coarse sandstone probably taken from the river bed, shows really superb workmanship, and no modern fabrication could be better suited for its purpose.

"Also, dear visitor," the director seems to say, "some of the pits have been left open for your examination. Use your imagination. Here, at the bottom of one of them, is the skeleton of someone whose legs were flexed at burial. Why, when the custom at this site seems to have been to inter the deceased supine and extended? And this person, as you see, has no ornaments buried with him, whereas all the others were found with the little trinkets that they must have treasured during their lifetime. Was this possibly a slave? The Missouris occasionally had slaves, as we know. Or was it some member of a tribe with different burial habits, who had wandered into this village and died among strangers?

"And then, have a look at these trash pits. There is evidence that each family may have had its own garbage-disposal pit in back of the 'house.' These trash pits are extremely interesting. They show what the family intentionally discarded, but occasionally there is also an object that was not thrown away intentionally. This arrow point, for example, in perfectly good condition. Plentiful as the supply of flint might have been, they didn't throw away good points. Or this bone awl. Surely, that went out with the garbage accidentally; just as the housekeeper sometimes loses a good silver spoon with the potato parings."

No wonder more than 3,000 visitors delightedly roam around the excavations on a broiling July day. Most of them surely found that they were not merely visitors, but participants in the fascinating reconstruction of life in this village in the seventeenth and eighteenth centuries.

The prehistoric old fort west of this excavation is, of course, of an entirely different nature and period. We have mentioned that artifacts from this vallated earthwork disclosed the Hopewellian culture so commonly found in Ohio and the surrounding states. This is perhaps "farthest west" for such a culture. The outer lines of the fort followed the natural contour, and enclosed about six and a quarter acres. The shape is rather ovoid. Though called a fort, this was more likely a place of religious ceremony. Erosion has softened the outlines, but the forms are still readily apprehended. Many good-sized trees have sprung up in this area, which will be a subject of revealing interpretation at Van Meter in time to come.

This fine park occupies ground that has been fortunately preserved in a state where so much archaeological evidence has been destroyed by land use. Here, though seekers for trophies and mantelpiece ornaments have been busy with their spades over a long period, the actual disturbance has not been great. The visitor is indeed in the center of a great area where evidence has been found of ten thousand years of human occupancy. The winding Missouri was not alone a waterway of adventure for the white man migrating toward the setting sun. Others, many others, had passed that way before.

PART 5

THE WEST

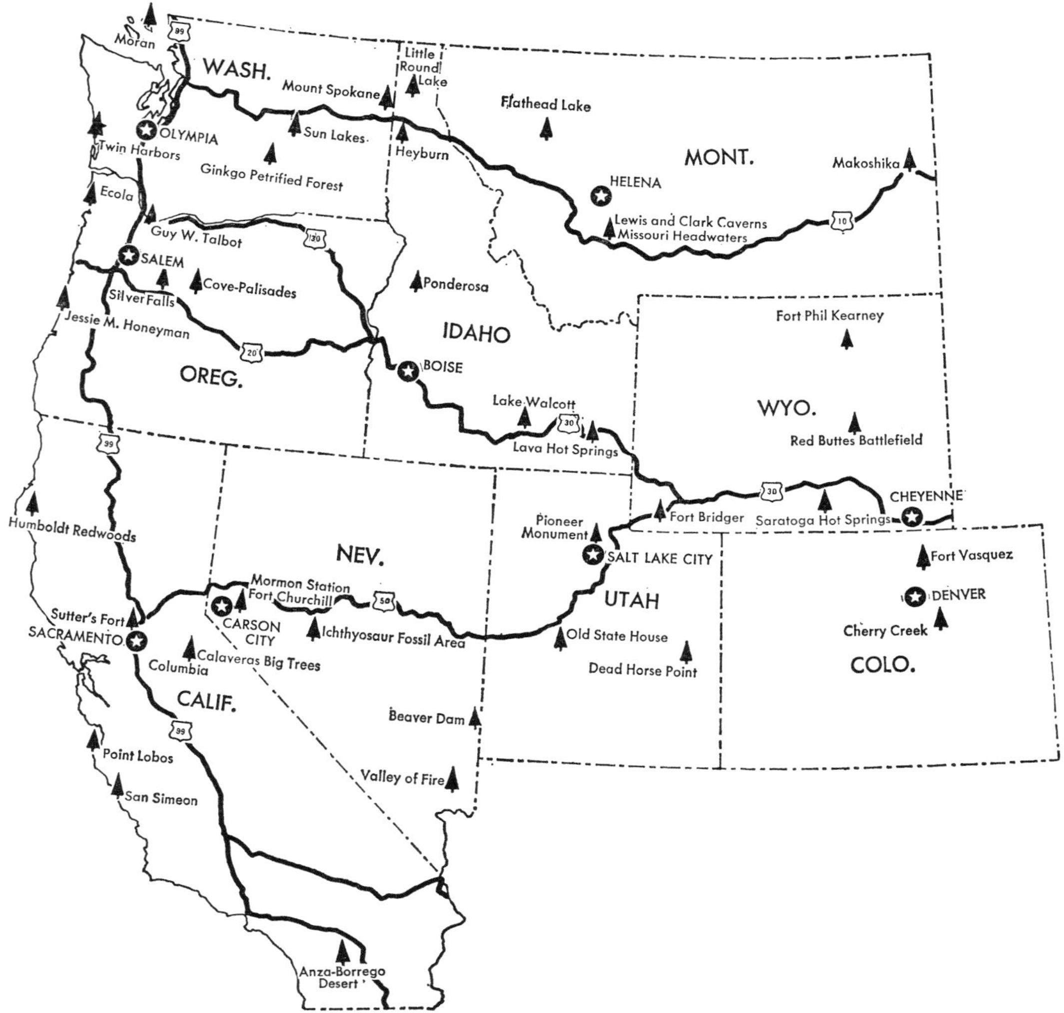

WASH.
OREG.
CALIF.
NEV.
IDAHO
MONT.
WYO.
UTAH
COLO.
OLYMPIA
SALEM
SACRAMENTO
CARSON CITY
BOISE
HELENA
SALT LAKE CITY
CHEYENNE
DENVER
Moran
Twin Harbors
Mount Spokane
Sun Lakes
Ginkgo Petrified Forest
Little Round Lake
Heyburn
Flathead Lake
Makoshika
Lewis and Clark Caverns
Missouri Headwaters
Ecola
Guy W. Talbot
Silver Falls
Cove-Palisades
Jessie M. Honeyman
Ponderosa
Lake Walcott
Lava Hot Springs
Fort Phil Kearney
Red Buttes Battlefield
Fort Bridger
Saratoga Hot Springs
Pioneer Monument
Fort Vasquez
Cherry Creek
Humboldt Redwoods
Sutter's Fort
Mormon Station
Fort Churchill
Ichthyosaur Fossil Area
Old State House
Dead Horse Point
Columbia
Calaveras Big Trees
Beaver Dam
Valley of Fire
Point Lobos
San Simeon
Anza-Borrego Desert
99
30
20
10
50

(I)

ANZA-BORREGO DESERT STATE PARK

CALIFORNIA

Ninety-four miles northeast of San Diego,
north of Highway 78,
between Julian and the Salton Sea

WHEN, on the last day of the year 1928, the California State Park Commission presented to Governor Young the report of Frederick Law Olmsted's *State Park Survey of California*, they used the words "a magnificent report which deals with the problems in hand in a masterly fashion." They were speaking with restraint. The Olmsted survey remains a classic, not merely for California, but for any state that aspires to set aside portions of its natural domain while there is yet time for preservation of the landscape and all qualities therein, in all possible integrity.

Olmsted, with his sensitive eye and soul, was the man; and, to do them justice, the Californians were the people. Before the Olmsted report was in print, the people of the state had bonded themselves in the amount of six million dollars to be used on a fifty-fifty matching basis for the purchase of park lands. Therefrom, and with the accomplishments of the Save-the-Redwoods League as a potent educational background force, there came into being one of the great park systems of the world.

For our present purposes, let us hear what Olmsted had to say of the desert:

"Certain desert areas have a distinctive and subtle charm, in part dependent upon spaciousness, solitude, and escape from the evidence of human control and manipulation of the earth, a charm of constantly growing value as the rest of the earth becomes more completely dominated by man's activities. This quality is a very vulnerable one. Its bloom is easily destroyed by comparatively slight changes made by man. The very conditions which make a desert what it is, leave every man-made scar upon its surface so completely unsoftened by natural processes as to produce a rapidly cumulative deterioration of its precious wildness.

"The desert is in general worth so little for any other purpose than occasional enjoyment of its untamed character, and so much of it in southeastern California is within easy reach by automobile of so large a population, that it seems a clear duty of the state to preserve inviolate several desert areas large enough for future generations to enjoy in perfection . . . nowhere else are casual thoughtless changes so irreparable, and nowhere else is it so important to control and completely protect wide areas."

How could any man be so foreseeing? "Within easy reach by automobile of so large a population." This was 1928. Since then the population has exploded, as jargon has it. Automobiles stream into the desert, of a weekend, like army ants on the move. "Inviolate?" It was too late to attain that ideal in large measure. The desert is fast going the way of the Atlantic and Gulf seashores, and the inland lakes, and the larger streamsides desirable for cottage and shack.

This invasion of the desert for private recreative ownership is hard to believe until you have seen it. "Exploding population" for many refers only to the increase in population and to sprawling suburbia. But this stampede for personal ownership of a fraction of wilderness is more than that.

The magnificent Anza-Borrego Desert State Park, inholdings and invasions to the contrary, is the answer to California's needs. And it was achieved in the nick of time. Except for a few desirable arable and ranching spots in this desert-mountain country, a few years ago no one wanted it. Now luxurious hotels, motels, and expensive residences have sprung up all around.

Olmsted said "in part dependent on spaciousness." Well, Anza-Borrego is spacious: 460,000 acres, mostly virginal, and some yet unexplored. The ranger points out distant mountains. "Those are in the park." We come to a short stretch where he says, with a touch of sadness: "We don't own this strip." But soon you see more mountains, more canyons, more vast alluvial fans: all *that* is park.

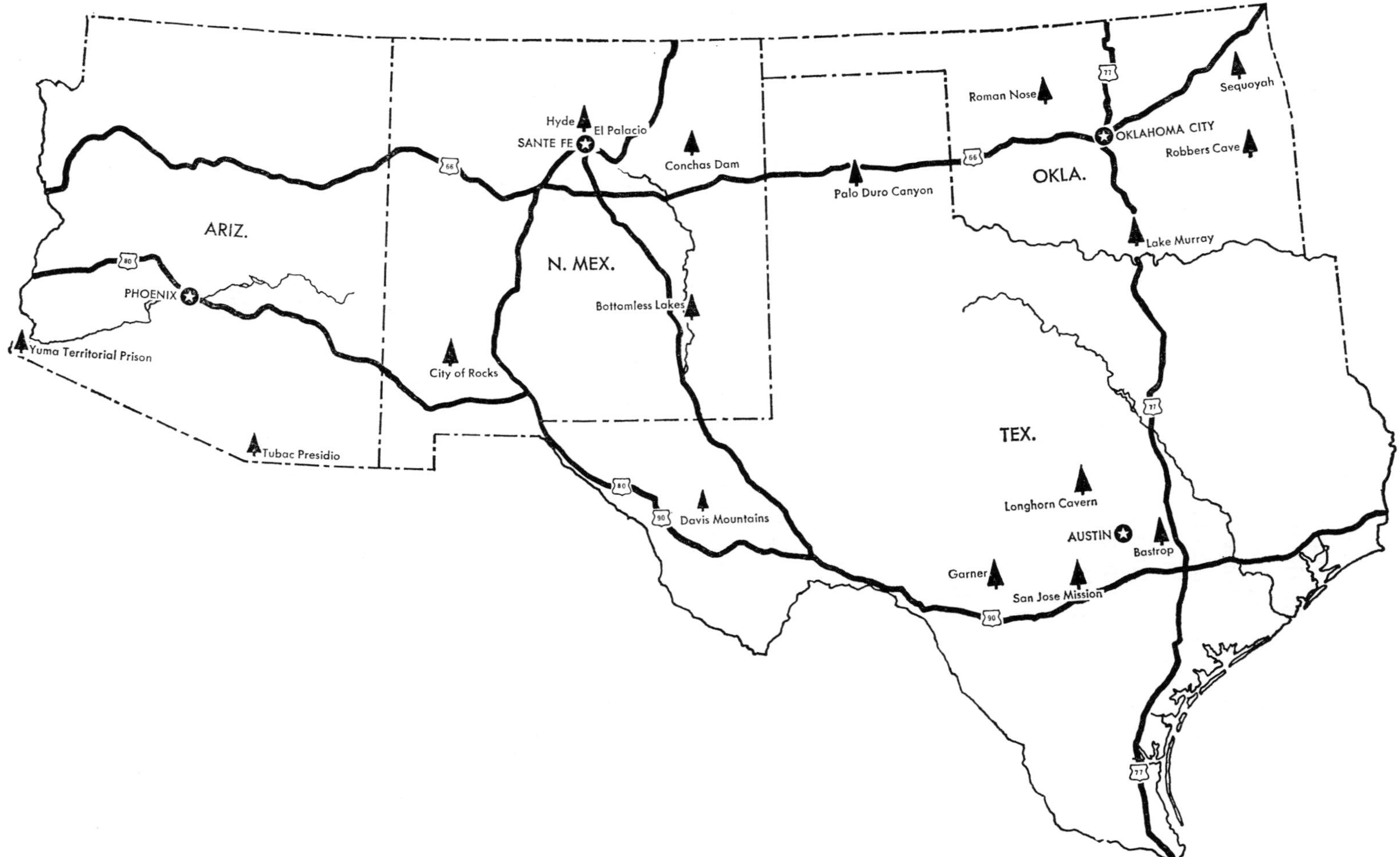
ARIZ.
N. MEX.
OKLA.
TEX.
PHOENIX
Yuma Territorial Prison
Tubac Presidio
City of Rocks
Hyde
El Palacio
SANTE FE
Conchas Dam
Bottomless Lakes
Davis Mountains
Palo Duro Canyon
Roman Nose
OKLAHOMA CITY
Sequoyah
Robbers Cave
Lake Murray
Longhorn Cavern
AUSTIN
Bastrop
Garner
San Jose Mission
66
77
80
90

You can hear remonstrants saying: "Why do you need so much land for a park?" It was said here; is still being said. Why, indeed? *Spaciousness.* Without that quality, desert is merely a place of pleasurable basking—or, in summer, rapid cooking. Solitude, or the opportunity for it, comes from spaciousness.

There are other reasons. The life that goes on in the desert is not, as you would think, meager. It is astonishingly abundant. But the competition is terrific. The community demands room. You kill if you crowd. And finally we recall the wise words of that Connecticut Yankee: "When you are in a park, all you see is in the park." Meaning sky, distant range, and possible scars and ugliness that are beyond the boundary but in your vision.

When Juan Bautista de Anza, with the Indian convert Sebastian Tarabal as guide, led his party of 240 from Sonoran Tubac across this desert and up Coyote Canyon in the year 1775, they made no scars on the surface of the beautiful land. The party moved across it much as the Indians did; and the aboriginal peoples, as Willa Cather noted in the story of her Archbishop, "treated the land with consideration; not attempting to improve it, they never desecrated it. . . . they seemed to have none of the European's desire to 'master' nature, to arrange and recreate."

Despite the invasion of resorts, most of this mountain-desert country looks today as it appeared to the eyes of the priests who kept diaries of the early Spanish transits. They had time. They saw the native palm trees that still furtively thrive in the remote canyon shelters. They passed the great stands of ocotillo, which flourishes here as I have never seen it elsewhere, and reminds one of the fact that, though desert lands may appear the same, the plant world knows differences in soil, elevation, rainfall. In the Mojave are found the superb Joshua-trees—though they do fairly well on the fringes. We think of the magnificent showing of agaves that climb the steeps of Casa Grande in Big Bend National Park. The ocotillo waves its many bare arms wildly and plays dead in the dry time, then becomes well clothed with leaves and tipped with bright red flowers when the rains come. Nowhere is the ocotillo so proud; proud, perhaps, of the fact that it is *not* a cactus; and it looks down in condescension upon the bisnagas, the determined creosote bush, and the brittle bush, and a hundred other desert plants, including, when the rains are well timed, the carpeting bloom of miraculously springing flowers.

Near Bow Willow Canyon Road is an ocotillo twenty-nine feet

tall. About nine miles up Carrizo Wash stands an eight-foot Bigelow cholla. Mystery upon mystery—you will see, if you are willing to use your legs, the "elephant tree." Except for just one small spot in the Santa Rosa Mountains, this odd relative of the Mexican copal thrives only in this desert park. It emigrated north; or perhaps it once grew here in abundance and these trees are what is left.

The Spanish emigrants moved quietly across this desert toward Alta California, to establish a presidio in San Francisco. They treated the land with prudent respect. But other people followed who left stripes on the face of the fragile landscape. Settlers with iron-shod wagon wheels, explorers on railroad surveys, John Butterfield's stage coaches. ("Remember, boys, nothing on God's earth must stop the United States mail!") The sound of the coach horn echoed in the desert then; and today the marks of the wheels are still to be seen on miles of the valley floor.

Through the lower San Felipe Valley, now called Blair Valley, the stage road went across the dry lake and mounted a rocky ridge on a grade so steep that the men passengers were asked to get out and push. "Foot and Walker Grade," it was called, with wry humor. The southern emigrant trail was cut deep into the granite here; gravity and erosion have somewhat changed the spot from what you would have seen had you been a walker-and-pusher in those westing days.

This is still mainly untamed land. If you really want to see at least a small part of what it has to show, you must exert yourself. You cannot sit back in a lordly sedan and get to know the desert. You may drive for some distance up Fish Creek Wash and stand between the walls of a remarkable sandstone and conglomerate exhibit. A great area here drains through Split Mountain on its way to the Salton Sea, following this wash. It was once a sea bottom. They say that even down to our time this wash had pools with small fish, and that floods following cloudbursts buried them deep under gravel and boulder.

The wash, as I say, you may see in part without straining your urban muscles. The fascinating Borrego Palm Canyon is also readily accessible, with a campground and the mile-and-a-half of good foot trail leading to groves of the native Washingtonia palms. A fine interpretive job by a competent naturalist is done for visitors there. Labels along the trail are numbered to correspond to the informative explanatory leaflet available to the hiker. Campfire slide talks are given in a little amphitheatre during the winter months. Did I say campfire? For many reasons, including lack of wood, this campfire will be different from any other you have ever known. I shall not explain. You will enjoy finding out. But let us not forget that in the desert a pile of charcoal will stand out like a wart on a human nose. The management has found a device that will supply the cheerful background of flame for the purpose.

The saying "when it rains it pours" must have come from a desert rat. Look at the boulders, which can be hurled down the canyons as easily as balsawood anytime the clouds decide to let go.

To get to know the desert-mountain country, you must have a vehicle with a four-wheel drive. A truck will do; a jeep is even better. Within the Anza-Borrego park there are four hundred miles of what are called, very accurately, "routes of travel." Most of these routes are up dry washes (dry normally, it should be added). With a four-wheel drive, you can reach Font's Point, named for the good *père*, and overlook the bare eroded clay hills called the Malpais or Badlands. Badlands are always the same, and never the same—South Dakota, North Dakota, Death Valley, Petrified Forest. This view from Font's Point will make the visitor exclaim. One of his first thoughts will be that nature has wasted a great deal of effort with very poor results. But nature's providence may not be exactly what he imagines.

On one of these trips you may see, if you will stop and be quiet (for birds don't fancy quick motions by unfeathered bipeds), that Sonoran aristocrat, the dandy phainopepla. It thinks the well-dressed bird has a dashing little crest and a velvety back suit. It might be right. It shows the elegance of simple garb.

Stop and look, too, at the many examples of "desert varnish" on the rocks. In a terrain where the temperature may hit 130 degrees in midsummer, even the rocks bake, you may say. The naturalist tells me that this varnish effect is due to "a complex mineral deposition on rock surfaces in extreme hot and arid areas." I say it's the same as a loaf of bread having a crust on it when you take it from the oven. Most unscientific, but it pleases me.

Look at a lot of little things in the desert. The panorama is splendid, true. But you will find the essence in small packages.

No phase of the work of natural forces, is in greater need of skilled interpretation than the desert. California has been wise to have a naturalist available for the visitors who wish to see some things with the inner eye.

You may see the Desert Bighorn, which once lived here in greater numbers. You *may*. The chances are that you will not. They melt into this gray landscape; into the side of a mountain that rises 6,000 feet. But there is something besides seeing the wild creatures. Feeling the certainty of their presence, with a rare chance of spotting them, is also adventure.

Or, if your interest lies more in the story of human occupation, you can ponder and re-create the passage of General Kearney and his troop, guided by Kit Carson; of Colonel Cook leading the Mormon Battalion to the California of 1847; of bearded prospectors frantic with the lure of gold. Of some of these, thirst-crazed, dehydrated, so weak that they could not free themselves from the hooks of a catclaw, it was grimly said that "they had gone in and stayed."

Let this vast, mysterious desert, first of all, describe itself to you. It can do it better than I, or any man. But, though in a few of its square miles it seems tamed, be warned. The desert tolerates no easy and patronizing familiarity. Even the personnel who serve the public in a great desert park like this must be fitted for the job. Many a ranger who would perform admirably in another kind of land finds that he cannot endure the desert patrol for long, whether he be bachelor or married, and though he be housed in the admirably designed fenced compounds, each with trailer house and outbuildings, in the patrol districts. The work here forces a man back upon his mental and spiritual reserves; he must get along with himself; and that is no easy thing.

Of all the guidebooks I know (and there are some very fine ones), I find the *Anza-Borrego Desert* of Horace Parker exceptional. A guidebook may have merit without literary quality—as a guide may. But this man, who loves the desert and feels himself a part of it, does not have a dull page in him. For those who wish to explore the Anza-Borrego area, there are some priceless safety hints at the end of Parker's book. The tenderfoot adventurer will be wise to heed them. But most pleasing, and philosophical, is what Parker says in conclusion:

"Don't be *afraid*. Over-caution can become burdensome; mental anxiety and fear make for a tense, dull day. The main thing is to have fun."

How true this is! You cannot enjoy what you are afraid of. The answer is to take sensible precautions; make practical preparations; treat the desert with respect; then trust it and enjoy the uplifting quality which the first philosophers knew: for *they* lived in arid lands, and saw the sky at night.

(11)

COLUMBIA HISTORIC STATE PARK

CALIFORNIA

Five miles north of Sonora, in the old business district of Columbia

RED DOG, Pokerville, Fiddletown, Bootjack, Mormon Bar, Squabbletown, Jackass Hill, Brandy Flat, Whiskey Slide, Sucker Flat. The gold seekers who swarmed like locusts in the Mother Lode after the discovery at Sutter's Mill laughed wryly at their hardships, their disappointments, their frantic way of life. The story of the forty-niners has been told many times. It can never be more effectively told than in the record they themselves left—the robust nomenclature of the mushrooming camps—Dogtown, Scratch Gulch, Hangman's Tree, Chinese Camp, You Bet, Rough and Ready, Greenhorn Creek, Bunkumville, Shirt Tail Bend, Ragged Breeches Bar, Henpeck City.

There were these and many more. We could mention Louse Village and Rot Gut, and a few others even less delicate. James M. Hutchings, in his *California Scenes* of the year 1855, mentions a boom town called Salt Pork Ridge. Implicit in that graphic name are frazzled homespun trousers, soap-hungry calico shirts, eager faces that needed the touch of a razor, and a food supply that invited scurvy. Far from home, lonely, lucky if somebody around could fiddle a tune, these men bought their nuggets at a price; and they attacked the gold-bearing gravels not merely to get, but to forget.

It was an epic time. And fortunately, among the hordes who were gophering the foothills of the Sierra, there were a few men capable

Redwoods in Pepperwood Grove, Humboldt Redwoods State Park, California

The Hearst San Simeon State Historical Monument, California

L

Dry Falls, Sun Lakes State Park, Washington

In Point Lobos Reserve State Park, California

Ocean front, Point Lobos Reserve State Park

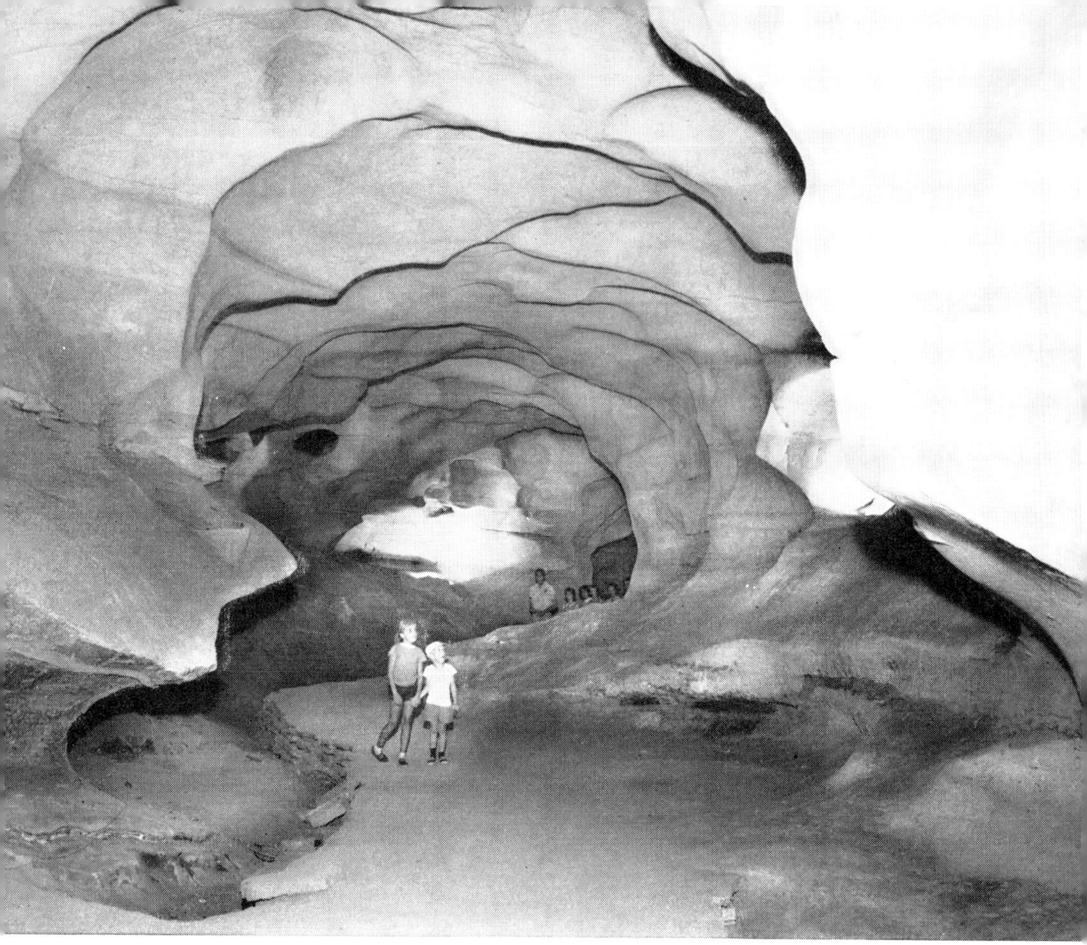

Hall of Marble, Longhorn Cavern State Park, Texas

Seascape, Ecola State Park, Oregon

The San José Mission, construction of which was begun in 1768;
San José Mission State Park, Texas

Petrified Tree Museum,
Gingko Petrified Forest State Park, Washington

CHEROKEE ALPHABET.

CHARACTERS SYSTEMATICALLY ARRANGED WITH THE SOUNDS.

Ꭰ a	Ꭱ e	Ꭲ i	Ꭳ o	Ꭴ u	Ꭵ v
Ꭶ ga Ꭷ ka	Ꭸ ge	Ꭹ gi	Ꭺ go	Ꭻ gu	Ꭼ gv
Ꭽ ha	Ꭾ he	Ꭿ hi	Ꮀ ho	Ꮁ hu	Ꮂ hv
Ꮃ la	Ꮄ le	Ꮅ li	Ꮆ lo	Ꮇ lu	Ꮈ lv
Ꮉ ma	Ꮊ me	Ꮋ mi	Ꮌ mo	Ꮍ mu	
Ꮎ na Ꮏ hna	Ꮑ ne	Ꮒ ni	Ꮓ no	Ꮔ nu	Ꮕ nv
Ꮖ qua	Ꮗ que	Ꮘ qui	Ꮙ quo	Ꮚ quu	Ꮛ quv
Ꮜ s Ꮝ sa	Ꮞ se	Ꮟ si	Ꮠ so	Ꮡ su	Ꮢ sv
Ꮣ da Ꮤ ta	Ꮥ de Ꮦ te	Ꮧ di Ꮨ ti	Ꮩ do	Ꮪ du	Ꮫ dv
Ꮬ dla Ꮭ tla	Ꮮ tle	Ꮯ tli	Ꮰ tlo	Ꮱ tlu	Ꮲ tlv
Ꮳ tsa	Ꮴ tse	Ꮵ tsi	Ꮶ tso	Ꮷ tsu	Ꮸ tsv
Ꮹ wa	Ꮺ we	Ꮻ wi	Ꮼ wo	Ꮽ wu	Ꮾ wv
Ꮿ ya	Ᏸ ye	Ᏹ yi	Ᏺ yo	Ᏻ yu	Ᏼ yv

SOUNDS REPRESENTED BY VOWALS.

A as *a* in *father*, or short as *a* in *rival*.
E as *a* in *hate*, or short as *e* in *met*.
I as *i* in *pique*, or short as *i pin*.
O as *o* in *note*, but as approaching to *aw* in law.
U as *oo* in *moon*, or short as *u* in *pull*.
V as *u* in *but*, nasalised.

CONSONANT SOUNDS.

G is sounded hard approaching to k; sometimes before e, i, u and v, its sound is k. D has a sound between the English d and t; sometime, before o, u and v, its sound is t; when written before l and s the same analogy prevails.

All other letters as in English.

Syllables beginning with g, except ga, have some times the power of k: syllables written with tl, except tla some-times vary to dl.

THE MISSOURI, KANSAS & [TEXAS] RAILWAY

Is the direct line through Central Missouri, South-eastern Kansas and the Indian Territory to Texas, Thence on to deep water on the Mexican Gulf.

THE MKT AND
MISSOURI, KANSAS & TEXAS RAILWAY

Was the first railroad ever built into the Indian Territory and the first to cross the border into Texas and push on through the thriving towns of the state to tide water. The KATY is always first to get out of the old ruts and improve its facilities for handling passengers and freight. As the early settlers moved from old log cabins to the more comfortable modernized houses, so has the KATY advanced and moved its passenger sim Pullman into

Wagner Palace Sleeping Cars

AMERICAN EXPRESS COMPANY

to do the express business of the Company. The above Express Company covers lines from the Atlantic to the Gulf, and stands higher than the AMERICAN.

THE KATY REACHES

from Hannibal, above St. Louis and Kansas City, to Houston, Texas, as the head of tide water, over its own rails, and passes through

Denison, Sherman, Dallas Ft. Worth Waxahachie, Hillsboro, Waco, Temple Belton, Taylor, Gainsville, Henrietta, Bastrop, Lockhart, San Macros, La Grange, Houston and Galveston.

RUNS THROUGH SLEEPERS TO

SAN ANTONIO

and affords comforts and conveniences to its patrons unequaled by any other Southwestern Line.

Any persons wishing to visit ST. LOUIS, CHICAGO, KANSAS CITY, HANNIBAL or the productive plains and prairies of MISSOURI, KANSAS AND THE INDIAN TERRITORY, should by all means take the

Missouri, Kansas & Texas R'y

as it is the most direct, best equipped and runs THROUGH WAGNER SLEEPERS to all above points WITHOUT CHANGE where direct connection is made in Union Depots for all points North, East and West.

FREE RECLINING CHAIR CARS ON ALL THROUGH TRAINS.

For further information as to artes, routes, maps, time tables, sleeping car reservations, etc., call on or address your nearest Ticket Agent or

JAMES BARKER,
Gen'l Pass. & Tickent Agent, Mo., Kan. & T. Ry'System, ST. LOUIS,

EDWIN ADAMS,
General Ticket Agent, Kansas & Indain Ter., PARSONS,

J. W. WILLIAMS,
Agent, MUSCOGEE, I. T.

WILLIAM F RASMUS,
Tahequah, Che. Nat. I. T.,
Attorney & Counselor at Law

Practices before all the courts and Departments of the Cherokee Nation and the Courts and the Departments of Muskogee, Choctaw, Chickasaw and Seminole Nations of Indians: Also practices before the U. S. District Court at Fort Smith, Ark., and the U. S. Court at Muskogee Indian Territory. Is a duly authorised and acting

NOTARY PUBLIC,
First Judicial Division Indian Territory

U. S. COMMISSIONER,
U. S. Dist. Court. Western District Arkansas

COUGHS and COLDS
ELY'S PINEOLA BALSAM

ELY'S PINEOLA BALSAM

The results of Sequoyah's genius—
the Cherokee language in print,
Sequoyah State Park, Oklahoma

North Falls, Silver Falls State Park, Oregon

Lake Chatcolet, Heyburn State Park, Idaho

Mormon Station Historic State Monument, which marks Nevada's first settlement

Native palms, Anza-Borrego Desert State Park, California

El Palacio, America's oldest public building;
El Palacio State Monument, New Mexico

Recreation facilities, Sequoyah State Park, Oklahoma

of giving a moving description of the period: not just the two who were to become famous in the world of letters—Mark Twain and Bret Harte—but many a newspaper man and homely philosopher with talent and style.

Of course, the turbulent and seamy side of an unpoliced new country was bound to be exaggerated in history. The few hangings were actually the spontaneous outcome of a feeling for social order on the part of an unorganized society of mainly clean and decent men. There were mistakes, yes. The much-publicized gambler throve on a craving for recreation by men who had engaged in the back-breaking toil of shoveling a mountain of dirt into insatiable riffles. Besides, there was the normal admiration for skill in anything. Not everyone can deal himself aces from the bottom of the deck more quickly than the eye can see.

The prodigious pure gold, which was to affect world economy and to establish a sound basis for the nation's paper money, had been waiting a long time for John Sutter to build a sawmill on the south fork of the American River near what is now Coloma. Indeed, the gold rush could have started five years earlier than it did. Sutter, a great landowner, had a supervisor named John Bidwell, and under Bidwell were many Mexicans. One of these, who had placered gold in the mountains of Sonora, told Bidwell that this foothill country looked promising, and offered to do some panning if he was supplied with a *batea.* But Bidwell did not know what a *batea* was and fancied it might be some expensive instrument, whereas it was simply a wooden bowl resembling the metal pan used by miners later. So the gold, which had patience, waited a while longer.

Some of the placer miners saved their nuggets and dust, returned home or went into trade in California, and did very well. For most, however, the net result was not much more than a day's pay anywhere, except that they got a dividend of excitement and rough fun. The great fortunes that resulted from the gold operations came to men who had nimble wits and quiet hands, men who mined the market that miners created.

There were many ways of doing this. In Jacksonville a man like Julian Smart could do well by starting an orchard and vegetable garden and offering to the Salt Pork Ridge boys a *vegetable* dinner at $2.50. In Placerville a man named Studebaker manufactured wheelbarrows, then went back East to build wagons, and much later, automobiles. Mark Hopkins had a grocery store. Leland Stanford had a general store in Sacramento. John B. Stetson, who later created the famous hat which ranges from one to ten gallons depending on the part of the country it is in, also traded in miner's supplies. Grocers were in a particularly favorable position to seize an opportunity. They had a firsthand knowledge of everything that happened. So had butchers: Philip Armour went from a little shop in Placerville to the heights of the meat-packing industry. Mills, Flood, Fair, Mackay, Crocker, Hopkins, Stanford . . . the list of great enterprisers who waxed upon the outpouring of precious metal is endless.

And what of the mining towns that produced, this one ten million, that one a hundred million, during a short life span when populations of five or ten thousand crowded together on hills that hear no shouting now? Most of them are gone. The buildings were of wood, and matches were handled carelessly. Sometimes the structures were undermined by feverish prospecting into their foundations.

In the thirties I made a trip through the Yuba country with Robert Wells Ritchie, who was writing a Mother Lode book, and we found a ghost town like North San Juan, full of houses the owners had seemingly just moved out of, leaving furniture, pictures, and the family Bible. There was an apple orchard, too, the trees heavy with luscious fruit, no wormholes, no scab—and nobody to pick them.

Three quarters of a century after the discovery at Sutter's Mill, Californians decided that the gold-rush period, so vital in their history, should be commemorated in a permanent and dramatic form. The historically minded had hope and enthusiasm; but this was not enough. Action was needed—and soon. The houses and stores of the old mining camps were melting back into the landscape like overripe toadstools after a heavy rain.

Where was the typical gold-rush town which still retained, relatively unspoiled, the characteristics that in the years to come would make it memorable to the visitor? There were individual buildings in a number of places, in Hornitos, in Sonora, in Vallecito, in Murphys, in Volcano, and in the northern end of the old lode foothills. Some of these structures could be restored, having defied the elements by virtue of the heavy iron doors and shutters that the builders had installed to make them proof against the fires that cursed the camps.

To reconstruct a ghost town was obviously undesirable. Preferably it should be an inhabited community, even though breathing with difficulty. It should contain a considerable number of the original buildings of gold-rush days, even if these were unoccupied and in urgent need of restoration. The atmosphere had to be real. Neon lights and realtors must not have intruded. Did California still have such a town?

It did—Columbia. Columbia had not died. It had kept a pretty constant population of about 500 people, mainly colorful descendants of the original prospectors and merchants. Though it came into prominence fairly late, this town has achieved a measure of prosperity; it had been called the "gem of the southern mines." It had a picturesque setting among odd, weathered limestone boulders. Good marble had been quarried on the outskirts, and not only used in local construction and in the cemetery on the hill, but had also been exported.

On July 15, 1945, the state legislature, with the approval of Governor Earl Warren, created Columbia Historic State Park, and the Division of Beaches and Parks began the restoration, which will eventually be a significant showcase of the American past. This is a long-range program. A great deal of progress has already been made; but it will be twenty-five years, perhaps more, before the job is completed.

Even now, you can walk the main street of old Columbia with the feeling that you are elbow to elbow with the pioneer of the gold-rush days. When the restoration is complete, you will be able to walk in the shoes of a bearded miner trading at Sewell Knapp's general store. Clever, resourceful Maine Yankee, that Sewell Knapp. He not only sold commodities, he delivered. His wagons went out to all the adjoining camps, and miners who were getting a daily two ounces of gold from the diggings were willing to pay well for that convenience. Knapp's store is now a museum, full of interesting relics of the period 1850–70, thanks to a generous donor, William Cavalier. There was the French store, too; it seems to have changed owners often, but always the buyer was a Frenchman.

In March 1850 Thaddeus Hildreth and four companions came to this spot among the limestone boulders, prospecting. They came in the rain, and that night they shivered in a cloudburst. While they were drying out next morning, they panned some of the earth among the boulders. Nearby was a limestone outcrop where the Indians of olden days had ground their seeds and nuts in mortars carved into the rock.

This was it! Rich dirt? Out of the Wells Fargo Express office on Main Street more than $50,000,000 of gold was shipped in the short period of exploitation. Not much less than $100,000,000 was taken from Columbia and the immediate area. This was Hildreth's Diggins—later to be patriotically rechristened. Within a month from the time the Hildreth party "struck it," there was a roaring camp of six thousand men. Not long afterward, the population had jumped to fifteen thousand. It was a city—and unlike some of the "towns" that sprang up around other diggings, it felt like one, even though, because of the lack of water for washing the gravel in the dry season, the population fluctuated. There was a good spring of water in back of the town, but it was not that good, and water was always a problem even after distant streams were diverted into flumes and ditches.

The pioneer enterprisers were stopped by no obstacles. Imagine an aqueduct that wound its way into Columbia sixty miles through the mountains! It cost a million dollars, but they had it. And then the store of gold laid up by nature through millions of years began to peter out. The miners drifted to other eldorados; the girls in the fandango halls painted and dolled themselves up for a waning patronage; the gamblers packed their gripsacks and headed for fresher pastures.

Columbia declined, but it lived on. And it will live on and on; for the State Park Commission of California intends that the shops again be real shops, the merchants genuine businessmen, the drugstore a useful purveyor of pills. If, for example, the vagrant from as far away as Fresno should happen to get it into his head that the justice's courtroom on the main street is merely a showpiece, he will be sternly educated. A descendant of the pioneers presides there. The drunk and disorderly get thirty days, if they don't sass the court. Contempt calls for severity.

Fire almost wiped out the town in the summer of 1854, and thereafter the construction was of a better order, with brick, stone, and massive iron doors. But in these remote hills the hauling of brick was a great chore; sometimes home-cured adobe was mingled with the brick. By the time the restoration was begun, time had attacked the footings; the mortar on exposed surfaces had been spirited away by lime-hungry insects and birds. The work was done in the nick of time. In one structure the weathered brick was lovingly disassembled and turned about so that the fresh side is now exposed.

Columbia, in its prosperity, took steps against another conflagration. There were four fire-fighting companies who turned out and pumped the "Papeete" and the "Monumental," both pieces of equipment that had seen service in San Francisco. These historic pumpers are housed in a temporary shelter till the old fire station is restored.

The Wells Fargo express office has not changed much. The assayer had his laboratory here—furnace, cupels, scales, and a big shelf of numbered samples in bags. Imagine that the Stockton stage is expected—due at 8:15, but delayed because a boulder rolled down into the road. Sole-leather trunks, bags, bundles, bedrolls, miner's kits are piled up in the main room. Then the horn is heard, and the coach comes galloping in. Two Chinamen of a large local colony of Orientals sit impassively amid the bustle. This was the Columbia of 1850-70.

There were no automobiles in the main street then; and there should not now be. That, it is hoped, will soon be adjusted. The surface of the streets will eventually look more like that of boom days. It will be a short walk from parking spots to the business section and its historic treasures.

One of the old boarding houses will be restored, and the modern traveler will be roomed and boarded there in somewhat the manner of gold-rush times. In "Articles in a Miner's Creed," published as a broadside by Hutchings in 1855, the forty-niner who wrote it included the articles:

He believes that the feathers in straw pillows should not be over six inches long and an inch square;

He believes that sheets in hotels should not be considered clean after five weeks without washing;

He believes that hash set upon the table twice a day for two weeks, after that should be considered pickles.

So mote it be.

All right, Forty-niner, all right. These defects will be missing in our restored hostelry. The wayfarer will eat and sleep well. So mote it be.

(III)

ECOLA STATE PARK

OREGON

On old U.S. 101, two miles north of Cannon Beach on the coast

When Talapus, the coyote god of Indian legend, shaped the four-hundred mile coast of Oregon, it is certain that he did not have the automobile in mind, or for that matter any means of transportation other than a pair of moccasins. The coastal strip, of singular beauty, from the California border to the mouth of the Columbia, is never wide. The foothills of the Coast Range leave a few miles of plain in some places, but again and again the traveler of U.S. Highway 101 finds himself leaving the shore to climb over a shoulder of considerable height where a rocky promontory juts to the ocean edge and ends in a precipitous cliff.

This inaccessibility explains why, so many years after the Willamette Valley and other inland places thrived, there was so little development along the Pacific front. Many inhabitants of Newport will tell you how they used to follow the beach and keep a sharp eye upon the tide all the way down to Yachats. When Benjamin F. Jones of Newport proposed the coastal motor road that has now become world-famous for its scenic beauty and variety, he got scant encouragement. Indeed, it must have looked visionary. But the highway was completed in 1932, and a few years later toll-free bridges made it possible easily to cross the four bays and the river which opened the widest gaps.

At Newport, where a great bridge crosses Yakina Bay, there is a small state park. It overlooks the bay and the fingering jetties that make it possible to use the place as a safe harbor. We remember, seeing the boats come up between these jetties, that Drake, navigating along this coast, complained that the only place he could anchor was in "a bad bay." Captain Cook made the same complaint in 1778; and we learn from the bronze interpretive marker at Yakina Bay State Park—set against a tangle of wind-blown jack pines, wild currant, and huckleberry bushes—and in sight of the old Yakina Bay Lighthouse:

. . . The earliest aid to navigation standing within range of the first recorded landfall made from ship to the shores of the Pacific Northwest. Captain James Cook made this landfall on March 7, 1778. At noon he named Cape Foulweather. On account of the heavy weather he was compelled to stand out to sea and only approach the land in the afternoon so that he was unable to find any harbor along the Oregon coast. News of his voyage . . . aroused in Thomas Jefferson an interest that led to the Louisiana Purchase. . . . and the dispatch of the Lewis and Clark expedition.

Small but neat and pretty, flowered with the rhododendron in season, and with modern utilities for the use of the picnickers who come here in large numbers, Yakina Bay State Park invites us to linger and loaf. But we must follow the path of history as it was outlined in that bronze marker. We must go northward to an Oregon state park set in the very locality that Jefferson's intrepid explorers, Lewis and Clark, came to know well during their hungry winter at Fort Clatsop. Yes, Ecola.

Ecola, with its beautiful approach through the great hemlocks; with its six miles of frontage on a shore of infinite charm; with its beetling offshore rocks where the sea lions bask and bellow and the marine birds make their nest and raise their fledglings. Ecola, with its clamming beaches: razor clams at Crescent and Indian Beaches, and butter clams below Ecola Point. To one who knew the North Atlantic Coast in the old days when you could dig clams at will in unpolluted water and have only the gulls as companions, it seems impossible that there remains such a clam wilderness. But so it is. The deer, unafraid, eye the visitor from the undergrowth. The view southward along the coast—white breakers pounding at the foot of the offshore rocks and creeping landward to the edge of a green shelf—would mellow any heart. This is Ecola State Park, one of the larger of the shoreline preserves that Oregon has set aside for the physical and mental well-being of its people.

Late in 1805 Captains Lewis and Clark had completed their epic task of "finding a route to the Western Ocean." They had followed the Missouri to its headwaters, crossed the Rockies to the Columbia, and now, after looking upon the blue water of the Pacific, they were scouting for a suitable location for fortified settlement. They chose a place near the river that now bears their names, on a bay—as Clark entered in his journal—"which I call Meriwether's Bay, the Christian name of Captain Lewis who no doubt was the 1st white man who ever surveyed this Bay. . . . This is certainly the most eligible Situation for our purposes of any in the neighborhood." Captain Clark was in error when he credited Lewis with the discovery; nevertheless, it was a gracious gesture commemorating an unfailing friendship between these two leaders. The party now erected rude huts around an open square, and were ready to take cover by Christmas Day.

For many months the expedition had been living off the country, most of their supplies exhausted, except for the precious gifts and trading goods they needed to establish relations with the Indians they encountered. Now they had fish and they had enough of what Clark set down as "pore elk," but they lacked salt. Clark seems to have been the only member of the party who did not crave this seasoning, even when, as on that first Christmas at Clatsop, "our dinner consisted of pore elk, so much spoiled that we ate it thro' mear necessity."

The visitor may see at the southern end of the promenade in the present town of Seaside the remains of the cairn where the soldiers of the expedition boiled down sea water to obtain their salt. Then some families of "Killamuck" Indians proved friendly and brought the salt-makers "a considerable quantity of the blubber of a whale which had perished on the coast near them . . . it was white and not unlike the fat of Poark." Lewis had some of the blubber cooked and liked it, as did his men.

Ecola State Park was named for Ecola Creek, and *ecola* was the local Indian's word for whale. Afterwards the name became Elk Creek, perhaps because it had been forgotten that when Clark named it he had a good reason. "Capt. Clark determined this evening to set out early tomorrow with two canoes and 12 men in quest of the whale, or at all events to purchase from the Indians a parcel of the blubber."

At this point occurs a rather delightful passage in the Lewis and Clark saga. If the reader has read the immortal diaries of the expedition, he will recall brave little Sacajawea, the wife of Charbonneau the French Canadian guide and interpreter. She was of the Shoshone people, had been stolen by raiding enemies and finally sold to this voyageur. You see her, many times during the long march, as she trudges with her little son on her back; and unforgettable is the dramatic moment when, the expedition having reached the Shoshone lands, Sacajawea met again her long-lost brother and wept upon his shoulder.

Neither Lewis nor Clark was sentimental about Indians, though if either had had his way about it, there would have been a policy of fair treatment. But Sacajawea must have charmed them all. Clark named a landmark in Montana "Pompey's Pillar" for her little boy.

So Clark set out to see the *ecola,* or whale, after an early breakfast. "Charbono and his Indian woman were also of the party; the Indian woman was very importunate to be permitted to go, and was therefore indulged; she observed that she had traveled a long way with us to see the great waters, and that now that monstrous fish was also to be seen, she thought it very hard she could not be permitted to see either. . . ."

"Very importunate," was she? But just a few days before, Captain Clark recorded the fact that when he coveted two fine otter skins made into a "roab," and the Indian owner refused to deal unless he received the "belt of blue beeds which the Squarwife of our interpreter Charbono wore around her waste"—straightaway little Sacajawea had taken off her precious belt and handed it over. The faithful "Squar-wife" (squaw) had fully paid her way! And she did go; she did see the biggest fish. It has been said that of all her adventures on that famous journey, the incident she never tired of telling in later years was her visit to Ecola Creek. Ecola State Park sits astride historic ground, you find.

The nucleus of Ecola State Park—the first 450 acres—had been owned by a corporation. Rodney L. Glisan, Florence G. Minott, Caroline Flanders, and Louise Flanders held forty-nine per cent of the stock. These four had built summer homes on the property, and loved to vacation there, but they became convinced that it should belong to all the people. A bronze plaque in the park rightly perpetuates the memory of their generosity; and to be fair it must also be said that the majority owner sold to the state at a very reasonable figure.

In the fall of 1934 a CCC camp was established at Ecola. It had been difficult to get to the park over the old road. At one place it bordered the ocean, and after a tempestuous sea wind there was always a blockade of great drifts of sand. Besides building a new road, the CCC outfit, under the National Park Service, put in water systems, picnic areas, and a number of utility buildings. "Without the aid of the CCC our parks would have been years in arrears in their development," wrote Sam Boardman, when he was superintendent of Oregon parks.

Ecola State Park is, of course, but one cluster of scenic areas in that truly regal chain that the highway department of the state has created from the California line to the mouth of the Columbia. The drive, from one end of this chain of parks—so well kept and each so highly individual—to the other is a memorable experience. There are fine beach parks in many states, but this Oregon coastal chain is unique.

The Umpqua Lighthouse State Park is just south of Winchester Bay, skirting the shore for two miles and a half with sand dunes that rise to a height of 500 feet. Around its two lakes, among the spruces and hemlocks, the rhododendrons make a brave showing in late May and early June.

South of Coos Bay is a group of delightful parks: Cape Arago State Park; Shore Acres State Park; Sunset Bay and Simpson. This shoreline is different even when compared with the typical Oregon ruggedness. Here sandstone cliffs, with tops fifty feet above the waterline, have been undermined by the ocean's assault and tilted to an angle that catches the force of the incoming breakers and hurls the spray skyward, to pour downward again in a veritable cascade. Shore Acres was once the estate of L. J. Simpson. He and his wife were among those generous people who grace the story of park creation in the state. At Shore Acres may be seen an extraordinary arboretum put together in the "Cappy Ricks" days when fast sailing ships were bringing home to this owner shrubs and plants from all over the world.

Cape Sebastian State Park, likewise a cluster of units, is built around a towering headland from which looks down a 700-foot sheer drop to the surf below. This, too, is a mecca for lovers of flowers—in the season of bloom the wild azaleas, rhododendrons, blue ceanothus, and blue iris are gorgeous masses.

At Cape Lookout State Park there is stand of virgin Sitka Spruce; and on the tip of the cape a great colony of murres—sometimes known as "foolish guillemots"—maintain a rookery. The only thing ever foolish about this kind of auk was his trust in the good will of human beings. But here at Cape Lookout he is safe.

Farthest north of the coastal parks is Fort Stevens, near the site of the historic place where a garrison once guarded the south side of the mouth of the Columbia.

And though it is not one of the coastal areas, it would be a pity not to mention the superb reserve of virgin forest through which one drives for several miles on the way over the Coast Range from Salem to the sea. The H. B. Van Duzer Forest Corridor Wayside is "undeveloped," according to the folder. In the shade of those noble spruces, firs, and hemlocks, the delighted traveler through this forest may wish that it will ever remain so.

(IV)

EL PALACIO STATE MONUMENT

NEW MEXICO

In Santa Fe

EVERYBODY has heard of the old palace in Santa Fe, New Mexico. A rambling, one-story adobe structure, with walls in places six feet thick, and hard as friable stone, it covers the whole of the north side of the plaza.

Authentic history connects it with the occupation of the Cibolan region by the Spaniards; while traditionally every room in it is the habitat of ghosts more or less numerous, of which some are said to mutter their tales of woe in the vernacular of the Pueblos, some in the liquid Castilian of Isabella, some in what a lively French ambassadress, wishing to flatter me, once called 'American English.'

The second door from the west-end plaza front opens into a spacious passage; and does one seek a conference with his excellency, the governor of the territory, he must knock at the first left-hand door in the passage. Back of the executive office is an extensive room provided with a small window and one interior entrance.

The walls were grimy, the undressed boards of the floor rested flat upon the ground; the cedar rafters, rain-stained as those in the dining-hall of Cedric the Saxon, and over-weighted by tons and tons of mud composing the roof, had the threatening downward curvature of a shipmate's cutlass. Nevertheless, in that cavernous chamber I wrote the eighth and last book of *Ben Hur*.

So wrote General Lew Wallace in his autobiography. And today, in the Territorial Room of the Palace of the Governors, the visitor may see a portrait bust of the famous author and the chair on which he sat as he put the finishing touches to a book that has not ceased to charm readers all over the world.

General Lew Wallace, a figure of some importance in the Civil War, was appointed governor of New Mexico in 1878. He traveled on the railroad as far as Trinidad, Colorado, and then it was a two-day trip by horses and buckboard to reach his post. Mrs. Wallace, also an excellent writer, joined her husband the following year. Let us see Santa Fe and El Palacio through her eyes:

"The narrow streets are scarcely wide enough for two wagons to pass. The mud walls are high and dark. We reached the open plaza. Long, one-story adobe houses front on every side. And this is the historic city! Older than our government, older than the Spanish conquest; it looks older than the hills surrounding it, and worn-out besides. . . . I used to think Fernandina [Florida] was the sleepiest place in the world, but that was before I had seen Santa Fe. The drowsy old town, lying in a sandy valley enclosed on three sides by mountain walls . . . resembles an extensive brickyard with . . . kilns ready for the fire.

"Yet, dirty and unkempt, swarming with hungry dogs, it has the charm of foreign flavor and . . . retains the grace which lingers about, if indeed it ever forsakes, the spot where Spain has ruled for centuries. The archives of the leaky old Palacio del Governador hold treasures well worth the seeking of student and antiquary. The building itself has a history full of pathos and stirring incident, as the ancient fort of Saint Augustine, and is older than that venerable pile."

Although the dogs of Santa Fe are now well fed, and the Palacio is no longer leaky, or the town unkempt, "the charm of foreign flavor" still clings to Santa Fe; much more than it does to its great rival in early days, Saint Augustine—the latter having diluted its personality with neon lights and other lures for tourist wealth. Santa Fe has a certain "we don't care whether you come or not" attitude toward the visitor, with the result you might expect: the tourist insists on coming.

Three hundred years of weathering and use are hard upon any structure, and especially rough upon one of "puddled" adobe walls —a technique somewhat similar to the modern method of pouring concrete between wooden forms. Many changes and much destruction have taken place over those long years which included war and insurrections interspersed with periods of ostentation, sleepy governmental function, and neglect. There was even a period of mild architectural insanity when it was the fashion to add a Victorian Gothic touch to defenseless buildings. This Palacio, built with such fidelity to the countryside and climate, was at one time decorated with a noisy balustrade across the length of the parapet! But this offensive addition is no longer there.

Don Pedro de Peralta was the third governor of the Province of Nuevo Méjico. He came upon the place that the Pueblo Indians had named Kuapoga (the place of the shell beads near the water) in the winter of 1610. It was to be ten years before the Pilgrims came from their exile in Holland to Plymouth Rock. There had once been a Tano village here, but the adobe had become part of the landscape before Peralta came.

It was a walled city still, we have seen from Mrs. Wallace's account, when General Lew took over. Here and there, a bit of the wall may still be seen. From rooms in El Palacio sixty Spanish governors ruled a vast expanse of territory over a period of 212 years. In a mere seven years from the day when Don Pedro arrived the Franciscan Friars had built eleven churches and converted 14,000 Indians to the faith.

Or were they converted? The wiser fathers knew that conversion was not absolute; that always it was expedient not to hurry the neophytes too briskly away from certain of their ancient practices and beliefs. Most of the friars were wise; some were not: too stern an insistence brought trouble. The northern Pueblos revolted in 1680, and those of the colonists who were not massacred fled into the palace, where for a time they held off the Indian attacks, but in the end they had to retreat to El Paso del Norte.

For twelve years the Indians held the city and the Palacio. Their leader occupied this venerable building, and its chapel was converted to a kind of *kiva* for the worship they relapsed into.

De Vargas led the Spaniards back to the city and the Palacio in 1693, and once more the old walls saw the colorful etiquette and official parade of a new succession of governors, who, since they had to pay the costs of furniture and entertainment out of their own pockets, levied heavily upon the territory for reimbursement.

There was reasonable Spanish suspicion, in the early part of the nineteenth century, of the English-speaking traders who were moving into New Mexico in ever increasing numbers. The dungeon on the west side of the palace received some of these intruders: the Baird-McKnight party, Pierre Chouteau, David Merriweather (who had his revenge many years later by revisiting the palace as American governor), and Zebulon Pike, who was detained here before being sent south to trial in Mexico City.

The Spanish commandants gave way, after Mexico revolted, to a series of new men who did little to keep the buildings in repair. Finally, General Stephen Kearney hoisted the American flag over the palace, and except for a short time during the Civil War, when the Confederate forces occupied the city, the Stars and Stripes have remained.

Yet Spain is still there in a very real sense. Those two centuries when the Chihuahua Trail linked Santa Fe with New and Old Spain have left indelible marks. "The cowboy who clicks along the sidewalks . . . inherited his trade, his horses, his outfit and his methods from the first settlers; the old man who takes his siesta on a bench in the plaza may count among his ancestors a don who owned a rancho as big as Delaware." At least half of the people seen by the visitor bear Spanish names and still speak the musical language of the conquerors.

Originally El Palacio was only a part, though the most imposing part, of a fortress that included both military and civil units. All the buildings within the walls were known as Casas Reales, or Royal Houses. A pair of low watch towers stood at either end on the plaza side of the city; the east tower contained the chapel. The present restoration, which follows some old plans fortunately exhumed in the British Museum, was done in 1909. It is a state monument, but it is administered by, and is the headquarters of, the Museum of New Mexico.

Although the original palace was a much larger structure, the restoration is faithful in all respects. A long portal, with projecting vigas, covers the sidewalk in front of the palace, and here the local Indians gather to sell their crafts.

Of course, the hollow rectangle with the pleasant patio in the center is itself the primary museum piece, for here the visitor sees a type of construction which came straight from the cut-and-try experience of the native architects who built the pueblos from the material at hand—the soil beneath their feet. There are no arches. Whether true or not, it seems to have been thought that adobe would not stand the stress of arched doors and windows. The flat roofs and roof beams (vigas) were adapted straight from the native dwellings.

The museum collections inside are exceptionally fine, representing not only every period of the long occupation, but including also displays of artifacts from several ruined pueblos that have been excavated by the Museum of New Mexico over the years.

(V)

GINKGO PETRIFIED FOREST STATE PARK

WASHINGTON

Two and a half miles west of the Museum (Vantage, Washington), on U.S. 10

On a high bluff overlooking the Columbia River and the little settlement of Vantage stands a fine building, the Museum of Ginkgo Petrified Forest State Park. The visitor will find here, besides an excellent series of exhibits that tell the geological story of the area, a little concession where mementos may be purchased. One of these days it may be desirable to canvass and reappraise the field of gift-shop concessions in state parks. This one at Ginkgo may be recommended. It contains only objects clearly associated with the locality and the preserve.

Mrs. Ruth Peeler, who administers the shop, is one of the outstanding women in the field of state parks. In 1955 she received the Cornelius Amory Pugsley silver medal, awarded through the American Scenic and Historic Preservation Society. Well-known to National Park Service folks, her tireless efforts to create an adequate system of parks in her own state have had happy results. In the words of the president of the society that presented the Pugsley medal, Mrs. Peeler, "following World War II, started a one-woman crusade" for more and better parks. Several fine historical areas are preserved because of her energy. And she was active in saving Ginkgo, one of the most significant parks in the country.

There is nothing unusual about the occurrence of fossilized wood, as such. In the more recent geological deposits of the west, erosion is constantly bringing to view scattered logs, stumps, roots, fragments. In some places you may walk over a mesa the ground surface of which is littered with small "stones" that once formed parts of living trees—perhaps of species that no longer exist in the region.

But fossil *forests*—aggregations of well-preserved trees, standing in place or as logs that were washed down from some higher elevation where they grew—are rare. In this country the great exhibits are in Petrified Forest National Monument of Arizona, in Yellowstone National Park, near Calistoga north of San Francisco, in the Black Hills of South Dakota, and in east-central Oregon and Washington.

The mighty fossil logs at the Arizona monument are representative of a much older forest than that of Ginkgo. None of the logs there are of any species that now grow in the United States. They are closer to the monkey tree of the southern hemisphere. In Yellowstone the still-standing trees were petrified within a tomb of volcanic ash. The species represented are few—three coniferous trees and seven broad-leaved trees have been identified. The petrified redwoods of Calistoga were preserved in volcanic mudflows, and are indeed thrilling to the imagination since they are shaded by living trees of the same kind—a past-and-present picture expressing the continuity of the life stream.

Before we consider why the Ginkgo Petrified Forest is unlike these other classical examples, let us look at the tree from which the state park gets its name. The ginkgo trees now growing (many have been planted in various sections of the United States) are nursed survivors of a race of trees that were once plentiful all over the temperate zones both north and south of the equator. Fossil ginkgos have been found in rocks in Greenland and Australia. For some reason, the ginkgo could not meet changing conditions, either of climate or some other factor, and ceased to exist under natural conditions all over the world, except as preserved as a semi-sacred tree in China. It is sometimes called "a living fossil."

The disappearance of the ginkgo as a naturally self-propagating tree seems mysterious in the light of the fact that it was noted in a published Chinese botany book of the eighth century. Apparently it was then valued for its pretty fanlike foliage and for its white nuts, which, when freed from a pulp of nauseating odor, were roasted and eaten with relish by the Orientals.

Long before the present Cascade Range was born, the "maidenhair tree," or ginkgo, flourished in the part of the country now called Oregon and Washington. Geologists have pictured the scene for us. The Columbia River was then following a course that took it more directly to the ocean. Between the place where the Grand Coulee Dam stands and the southern part of Washington, there was a great basin, surrounded by mountains. Since there the Cascades did not exist to block the Pacific storm winds, the climate was warmer and wetter.

On the higher elevations of this great basin, cone-bearing trees like the firs, spruces, pines, and sequoias grew. The lower slopes had broad-leaved trees: beeches, sycamores, hickories, oaks, maples, chestnuts. In the bottom lands were trees such as we see in the deep South today—tupelo, cypress, magnolia. And, in addition to these, the revered tree of the Orient—ginkgo.

Then—of course a geologic *then*, consisting of extended time we can hardly realize—this part of the country underwent a series of radical changes. Not with explosive violence but in a casual, placid sort of way, lava began to issue from vents in the earth's surface. Flowing, resting, flowing and resting again, the lava pushed ever northward and blocked the course of inflowing rivers. The basin became relatively flat and its streams meandering. In the resulting swamps and around the quiet waters of lakes another wetland forest sprang up. The volcanism continued at intervals, flow after flow. Finally all organic life was expelled, destroyed, or submerged. Whatever remained in a fossilized condition, because it had been enveloped in the lava, reappeared when the region was again uplifted and erosion wore down the hills.

Ginkgo is unique. Consider the limited number of trees found in the classic fossil forests we have mentioned. Then look at Ginkgo. The discovery of this forest is credited to George F. Beck of Central Washington College, who hiked over these dry hills in 1931. But it was some years after, when microscopic examination of the fossils revealed their genus and species, that even Dr. Beck realized the progidy he had turned up. More than two hundred species of trees, representative of at least fifty genera, have been identified from the specimens uncovered in these hills near Vantage.

Most fossil forests are preserved in a matrix of acidic lava; that is, a lava that contains abundant silica in solution. As the slow process of decay took place and each particle of organic matter was removed, its place was taken by the silica. By this or some similar process, the original wood structure was preserved with remarkable fidelity, so that a thin section of fossil wood will show, under a microscope, almost the same features as living wood. In the case of the pine, for instance, the resin ducts, which in the living tree are filled with the pitch that exudes when a branch is broken, are clearly seen in the fossil.

Examination reveals among the logs of the ginkgo forest a collection of petrifacts which include such widely different growths as the firs—true fir and Douglas—the redwood of present time, the "dawn" redwood or metasequoia, yews, maples, buckeyes, birches, persimmon, witchhazel, red gum, mountain ash, elm bay, oak magnolia, ginkgo. Since trees of such widely varied habitat could not all have been enveloped in a lava flow as living trees, how do they come to appear scattered on the surface of these arid hills?

The only satisfactory explanation is that the trees of the upland forests—the conifers of higher elevations and the broad-leaved trees that grew in foothill country—fell to earth as the result of old age or the accident of tempests, and were floated or "worried" down to the region of the wetland trees. They then cruised around, having lost limbs and bark on their journey, till they became waterlogged and sank into the mud, there joining sunken specimens of the swamp species. When the incandescent lavas flowed into the low lands, all the surface vegetation was consumed. Even floating logs would have burned. But, protected in the mud, the well-submerged logs were preserved in an almost undamaged condition in the sticky mass that cooled into rounded pillows known as palagonite. If the replacement theory is acceptable, the silica and other minerals that have taken the place of the wood cells and produced the opalescent petrifact characteristic of this fossil forest—opal being a silica mineral but softer, less dense, and containing more water than agate—could have been derived from the steams and gases of the successive laval flows of the region.

In the Ginkgo Petrified Forest State Park, on the basaltic cliffs palisading the Columbia River, there are some unusually interesting Indian picture writings, or petroglyphs. As in other regions where these petroglyphs occur, the contemporary Indians have no knowledge of their meaning. That they mean something—religious experience, news reports, directions to later travelers, or whatever—is likely, though patient study of them has left students perplexed and baffled. Some skeptics have concluded that these petroglyphs are nothing more than the "doodlings" of our prehistoric brethren who had time on their hands and the same passion as the park visitor who today exercises it with a jackknife.

It could be so, but it does not seem likely, since certain mystical figures reappear in widely separated places. An Indian of today has suggested a translation that gives the writings a coherent ethical meaning. Who shall say?

The picture writings now incised on the basaltic columns at Ginkgo are doomed to disappear forever beneath the flowback from the Wanapum Dam, now in the process of construction. Fortunately, a number of the rock tablets have been removed and placed in the Ginkgo Museum. It was no easy job to salvage these. To bring them up the steep bluff directly to their present location was out of the question. So they had to be detached and loaded upon a barge, ferried across to the opposite bank of the river, then trucked over the road.

The Wanapum Dam bears the name of an Indian tribe that once fished and hunted these reaches of the Columbia. In the mid-nineteenth century the chief of the Wanapums, one Smohalla, was greatly given to trances and visions. A native sect and ritual based upon his revelations spread among the Indians of Washington, Oregon, and Idaho. They called themselves Dreamers.

Among his many visions, Smohalla seems to have missed one: he did not foresee the dam that would wipe out the ancient picture writings. Or, at least, if he did have this dream, he kept it to himself.

(V I)

HEARST SAN SIMEON STATE HISTORICAL MONUMENT

CALIFORNIA

In San Luis Obispo County,
approximately five miles off State 1

I CANNOT HELP wishing that the late Calvin Coolidge had left us a Pepysian diary. For when Coolidge was President, he was one of the many distinguished guests of the San Simeon castellan, William Randolph Hearst. So was George Bernard Shaw, and so was Sir Winston Churchill; but I would like to have heard what Calvin, of Plymouth Notch, Vermont, thought about it.

George Hearst, one time United States senator from California and an early enterpriser in the Far West, bought the Piedra Blanca Rancho—40,000 acres—in 1865, added 200,000 acres, and began cattle ranching. The original buildings, white wooden structures that fit gently into the landscape, are still in active use at the foot of the Santa Lucia hills. From a favorite spot commanding a full-circle view of blue ocean and parklike grazing lands studded with native oak, George Hearst could look around upon a domain whose boundaries were always beyond view and say with Selkirk: "I am monarch of all I survey; my right there is none to dispute."

Charming pastoral scene. At any time of year it has a melting beauty; in the early days of spring, it provides a balm for the soul. For though the mountains are furrowed with canyons, the outlines everywhere are soft, so that you seem to be looking at a vast carelessly folded world of green plush. The hilltop came to be called "la Cuesta Encantada" (the Enchanted Hill), but I do not know just why, since it is not the hill but the visitor who is placed under a spell.

It was upon this hilltop, so agreeably associated with his childhood adventure, that William Randolph Hearst built La Casa Grande and the other famous structures, a fairy creation as seen by travelers along state route 1 at the edge of the ocean below. Once, on a foggy morning, I saw the Cité of Carcassonne in Provençal France hanging in the clouds with no roots on the earth. It was like that. Legends sprang up about this wondrous "Hearst Castle," but what chance did the average citizen have of ever being invited to visit it? Now anyone can do so, though you may have to stand in line for a ticket.

Incidentally, it isn't a castle and Hearst never called it one. He referred to it as his "ranch house." This seems an overmodest term for a development on which was spent, over a long period of years, not less than a million dollars a year—$50,000,000 in all.

Hearst was no run-of-the-mill rich man's son. He asked his father to buy him a newspaper, and his father obliged. The young man, with a touch of genius, developed the paper into a publishing empire—newspapers, magazines, books, and whatnot. The brilliant Arthur Brisbane aided him.

Hearst discovered that a vast number of people in the United States had just become literate and could read words instead of pictures. But the words had to be short and printed in large type. And both news and opinion had to be shouted. Joseph Pulitzer made the discovery about the same time, and when young Hearst invaded New York journalism, there was a pretty battle, from which veteran Pulitzer emerged with scars.

Upon this hill of enchantment, 1,800 feet above the Pacific sea, the son of pioneer George Hearst, now himself mining a richer ore than his father had known, began what a biographer has called "a carefully planned deliberate attempt to create a shrine of beauty." The year was 1919. He had the full-time services of the architect Julia Morgan, whose days were not humdrum, for Hearst's waxing imagination created projects faster than she could draw or workmen could build. First to be constructed were three great guest houses; and three years later the main building, La Casa Grande, was begun. Up the winding road from the port were hauled materials from all over the world, mature trees for transplanting, objects of art, a stream that stopped its uphill progression only when the owner died at the age of eighty-eight.

As Hearst built, he bought; and as he bought, he built. He bought from catalogues of rare objects, he bought through agents; to European monastic vendors and impoverished nobility, Hearst became the prime American export market. From Luxor, up the Nile, came granite sculptures of strange gods. Greek and Roman temples, walls and ceilings and even travertine floors from wrecked middle-age edifices, Gothic fireplaces, crystals, marble, bronze. . . . When Hearst ceased buying there were enough rarities in storage to fill another great mansion, and then more, and more.

The state, which now possesses all the riches, often longs for a catalogue of some of the treasures, and finds itself wondering what some of them are. Hearst once remarked that one does not catalogue one's home furnishings; and this is good evidence that he never thought of creating a museum. Even the ornately carven bed in which Cardinal Richelieu used to recline sleeplessly is therefore to be considered one of those homey things that one would naturally have around the house if. . . . if one were spending on this scale.

There were books, too: first editions, famous autographs, superb bindings. But books were never as favored as sections of French chateaux and Italian convents.

You cannot look out the window of the room where Cardinal Richelieu's bed stands and see a zebra grazing on the lawn. But there are zebras nibbling grass, for Hearst was a collector of wild and strange animals, too. As the buses draw the visitors up the five-odd-mile winding road, the fortunate ones may see not only zebras (I saw three, including a charming little foal) but gnus, fallow deer, aoudads, axis deer, sambar deer, and tahr goats. These grazing beasts are what remain from a large zoo that formerly entertained the ranch guests. I believe there was an elephant, as well.

It makes this monument no less interesting to observe that it was never finished. Indeed, I think this fact induces some philosophic thoughts. You see raw concrete which was destined, had the castellan lived, to be clothed with Utah limestone; even in the kitchens there are bare spots where tiles of artistic merit were planned to lie. The tessellated mosaic floor that once ornamented the house of a Roman gentleman in Pompeii, and now is walked upon by those who cross the first-floor vestibule of La Casa Grande, will give the visitor pause. The volcanic eruption that buried Pompeii deep in ash interrupted what the Roman gentleman had become accustomed to think an entrenched way of life. As in nature, no human aspiration is ever finished. There just isn't time enough.

When the Hearst family and corporation offered to deed these

123 hilltop acres to the state, there were grave doubts in the minds of the Director of Beaches and Parks and the other state officials involved. It was tempting: there had never been an offer like it. But they thought of the expense and difficulty of maintaining the place. State Route 1, the scenic highway along the coastline, is not a heavily traveled road. The location was "out of the way" for tourists. Above all, the visitor would have to be shuttled five and a half miles from the parking lot. This would probably be merely a summer operation, and the overhead would be high.

But the success of this tourist attraction has been phenomenal. The place was opened to the public on June 2, 1958, and less than two years afterward 430,000 visitors (at the time of my visit) had passed through the gates. On a holiday morning in 1960 there were 1,000 people in line for tickets at seven in the morning, and at eight it was a sell-out for the day, for the admissions are by necessity quite limited.

Does this monument "pay its way?" That is a question that will interest all state park officials. The answer is yes—but. The bookkeeping does not reveal the delicate nature of the priceless contents of these structures—treasures that, lacking expert care, can so readily deteriorate.

A more serious problem at the "castle" is that of interpretation. Just what is this monument? What does it mean in American history? Or, if it means a number of things, what are they? Does it tell the story of an individual, or of an economic phase that can never return? Surely it is not merely dedicated to the gods Plutus and Whim.

As in all California's parks, the staffing is admirable. The guides are well trained; the interpretation has been most carefully studied; the whole effort is on the highest plane. And it must be so. The concept of the monument could deteriorate quite as readily as the fragile objects of art within it.

(VII)

HEYBURN STATE PARK

IDAHO

Nine miles east of Plummer, on Highway 5, off U.S. 95

To HAVE Idaho called a frontier would irritate most of the people of that state, even though a few might relish the designation. Certainly the cultivation of the humble potato is not an achievement of a pioneer nature. The Idaho potato—long, mealy, flavorsome—is not merely the ideal partner of steak and chop; some delicate palates, buttering it with no stingy hand, are known to make it the mainstay of a worthy meal.

But, if in this oddly shaped commonwealth there should still be something of the pioneer spirit, look to the unusual origins of the region. Its boundaries respond to hardly any topographical features. There is something of western Washington, something of the Nevada desert, a touch of Montana; and it partakes of the high country of the Tetons. Yes, more than that, for it was from what is now the Idaho side of that glorious alpine range that the early French *voyageurs* saw the three famous peaks—"*les trois tétons.*"

At first it was all vaguely "the Columbia River country." Then, after 1820, people began to speak of "the Oregon country," and they included in that term not only what is now Oregon, Washington, and Idaho, but a part of British Columbia, western Montana, and western Wyoming. So late as 1863 Idaho became a territory. Its borders were fluid. Part of it was joined to Montana; another big wedge was given to Wyoming. Finally there emerged the fry-pan shape with a panhadle whose upper edge is on the Canadian line. There was no logic in the carving of it; but there Idaho stands!

Strange and beautiful geological wonders greet the eye wherever one travels on Idaho highways—whether on its mighty dissected granite batholith, or the lava beds, or the canyons of the Snake, or the dashing streams like the Salmon which Captain Clark entered in 1805, to fight its mad waters for fifty miles and finally acknowledge defeat.

It is the Panhandle, though, which we shall consider first. Or perhaps we should say, the "upper part of the panhandle," for the boundary line has a way of sidling so gently toward Montana that one hardly knows the spot where it ceases to be a handle. Here, if the tourist has just come up from the fertile irrigated acres that lie between the Sawtooth foothills and the Oregon line, is revealed one of the loveliest regions of the primitive American scene, an altogether different Idaho.

A local writer has well pictured it: "An area of surpassingly lovely lakes and of great evergreen forests, with cities standing within the shadow of larch and hemlock and pine . . . some of them, built within the forests themselves, look from a distance as if the trees had grown up through the sidewalk and pavement and front yard. They are all drenched with the smell of conifers and fresh water lakes and cool mountain reaches."

This region was at a remote time in earth history a huge lake. The great body of water left an astonishingly large family: great lakes, medium-sized lakes, gemlike little lakes. Pend d'Oreille is one of the largest fresh-water bodies wholly within our national boundaries. There is water everywhere, abundant water in a setting of dark forest; and if the fisherman is willing to toil back into the places where fish are still innocent of the ways of a wicked world, he can have choice experiences.

Some of the rivers flow into a lake and then out of it to another, reminding the visitor from Maine of his home "stream" of the Katahdin and Allagash country. The Kootenai and the Clark Fork flow across this Panhandle; the Coeur d'Alene and the St. Joe flow into Lake Coeur d'Alene and the Spokane River flows out of it; and then there are the Priest and the Potlatch and the Lochsa and the Palouse—waters sparkling in that sunshine to which Idaho lays special claim, perhaps because the Indian word that names the state meant that "the sun is coming down the mountain," a charming way of stating that "the day is beginning." Homer's "rosy fingers of the dawn" is not better than this Indian fancy.

In such a delightful setting, no state park could fail to be, in its natural attributes, an alluring adventure. Lying in a great basin, with its nearly eight thousand acres, more than a fourth of which are water surface, the mountains look down upon Heyburn State Park from all sides. The park touches upon the southern end of Lake Coeur d'Alene, making possible a boat trip of scenic delight upon this great body of water, and upon the St. Joe River. But the smaller lakes, Chatcolet, Benewah, Hidden, and Round, prove even more engaging to most visitors. Chatcolet is especially beautiful; a sparkling cup with evergreens growing down to the water's edge. Naturally, waterfowl find such conditions ideal. Of the many thousands who come here in the fall, a large number fail to continue their journey on the wing, as "duck hunting is at its finest in the park," according to the folder issued by the resort owners. But except for this seasonal bird shooting, hunting game creatures is forbidden.

The Village of Chatcolet, within Heyburn State Park, "supplies all your needs, from gasoline to furnished cabins, fine meals and groceries, fishing tackle, rental boats and telephones." These are at a price, of course; but another need of the worldweary human being can be had absolutely free. This is the soothing sight of the deer who come down to the edge of a lake to enjoy the cool dusky hours. Still wild enough to be a little cautious in your presence, they are yet confiding enough to let you take their picture.

Once a part of the Coeur d'Alene Indian Reservation, the lands included in Heyburn State Park were acquired by Idaho from the federal government when William Howard Taft was President. The conveyance stated that "the lands are to be held by said State, used and maintained solely as a public park, and for no purpose inconsistent therewith. . . ."

This brings to mind the Indian people that formerly lived here. Members of the large Salishan family of tribes, they called themselves Skitswish. Captains Lewis and Clark wrote the name down as "Skeet-so-mish," and though these great explorers of the Northwest never took any prizes at a spelling bee, they had keen ears for native dialects, so we can assume that the word was spoken very nearly in that way. Except for a few mild skirmishes with those whites who had treated them with cynical injustice, this tribe seems from the first to have been friendly.

When Captain A. A. Humphreys and Lieutenant G. K. Warren were making a survey for a railroad into the Oregon Territory, they reported that the Skitswish, under the guidance of the Jesuit fathers, had made considerable progress in agriculture, lived in comfortable log cabins, and kept much livestock. "They have abandoned polygamy, have been taught the rudiments of Christianity and are greatly improved in their morals and in their comforts of life." By other visitors they were reported to be "self-respecting, industrious and docile."

How, then, did these friendly Indians get the name of Coeur d'Alenes? In French *coeur*, of course, means *heart*, and *alêne* is a shoemaker's awl. "Heart of an awl." The combination is interesting. Is it possible that, in their first contact with the white man, French trappers from Canada, the name resulted from a bit of frontier irony? The *voyageurs* described these Indians as "hard-bargainers and very shrewd in trading." Could the natives have discovered that, if they didn't meet sharpness with sales resistance, they would get the worst of it? You can only guess who threw the first verbal brick—who it was that said the other party had a heart that was no bigger than a shoemaker's awl?

It would seem that Idaho, after acquiring this charming scenic area, lapsed into a period of forgetfulness. Nothing seems to have happened here until the CCC moved in and constructed cabins, caretaker's quarters, docks, wells, and a water system. In the late forties a state parks organization, administered by the State Land Department, began the development of roadways and camping and picnic grounds.

In 1948 the Idaho legislature passed a bill to appropriate $32,500 "for the sole purpose of the care, maintenance and development of Heyburn State Park." This park still receives a separate appropriation from state funds, and any income derived from cabin rentals, boathouse dock fees, or concessions must accumulate in a special fund for the benefit of Heyburn alone.

(VIII)

HUMBOLDT REDWOODS STATE PARK

CALIFORNIA

Extends north along the Redwood Highway from Miranda to Red Crest

HOVERING OVER the acquisition of a beautiful and significant fragment of our natural heritage, to be preserved for posterity as a state park, there seems always to be a menacing shadow, observed only by the few who judge from long experience. The shadow is not thrown by the frankly commercial opponents of the preservation. One knows where they stand; they win, or they lose, and there's an end to it. Ironically, the danger may come from those who are mainly well disposed, or even mildly enthusiastic; and it takes two shapes.

First (usually uttered with a show of impatience): "We are with you in principle, but why do you want *so much* land?"

Second: "Why are you in such a rush? Another ten years will be time enough to think about it." And, less than ten years afterward: "Well, it's really too bad. But it's too late to think about it now."

To make the foregoing less cryptic, let us proceed immediately to the tragic case in point. Yes; here in the magnificent Humboldt Redwoods State Park.

Remember first with what joy the news came to the public that the incomparable Bull Creek grove of coast redwoods (*Sequoia sempervirens*) was at last in the custody of the state of California The year was 1931. Thousands of people all over the country had given money for the purpose: garden clubs, women's clubs, individuals. John D. Rockefeller, Jr., had contributed a million dollars and in addition had pledged to match contributions. The Save-the-Redwoods League and the state had done the rest; and the final amount was a great sum in the early thirties—$3,212,226.

Dr. John C. Merriam, one of the founders of the League and later head of the Carnegie Institution in Washington, said: "This great project carried out by the Save-the-Redwoods League with interested members all over the country and with cooperation of the State of California protects one of the unique features in the primitive life of America. This forest constitutes one of the greatest assets of California and of the United States and will have increasing value as a spiritual influence in the life of the people of the State and of the Nation."

California and the League had already done handsomely by their state inheritance; grove after grove of the famous trees had been saved from destruction. But the Bull Creek grove—well, let a man seasoned in the study of plant physiology tell it in measured terms: "It seems to me to be the most remarkable aggregation of trees that I have ever seen anywhere. The beautiful symmetry of the trees, the pure stand, their large number and great size, make this forest unique. . . . Evidently the redwoods along Bull Creek must have developed under optimal conditions. Should such be the case, it is very doubtful if their like could ever be developed elsewhere, and should the grove be destroyed . . . it is certain that its like would never again be produced."

In 1931, then, the Bull Creek Grove, later named the Rockefeller Grove, was in the hands of the state, safe from all harm. Or was it?

What the state acquired was about 8,000 acres of redwood forest and 1,400 additional acres of the Bull Creek Flats. But Bull Creek Basin represents a watershed of some 28,000 acres, lying back from the coastline a short distance, rising sharply from the flats to a height of 3,400 feet. The rains that fell upon this big watershed found their way finally to Bull Creek and thence to the South Fork of the Eel, but the creek was not dramatic. The steep hillsides and canyons were covered with a rich forest growth, firs on the slopes, alders and maples along the brooks, and an accumulation of duff that retained the precipitation and released it in dribs like any prudent treasurer.

Into this watershed, denuding the steep hills, came the loggers. Not the big lumber companies, who have learned the tactics of a wise invading army—to exploit but not to lay waste. No, these were wildcatters, hand-to-mouth smalltimers, guerillas of the trade. Today you climb the winding roads to the top of the ridge and look upon a ruined land. A few gaunt dead trees, weedy shrubs that seemingly can live on nothing, old skidways that become deeper with every storm, a denuded landscape. Year by year the waters of the basin, once so clear and pure that the salmon sought them, became increasingly muddied. Fires devoured the humus of centuries. Then came the deluge.

In 1955 it rained for many days, ending with a cloudburst. With nothing to hold back the water, and every skidway a widening conduit, Bull Creek went mad. Carrying mountainous loads of debris, the stream bore down upon the creekside giant redwoods, undermined them, made huge dams of them, and flooded back into the grove, laying down a deposit of sterile basic sediment that buried the understory plant life and "looked like snow," as a ranger said to me.

The first onslaught downed 420 noble trees, and every season since, the toll has grown. The banks continue to be undercut. At the time of writing, the Chief of Beaches and Parks considered that hundreds of 300-foot redwoods stood within inches of destruction. The stabilization of the banks of the stream is being carried out as a stop-gap measure, but the menace is in the steep watershed, and no gabions can take the place of nature's own blotting paper when the rains fall. It is hoped now that the whole of Bull Creek Basin can be acquired and some natural cover gradually restored. This will be expensive, but the Save-the-Redwoods League, bent upon preserving what had been thought of as preserved, is acting with all vigor.

Of these redwoods, surviving and flourishing along the coastal region of California from Big Sur to (and barely across) the Oregon border, many fine words have been written. Painstaking scientific study has revealed their extraordinary history. They are indeed survivals, for they flourish today, in amazingly pure stands, as the remnants of a plant race that for millions of years was spread over the world, as evidenced by fossil remains.

Cousins of the massive Big Trees of the high Sierra (*Sequoia gigantea*), they show marked differences from those mountain titans. They do not attain such girth as the Big Trees, some of the noblest of which the state of California is also preserving in the Calaveras groves. But in height they have no rivals in the arboreal world. On the river benches, where the soil is deep and constantly moist, great groups stand, so closely packed that it is a mystery how the necessary plant food is available to them. They rise more than three hundred feet; and, before it lost a section of its top, there was one tree in Bull Creek Flat which measured more than 368 feet. As to their age, these coast redwoods are known to reach 2,200, for that was an actual count of annual rings. That, to be sure, is still but middle age compared with the ancients of the Sierra heights; but the coast redwoods are still growing lustily, and man, with his meager term in nature, may only guess how this rivalry of two elders will finally end.

The seeds of the redwood, which result in a grove of giants so densely placed that the sunlight merely filters through, are such tiny things that it takes thousands of them to weigh one ounce. Yet in that seed is history; and who shall say that it does not also contain something akin to intelligence? The redwoods survive forest fires because of their heavy bark; as they also repel most insect pests. But occasionally they do suffer severe burns. Immediately, they start a healing action. In the Henry Cowell Redwoods State Park in the Santa Cruz Mountains there is a tree which was damaged 250 years ago. It sent down from 100 feet above the wound two growths that completely covered the burn and now support the tree.

Lacking a taproot, what would you think of the engineering task of maintaining your stance if you had the tonnage of a mature redwood to support erect? If you realized that you were in danger of falling, as a result of an accident, would you grow a compensating buttress, like the kind an architect constructs to support the thrust of his wall? The redwood does this, and many other things as well. Tell us, wiseacres, how the redwood comes to do so! Oh, very well, then, it is instinctive. It has become, over the history of the species, the way of life. However, as J. H. Fabre remarked of his beloved insects, there must have been a single being, once, which had no benefit of an inherited trait. Sometime, somewhere, an individual organism must have *thought it out*, or—what else?

What will your feelings be, when you find yourself in one of these redwood groves preserved for you and yours by the state of California? Who can say? To each visitor they mean something special. Joseph Hergesheimer, having strayed into the subdued light and stillness of a redwood grove, felt exalted "by the grace of the towering trees masking their gigantic span." He beheld "the ground, in perpetual shadow, holding only flowering oxalis and emerald ferns," and "the fallen trunks, too great to see over, green with moss." He heard "the whisper of the wind, barely audible, far off, reflective; the gloom in the trees was clear, wet and mild." And he thought "this was the redwoods' secret, their special magic, that they absolved, blotted out the fever of time, the wasted years, the sickness of mind, in which men spent the loneliness of their lives."

To Duncan McDuffie, entering the grove of redwoods on Bull Creek Flat was "to step within the portals of a cathedral dim, lofty, pillared, peaceful . . . its nave loftier than that of Amiens and longer than that of St. Peter's. Its wine-red shafts . . . more numerous than the pillars of Cordova; its floor carpeted with a green and brown mosaic more intricate than that of St. Mark's. . . ."

You may not have the poetic insight of these exceptional visitors, but you will not emerge from one of the redwood groves the same person as you first entered it. And you may find yourself and attain at least a shadowy sense of your place in the natural world. Since I myself believe this, I like best of all what John C. Merriam said about these redwoods and what they may mean to the thoughtful man.

"These trees," he wrote, "connect us as by a hand-touch with all the centuries they have known. The time they represent is not merely an unrelated, severed past; it is something upon which the present rests, and from which living currents still seem to move. . . . It is as if in these trees the flow of years was held in eddies, and one could see together past and present." "A Living Link in History," Dr. Merriam called his chapter on these redwoods. To me, they are just that.

And what uplift of heart one may derive from this conviction of the continuity of life! For we are living today in an uneasy and dangerous world—of our own making, to be sure, but none the less filled with unspoken alarms. Our faith in the continuity of existence, and therefore in its meaningful if unknowable spiral ascent, is being shaken. It seems that we can only witness with a grim passiveness the retreat of that irreplaceable faith. This is not the sense of alarm that comes during an earthquake or an outburst of fire and lava and volcanic rock and cinder, for we know that is local and will come to a stop. No, we face the challenge of a faith in a *necessary* continuity of the life spirit. If not in these redwood groves, with their background of millions of years and their sturdy well-being of today, where may we resort to find consolation?

Although this chapter has the heading "Humboldt Redwoods State Park," partly because this preserve has the greatest acreage of the eighteen which contain choice specimens of these marvelous trees, the achievement of the state and the Save-the-Redwoods League should be considered in its entirety. Five redwood parks are south of San Francisco Bay—Portola, Big Basin, Butano, Henry

Cowell, and Pfeiffer–Big Sur. And although it is said that not until one gets north of Garberville does one enter the truly great domain of these trees, the more southerly groves are not without their giants and the sense of grandeur and solitude can also be found within them.

Each grove seems to have its own individuality. If you go from the Humboldt groves northward to those of Prairie Creek, for instance, you first merely sense that this is a slightly different way of forest life. With somewhat more openness and light, the understory of fern and smaller plants appears more thriving. A greater number of the broad-leaved trees, heavily plushed with saffron lichen, furnish a touch of gayer color. Finally it dawns upon you that you have entered a redwood region of greater rainfall. There is in Prairie Creek a perceptible shift to the rain-forest aspect that will steadily increase as one goes north along the coastline. South of Crescent City, in the Del Norte Coast Redwoods State Park, and northeast in the Jedediah Smith Redwoods, the effect of increased rainfall is even more marked.

Yes, each of the forest wonderlands has something of its very own to show. There are those, indeed, who think that Prairie Creek offers a little more than any of the others. To be sure, this lies within the realm of personal taste. Yet, Prairie Creek certainly offers a wonderful prospect for the future, with its potential nine miles of ocean frontage, its herd of Roosevelt elk, and (I am tempted to add, even though it sounds trivial in the light of so much beauty and inspiration) its singular lack of that predatory plant, the poison oak.

Fine creatures, these Roosevelt elk, protected in a domain where they thrive happily! In a meadow near the utility buildings of the park, the mothers and their fawns were grazing confidently, only now and then looking up curiously at us, sitting and watching them from our automobile. But, said the ranger, when you surprise a buck in the forest, he shows a fleetness short of the speed of light.

California's coastal redwood parks embrace a total of more than 50,000 acres. Additionally, the 5,437-acre Calavaras Big Trees State Park preserves two magnificent groves of the Sierra Redwood (*Sequoia gigantea*).

Of the management of these superb California parks, what more need be said than that these are career men, carefully chosen for ability and sound judgment. "The men in the field develop the details of protection and maintenance," said one of them to me, with pardonable pride. Good, good. The results show the wisdom of this.

(IX)

LAKE MURRAY STATE PARK

OKLAHOMA

Two miles east of U.S. 77, and four miles south of Ardmore

WHILE I was at Lake Murray in Oklahoma, not far from the Texas border, the Southwest Park and Recreation Training Institute was in session at the commodious modern lodge, which has a much-used convention hall seating five hundred persons. Of such institutes, and their workshops, the public knows little; nor does it need any familiarity with them. Yet these are the meetings of the men who provide the finished parks for the people; the behind-the-scene folk who explore all the possibilities that will lead to the finest enjoyment of outdoor recreation.

The workshop subjects may not sound provocative to the millions who use the parks. "Proper Use of Equipment." "Special Grasses for Turfs." "New Chemicals for Insect and Weed Control." "Safety to the Public." These appear a little dry, perhaps. But they result in public security and delight.

Sitting in at one of these sessions, I heard a colloquy that gave me much to think about. The astute city manager of a Texas metropolis was speaking of the part played by the municipal parks in his domain. In the course of his talk he happened to say: "Of course, we have to remember that the parks and their varied activities are for minorities. Relatively few people in a community use a golf links. Same with a tennis court. Many people never use our parks at all." The director of a Rocky Mountain city park was inclined to challenge this statement. "*All* the people use these parks, he said, even though they do not realize it. Even those who merely drive through a park on the way to and from work are unconscious beneficiaries. The influence of these beautiful and health-giving breathing spots is extended to those who apparently never use them."

It is not necessary to enlarge on these two points of view. Both men were right. There was no real conflict here. The city manager was speaking as a man who allocates the municipal funds. The other was viewing the situation as—as, well, a park manager.

When you come to think about it, you see that *all* the people of the nation benefit from the national parks. Despite the great and growing numbers who visit these preserves, there are millions upon millions who have never visited a single one. Put it to a vote of those millions as to whether they would like to have our national parks abolished. You would not get fifty ayes. They look forward to visiting the parks some day; their children read about them in school; they enjoy them by picture; they feel a pride that they are *theirs*: but most important, they know that, visit them or not, they are part of their cultural heritage. Yes; all *do* use the parks; one way or another.

Yet, in another sense, almost every public service may be said to be set up for a minority. There is a good illustration in Oklahoma, on the road from Davis down to Ardmore, where you leave the main highway for Lake Murray State Park. Between Davis and Ardmore you drive over the Arbuckle Mountains. They are called mountains, though they are of no great elevation. Yet the Arbuckles are the worn-down roots of once majestic heights that rose in the dimly realized geologic era known as the Paleozoic. Time has weathered them to what you see—like the tooth stumps of an aged ruminant. Along this highway, at intervals, there are signs telling you what sort of rock you are passing through. Many, many layers there are of limestones, laid down at different periods beneath an advancing and receding inland sea. You will learn that the rock of the ancient uplift was Ordovician. Sign after sign, very legible and concise, will give you a little lesson in geology as you ride. The Lions Club of Ardmore put up these markers, and I know of no finer feeling for popular education than that which this service organization has shown here.

Was it done for a *minority*? Of course it was. The Lions Club knew that. Anyone with the intelligence for this public service would not have to be told that only a small proportion of the people who drive along that road will be directly benefited. But there may be more than you think. A father goes home and looks up "Ordovician" in the dictionary; the children tell the teacher what they saw: who knows where these things stop.

But on a Sunday morning in Lake Murray State Park, not all the visitors are as serious as this philosophy might imply. The sky is bright overhead, but there is bite in the air from the northern plains. Most of the fishermen, who were early on hand, are ranged around the pool within a warmed house floated on oil-barrel pontoons. This, on a cold day, is fishing de luxe. Of course, the basic idea isn't new, for the fishermen of the Great Lakes have been using warmed huts for a long time. But it's quite the thing nowadays in Oklahoma and Texas reservoir parks. A few hardy souls fish outside in the wind. Those inside read the newspaper, smoke placidly, and occasionally haul a crappie out of the 30-foot-deep water. *Crappies* they are called some places: in Oklahoma they are *croppies.*

All the lake parks in Oklahoma have these warmed floats. The biggest one, I think, is at Lake Texoma State Park. There, also on a Sunday morning, I saw no less than fifty fishermen seated around the four open pools. I suggested to one of them that it would be wise on the part of some neighboring parson to come down there and give them a sermon. The notion was received with more surprise than approval. However, I still think there is merit in it. What better place for fishers of men to speed the word, than among quiet, receptive fishers of fish?

This brings us to a distinguishing feature of Oklahoma state parks, and it no doubt is a feature of other southwestern states as well. The desire of people to get to the waterside, whether it is the ocean or an inland lake, is general all over the country, but in Oklahoma this desire reaches an extreme point. The director of state parks described it to me as "water-hunger," and then added apologetically, "maybe that isn't the way to say it." I responded that I thought it a very effective way of describing this yearning.

"Maybe, coming from back East," continued the director, "you haven't much idea of what water means here. The people just can't get near enough to it. They want to camp where they can reach out their toes and dabble them in the lake. We built a fine camping ground on a knoll with a grand view of the scenery. Would they camp there? No, sir! They all try to get a spot on a little peninsula where they are almost surrounded with water.

"Walking trails? Our people don't walk them. The adults have almost given up riding the horse trails, though the younger folks still like to ride. I tell you, they want to be either in or on the water.

"What's more, things have changed in the last few years. The camper used to come with his family in an old Ford or Chevy, and have a good time camping in a patched tent for a few dollars. Now we get Cadillacs with all the latest camping equipment and a boat trailer—some put $3,500 into the camping outfit alone. Eighty per cent of them have air conditioning in their homes. Still, that isn't being in the fresh air and close to water. Take our park at Beavers Bend. There is just a mountain stream there, but everyone wants to camp as close to the stream as he can get. So, as I say, our folks don't want nature trails, and instead of developing them, our present tendency is to develop the horticultural side, to beautify as we would a city park."

The lodge and the cabins are the last word in luxury. That, too, is what these people want, and for the height of the season reservations are made long in advance. "Another thing," added my mentor, "our people like to be able to drive right up to the front door. In fact," he added, with a grin, "they would like to drive right up on the porch." All the facilities must be close by.

Lake Murray is surely a startling example of the reservoir-lake created for the single purpose of recreation. Six thousand acres are water surface, but there are fifteen thousand acres of land. Indeed, this state park is large enough to be far more than a place of physical romping at such time in the future as the public might demand more from it. There are already a thousand deer roaming its land.

Lake Murray was formed by a 130-foot-high dam erected at a point where Anadarche Creek cut a gap 1,000 feet wide through a heavy sandstone rock, to form what was known as Lower Devil's Kitchen. The water extends along the valley of West Anadarche Creek about eight miles, and almost as far up East Anadarche and Fourche Maline. The lake is large and deep enough for heavy boats, and water skiing is the top sport. The beautiful wooded section near the southern edge of the Arbuckles was once the cherished home of the Chickasaws, after they were evicted from their earlier homelands east of the Mississippi.

(X)

LONGHORN CAVERN STATE PARK

TEXAS

Eleven miles southwest of Burnet, off U.S. 281

THE LONGHORN, that mournful-faced bovine critter, half horn, half muscle, and draped in a bargain-basement hide, once roamed the sweet grasses of New Spain in great numbers, making light of flies and ticks and seemingly immune to the ailments that afflict the proud Herefords and Brahmans of the present day. New Spain, or part of it, has become Texas; and the only longhorns seen now upon the range are those preserved from sentiment.

What a fine sentiment it is, too! In the historic past that lives in the names of Davy Crockett, Houston, Austin, Travis, and the Alamo, the longhorn finds its rightful position. In Texas you may sleep in a longhorn motel, toss a glass in a longhorn bar, eat in a longhorn restaurant, and frivol in a longhorn night club. I saw, the other day, a sofa that some ingenious person had constructed from the horns of these animals. It was cleverly done, and looked as comfortable as a couch of cholla cactus.

There is no reason for the state park cavern, a few miles from Burnet, not to be called after the longhorn, too. This was longhorn country, and as you enter the mouth of the cave you see a big recess in the limestone where, on the approach of a cloudburst, the cowpokes lucky enough to be nearby have taken shelter and waited out the storm. (By the way, I have called the place both cave and cavern. Is there any difference? Webster makes the words synonymous, but adds that a cavern is "usually a large cave, or one of indefinite extent.")

Longhorn is certainly a large cave, and one of indefinite extent. The part open to the public is only one level of at least three, and only a two-mile walk of the eight miles that have been explored. The actual extent of this underground hollow is a matter of guesswork on the part of speleologists. Some experts believe that the cavern may stretch along for hundreds of miles in this ancient limestone formation.

Speleologists are geological specialists who study caves. With them it is a profession. Then there are spelunkers, the enthusiasts who risk their lives in such explorations for the love of it. You would think that a spelunker would be a poor insurance risk. The truth is, he is seldom in trouble, just as expert mountaineers are safer on the climb than in highway traffic—because they know their stuff. Item: don't go exploring caves unless you have a practiced spelunker with you. I mean, of course, caves that have not been developed for public visits.

No cavern could be safer or easier to enjoy than the Longhorn, situated at almost the geographical center of the second largest state in the Union. You pass through the administration building, into a natural rock amphitheater, go down a few short flights of steps, and proceed under the earth surface along an incline so gentle that it seems level ground. Before you realize that you are underground, your attention will be caught by the shining calcite crystals around you. The lighting has been artfully done; the actual lights are well concealed and not overplayed.

The rock formations, as they were left when the percolating waters of long ago completed their work, have been given names like the Queen's Throne, the Queen's Watchdog, Liberty Bell Dome, Eagle Wings, and the like. There is even a recumbent Abraham Lincoln. It did not look too much like the martyred President to me, but if you should happen to see in it a remarkable likeness, you will probably admire the good taste of Nature in honoring a great man. You would be wiser perhaps to fix your attention upon the marvelous process known as crystallization, by which Nature directs that each mineral shall attempt to perfect its form in a certain inevitable way. That the minerals seldom attain perfection, owing to a myriad of reasons, is another matter. And it can be seen here how millions of calcite forms, so crowded together that a perfect crystal could not result, have at least contrived to achieve one facet or two.

The temperature of the cavern is a constant sixty-four degrees, no matter what the season of the year. Because of the natural air shafts that extend to the ground surface, the ventilation is exceptionally good.

To stand, in awe of its beauty, in the magnificent Chandelier Room, where the crowding stalactites hang from a dimly seen ceiling, is to realize that what we perceive as beauty does not exist merely on the surface of the earth, but is everywhere we may go—in a subterranean world, in the ocean, in the sky. Whether we should see it so in other planets we may soon discover.

The Ellenburger limestone in which the Longhorn Cavern is found is the cemented and hardened mud of a sea bottom that existed in Texas in Ordovician times. You need not pay too much attention to the word "Ellenburger." It is a name employed by geologists to relate certain rocks when they prepare their charts and timetables. And the term "Ordovician," describes a long, long time within an era of much longer duration. Suppose that the Ordovician means 400 million years ago: it is difficult to grasp this figure. But we can relate this limestone to something else that we have seen. If you have been in the low Arbuckle Mountains of southern Oklahoma, you have passed through highway cuts of rocks of this same period—Ordovician. Yet the rocks of this period are far from senile in the whole story of the earth. This limestone of Longhorn Cavern is in contact with granites that were ancient when Ellenburger was limy mud.

There were times when the inland sea receded and times when it returned—marked by deep layers of sediments upon the old limestone of the cavern—but finally the land emerged to remain until the present day. At Longhorn, those later sediments, hardened to rock, have long since been pulverized by time and have gone along the streams to the ocean. Now you have only to go down a few short steps to enter the rock of 400 million years ago.

It was at a comparatively later time, scarcely a million years ago, that the formation of Longhorn Cavern began. That was when glaciers, or glacial ice, covered the northern part of what is now the United States. The ice never came down as far as Texas, but the climatic change that accompanied its advance was to have great effect there. The rainfall was far greater than what we now experience. The water table was raised so that the limestone, easily soluble, began to disintegrate. Then, only a brief 4,000 years ago, a drier period came and the water surface began to drop; the openings in the limestone were subject to wear by streams carrying abrasive debris which flowed into the entrances to the cave after every heavy downpour. In the latest stage ot development, the dripstone deposits began to form.

An unusual feature of Longhorn Cavern is the three-way natural bridge that remained over what is now the visitor's entrance, after the collapse of a "sink." This bridge is part of the original "roof."

The crude stone tools and beds of ashes and charcoal indicate that a prehistoric people were familiar with this cavern on the triangular-shaped plateau known as Backbone Ridge, but apparently it was used by them as a refuge rather than as a residence. The human remains which have been found are probably those of the victims of the notorious outlaw Sam Bass, who used the place as a hideout during the 1870's, after his forays in the countryside.

The Texas Rangers finally gave Sam his come-uppance in a pitched battle near Round Rock in 1878. There is a legend that before the bandit died he told someone that within the cave there was concealed the vast amount of loot he had accumulated. So far nobody has found it, though rusted pistols and flattened bullets suggest that gun battles took place in the underground chambers. What is certainly known is that the Main Room of the cavern was used just before and during the Civil War to manufacture gunpowder for the Confederate Army. Somebody carved the date "1860" on the wall of that room.

Nearly all caves have their romantic legends, and several colorful ones have blossomed in connection with Longhorn. What features of these stories are authentic and which are fancy, it is difficult now to decide. A perfectly credible story is that of a fight between a party of white men and a band of Comanches which took place here in the stirring days of young Texas.

In a raid upon San Antonio, then a thriving trading town of the frontier, the Comanches had captured thirteen whites. Logan Van Deveer, a veteran of the battle at San Jacinto and at one time owner of the townsite which is now the city of Austin, was one of a group that attended a council with the Indians in an attempt to have the captives returned. Fearing that any plan for a rescue by forcible means would result in the death of the prisoners, the townspeople invited the Comanches to come and smoke a peace pipe and agree on terms.

The council seemed to be a success. One of the chiefs promised, in flowing oratory: "When the moon appears in the East, my brothers, soon after the sun hides in the West, we will return the captives." The promise was made in colorful terms, but the performance, at the next full moon, did not equal it. The Comanches brought only one of the white captives, claiming that the others has gone to other tribes and were not within their jurisdiction. A bloody brawl ensued, which resulted in some Indian deaths; but no white prisoners were returned to San Antonio.

Van Deveer started off on his own. He followed the trail of the Comanches till he reached the Colorado River, in search of the Indian village where the prisoners might be found. At one spot he found a lacy handkerchief and farther on a bit of ribbon, an indication that at least the woman who had been abducted was still with the raiding group.

The trail led to Marble Falls and thence to Smithwick Mills, where Van Deveer met a Captain Magill and a Colonel Smithwick "just returning from a bear hunt." What a picture that presents of frontier life! Bear hunting one day and fighting Indians the next. But that was indeed the real wilderness existence. The three men picked up the trail again and followed it into Backbone Valley, where it ended abruptly at Sherrard's (Longhorn) Cave. They were now at one of three entrances, the one in a cedarbrake some miles to the west of the main opening. The odor of broiling venison ascended from the cave. They lurked outside until dark came, then crept in.

The Comanches were squatting around a fire, and the white woman, her hands bound, leaned against the crystal-studded wall behind them. Each of the white men selected his target and fired. The Indians, unaware that their attackers were but three in number, fled along the underground passages. Only a single man, a leader, remained behind to fight it out, or perhaps, in a burst of last-stand hatred, to kill the prisoner.

But the chief was slain before he could harm the girl; the three white men carried her to safety and rode all night toward San Antonio to return her to her family. The name of the distressed damsel was Mariel King. Van Deveer married her. It sounds like a movie, but there is no reason to question a word of it. Living in the Texas of those days was just like that. The pioneers did not invent romances; they lived them.

As a result of the many battles between whites and Indians, including the fight in the cavern, Fort Croghan was established at the foot of Post Mountain. Robert E. Lee was at one time in command there.

This is charming hill and lake country, around Longhorn Cavern State Park. There are facilities for picnicking and for camping in the area, though the visitor must not expect all the modern devices.

(XI)

MISSOURI HEADWATERS STATE MONUMENT

MONTANA

Three miles east of Three Forks, then three miles north of U.S. 10

In another chapter I have told of the delight the visitor experiences when he stands at the spot where the Mississippi River is born; of the little rivulet that flows from Lake Itasca in Minnesota, seeking its way so modestly northward between alder-clad banks till finally it turns upon its long journey to the Gulf of Mexico and the Atlantic.

Not many miles from the Continental Divide, we find a complement to the story of one of the great watersheds of the world. With our imaginations fixed upon the "Father of Waters," it was easy to forget that the tributary streams that make the Mississippi what it is are mighty rivers in their own right. One of these is the Missouri. Indeed, the Missouri is so proud of its own identity, and so stubborn about any relinquishment, that for miles beyond the merging point above St. Louis you see its yellower water still pursuing its way alone.

Montana has done well to mark the headwaters of the Missouri. It is no flourish of oratory to call this a "river of destiny." It was the route of those great pathfinders, Lewis and Clark. Its sinuous course revealed the riches to be acquired in the purchase of Louisiana from France when Napoleon, aware that he could not prevent it from falling into the grip of his arch-enemy England, put it on the bargain counter for the young United States.

In truth, Napoleon had only a sketchy knowledge of what he was selling. But President Jefferson and his cabinet were equally ignorant of what they were getting for that $15 million, no small sum for a new and struggling nation. They sensed that they had acquired something great. And Jefferson, his Secretary of State Madison, and his Secretary of the Treasury Gallatin decided to find out. Hence the classic exploration party led by Captains Lewis and Clark, Virginia friends and neighbors of Jefferson.

There was a curious feature in the leadership of this momentous expedition into the western wilds. Lewis and Clark, by mutual agreement, had "equal authority." According to all military judgment, this fact should have insured failure. But the friendship of the two leaders never wavered. Competent, resourceful, natural commanders of rough and hardy men, they represented an inspired choice on the part of Jefferson.

The expedition had wintered in 1804-5 with the Mandan Indians near what is now the capital city of North Dakota. In early April they set forth again, this time with a French interpreter-guide named Charbonneau, who had a young squaw Sacajawea, whom he had bought from the Grosventre Indians after she had been taken prisoner during a raid on her Shoshone people. In our saga of western expansion little Sacajawea, the only woman in the expeditionary party, trudging along with a half-breed burden on her back, has become a romantic figure. She was to prove a great help to the explorers, partly because the presence of a woman assured suspicious Indian tribes that this was not a party bent upon war.

Late in April Lewis and Clark reached the mouth of the Yellowstone River. They had now traveled 1,888 miles from the junction of the Missouri with the Mississippi. They were getting into higher ground, faster water, and were seeing mountain sheep. The third week of May found the expedition at the mouth of the Musselshell and in really mountainous country. The nights were becoming colder, with frost on the ground in the mornings. The first Sunday in June they came to the mouth of a river so large that they were amazed. After several days of exploration, they decided shrewdly that the south branch was the Missouri, which they wanted to follow; they named the other Maria's River. The Missouri then began to be very clear water, and soon they reached the Great Falls.

Now the expedition was in a country that the little squaw Sacajawea knew. But she could not help them when, late in July, they came to a place where "a branch of the Missouri came in on the south," and within a mile another branch of the same size also entered the stream they were following. Three branches, and little to indicate a choice among them. Which was the Missouri?

It is no discourtesy to leave our two captains at the Three Forks for a brief space, while we indulge in something of a quiz problem. Actually we are not straying far with this interlude. Anything that helps to realize the wonder of the mighty Mississippi watershed seems worthwhile.

Millions of visitors, over the years, have watched Yellowstone's Old Faithful in its gorgeous and regular eruption, when, almost on the hour, tons of water are hurled into the air and fall in cloudlike spray. Few spectacles have been photographed by amateurs and professionals as much as this one. Now the question: where does that mighty spout of water finally go? For of course, with allowance for evaporation and ground absorption, Old Faithful's discharge is destined for the sea.

This water finally reaches the Gulf of Mexico and the Atlantic Ocean, despite the fact that the geyser is in the very northwest corner of Wyoming and in a basin surrounded by mighty mountains. The Firehole River drains the upper geyser as the Gibbon drains the Norris. Perhaps you will recall that it was where these streams join with the Madison that the early Montana venturers into Yellowstone sat around their campfire and made the great civic decision that this wonderland should be the property of the whole nation instead of a source of profit for the few.

The Madison, flowing out of what is now Yellowstone Park at the West Yellowstone gate, goes along at the very foot of the Continental Divide and makes its way in a northerly direction till it finds itself in close company with two other streams of about the same size. And these are the Three Forks of Lewis and Clark.

"In just a few days," said a diarist of the expedition, "the river [Missouri] became narrow and very crooked, and the commanding officers came to the conclusion that the Missouri should lose its name at . . . this confluence." They gave the three branches, or forks, names. The north fork they called the Jefferson, in honor of the President. The west, or middle, branch they called the Madison for the Secretary of State. The south branch was named for the Secretary of the Treasury, Albert Gallatin.

This spot, then, was the place where the Missouri could be said to originate. And this is where many thousands of tourists, from all over the world, come every year to visit the monument of the Missouri headwaters.

But this nine-acre preserve, with its modest accommodations for campers or trailer folk, is far from being just a memorial to the far-flowing Missouri River. In this vicinity are packed a host of pioneer memories and thrills. Here the good little "bird-woman" Sacajawea began to recognize her home country, from which she had been kidnapped and enslaved. Ah, the burst of happiness that came into the young mother's heart when the expeditionary party met a band of the Shoshones headed by Chief Cameahwait, her own brother!

It was not far from this monument that Manuel Lisa established the principal trading fort of the Missouri Fur Company. Nearby is the cliff of the "buffalo jump," where the Indians drove the animals over the edge, to slaughter them when they fell to the ground below.

The economy of the plains Indian was built around the bison—food, lodging, clothing, utensils, almost everything needful. Here, near the Missouri headwaters, many trails were found, and many sites where the Blackfeet from the north, the Bannacks and Crows from east and south, Flatheads and Kalispells from the west, and the Shoshones from the northwest, camped in preparation for their seasonal hunting. It has been said that during the bison hunts there was a moratorium on tribal warfare. This may have been true at some time, as the quarrying of pipestone in Minnesota was a matter of "sanctuary," but the warlike Blackfeet were not long so readily curbed as that.

Here is the rocky plateau which Captain Clark described in a letter to Jefferson: "This would make the best place of anywhere along our route for a fort . . . it is almost inaccessible; just two little points which would have to be fortified." From this vantage point one looks out over a countryside of notable charm. Finally, not far from this spot, over on the Madison River, John Colter had his nearly incredible escape from Indian captors. Colter was one of the first white men to view the marvels of Yellowstone Park, but how flesh and blood could have endured such travail as his, and survive to recount it, is more than modern sedentary and motor-cradled Americans could possibly understand.

Colter was one of the soldiers in the Lewis and Clark party. When the expedition had triumphantly made its way to the Pacific Ocean and was on its way back to St. Louis, things began to be a little tame for Colter. He had tasted the freedoms of the wild, breathing tonic air under the star-studded skies at night, and he could not see himself going back to a boarding house. For John the life of the mountain man, with a trapline for beaver in the streams of the Divide!

Since the Lewis and Clark expedition was finished, Colter was discharged and he took up with a fur hunter named Potts. Within a short time John got more excitement that he had bargained for. A raiding party of Blackfeet caught the two trappers one morning as they were paddling their dugout down the Madison; they killed Potts outright, and decided to have a game of fox-and-hounds with Colter.

First, the Indians asked Colter if he was a good runner. He sensed what might be coming and replied that he was indeed a very poor one. He was stripped to his skin and told to try to save himself by what speed he had. Thus, across a cruel terrain carpeted with creeping cactus, Colter started running. He showed the speed of a greyhound in crossing the plain that led to the banks of the Jefferson, his sole hope of escape. Hardened and fleet as he was, he spurred his strength till he was hemorrhaging from nose and mouth. He caught his nearest pursuer by surprise, wrested a spear from him, and kept going till he was at the river. There he dived under the driftwood and kept only his mouth and nose above water till the Blackfeet gave up their search, concluding that their quarry must have drowned. Colter finally made his way through the wilderness to that wonderland which is now Yellowstone National Park. His name is commemorated there.

Some years ago a devoted group of history-minded Montanans, aware of the importance of the Three Forks where the Missouri is born, decided to preserve it for the people of the state and for visitors from elsewhere. A Park Commission existed, but there were no funds to develop the site, even though Clark M. Maudlin of Anaconda, the owner of the land, offered to donate it to the state. There was an unsightly gravel plant on the grounds, and a considerable sum would be required to restore the area to what it had been in pioneering days.

The Founders Club of Montana was formed. "This is an all-Montana project," said the promoters, among whom were Governor Bonner and an ex-governor, Sam Ford. "Our headwaters of the Missouri is one place we have which represents all Montana—it *is* Montana." Many organizations participated in the plan, including mining unions in Anaconda and Butte. Through the sale of a historical booklet, local clubs collected funds. On June 19, 1947, the State Board of Land Commissioners formally accepted title to the land offered by Mr. and Mrs. Maudlin.

There are suitable and well-written historical markers on the site. These will remind the tourist of the interpretive signs along the highways of Montana, for many years a source of delight to the out-of-state motorist.

(XII)

MORMON STATION HISTORIC STATE MONUMENT

NEVADA

In Genoa

THE OVERLAND STAGE, galloping into Carson City on a day in mid-August, 1861, unloaded at the doorway of the Ormsby Hotel some dusty baggage and the two dustier Clemens brothers—Orion and Sam. It was a thrilling day for the brothers, and though the small hopeful population did not know it then, it was really quite an event for Carson City. Orion, to be sure, in spite of his name, was never to emit more than a feeble ray of starshine. But Sam was later to be known, wherever the English language was read, under the inspired pseudonym of Mark Twain.

Carson City was so new that the pitch was still weeping out of its pine shingles. The Clemens boys were even greener than that. Every mile of sagebrush they had seen since leaving Salt Lake City had made them more homesick for the lush verdure of Hannibal, Missouri. Sam was later to write in *Roughing It:*

> Even at this day it thrills me through and through to think of the life, the gladness, and the wild sense of freedom that used to make the blood dance in my face on those fine Overland mornings.

Don't believe a word of it! This was one of those sweet afterthoughts that come to an author when years have blunted the sharp angles of fact. Here is what at the time he wrote to his sister Pamela:

> Some people are malicious enough to think that if the devil were set at liberty and told to confine himself to Nevada Territory, he would come

here and look sadly around awhile, and then get homesick and go back to hell again. . . . Why, I have had my whiskers and mustaches so full of alkali dust that you'd have thought I worked in a starch factory and boarded in a flour barrel.

The time came when Mark Twain wrote in terms of reverent admiration of the beauties of the Lake Tahoe shores; he even came to appreciate the luminous integrity of the desert, as most others do when they really know it. But that was later.

Observe that in 1861 Sam Clemens was already calling the region "Nevada Territory." But the designation was span-new. Officials in Washington had been calling this vast expanse of western land West Utah, not knowing much about it and caring less. Brigham Young and his followers spoke of it as Deseret—part of a huge domain flowing with milk and honey after Mormon industry and intelligence had a chance to make it so.

Ah, this was in truth a wilderness! The hordes of seekers for gold in the California foothills passed through the parched desert with merely a curse for the lack of water and firewood along the trail. A few enterprising souls noted an oasis here and there, even did a little prospecting for minerals. There were no laws, and nobody to enforce them, had there been. There was no place to establish land ownership; just the rudimentary rule of claim and squat.

But the federal government had finally recognized that there was such a spot on the map, and had sent James W. Nye, a politician of pleasant manners, to become territorial governor. Orion Clemens had influence with a member of Lincoln's cabinet, so he was to be the governor's secretary. Sam went along for the excitement, and, incidentally, paid both their stage fares out of his savings from piloting riverboats.

Carson City was not quite ten years old—even as a microscopic trading post—when the Clemens brothers arrived at the Ormsby. The furious pace of occupation and development which followed the gold strike at Sutter's Mill is difficult to believe. Carson City was certain to be the territorial capital when Governor Nye arrived. The shrewd Abraham Curry, sniffing the coming separation from Utah, had surveyed the place as a townsite and sold the idea to his friend Major Ormsby. The Major did not live to profit from it. He was killed, with sixty-four others, in a fight with the Indians near Pyramid Lake.

Anyway, Carson City had stolen a march on Genoa, the settlement in the fertile Carson Valley a few miles to the south. Genoa, where once a log cabin was doubtless the only house in all of what is now Nevada, had every right to be irked. *They* were the old folks, the originals. Carson City was an upstart, lacking traditions and culture. But when Nye came, he summoned a legislature to convene there; the only place they could gather was at a hotel.

And what, really, was Genoa? Well, Genoa was truly Mormon Station, under a fancy name. Named for the Italian city where Columbus was born? Possibly. But perhaps for a town in New York State.

The towering bulk of the high Sierra casts a dry shadow for many miles to the eastward, so that rain is scant in Nevada except where the state's own high peaks reach out and wring the passing cloud. But there is a slight rift in this dike. At the eastern foot of the great scarp nestles a genial oasis, with the Carson River running through it. The Mormon pioneers, less interested in picking up nuggets than in creating a far more valuable agriculture, moved in upon these fertile acres, and as they were keen to capitalize on any good chance, they traded with the feverish gold hunters who straggled through. So it became Mormon Station. Where Hampden Beattie had placed his roofless stockade in 1849, John Reese built a store two years later. The stockade remained, a protection from raiding Indians which enclosed more than an acre. Turnips were raised that sold for a dollar a small bunch. Gold is good; but when scurvy threatens, a juicy turnip is better.

It was Judge Orson Hyde, probably, who changed the name to Genoa. With a newspaper, a gristmill, a sawmill, and a telegraph line, Mormon Station flourished. Here lived the valiant "Snowshoe" Thompson, who, during the deep winter snows, packed the mails across the mountains. There was a typical "bad man," too—one "Fighting Sam" Brown, who boasted that he had filled a graveyard. He reigned until one day he made the mistake of antagonizing a peaceable Dutchman named Van Sickle. Van Sickle killed him, and Sam went to join the others in his well-filled graveyard.

As for Judge Hyde, he and his fellow Mormon settlers had to leave the region hurriedly at the call of Brigham Young when the latter was having difficulties with the federal government. Hyde and the others had to sell out their valuable holdings for anything they could get. The prices were, therefore, picayune, which caused Judge Hyde to lay a curse on the greedy buyers, saying that he "placed his suit in the Chancery of Heaven." As the prospective defendants did not know where the Chancery of Heaven might be, and had no hopes of getting there to stand trial, they laughed it off. Tradition has it, though, that a flood, a fire, and other subsequent mishaps indicated that they had been tried and found guilty *in absentia.*

Nevada does well to preserve this precious memorial of its earliest territorial days; effective interpretation will not only present a vivid picture to the state's adults and children, but will delight visitors from far away. For here, in a small area, in a countryside of charm, can be realized the typical boom and decline that was the fortune of so many pioneer developments. The discovery and rush to the Comstock Lode; the stripping of the forest slopes of the Sierra for mine timbering and for the locomotives of the Virginia City–Truckee line; the impact upon the neighboring Indian lodges who saw first with surprise and then with helpless anger the devastation of a principal food supply, the nourishing and delicious nut of the pinyon pine. This thoughtless raiding of natural resources was a story enacted again and again in the western expansion. And after the storm, the calm: Genoa (Mormon Station) faded slowly away. New roads built to surmount the Sierra bypassed the stopping places of the stages and pony expresses.

Sooner or later, after the whirl of get-rich-quick excitement, the land surface is almost always certain to go back to serving its best purpose, whether that is in forest or cultivated fields, or in wildlife refuge, or in a cultural preserve for American posterity. It is interesting to look back to the day when Samuel Buckland first saw this fertile land of the Carson Valley and decided that it offered a surer and nobler way of enrichment than panning placer gravel. Samuel, from Ohio, had tried both. He was a generous-minded man, too, it seems, for in the rough winter of 1860 he had opened a "tent hotel" at his stock station, and "all who stopped there were welcome to sleep on the floor or in his nearby haystacks without paying."

Another glowing picture of the time: territorial election day in 1861. The men from Fort Churchill (not far from Mormon Station) rode into the Buckland rancho and demanded the right not only to vote but also to have all the whisky they could drink. With neighboring ranchers on their way to the polls, Buckland smelled trouble. Soon there were fists flying. The soldiers had their way; they not only got liquor but they also registered their votes; this being, it was said, the first time that federal troops had thus been electors.

The original Mormon Station building burned down in 1910, and of course the old stockade had long since disappeared. But the reconstruction is faithful and there is no lack of period museum pieces to show the visitor the tools with which the pioneers labored.

(XIII)

POINT LOBOS RESERVE STATE PARK

CALIFORNIA

Four miles south of Carmel, six miles south of Monterey

FROM BIRTH, *man carries the weight of gravity on his shoulders. He is bolted to earth. But man has only to sink beneath the surface and he is free. Buoyed by water, he can fly in any direction—up, down, sideways—by merely flipping his hand. Under water, man becomes an archangel.*

Jacques-Yves Cousteau

THIS IS high talk about the new sport of skin-diving. The cynic might say that it is an exalted way of stating that the sport of imitating birds has palled upon some people and that these have now taken to imitating fish. At Point Lobos Reserve, skin-divers have become a nuisance. From all points of the compass they have swooped down into the 775 tidal and submerged acres adjoining this lititle miracle of sea-and-land loveliness and significance. Many have come to look and admire. Others, alas, have less innocent designs. The one-time nearly extinct sea otter lives blithely in this fringe zone. On the offshore rocks the pigeon guillemot, the brown pelican, the black oyster-catcher, and many other marine birds, nest and rest. These creatures, for whom the reserve was designed as a sanctuary that would likewise offer delight and education to man, are equipped to do their own skin-diving and do not thrive in the company of strangers. Something has had to be done to safeguard this domain.

The California State Park Commission is mindful of its pledge. This famous spot of earth was from the first day of acquisition to be "preserved and protected as a *reserve,* accessible to the public in such ways as to permit its enjoyment without impairing its excellence —safeguarding for all time its unique inspirational, educational and scientific interest."

Skin-diving will be permitted, but only for photographic and observational purposes; and even these, if found to be adverse to the integrity of the life forms over and under water, may be subject to further appraisal. Skin-divers must obtain a permit upon entry into the park, and must not enter the submerged extension of the reserve from adjoining property. The Commission is not without concern for the diver's safety, either. He must conform to certain regulations for his own protection.

Here is something new in the administration of state parks. To the many kinds of protection for the visitor, we now add that of safeguarding the skin-diver. But protecting a park from skin-divers— *that* rates as front-page news, as when a man has bitten a dog.

In the field of parks, a word is frequently bandied about: *purist.* The dictionary gives it a sneering connotation: overnice, fastidious, prissy. John Ruskin was a purist, admittedly a hard man to get along with, for he believed that if you set a high standard in art or life and then retreat from it, you are likely to end, not with a lower standard, but with no standard at all. On the other end of the measure you find the butcher of landscapes, who may be a commercial exploiter of natural resources or a highway engineer; let the dictionary call such folks *impurists.* Between is the middle-of-the-roader, who prides himself that he is reasonable, and realizes the necessity of making concessions, and is always ready to "give the people what they want." But people, as people, do not originate and seldom declare for cultural development. Their ultimate power is in dissent. Eventually they will sharply indicate what they do *not* like.

Judge whether these comments have validity when you consider the quarter century during which Point Lobos Reserve State Park has, in its purist integrity, delighted the eyes and minds and souls of Californians and other visitors. Francis McComas, the artist, called this six-mile shoreline on the south side of Carmel Bay "the greatest meeting of land and water in the world." Whether or not he agrees with such a superlative, the person who stands in the midst of all this beauty is not at all of a mind to challenge the statement. It will suffice; for really all the artist meant was: "I can imagine nothing finer." Yet the aesthetic impact is far from all. In a mere 356 acres of land, it would be difficult to find—at fingertip, so to speak—a more complete presentation of the organic and inorganic manifestations of nature, and of the forces that bring land forms into being, only to tear them down again.

Over the centuries and the ages, Point Lobos and the surrounding region saw many a natural change and many historic adventures. There are signs of prehistoric camping, and more concrete evidence of occupancy by later Indians. The early explorers of Spain probably saw this rocky headland from the sea, though they would not have thought it important in their search for riches. You may be sure that Father Junipero Serra, that tireless walker, came here from his beloved Mission San Carlos and meditated, beneath the cypresses and pines, upon his extensive cure of souls. The native *vaqueros*, tamed by the fathers, ran their cattle here, and it is even said that they threw their lariats over predatory bears along San José Creek. Then the church properties were secularized, and from the river of Carmel to the mountains and south as far as Palo Colorado Canyon this land became a grant to one of the King's stewards.

The land barons of the early days treated their holdings lightly; it is said that the great rancho was wagered and lost at dice or cards. The title claims became dizzily obscure, till finally outright exploitation of the natural resources of land and water was begun by the newer Americans. The hulk of a whaleboat, a derrick ring in one of the rocks, and the skeleton of a ninety-foot whale remain within the reserve to remind the visitor that the acrid odor of rendered whale blubber and the shriek of hungry gulls filled the air around Carmelito Cove.

Then some attempts were made to wrest a fortune from coal seams nearby; there were flurries of gold mining; fishing and packing of abalones for the Oriental trade—until finally the ubiquitous resort subdivider came on the scene with plans for a seashore development. Fortunately, this effort failed, and it remained for a man named Allan to realize to what fine use this small paradise could be put. He knew that this was a singular and irreplaceable landscape, that in this wonder spot people would "loaf and invite their souls"—so he set up a toll gate and charged admittance, and he did well. Perhaps he knew also that Dr. David Starr Jordan had reported to the government in 1880 that this Carmel Bay area was "the most picturesque spot on the Pacific Coast."

This precious spot of earth, showing no fatal scars from the commercial ventures practiced on it, was finally acquired for the state of California in 1933. An interesting date for an investment in sheer beauty and culture, when you recall that this was the very depth of the great economic depression. Was it good fortune that when the state's available funds needed to be matched by private gift the Save-the-Redwoods League was able to come to the rescue? You might have thought that this fine organization had its hands full with the threat to the redwood groves; but the League was led by men eager to redeem threatened beauty anywhere. It cost the state $631,000 to acquire Point Lobos.

Rather than to describe in detail the natural outdoor museum which is Point Lobos, and the adventure into beauty available there —as demonstrated by pictures known throughout the world—it may be more interesting for our present purpose to note the unusual wealth of human talent that has been directed to the formation and administration of the park. Frederick Law Olmsted, John C. Merriam, Ralph W. Chaney the paleontologist, Willis Jepson the botanist; Herbert L. Mason, with his study of flowering plants; Grinnell and Linsdale in the field of land and marine animals; Fisher and Leitch on intertidal animal life; the Drury brothers—did ever a state park come into existence and have its maintenance under the scrutiny of such a roster of able scientists and men of taste?

Olmsted, for example, the great master in the world of landscape architecture, looked with understanding not only at what is evident to the eye but also at the hidden, more precious values which link man and nature. Jepson disclosed the strange story of the Monterey cypress—storm driven as you see it where the tumultuous seas roar upon it and spray it along the ocean edge—this relic of the Pleistocene period, migrating under changing geologic conditions till it perhaps will wear out its life upon Point Lobos.

The bold rocks of shore and island where the Steller and California sea lions and the great flocks of pelicans, cormorants, and other waterfowl are seen; the story of the rocks themselves, alternately raised and submerged during eons of time; the flowers and the many animals of forest and grassland—all these have thrilled the men of science who came to Lobos to study them. The visitor, less of a specialist, may find even greater reward, that of mingling with unspoiled wilderness.

The statement prepared by the California State Park Commission, when the "master plan" for the future of Point Lobos was being formulated deserves to be quoted: "To keep at a high level of perfection the unique natural conditions upon which the greatest values of Point Lobos depend, in order to make these permanently available for the enjoyment, education and inspiration of the public."

In the preservation of delicate landscape two possible destructive invasions must be anticipated. One is the pressure for improvements or extraneous public facilities that do not belong there. The other is the impact of public use on the land. With no thought of doing harm, the public may, by mere use, eliminate the very features that have been preserved for its delectation. With this in mind, the Park Commission reduced the automobile roads within the park by half; the finer areas can be entered only afoot. "Marauders of landscape," said the planners, with a certain acidity that comes from experience, "do not so readily mobilize on foot." Camping and gatherings of convention size are out; but picnicking where it will do least harm is permitted. The clean-up of fallen wood and other natural, vegetative decay is practiced with great restraint.

Can such rigid trusteeship work in a democracy where, we are so often told, people will say: "We own this and we insist that we have a right to use it even to the point of *using it up*?" At Point Lobos it has worked. It has worked for the simple reason that intelligent people recognize and respect the wise administration of their assets. Instead of insisting upon its rights, the public can learn to take pride in its responsibility. But the guiding hands must demonstrate that their inflexibility is the fruit of wise decision.

So considered, the success of a rigid policy at Point Lobos Reserve State Park must inspire courage and hope in preservationists everywhere.

(XIV)

SAN JOSÉ MISSION STATE PARK

TEXAS

On U.S. 281, at the southern city limits of San Antonio

THE Missionary College of Guadalupe in Zacatecas sent Father Morfi to San Antonio, Texas, in 1777 to report on the condition of Mission San José y Miguel de Aguayo. The long name of the mission honored both a saint and an important personage. The Marquis of San Miguel de Aguayo was then governor of this northern frontier of New Spain.

When Father Morfi arrived in San Antonio, the mission was already fifty-seven years old. Observe the date of its founding—1720! Benjamin Franklin, a youth of fourteen, was a printer's devil on his brother James's newspaper in Boston. The readers of that newspaper knew little about New Spain. George Washington and Thomas Jefferson were not yet born. Great Britain and the American colonies were bound by ties that nobody then dreamed would be severed.

Father Morfi inspected this Franciscan religious outpost and was pleased. No; that is too mild a term. He was ravished both by its beauty and by its religious prosperity. He reported, joyously: "San José is Queen of all the missions of New Spain in point of beauty, plan and strength, and is a symbol of the faith, courage and vigor of the Franciscan Fathers."

Queen then; still queen. Years of neglect were to ensue, when the noble vaulted stone roof, the dome, the cupola of the church were to collapse; the stone walls around the compound were to disintegrate and become good quarrying for builders; the very location of the walls and some of the buildings was to be forgotten. But the mission continued to exist, even if only in that the family of Pedro Huizar still lived in the granary, and the fields of the old mission farm still were watered by the aqueducts so artfully built by the first directors.

This Pedro Huizar was the master artist of Mission San José. It is said that his ancestors were among those who had chiseled the delicate tracery of the Alhambra. The King of Spain, Philip V, was interested in this overseas post and sent his favorite sculptor to execute the carvings, which, though weathered by nearly two centuries, are today all the more affecting in their loveliness for the dimmed lines that hint at the inspired original.

Father Morfi did not see the completed church, which was begun in 1768, with Don Hugo O'Connor (the name reminds us of the many Irishmen who fled to Spain and preserved their family names for a posterity that spoke only Spanish) laying the cornerstone. The walls were mainly of tufa, a soft and easily worked rock; but where Huizar was to exercise his art a tougher limestone was used.

When the church and the mission were at the height of their florescence, what did the wayfarer and the inhabitants see? No stark structure, nor uncolorful. The façade was magnificent. Figures of virgins and saints with draperies that imitated drapery as the portrayed lace of Frans Hals resembles real lace. Heads of cherubs, sacred hearts, ornate pedestals—and the doorway and arch with a touch of the Moorish. What delighted both Spaniards and Indians alike were the bright pigments that decorated the plastered walls on three sides. All but a vague spot of this cheerful coloring has long since gone, but the visitor may see what it looked like from the small restored sample on the south wall of the tower.

Father Morfi's pardonable exultation over the Queen of the Missions was not due, you may be sure, to the beauty of an edifice. He was thinking of the wholesome prosperity of an institution that was carrying the Cross and the ways of civilization to the Indians—the Pampocas, Mesquite and Pasyas, the Camanas, the Tacames, the Cannas, the Aquastallas, the Zaunaes—three hundred and fifty of them who were sleeping (*in beds,* mind you!) and had gunny-sack sheets and buffalo-hide mattresses. They had a carpenter shop, brick kilns, a forge. The farm below, taking for irrigation the water from the mill, was lush with corn and cane, cotton and beans, melons; and there were peach trees that had fruit weighing a full pound.

Of this Indian population forty-five had guns and sixty-five had bows and arrows. When Father Morfi said that there was not a presidio (army post) along the entire frontier that could compare with San José, he was not thinking in warlike terms. The mission fronted an unknown west, from which any day could come a foray of unconverted Indians who would give quarter neither to proselyters nor to backsliders from the pagan rites. Indeed, the Fathers, from long experience, had learned to be patient with their charges, who had a way of lapsing into their native "mitotes" and craving the celebration of festivals that, though pleasant, did nothing for their souls.

"The Indians," said Father Morfi, "go about well dressed, are abundantly fed and arouse the envy of the less fortunate settlers of San Fernando, the indolence of many of whom obliges them to beg their food from these Indians who enjoy so much plenty."

One wonders what became of these converts when the Texas missions were secularized and the lands divided, in 1813. One hopes that the Franciscan priests took them along when they went back to Mexico, because a Christian Indian left in this wilderness, and somewhat softened by civilized security, was on unstable ground.

It was more than a hundred years before the Franciscan Fathers returned to the Queen of the Missions. Restoration of the church was begun in 1920 but abandoned for lack of funds, but the work was resumed later by the Archbishop of San Antonio. Through his interest, and later that of Archbishop Robert E. Lucey, the church has been completely rehabilitated, with restorations of the façade, the altar, and two of the arches. The creative interest of Archbishop Lucey, not merely in the church, but in the restoration and presentation of the whole mission picture, has been a factor, along with the surprising number of historically minded San Antonians, in recreating an unparalleled scene of early America. Not without good reason did the National Park Service declare San José Mission a National Historic Site.

The administration of the Mission is sufficiently unusual to deserve mention. On the operations board are representatives of the Texas State Parks Board, the Archdiocese of San Antonio, and the San Antonio Conservation Society. The advisory board also includes representatives of the National Park Service and the county of Bexar—a county, by the way, whose pronunciation trips up the unwary tourist. Call it *Bear* county. That is not precisely correct, either, but it will suffice.

Of the famous rose window of the baptistry, let us give the judgment of Harvey Partridge Smith, the San Antonio architect whose taste and talent have contributed so much to the restoration. "This one piece of work alone is worth coming a long way to see and is considered by connoisseurs to be the finest single original piece of Spanish-colonial ornamentation existing in America. Its curves and proportions are an ever pleasing sight to the laymen as well as to the professional and it is forever revealing some fresh and hidden beauty in leaf or mould. The carving is bold and daring, but exquisite in line and curve, with a freedom and freshness in its composition that denotes the hand of an inspired genius." Oscar Wilde said it was "the most beautiful thing in America." Wilde was a man of special tastes, which ran in many directions, but this declaration will find support from many lovers of sculpture.

There is a legend to the effect that the rose motif in the window refers to a certain beautiful *señorita* named Rosa with whom the artist was deeply in love. She was to follow him to the Americas, but the ship on which she traveled was lost at sea. "The heartbroken Pedro spent five years carving into the limestone the essence of his love and sorrow." Generations of Huizars have passed down this story, and a legend so insistent is difficult to disregard. But the artist will express his love of beauty, sweetheart or no, and the five years spent by Pedro upon this masterpiece find justification in the rapture of the millions who have seen it.

There is another feature of the church that must not be missed. "In the angle made by the tower and the main wall of the chapel is a peculiar winding stairway of solid oak-hewn steps to the second story of the belfry. From this level to the roof are unique stairs made of solid tree trunks, the steps having been notched out with the axe." Again I am quoting Harvey Smith.

After two hundred years these ingenious steps, held in place without nails, screws, or bolts—merely placed atop one another—are still in place, as though they had been made of structural steel and were well protected.

The preservation of the secular part of the Queen of Missions has been a triumph of devoted enthusiasts, working principally through the remarkable San Antonio Conservation Society. This achievement is, to be sure, only one of a long series of successes by the Society, but it will probably always remain its greatest. Here is the place to refer again to the wonderful good fortune that has made the restoration possible—the existence in San Antonio of a considerable group of people that could not bear to see the city's treasures disappear. From the time when work on U. S. Highway 281 revealed the remnant of the foundation of the mission walls, and a historically minded highway engineer, appealing to an interested county judge, managed to reroute the road at considerable expense —from that day to the present there has been a continuous victory of love, energy, and purpose over the usual discouragements and popular inertia.

The pamphlet written by Mrs. Ethel Wilson Harris, *San José Mission,* which every visitor to this monument should read, gives special mention to Mrs. Lane Taylor of the Conservation Society, to Harvey Smith the architect, and to Jack Beretta, engineer in charge of restoration of the old granary, mill, prefect, and soldiers' quarters. It modestly does not mention one of the most devoted redeemers of San Antonio's historic possessions, Mrs. Harris herself. She has been tireless, charged with rich imagination and understanding of people. And, of course, many others have made valuable contributions also. The Colonial Dames, Ernst Schuchard, the federal government, the county of Bexar—the list is long.

It is always presumptuous to tell the visitor to such a museum as this how he should proceed to enjoy it most. For myself, if I wished to capture the spirit of the Franciscan Mission in those early days, I think I should first look at the fine scale model in the granary. This was a fortified place; a walled city in the wilderness, if you please. These men even managed to drag a small cannon up the winding stairs of the tower, if tradition is to be credited, and used it during a hostile Indian attack. Within these walls then, went on the life of a large community. Along the walls, in separate quarters, lived the Indian neophytes—eighty-four apartments in all. Each had its bedroom and kitchen.

The granary is the one building which has been in continuous use for two centuries. The oldest part of the mission, it is also, dating from 1726, a relic of the very oldest San Antonio. When the Conservation Society bought it from the Huizar family, they got with it a deed that dated from a royal grant to Pedro the artist. With its unique flying buttresses and vaulted roof, the granary is a testimonial to the resourcefulness of the mission founders, who worked without modern equipment to achieve near perfection.

How in the world would *you* erect a structure like this, with massive walls and a vaulted roof? Just the way they did, if you had the skill. As the walls went up, earth was constantly filled in between them; when the walls were high enough, the mound of earth was rounded off, the stones locked in place upon the curve; then the earth was gradually removed and the buttresses built to take the outward thrust.

The same ancient simplicity and nearly perfect results marked the construction of the old mill. A reservoir supplied water that poured upon a turbine with a pressure of about ten feet. The horizontal water wheel, with a vertical axis on which millstones were mounted directly, did away with the necessity for intermediate mechanisms. It was a device as old as Rome in Pliny's time—and no doubt far older than that. The water, having served its purpose at the mill, ran through a ditch to the fields below the mission compound.

On the first Sunday night after each Christmas many hundreds of people come to the mission to see and hear a Yuletide play of an extraordinary kind. It is called *Los Pastores*—the shepherds. Only in places where the Franciscan Order has had influence is this medieval miracle play performed. Except for a somewhat similar observance in New Mexico, this annual play at San José may be the only one of its kind in the country. No original manuscript has ever been found. The many different versions have been handed down by oral tradition, and perhaps no two are alike.

It may be that *Los Pastores* was first written by St. Francis of Assisi. The miracle play derives its charm and significance from the fact that the performers are the lowliest laborers of the vicinity, sometimes unable to read or write. The acting—if it can be rightly called that—is full of the persuasiveness of perfect faith and the identification of self with the character impersonated.

If *Los Pastores* was in fact always and uniquely Franciscan, it is fitting that it should have come home to San José Mission in San Antonio.

(XV)

SEQUOYAH STATE PARK

OKLAHOMA

On State 51, between Wagoner and Tahlequah

WHEN THE Indian Territory was standing on the threshold of statehood, there was a chance that it would be named "Sequoyah," in honor of the remarkable Cherokee who not only gave his own people a written language but had visions of doing the same for many another Indian nation. It was a mere chance, of course. The state entered the Union as Oklahoma. But the Cherokee philosopher has at least been honored in the region to which his people came when insensate greed drove them from their homes in the southern Appalachians. Sequoyah State Park is a monument to a great American.

Visitors to the gift shop in the fine Western Hills Lodge—one of the string of modern hotels that Oklahoma has built in five of its state parks—may observe a strange four-page newspaper, for sale at the price of a dollar. The first page, with its Cherokee-language banner meaning *The Advocate,* is printed in a type face that looks as exotic as Egyptian hieroglyphics. The remaining three pages are in the English language. A whole dollar for a four-page newspaper may seem unusual: but this is a memento worth taking home. It is a facsimile of the newspaper that made the Cherokees a literate people. Moreover, the money accruing from its sale is to go toward the erection of a statue of the great Indian, and this memorial will one day stand in front of the lodge, and look out upon the charming 20,000-acre timber-lined lake formed by the Fort Gibson Dam. A worthy enterprise, indeed!

Of a piece with this curio, in revealing the fact that Sequoyah

State Park is full of historic significance in addition to recreation opportunities, is the little folder that the visitor will also receive. It describes four tours of the Cherokee country that may be made from this pleasant base of operations. If you take all four of these tours, you will have traveled nearly 500 miles. But not only will you have seen the quiet beauty of the Cookson Hills—or the "Ozark" Hills, if you like—but you will have had firsthand experience of one of the country's most fascinating historic spots. Tragic history, some of it; the revelation, in one light, of a ruthlessness which has in later days brought a blush to any sensitive white man's cheek. But there is a brighter aspect. It encompasses the story of nobler impulses, of stubborn fortitude, of the iron will to survive. The crime of 1838, the brutal expatriation of a happy people, the death march to alien lands, is bitter reading, and need not be repeated here. But the Cherokee Nation still lives, even though not as a political unity.

I like, and I know the reader will like, the words on the park folder which conclude the tour of the fourth day. "From Muskogee, turn towards Sequoyah State Park by way of Wagoner. You've seen the park, and you've covered the surrounding countryside. We hope the places you have visited have brought pleasure and a deeper understanding of the forces that have made Oklahoma." It isn't only the simple friendliness of these words, though I find in them a particular graciousness. They so neatly make the point that Sequoyah State Park offers much more than physical recreation, however fine and desirable open-air activities may be. Sequoyah fosters "a deeper understanding of the forces that have made Oklahoma." *That* is what makes the difference.

In addition, there are fine opportunities for physical recreation. The fishing in Fort Gibson Reservoir is notable. The atmosphere of the "old West" is brought to life by trail rides and stagecoach trips, and hay rides for groups, with an occasional rodeo and chuck-wagon feast. The bison, antelope, and Texas longhorns offer another and photogenic touch of the West that was. Very modern are the facilities—airstrip, driving range and putting greens, water skiing, ski tows, and a school for the beginners. About every kind of game that can be played outdoors or indoors is available. The beaches are good. You may even get a baby-sitter. There are, of course, those who just like to rest, look down the lake at the waving line, wooded to the water's edge by the damming of the former stream, meditate, dream, vegetate. A good place for that.

And yet—and yet—somehow it is the romantic countryside, as a whole, that makes the place and the holiday supremely worthwhile.

Not far from the lodge and the modern housekeeping cabins is Tahlequah. Still smacking of the frontier, though modern in many ways, Tahlequah was the seat of government of this Cherokee Nation that would not die. The original capitol is now the county courthouse. I went in and got acquainted—Oklahomans are easy folk to greet—and the pleasant justice of the peace mentioned a booklet of local lore written by one of the old-time residents. I got the thin volume at the drugstore across the street. Disappointing, yes; like most local histories, it is so close to the hearth that it cannot distinguish between the important and the trivial. Yet there is salt in it, and I thank Mr. Ballenger for putting down some of the color of Tahlequah before it fades.

For instance, can you see this picture? The year is 1841. Major general Ethan Allen Hitchcock is attending a council meeting, under the big shed in the center of Tahlequah Square. Chief John Ross (Cherokee) rides into the middle of the council ground and ties his horse to a tree. He speaks in English, and Chief Justice Bushyhead interprets. On the outskirts of the crowd are Osage Indians, clothed in blankets, with shaved heads and feather ornaments. And the curious Cherokees "gather around the Osages and gaze at them as if they had never seen an Indian before." How significant a scene enacted by these Cherokees who had been raised to civil superiority by means of the written language Sequoyah had given them. They were a superior nation of Indians by nature, but what a difference it made, having their own literature!

The old Cherokee Supreme Court building still houses the original steel vault of the Cherokee national treasury. The first newspaper in Oklahoma was printed there—this same *Advocate* that you can buy in facsimile. In the courtyard is the bust of Stand Watie, the only Indian general of the Civil War. Watie sided with the Confederacy—a not altogether popular preference among his people, and his partisanship had an unpleasant aftermath.

On the way to Tahlequah you may have come north from Wagoner, through Chouteau. Here was the first mission in Oklahoma, founded in 1820. At Salina the first white settlement was begun. There Jean Pierre Chouteau, the youthful agent of the fur traders of St. Louis, came floating down the Grand River and established a trading post. This is the scene of the Westward expansion of young America which was finally to settle the shore of the Pacific and bring into the Union of States an empire of which our forefathers of the Eastern seaboard never dreamed.

All this is a day's stimulating historical journey. Tomorrow, if you are wise, you will go to Sallisaw, where Sequoyah, in his turban and moccasins, worked at silversmithing, tended the salt kettles that arose from a little salt-lick monopoly given to him by his grateful people, and in his leisure indulged in painting. Sequoyah was an artist as well as a philosopher. He was a better philosopher than artist; yet they say he painted horses well. The little cabin of Sequoyah has been enclosed in a stone building for its preservation.

When you look upon this humble structure, you are in the presence of one of the most remarkable men in the Western world. This Sequoyah, the illiterate son of a white man and a Cherokee mother, sometimes called himself George Guess or George Gist. His father, then, may have been the Nathaniel Gist who was a friend of George Washington. But he was brought up in the Indian manner and looked like a full blood. He never learned English.

I have seen somewhere, probably in an old schoolbook, the quotation: "Blessed be Cadmus the Phoenician, or whoever it was that invented letters." You may say that Sequoyah was a second Cadmus. He was that, at least, to his Nation.

Sequoyah was no warrior, though he had served when Andrew Jackson persuaded the Cherokees to help him in the battle against the Creeks at Horseshoe Bend. But he loved better to sit and ruminate on the way of the world, puffing at his long-stemmed pipe. The great puzzle ever rose in his active brain: Wherein lay the extraordinary power of the Englishman—of the white man—which enabled him to sweep all before him? It was not physical courage. The red man had plenty of that. It was organization, no doubt. But whence came that?

A bit of writing that had been taken from the pocket of a captured white man was examined carefully. *This* ability—to set down thoughts on paper, and preserve them into the future—might be the answer! The spoken word was a thing written on sand, which the next wave erased; or, even if committed to memory, was a frail thing subject to lapse of memory. These white men communicated with a nonperishable instrument. Why couldn't the Indian have something like it?

From these reflections arose the "syllabary" of Sequoyah, though not until after many fruitless attempts to set down the Cherokee tongue, with its special sounds that had no English equivalent. From an English spelling book, which he could not read, George Guess copied certain letters of the alphabet. To these he added strange, and rather difficult, letters of his own devising, to express the native sounds. The syllabary had clumsy features. But it could be learned. At first it seemed like foolishness to most of his people. Turtle Fields told George that he was indulging in nonsense. The white people had magic.

"We can learn similar magic," responded Sequoyah. And the day came when Big Rattling Gourd, a skeptic, came to the philosopher and said: "I couldn't sleep last night. What you told me yesterday seemed silly. But all night I have wondered at it. Sequoyah, show me those signs you made. I am coming to believe."

The type for Sequoyah's language characters was cast in Boston. The first result was the publication of the *Cherokee Phoenix* in 1829. The Cherokee Nation had, as a result, a language and a new life. A heroic feat, indeed. If it came too late to save the Indian from political annihilation, it was not the fault of this thinker.

And what became of George Guess—Sequoyah? When he was over seventy, he made a trip to Mexico, looking for a supposed lost tribe of the Cherokees—and disappeared.

There is a genus of mighty tree in California now known as the sequoia. The Big Trees of the Sierra are called *Gigantea.* The coast redwoods are *Sequoia sempervirens*—Ever Green. Ever green, too, is the memory of our second Cadmus.

A short distance from Sequoyah State Park is another interesting historical monument. Fort Gibson was founded in 1824 by Colonel Matthew Arbuckle. It was then the point farthest west of a chain of north-south forts to guard the frontier. During its life as an active post, more than a hundred West Point graduates served there, one of the most famous, in later days, being Lieutenant Jefferson Davis. It was for a time the headquarters of General Zachary Taylor. Abandoned in 1890, the fort fell into decay, but in 1935-6 the WPA and the state of Oklahoma restored it to its original state. The first logs of the stockade were willow, but oak has been used in the reconstruction, since the early material is no longer available.

Sam Houston, one day to be president of the Republic of Texas, was here in 1829-32, operating a trading post about two miles across the Grand River from Fort Gibson. Here he married his Indian wife, Diana. She was a Cherokee damsel, and Houston became an ardent friend of the Indians, pleading their cause on every occasion. It was great pity that he had to say, on one occasion, that he had "never known a solemn treaty between the white man and the Indian that was not first violated by the whites."

And to Fort Gibson, also, came Washington Irving, the beloved journalist and creator of Rip Van Winkle and the Sleepy Hollow folk of fiction. "It was early in October, 1832," says Irving, "that I arrived at Fort Gibson, situated on the Grand, or Neosho, River near its confluence with the Arkansas." Like a practised hand, Irving wasted no words on what was a typical frontier post, but gave us, in *A Tour of the Prairies*, a charming account of his adventures in the company of Charles Latrobe and the Count de Pourtalès in the nearby Pawnee hunting grounds.

Near Fort Gibson, Irving saw the Osage Indians for the first time. He thought them, with "their fine Roman countenances and broad deep chests, their bust and arms bare and their blankets around their loins, the finest looking Indians I have ever seen in the West. . . . They have not laid by their simple Indian garb."

Much more—much more of the past is all around you at Sequoyah State Park. It is ground that tingles the imagination. You will do yourself a service by taking it in leisurely fashion—a little fishing, a little boating, a little riding, interspersed with enjoyable appreciation of a vivid history.

(XVI)

SILVER FALLS STATE PARK

OREGON

Twenty-six miles east of Salem, on State 214

NATURE does very well in her plodding way, but whenever she fails to provide the necessary thrill in one of her productions there is always some human being ready to assist. This was the case at the South Falls of Silver Creek, a torrent that comes tumbling down off the Cascades about twenty-five miles east of Salem. Silver Creek is a stream so impatient to get to sea level that it leaps fifteen times in an area of hardly more than three square miles: no mere cataracts, but distinct falls, at least five of which are of notable height.

Before South Falls was acquired as part of this lovely state park of more than eight thousand acres, it was owned by a man who thought he knew what the natural scene lacked to make it attractive: a good stunt. He built a low dam just above the lip, contrived a canoe into which a man would just fit, ran a wire from a ring in the bow to an anchor at the plunge pool 184 feet below, and advertised for spectators. They came; the occupant of the canoe went. When he was fished out of the pool, he had a set of broken ribs; whereupon the stunt was discontinued.

The owner of the falls resorted to another educational device. He pushed antique automobiles over the brink into the pool. But the new venture also failed. Even now, however, a fisherman at the pool sometimes feels a tug on his line and reels in a rusty carburetor.

On a rainy day in 1929 Samuel H. Boardman—Sam Boardman—drove up the zigzag dirt road from Silverton, dodging the potholes with the skill of a man who knew rural Oregon, to have a look at these South Falls of which he had heard so much. As he neared the falls, a watchful lady toll-collector came to the car and stuck out a plump palm. "Ten cents." She worked on a five per cent commission basis for the owner of the property, and made as much as two dollars on a fine weekend. Not an excessive admission fee; but before this official visitor left South Falls, he envisioned a state park that would preserve for all time, for the coming generations of Oregonians, a significant geological inheritance, a fir forest that still had many acres of virgin trees. Two years later, the Highway Commission recommended the purchase, and it now seems a great bargain, of "this nest-egg which hatched into a complete Silver Falls State Park."

When Sam retired in 1950 from his job as superintendent of state parks, he was hailed as the "father of the Oregon state park system." For several years after retirement, he came down to the office regularly and labored at the job of setting down (sometimes in the form of private letters, sometimes in communications to the newspapers) the fascinating story of the efforts by which the state had acquired the lands for its parks. These priceless reminiscences have been published in pamphlet form in the Oregon Historical Quarterly. We are reminded, when we read Sam's blunt, racy recollections—sometimes soaring into purplish prose, sometimes as earthy as the small talk of a longshoreman, but always, even in their humor, touched with the fervor of the humanitarian—we are reminded of many similar victories, defeats, generosities, hopes, and performances in other states, the record of which is forever lost.

What a revelation Sam's account is! Would you, for instance, believe that Sam Boardman once almost acquired a state park for Oregon in the neighboring state of Washington? "I greeted the Chairman of the Highway Commission one day," says Sam, "with the information that we had a new park." The chairman was Henry Van Duzer, a state park enthusiast. He smiled. "Where is it, Sam?" he asked. "Beacon Rock" was the reply. (Beacon Rock stands at the edge of the Columbia River, on the Washington side—a huge basaltic tower 900 feet in height.)

Beacon Rock was in danger of destruction by the Army Engineers who were building jetties at the mouth of the Columbia. This trap-rock was made to order for them—so easy to transport, so ideal for the purpose, and of "no practical value otherwise." The owner of the rock thought otherwise. He believed that it was of inestimable value as a show piece of Washington's original past, and he offered it as a gift to the state, for preservation. He was turned down. The owner then offered the property to the state of Oregon for one dollar "if you can legally and properly care for same." The Portland *Oregonian* published an editorial celebrating the coming gift. "So far as we know, no state in the Union now owns a park in another state. . . ."

That did it! The Washington newspapers grew adamant. The idea of Oregon having a state park on Washington soil! What effrontery! But, some of the park-minded people of Washington wrote in rebuttal, it would be preferable to have Beacon Rock belong to Oregon than to see it demolished. With that, the area became a Washington state park, and a choice one.

Sly promotion on the part of Sam Boardman. He probably never really wanted it for Oregon. He wanted it for Washington. He wanted every state to save its precious cultural assets while there was yet time to do so.

Sam Boardman came to Oregon from Massachusetts by way of Wisconsin and Colorado. He has sometimes been called a great salesman, and if the word is used in its highest sense, Sam was indeed that. He had the gift of infusing his own boundless enthusiasm for preservation into the men who owned land that was desirable for park purposes. The list of his successes is too long to be noted in a short chapter. However, one result of his many friendships involves Silver Falls State Park. As Sam Boardman himself told it: "Elmer Bankus of Brookings gave me two myrtle logs five feet in diameter and forty feet in length. . . ."

We might interrupt Sam at this point to explain. Do you know the famous myrtle of the northwest Pacific Coast, a tree of consummate grace, whose lovely mottled grain makes its wood unlike any other in the world? The myrtle has disappeared rapidly under eager demand. Fortunately Oregon is preserving small virgin forests of myrtle at Maria C. Jackson State Park, at Coquille Myrtle Grove State Park, at Sweet Myrtle Wayside, and at a few other places.

Five feet in diameter and forty feet in length! That was indeed a gift, even thirty years ago. But we let Sam resume: "I found a one-man sawmill about five miles north of Brookings where I got the material cut to dimension for furniture. How the sawmill man ever handled these large logs with his teapot mill will ever be a mystery to me. CCC trucks got the material to Corvallis where they went into the Oregon State College experimental kiln weighing 18,000 pounds and came out sixty days later weighing 8,000 pounds.

"I got interested in the design of furniture at Timberline Lodge and called upon Mrs. Margery Hoffman Smith of the Oregon Art Project . . . who had designed the lodge." She and her staff designed the furniture of myrtle wood the visitor now sees in the concession building at Silver Falls State Park. True, the preserver of natural beauty is generally more interested in live trees than in dead ones. But there are connoisseurs of beautiful dressed wood, too, and such folk come from far to see this myrtle furniture.

From the two logs given to Boardman were produced twenty-five tables with tops three inches thick, eighty-two chairs of the same heavy construction, eleven wall and fireplace benches, and one large dining bureau. The furniture was two years in the making, but the total cost was only $500. What its value, cut into souvenirs, might be is for anyone to guess. Looking at this exquisite furniture, one wonders whether some of it should not be in a museum. Yet it is so sturdy that (with the tabletops protected by glass) it defies ordinary wear.

All virgin forest, of whatever genus and species, is pure, uplifting wilderness to which a tired soul may resort. Yet each type of forest has its particular expression and invitation. At Silver Falls, the foothill stands of almost wholly fir—with a touch of hemlock and spruce woven in—have a note of cheerfulness. This is dense shade—yet the sun is felt, which is not true, for me, in the coastal forests, magnificent though they are. All the fine youth-group camps in the area have the same warm and joyous note—the one on Smith Creek in particular.

The place now used for picnicking and parking at Silver Falls State Park seems to have been the site of the first land occupation in the Silver Creek Basin. This was optimistic land-platting, which, by the way, Herbert Hoover as a youth helped his uncle to complete. The "city" (Silver Falls City) once consisted of a church, a store, a blacksmith shop, a dance hall, and a few dwellings. No one knows just why the creek was called Silver Creek. Some think that in the first days of the settlement there were strikes of silver ore in the upper reaches. The Falls are silvery, too, especially when the visitor takes the trail to the "cave" in the lava cliff at South Falls, and views the curtain of spear points of dashing water from that sheltered rear side.

Among park planners, Sam Boardman will always be remembered for his "confession of sin," which he made in connection with a threatened piece of Oregon scenery. "In the Joseph State Park adjacent to Guy W. Talbot State Park is the second, or upper, Latourell Falls," Sam explains. "This is a double falls, the first plunging into a whirlpool, then over a rocky lip in a final plunge. I conceived the idea that it would be a wonderful thing if a trail were constructed along the face of the cliff where the hiker could stand between the two falls. The trail was blasted into the face of the cliff. The hiker was provided with a passageway to the beauty spot.

"*But what had happened?* [The italics are mine.] The very foundation upon which depended the beauty of the entire picture now has a great gash across it. The aesthetic sense of the individual is curdled before reaching the beauty spot.

"It was fortunate that this lesson came to me early in my career, for it taught me that man's hand in the alteration of the Design of the Great Architect is egotistic, tragic, ignorant. . . . From then on, I became the protector of the blade of grass, the flower on the sward, the fern, the shrub, the tree, the forest. Custodian of His creation, I became; for I found that man could not alter without disfigurement. . . . My error of the Falls taught me humbleness. . . ."

The lesson is for all of us who are similarly tempted.

(XVII)

SUN LAKES STATE PARK

WASHINGTON

Six miles southwest of Coulee City, in Grand Coulee Canyon

On an early spring afternoon the sun will continue to shine for several hours on the plateau above the Grand Coulee, although below, on the border of Park Lake, it may have dipped behind the brownish-black west wall. The rays bronze the basaltic palisades of the east wall, which is gaily colored with yellow and orange lichen. Clearly visible are the successive layers of lava, and the intervals, when in far-off time the surface of each flow weathered into soil that beckoned vegetation back again. One of these long intervals is recorded on the shore of Blue Lake, not far away, where a forest came in below the sixth lava layer from the top. They were big trees, but the lava ate them up, leaving only casts to show where they stood. Six or seven persons can stand in these molds.

The birds sing as evening comes on. Off in the scrubby foothill brush is a band of fallow deer. In the premature twilight at the foot of the west canyon wall, these animals look snow white. Perhaps at close range their wool is a pale yellow. They are not naturally residents of central Washington. These specimens came from William Randolph Hearst's ranch at San Simeon in California. Hearst had a strange passion for picking up objects all over the world and setting them in incongruous places. When he dispersed his zoo at San Simeon, some of the deer came here. They get good browsing, and do very well. Occasionally they may hear a noise like that of a tiny rooster who is not sure what he wants to say; that is a cock quail.

In the sharp-edged rock talus the rockchucks live—marmots who spend so much time in hibernation that it really doesn't seem worthwhile for them to wake up at all.

The visitor is completely comfortable in this admirably managed concession, which provides cabins, boats, and even a general store. To anyone interested in state parks, the concession itself commands attention, for it is a sort of pilot experiment on the part of the State Parks and Recreation Commission. The lessees are on a forty-year term, paying the state a stipulated sum yearly or five per cent of their gross business, whichever is greater. An arrangement like this, whereby the concessioner and the park manager share authority, presents problems. If the concessioner is well chosen, there are unquestionable advantages. In this case, the state seems to have made a good choice, for everything is spick and span, the service courteous and professional, the visitor well housed and fed.

The people who come to Sun Lakes State Park solely for physical recreation find themselves in a delightful area. If they remain long enough, they can hardly fail to realize that they are rubbing elbows with one of the greatest geological exhibits in the world. They look up from the bottom of a deep trough that was eroded into the second greatest outpouring of molten rock which ever took place in the knowable life of this planet. It is said that the lava region of the Deccan, in India, covers a greater extent of surface. Very well; but this one is quite big enough to rate as a world wonder.

The crust of the earth in this part of the northwest had mightily warped. Prodigious floods of lava came pouring out of the earth from the southward regions, unthinkable wave upon wave, till the flow finally covered 250,000 square miles. It was not all effected in one outburst of molten material. There were long periods of quiet, absolute quiet, for wherever the lava went, all organic life disappeared, save in those rare accidental preservations which are in themselves remarkable. So enormous was the volume of lava that, when the great convulsion ended, a plateau had been built up to a height, in places, of 4,000 feet.

Whenever one of the rivers then existing met the oncoming molten rock, it had to change its course. In our mind's eye we can see the steam and the hissing fountains when fire met water head-on; and we can imagine the south-flowing streams being driven back to new courses, time after time, till the tongues of lava ceased to pursue them.

One of these frustrated rivers was the great Columbia, which then, as now, had its source in the Canadian highlands. Turned from its earlier valley, this river found a new way around the margin of the lava barrier. Thus was created what is called "the big bend," and this new course is the one seen on the map of Washington today. Later, when the lava plateau began to be slowly uplifted, the stress created weak lines in the structure, called "downwarps" by geologists. One of these was in the vicinity of Soap Lake. After visiting the Ginkgo Petrified Forest State Park, the tourist who also wishes to see Sun Lakes State Park and the manmade marvel of the Grand Coulee Dam would probably take the road from Vantage which brings him up by way of Ephrata along the edge of Soap Lake. The other downwarp was just north of a present-day settlement with the optimistic name of Coulee City.

This specific information sets the scene and gives the geological background for a phenomenon that lies within the boundaries of Sun Lakes State Park—the *Dry Falls*. "And why," the tourist may ask, "should I want to travel anywhere to see *dry* falls? Surely it is more impressive, and a finer sight, to stand and watch a great river leaping from the canyon lip, hurling its flood waters in a rainbow-tinted, foaming cloud down to a roaring pool far below! Once I have seen that picture—at Yellowstone, Yosemite, Niagara or even South Africa or Brazil—what attraction will there be for me at a spot where not a trickle finds its way over the edge of a precipice? Still we say—see Dry Falls! There is nothing in the world like this natural wonder.

Over these lava cliffs, rushing southward through the Grand Coulee, once poured a volume of water so great that the falls of the Niagara seem in comparison only a model. Had there been human ears to hear it, the booming sound would have carried to them for many miles. The colossal proportions of this waterfall can best be judged by making a short journey from it to the north, and gazing at the Grand Coulee Dam. This is one of man's most massive achievements. Its total length, from one bank of the Columbia to the other, is 4,300 feet. Yet that is less than one third of the total width of the stream that once poured over Dry Falls. From the roadway across the top of the Coulee Dam to the river below, it is 375 feet. That is not as great as the jump made by the diverted waters of the Columbia when Dry Falls was a living cataract.

The *diverted* waters. That word reaches back into the remote past for the story of how Dry Falls came to be. A few steps from the refreshment and gift shop at the brink of the west wall of Grand

Coulee is a stance with guard rails from which the visitor may look down the dizzying drop to the floor of the canyon, and across at two arcs of cliff edge where the flood once rushed. It is an imposing sight; yet it remains only a spectacle for the eye until one knows the geological story. On the veranda of this little concession you may take a refreshing drink on a hot day and listen to a tape recording explaining in simple terms what happpened. You then begin to understand the meaning of the strange landscape before you.

We have seen how the great lava flows, piling on one another with thin layers of soil between them, like a many-layered cake thinly interspersed with filling, forced the great Columbia to change its direction. Imagine, then, a long, long period. Call it some millions of years. There were no further invasions of white-hot lava, and vegetation returned, as soil was created by the tiny organisms that break up the hardest rock—a period of comparative rest. But another prodigious earth force was gathering, one that would further change the face of the country, and eventually produce Dry Falls, or rather, what we now call Dry Falls.

Nobody knows why—there are shrewd guesses, that is all—but in the Pleistocene Age the ice of the far north began to move. It moved with the deliberation of the coldest molasses, but it moved. Emanating from several centers, it covered finally a considerable part of the present United States. In the Pacific northwest it finally reached the region of central Washington, and dammed the Columbia at a point somewhere in the vicinity of the "farthest north" of the Big Bend swing. In the valley of the Columbia a great lake began to form. Having filled the river valley, the water reached such depth as to overflow upon the plateau of lava. Then, by following the lower parts of the contour, torrents cut across the big bend and began to gouge the canyons, here called coulees, which now give character to this whole region. The greatest stream created the Grand Coulee.

The first great falls that were created as the result of the erosional power of the water were at the two points of weakness in the lava structure—just north of Coulee City and down at Soap Lake. It may be that the upper fall was once far greater than the dry one now seen in Sun Lakes State Park. It could have been 1,200 feet in height; anyway, as is the tendency of all waterfalls, it destroyed itself. The lower fall at Soap Lake gradually worked back till the water ceased to flow—at Dry Falls. The cutting back through the lava rock probably proceeded at a high rate. The visitor knows why when he examines closely the walls of the coulee. Those intervals of organic growth and soil between successive invasions of the molten rock gave the rushing waters a fine chance. At the soft intervals, the material washed quickly away, leaving a basaltic column that the suction plucked off easily. And once the basalt fell into the whirlpools below, it disintegrated rapidly.

The glaciers retreated and the climate became moderate. For many years after the Columbia was released to return to its big-bend channel, the great lake probably supplied plentiful water for the falls. But the end came at last. All that finally was left of the great water spectacle were the residual lakes now enjoyed by the visitor at Sun Lakes State Park—Rainbow, Perch, Deep, Dry Falls, Park. Blue Lake, too, of course, but that is not within the preserve area. Perhaps it should be, because in the coulee above it is one of the strangest relics of the lava flow. An odd species of rhinoceros was caught in the molten rock. This indicates that at that time there were mammals in Washington that we now see only at the zoo.

This particular unfortunate *aphelops* was an aquatic animal with short legs. A few bone fragments were found. Otherwise the animal exists only vicariously: as a stone cast marking the spot where he was trapped.

PART 6

THUMBNAIL SKETCHES

(I)

THE NORTHEAST

Camden Hills State Park: *Maine*

It would be hard to imagine a lovelier place to camp or to picnic than within these highly scenic boundaries—almost exactly 5,000 acres of green forest, with a bit of Maine's rockbound shore thrown in for good measure. Penobscot Bay is one of those flooded ancient valleys that cut this coastline like the teeth of a woodsman's cross-cut saw. From Mt. Megunticook, the second highest shoreline peak in the state, the visitor has a rare chance to observe the many islands that were once mountain tops before the land sank under the weight of glacial ice. There are twenty-five miles of trails, with thrilling outlooks. On U. S. Route 1, two miles east of Camden.

Cowans Gap State Park: *Pennsylvania*

Though not one of the largest of the state's recreation areas, this one, nestling in a small mountain valley of the Tuscarora Range, is a great favorite, as is shown by the unusual number of campsites provided. Unspectacular, just "comfy," it delights those who want more than anything to loaf and amble around looking at nature in her modest mood. Bird lovers say that the variety and number of the feathered folk is unusual here; one watcher reports that she has seen more pileated woodpeckers in this vicinity than anywhere else. There are interesting mountain trails. No motorboats except those belonging to the lifeguards at the swimming area. Not far west of Chambersburg, on U. S. Route 30.

Crawford Notch State Park: *New Hampshire*

Long before state parks were ever dreamed of, the Cabots and the Lowells, and their less distinguished Bostonian neighbors, journeyed through the Notch and "took in" the scenery. One of three famous White Mountain notches, Crawford was the scene of the landslide in 1826 which destroyed the Willey family; it was too good a subject for Nathaniel Hawthorne to miss. The state tells us of "twenty miles of unspoiled, rugged natural beauty within the White Mountain National Forest." The statement is modest enough, as generations can testify. On Crawford Pond the wildfowl come and go just as they did when the Cabots and Lowells drove through on Concord stagecoaches. Campsites along the Saco River and many other places. Twelve miles north of Bartlett via U.S. 302.

HAMMONASSET BEACH STATE PARK: *Connecticut*

This is perhaps the finest beach on the Connecticut shoreline, with two miles of gently sloping, fine sand, and a boardwalk; on Long Island Sound between Madison and Clinton on U. S. 1. In a sense, this beach is to the populous state manufacturing centers what Jones Beach is to the millions of Metropolitan New York. Excellent camping and picnicking facilities, public pavilion and bathhouses.

ISLAND BEACH STATE PARK: *New Jersey*

Still under development, this ten-mile strip from Seaside Park to Barnegat Inlet offers chances for picnicking and for year-round surf fishing. The area is exceptional, both in beauty and in scientific significance. Dunes and sea are always a fascinating combination, but here is an amazing botanical garden of beach and dune vegetation in all stages: wild heather gardens with hollies, cedars, bayberries, beach plums. The conquest of moving sand by plant life is a greater drama than ever man has written for the stage. Along State Route 35.

MOUNT BLUE STATE PARK: *Maine*

From the parking overlook on Center Hill, at 1,600 feet above sea level, the motorist can sit in his car and get a view of the surrounding mountains. He can; but it is not recommended that this should be his only experience in a park that offers so many foot trails with so many opportunities to know this northern forest, its trees and plants and wild creatures. The climber will aspire, of course, to go to the highest point—the fire tower on Mount Blue—where much of southwestern Maine is spread out beneath his eyes. On Lake Webb are picnic areas and a campground, a bathing beach and "Adirondack shelters." From Dixfield on U. S. 2 by State Route 142 to Weld; or leave U. S. 2 at Wilton by State Route 156; distance the same either way.

Mount Mansfield State Recreational Area: *Vermont*

The profile of this famous New England mountain is said to resemble a human face, upturned, with peaks representing the forehead, nose, lips, chin, and Adam's apple. But concentrate rather on the particular beauty of the Green Mountains; feast your eyes on the lush vegetation, the winding streams, the cool green forest land, and the blue expanse of Lake Champlain—as seen from the summit of Mansfield. Vermont has only two seasons, the natives admit—summer and winter. But good use can be made of both, for Mansfield is outstanding for the skier, and camping has a touch of paradise here. Reached from Stowe, by way of Smuggler's Notch. State Route 108.

Ricketts Glen State Park: *Pennsylvania*

There is a touch of pathos in the very name of this beautiful place. Colonel Robert Bruce Ricketts, after four bitter and soul-sickening Civil War years, sought the peace of unspoiled nature, and found it here. In his first deed he ironically gave his address as "Army of the Potomac." He kept adding tract after tract; brought heather from Scotland and planted it, where it still grows; and was buried at last beneath one of the towering hemlocks of his virgin forest. The state now owns 14,000 acres of this countryside north of Redrock, west of Wilkes-Barre, on State Route 115. Picnicking and camping facilities.

Roland C. Nickerson State Forest Park: *Massachusetts*

Here, on one of those large fresh-water ponds characteristic of Cape Cod, surrounded by wooded hills, the visitor seems far from the Atlantic Ocean; but the wind suddenly shifts easterly, and the briny odor comes in. This is a wonderful place to pitch your tent. A day on Flax Pond, with a picnic lunch, is also a pleasure for visitors. Nearly 1,800 acres of breathtaking landscape. On Route 6, just east of Brewster.

Walden Pond State Reservation: *Massachusetts*

On this sixty-four-acre pond, just out of Concord on State Route 26, Henry David Thoreau built himself a little cabin in 1845. There he sawed wood with a bucksaw. He said the wood warmed him twice; once when he sawed it, and again when he burned it. Emerson and Alcott used to come out here to see Thoreau; but he said frankly he liked his own company best, and that of the woodchucks. The reservation is small—91 acres—but precious to all conservationists. Picnicking, bathing beach, trails.

(II)

THE SOUTH

Babcock State Park: *West Virginia*

The Y-shaped gorge which splits this park has precipitous walls, hundreds of feet in height. There are fine views from points along the rim of New River, and from Island in the Sky, near the administration building. This is fine country for the climber-hiker. Trout fishing is available in Mann's and Glade Creeks. There are also cabins and facilities for picnicking. Twenty-seven miles from Beckley. The park entrance is four miles south of U. S. 60 on State Route 41 near Clifftop.

Chicot State Park: *Louisiana*

The very names of these Louisiana state parks are inviting. This one is in Evangeline Parish, eight miles north of Ville Platte, twenty-five miles from Opelousas, and seventeen miles from Bunkie. This is one of the largest state parks in the south, with 6,500 acres, a third of which consists of water in a setting of wooded hills and large bays filled with cypress. The lake has been well stocked with fish; state permits for fishing can be obtained at the park headquarters. There are cabins, but these are in such demand that reservations should be made well in advance. Camping and picnic facilities. Off U. S. 167.

De Soto State Park: *Alabama*

Within this large area—nearly 5,000 acres—the canyon of the Little River, deep and impressive, scores the mountain surface for part of its twenty-seven miles. A scenic road follows the rim of the canyon for a long distance. At De Soto Falls, there is a spectacular drop of 120 feet. This is a region especially rich in Cherokee Indian history. During the Creek wars it was the springboard for many military operations. Wild azaleas and rhododendrons—at their height of bloom in May and June—are seen here at their colorful best. Cabins and a lodge and good picnicking sites. Eleven miles northeast of Fort Payne; five and a half miles from Mentone and east of U. S. 11.

Devil's Den State Park: *Arkansas*

The picturesque Ozark Mountains cover a wide area. In Missouri the visitor never quite knows when he is in them, or out of them, the name being so inclusive. Arkansas has a good share of them, too. In this rugged northwest region of the state are the scenic ranges known as the Boston Mountains. This park takes its name from a snaky underground cavern several miles long and from two to twenty feet in width. There are many other strange rock formations, including the Ice Box, where the temperature in midsummer never gets beyond sixty degrees. Camping and picnicking sites, housekeeping cottages, and a swimming pool. Thirteen miles west of Winslow on State Route 74.

Fairy Stone State Park: *Virginia*

Staurolite crystals—in the shape of crosses—are frequently found here. Locally they are known as "fairy stones" or "lucky stones." This large state park, twenty miles northwest of Martinsville, off State Route 57, is a delightful place to pitch tent, hitch trailer, or have a picnic. You may rent a horse and ride fine bridle paths, or use the facilities of the 168-acre lake.

Florida Caverns State Park: *Florida*

These extensive limestone formations are three miles north of Marianna on State Route 167. Three quarters of a mile of trail through the underground passageways have been lighted and opened to the public, so that the stalactities and stalagmites may be viewed. Natural rock gardens are formed by the ledges and escarpments along the Chipola River. In view of the contemporary interest in bomb shelters, everybody should try to spend some hours in a good cave like this one, to become what the interpreter calls "oriented." The only creatures who do not need this apprenticeship are bats and spelunkers.

Fontainebleu State Park: *Louisiana*

Just east of Mandeville, on Lake Pontchartrain, this park occupies the lands that were once the summer plantation home of Antoine Xavier Bernard de Marigny. It is not hard to guess that a man with a name like that was a *bon vivant*. They say that he had much to do with importing into Creole life that fondness for good food, uplifting drinks, and the society of charming women, which still may be experienced in the parishes of the state. He founded the town of Mandeville, and all around was the beauty of the forest which ranged from upland pine to the cypress that has knees. A wonderful place for hiking, on nature trails; there are also camping and picnic facilities. On U. S. Highway 190; about fifty miles from New Orleans by land, though only twenty by water.

Fort Clinch State Park: *Florida*

When our young nation was building a chain of defenses along its vulnerable Atlantic and Gulf coasts, after the War of 1812 had revealed our weakness, this location on Amelia Island was judged strategic. The Civil War came before Fort Clinch was finished and Engineer Colonel Robert E. Lee made a personal visit here to inspect its possibilities. But Amelia Island had long been the scene of many struggles to control it. Jean Ribault sailed along its shore and claimed it for France, as early as 1562. The British general Oglethorpe named the island for the second daughter of George II; during the American Revolution the colonial troops skirmished here. The excellent museum should be visited by those who occupy the campsites for tents and trailers here, or who picnic and fish in this inviting region. At Fernandina, off Florida A1A.

Gambrill State Park: *Maryland*

There are two separate recreation areas here, one at the park entrance and the other atop High Knob, at an elevation of 1,600 feet on Catoctin Mountain, overlooking the Monocacy and Middletown valleys. The park is named for James H. Gambrill, Jr., of Frederick, whose "love of nature and outdoor life prompted him to be first to call attention to the beauty of this spot and its availability for the use of the public." In the western background is South Mountain, and southward one looks toward Harpers Ferry Gap—land that saw constant change of possession in the Civil War. Camping and picnicking, with fine hiking in charming and historic surroundings. Six miles northwest of Frederick, on Route 5.

Hunting Island State Park: *South Carolina*

A great barrier island in a semitropical setting is reached from Beaufort (pronounced "Bewfort" in this state, though in neighboring North Carolina the same name becomes "Bo-fort"). The ride across the sea-island country to reach the open sea is in itself a revelation to those who are not familiar with this stretch of the south Atlantic coast. Despite continued abuse by the armed services during our wars, some virginal forest growth still persists on Hunting Island. The palmettos make a crackling noise in the ocean breezes, and wet their feet on the very tideline. State Highway 285. Cabins, tent and trailer space, picnicking.

Kolomoki Mounds State Park: *Georgia*

One of the strange features of the American Indian is the general ignorance he displayed about his remoter ancestors. True, he had no written language in which history could be recorded, but when his forebears were so close to him as were the Kolomokis and the Weeden Islanders of this locality to the tribes of the Creek Confederacy, one would have thought the genealogy might have come down by oral tradition. The visitor here is impressed by the great Temple Mound which looms over the eastern end of the area. Bits of pottery, flint chips, and arrowheads are plentiful in the nearby fields. The park is on U. S. Highway 27 northwest of Blakely; it has a good lake, a museum, and a picnic and barbecue site.

Levi Jackson State Park: *Kentucky*

George the Third having been shorn of his transatlantic properties, the soldiers who had fought in Washington's army were offered "western Lands" in recognition of their services. One of the men who homesteaded on the Wilderness Road was John Freeman, whose grave is here. Later came Levi and Rebecca Jackson, who in 1800 built a home which stands almost in its original condition. There is also in the park a museum of pioneer relics, housed in an old log manor house, with smokehouse, barn, shop, and an ancient cider press. The cider was put down cellar in a bar'l and attained vintage condition the following spring, if there was any left. Good camping area; picnic sites and several miles of footpaths easy on the feet. Three miles south of London, just off U. S. 25.

Montgomery Bell State Park: *Tennessee*

Tennessee says that its Division of State Parks is "primarily a service agency and does not pretend to be self-supporting." Wherever you find that attitude, you find well-administered places which offer real rest and contain authentic preservations. This fine and spacious park, eight miles east of Dickson on U. S. 70, is a good example. This is redcedar country, and in the spring the redbud and the dogwood, those two blooming delights that nature contrived to form hillside bouquets, are seen at their best. There are many clear streams here, with two sizable lakes which offer fishing, swimming, and boating. Picnicking is available, too, of course. And the visitor will learn something about Montgomery Bell, the great ironmaster who supplied General Andrew Jackson with cannon shot.

Morrow Mountain State Park: *North Carolina*

In these Uwharrie Mountains of the Piedmont the visitor feels himself at a much greater height than is actually the case. Geologically, this is fascinating country, for the rock is much older than the present Appalachians—perhaps as old as anything in our country. From Morrow Mountain, from Tater Top and the other peaks, the Pee Dee River is seen flowing mildly through the rolling farm lands. Missing is the stirring quality of the Blue Ridge and other higher ranges, but camping here is delightful. North Carolina, too, is one of those states that supplies a naturalist guide in season. Many fine trails. Seven miles east of Albemarle on State Routes 27, 73, and 740.

Mound State Monument and Museum: *Alabama*

Where the Black Warrior River twists in a leisurely way through the foothills, a prehistoric people, peaceful and industrious, had a populous city with temples reared upon pyramidal earth mounds. Skillful excavation has recovered such evidences of the way of life of this people that the visitor comes to feel a real kinship with them. There were artists and craftsmen of talent among these early folk.

The visitor may see on this 300-acre monument not only forty mounds left by the ancient ones, but also a wonderful display of their artifacts in the museum. Of all preservations of this nature, Alabama's mounds are of great excellence. Seventeen miles south of Tuscaloosa, on State Route 69.

Natural Bridge State Park: *Kentucky*

Our ancestors, prowling around among strange rock formations, were inevitably reminded of the handiwork of the Devil. Satan was a character more feared for his malice and more respected for his power in those days, before man had invented devices that make his Majesty seem kindly by comparison. Sure enough, there is a Devil's Gulch here, and the nearby saltpeter mines are quite apropos. But the great feature of the park is the natural bridge, 30 feet wide at the top, 40 feet thick at the center of the arch, and 85 feet wide at the base opening. The Red River Valley, 57 miles southeast of Lexington, has much to offer the camper and hiker. Picnic areas, boating, and fishing. On State Route 77, off Highway 15, forty miles southeast of Winchester, five miles south of Slade.

Percy Quin State Park: *Mississippi*

This is pine-forest country primarily, though there are plenty of magnificent oaks. Situated not far from McComb, on Route 24 in south Mississippi, the gently rolling terrain affords may adventures along its trails for those who do not aspire to rugged climbing. There is excellent fishing in the large lake, and no license charge is made to visitors. Tent camping is permitted, but the camper is "on his own" as to facilities. Cabins and a lodge with dining-room facilities; a large beach and ample picnicking space.

Pickett State Park: *Tennessee*

This is a big area—1,752 acres in extent. Generally speaking (it is not invariably true), the bigger the park, the more room its natural features have in which to be their primitive selves. This one is in a rather remote region of the Cumberland Mountains, not far from the Kentucky border. Being typical cave-country, it contains rocks of strange formations. The lake is not large, but there is plenty of room for the camper and the picnicker. Horseback riding is a real adventure in these wild lands; bridle paths lead to unexpected nooks and views. Take State Route 28 from Pine Haven; about thirteen miles northeast of Jamestown.

SANDY POINT STATE PARK: *Maryland*

The park is a part of the farm that was patented in 1667 under the name of "Rattlesnake Point." When Baptist Mezick bought the place in 1833, it was described as "very beautiful, with the added advantage of an inexhaustible supply of *sea ore*." And what do you suppose "sea ore" was? It was seaweed, hauled from the shoreline in carts and used as fertilizer by the early settlers. French farmers on the other side of the Atlantic are still using this "wrack" to manure their fields. A short distance from the two sandy beaches are picnic sites, on a "first come, first served" basis. When the "run" is on, the crabbing here is famous. Students of marshland nature will relish this strip, with its varied flora and bird habitat. On Chesapeake Bay, just off U. S. 50.

SITE OF FORT CHRISTINA: *Delaware*

The Swedes landed at this place, "the Rocks," at the foot of E. Seventh Street in present-day Wilmington. This was in 1638 and the little colony they set up was not only the first permanent settlement in Delaware, but the first in the whole Delaware Valley. A fort was built here and named for the young queen of Sweden. The cultural, social, and religious influence of these Scandinavian settlers long remained, even after tough old Peter Stuyvesant came down from Manhattan Island with his fleet and claimed everything in sight for the Dutch.

STATE BEACH LANDS: *Delaware*

Along the southeastern edge of the state, these Atlantic barrier beaches stretch for nearly fourteen and a half miles between the ocean and Rehoboth, Indian River and Little Assawoman Bays. State Highway 14 extends through these lands from Rehoboth Beach to the Maryland state line. A trailer campsite with a restaurant is located at Indian River Inlet, and picnic and tent camping areas are provided along the highway. Bay on one side and ocean on the other offer a wide variety of recreation possibilities.

Table Rock State Park: *South Carolina*

This is scenic country, and no mistake. Against a background of high granite Appalachian peaks, the parkland, stream-cut, offers a great variety of hill and valley trail. At the foot of the stark rock is a dense forest in which trees of the north and south mingle—pine and hemlock, magnolia and gum. In the old days, before state parks, Table Rock was to the southern coastal folk what the White Mountains were to the Bostonians. Much unspoiled natural beauty has been preserved here. Two streams, leaping down from the heights, were dammed to create Lake Pinnacle, where a bathhouse and beach offer water sports. Ample picnic areas, family vacation cabins, and tent and trailer sites. Sixteen miles north of Pickens, between U. S. 178 and State Route 11.

Tishomingo State Park: *Mississippi*

Bear Creek, a tributary of the Tennessee River, divides this woodland park in the northeast corner of the state on Route 25. Its 1,400 acres supply the ample space and diversity desirable to those who wish to follow miles of nature trail through forest and among the limestone cliffs and shelter caves where the Choctaw Indians, led by Chief Tishomingo, fought their losing battle against the encroachment of the white man. Furnished cabins, swimming, boating, fishing, picnicking, and tent camping.

Tombigbee State Park: *Mississippi*

Here—near U. S. 78, about six miles southeast of Tupelo—the visitor will be in the center of a pine-clad, sharply ridged countryside that was the scene of stirring events during the Civil War. Just north of the park is Brices Cross Roads, where the cavalry genius, General Nathan Bedford Forrest, won a battle that has become a military classic. The topography that made it tough for mounted troops is just what supplies fine hiking for lovers of nature trails. Camping spaces, picnicking, fishing and boating on Lake Lee; cabins and a lodge.

Trap Pond State Park: *Delaware*

On this nearly level coastal plain, clad with pine on the higher parts and with cypress and other swamp growths on the lower, nature lovers will find a fine system of trails and a lake of sixty acres for fishing and boating. Picnic areas with shelters and a good modern campground in the pines. Five miles west of Laurel on State Route 24, then south one mile.

Vogel State Park: *Georgia*

The Blue Ridge Mountains come right down into the northern part of Georgia, finally to peter out as outliers—but always of the identical quality in structure and varied sylvan clothing. August Vogel gave to the people of the state, and their visitors, a fine piece of wilderness which was once beloved of the Cherokee. Neal's Gap was called, in the Indian language, "Frogtown," because of the evening concerts by what was either a heroic chorus of frogs or a solo by one heroic frog. These same Indians are alleged to have buried a hoard of gold somewhere on Blood Mountain. Natives still gopher for it. Lake Trahlyta offers water sports; there is a stone inn and cottages, and picnic sites. Eleven miles south of Blairsville, on U. S. 19 and State 129.

Watoga State Park: *West Virginia*

Most of West Virginia's state parks are large, and reveal nature's ways with complete integrity. This one consists of somewhat more than ten thousand acres, and contains the great Brooks Memorial Arboretum, besides a forest cover ideal for nature study. Deer multiply rapidly in the state, and there is a large herd in the park. When their numbers are too great, archers are permitted to try their skill in thinning them. They are tamer than in Robin Hood's time. Lodge and cabins; also campgrounds and picnic facilities. The park entrance is southwest of Huntersville on State Route 39.

Westmoreland State Park: *Virginia*

An ideal place to camp in pleasant surroundings while roaming through one of the country's richest historical regions. Sometimes it seems as though all our early great Virginians either were born here or frequented this orbit. Not quite true, of course. The park is forty miles east of Fredericksburg, just off State Route 3, and it fronts the Potomac River, with a sloping sand-and-shell beach. Trails, picnic and camping areas, log cabins.

(III)

THE MIDWEST

Angostura Dam and Reservoir: *South Dakota*

South of Hot Springs and not far from both Wind Cave National Park and the great Custer State Park, the manmade lake resulting from the damming of the Cheyenne River as part of the colossal Missouri River Basin Project, provides a welcome recreation area for the dusty tourist in a semi-arid land. There are beaches, picnic sites, and boat ramps. Both the prehistoric and the historic Indian came here, as shown by archaeological work done before the flooding. Petroglyphs above the water line are preserved in place, and challenge the beholder to interpret them. The reservoir extends from State Route 79 to State Route 87, a distance of eleven miles.

Arbor Lodge State Park: *Nebraska*

The old colonial mansion of fifty-two rooms, once the home of J. Sterling Morton, is only half the attraction of this cherished Nebraska preservation. Sixty-five acres of beautiful woodland surround the mansion, and through this forest growth, partly native timber and partly the plantings of the man who founded "Arbor Day," the visitor may roam, on foot trails or bridle paths. Picnic grounds are available in lovely locations. The T-shaped building houses precious historical relics. On U. S. Highway 75.

Baptism River State Park: *Minnesota*

Like Gooseberry Falls, this park is another spectacular site on the North Shore Drive of Lake Superior. Here is located the highest waterfall within the state. A wild torrent of the glacial period created the gorge and river mouth. The mountains from which the stream leaps are known as the Sawtooths. Picnicking and hiking are available, but the park is still undeveloped—you are free to use it and

Officers' quarters and parade ground, Fort Churchill State Park, Nevada

*The Dalles of the Saint Croix River, Interstate State Park,
the oldest park in the Wisconsin system.
Wisconsin seen to the left, Minnesota to the right*

State House, Annapolis, Maryland.
Here, where George Washington laid down his commission,
the Legislature still sits

Montauk Springs, out of which flows the Current River,
Montauk State Park, Missouri

Cathedral Gorge State Park, Nevada, seen from Miller's Point Lookout

Nineteenth century water-powered mill, Alley Spring State Park, Missouri

Sequoia gigantea, *Calaveras Big Trees State Park, California*

Sleeping cabin, Lake Hope State Park, Ohio

Caney Creek Cascades, Fall Creek Falls State Park, Tennessee

In New Salem State Park, Illinois

Manitou Falls, the highest in Wisconsin; Pattison State Park

Mound Builders State Memorial, The Newark Earthworks, Ohio

Fishing for trout in the Current River, Montauk State Park, Missouri

In Kershaw-Ryan State Park, Nevada

Fort Pike State Monument, Louisiana, seen from the moat

Devil s Doorway, Devil's Lake State Park, Wisconsin

not abuse it. Use your legs to climb into the tall timber and thrill to some of the grandest scenery you have ever set eyes on. One mile south of Illgen City on U. S. 61.

Copper Falls State Park: *Wisconsin*

The Bad River, rising on the divide between the Mississippi and St. Lawrence watersheds, flows north into Lake Superior. In this region, as it tumbles over the edge of the Keweenawan traprock, it produces inspiring cascades and waterfalls. This is rugged country. True, the forests have been logged by the white man, but it was long enough ago that in future years people will call them primeval. Some fine stands of hemlock and hardwoods escaped. Tramping the woodland trails here is real adventure. County Highway K leads from the city of Mellen (four miles) to the park entrance. Fine campgrounds and picnic sites. Off State 169.

Cuivre River State Park: *Missouri*

We are distinctly in historic and prehistoric Indian country here, and this expansive state park is interlaced with more than fifty miles of foot trails along which the hiker will find a great deal to arrest his attention. The winding creeks through the area are Big Sugar and Little Sugar. Thirty-nine old Indian campsites, villages, and mounds have been found within the park boundaries. An ideal place for those who avoid the highly developed recreation spots. Camp and picnic sites amidst quietude. Five miles east of Troy, on State Route 47.

Dells of the Sioux Co-operative Recreation Area: *South Dakota*

The Big Sioux River carved its way between walls of the brilliant red Sioux quartzite for three quarters of a mile at this place, making a deep and narrow channel. The thirty-acre park, surrounded by cultivated prairie country, half a mile south of Dell Rapids, is a welcome oasis for picnickers, but they must bring their water with them. Twenty miles north of Sioux Falls, South Dakota, on State Route 77.

De Mores Historic Site: *North Dakota*

In 1883 a young French nobleman came to Medora in the Badlands of North Dakota and began a cattle ranch, intending to establish a meat-packing industry nearby. Theodore Roosevelt also ranched not far away. The two men got along as well as could be expected, considering their pronounced individualism. The Marquis de Mores had good ideas, but his timing proved unfortunate; yet he enjoyed himself in the chateau he and the charming Marquise occupied near town. Most of the original furnishings can be seen here, now that the house is under the expert care of the State Historical Society. A unique preservation, reminder of a colorful frontier period. Near Medora on U. S. 10.

Fort Robinson State Park: *Nebraska*

Here is the headquarters building of what was in 1874 a military post established to keep the Sioux Indians quiet while the white men stole their lands. After Custer's defeat on the Little Big Horn, Chief Crazy Horse unwisely accepted an invitation to confer on peace at Fort Robinson. The evidence as to what happened was conflicting, but there was no doubt that Crazy Horse was dead. The museum tells the story of the conflict with the Plains Indians. Lodge, cabins, camping sites, and picnic grounds. About three miles west of Crawford, on U. S. 20.

Giant City State Park: *Illinois*

"There were giants in those days." Who else could have manipulated these huge blocks of stone and aligned them to form streets as straight as though a surveyor had laid them out? Truly a strange exhibition of the forces of nature. No doubt some great underground upheaval caused a bed of sandstone to slip over a deposit of shale. This rough, hilly section of the state, twelve miles south of Carbondale, is sometimes called "the Illinois Ozarks." There are the remains of a fort near the north end of the park, though some think it may have been an ancient buffalo trap of the early Indians. Camping and picnic areas; a lodge and cabins. Seven miles south of Carbondale on U. S. 51, then east three miles.

Gooseberry Falls State Park: *Minnesota*

To those who are unfamiliar with the Lake Superior shoreline northwest of Duluth, a revelation of wild beauty is in store. The Gooseberry River comes tumbling into the lake through the park. In hiking along this volcanic lava region, you pass from well-verdured patches of black spruce and birch, poplar and alder, into bald rock formations of strange design and of blue, rose, and purple coloring. In this rather remote part of the nation a camping adventure will be unforgettable. The park provides comfortable facilities for it. On U. S. Highway 61.

Hartwick Pines State Park: *Michigan*

The fortunate visitor to this tree wonderland will think with gratitude of Mrs. Karen B. Hartwick, who gave it to the state for the enjoyment of all who revere the small remnant of our primitive forest growth. It is a memorial to her husband, who died in World War I. The largest of Michigan's state parks in the lower peninsula—8,938 acres—it contains a block of eighty-five acres that have never felt the lumberman's ax. A white pine, "the Monarch," looms 155 feet, branchless for half that height. Camping with modern facilities is available. The abundant wildlife can frequently be seen. There is trout fishing, and attractive foot trails. Seven miles from Grayling on Highway M-93.

Hueston Woods State Park: *Ohio*

This is one of the newer park developments in Ohio, and a rare stand of virgin forest growth makes it of particular interest to those who like to feel themselves in a bit of primitive America. The total acreage of this park ensures elbow room, the manmade lake itself covers 625 acres. Housekeeping cabins with modern equipment may be rented. Campsites and picnic sites are available. Motorboat owners may use the lake, but nothing over six horsepower is permitted. The park is near Oxford, on State Route 732.

International Peace Garden State Park: *North Dakota*

Here is an unusual experience for the tourist—a state park that sits astride the great unfortified boundary between the United States and Canada. With the exception of the free access from Glacier National Park to its Canadian national neighbor Waterton, the world knows no finer example of amity than this. There are about 2,200 acres, of which 887 are in this country and the remainder in Manitoba. The location is almost the exact geographical center of the North American continent, and is in a region of scenic beauty in the Turtle Mountains. Overnight cabins, picnic facilities, and a rustic lodge that can house groups. Thirteen miles north of Dunseith off State Route 5, on Route 3.

Interstate State Park: *Wisconsin*

Along the dalles of the St. Croix River both Wisconsin and Minnesota have state parks. The French word *dalles* has been handed down from the early Canadian *voyageurs* who noted the likeness of the traprock of the gorge to the slabstones that paved the churches at home. Furiously the St. Croix has been pouring through this ever-deepening canyon, grinding great potholes in the rock with boulders that became spherical during the operation. Those on the Minnesota side are the largest and deepest potholes known. Interstate is near St. Croix Falls, on U. S. 8. Fine camping and picnicking.

John Brown Memorial State Park: *Kansas*

The log cabin that was once the home of the tragic figure of the abolition is now housed in a modern building. The interior of the cabin is furnished just as in the days when Brown lived here. It served as an "underground station" in the days preceding the Civil War. Nearby was fought the Battle of Osawatomie in 1856. On U. S. 169, south from Kansas City.

Lacey-Keosauqua State Park: *Iowa*

The name Lacey is a reminder of that stalwart preservationist, an Iowa congressman, who did so much toward placing the historic and scientific treasures of the nation under public ownership and protection. More than 2,000 acres have been set aside as recreation land, as a wildlife sanctuary, and as commemoration of the pioneer efforts that took place here. Ely's Ford, flanked by massive outcroppings of sandstone, was used by the first white settlers before there were any roads. Nearby is the site of a prehistoric Indian village. Camping and picnicking, a lodge and cabins, and many hiking trails. One mile southwest of Keosauqua, on the Des Moines River.

Lake Hendricks State Recreation Area: *South Dakota*

This small park is situated about 14 miles northeast of White, between State Highways 28 and 30 on the Minnesota–South Dakota state line. In 1960 there were 18,500 visitors, including 2,040 campers. Facilities for tents and trailers; picnicking, swimming, and boating.

Lake Metigoshe State Park: *North Dakota*

At a time when state parks were few and far between, the Historical Society of North Dakota led the country in the number of its preservations. Fifteen miles north of Bottineau, on State Route 5, is Lake Metigoshe, the largest body of water in the Turtle Mountains, near the Canadian border. Heavily wooded, with many deer and smaller game and fur-clad animals, this is an attractive spot for the camper and picnicker. Fishing, boating, and swimming are offered. There is also an interesting archaeological and historical museum. Good-sized sections are kept in their natural condition and are accessible by nature trails.

Lake of the Ozarks State Park: *Missouri*

The lake is manmade, but so huge that it seems like nature's own work. On the Grand Glaize arm of these 4,000 acres of water surface all the appropriate recreation features are available, except for cabins and a dining lodge. The spacious camping grounds overlooking the lake have the most modern facilities. Trailers are accommodated, too, but there are no electrical or sewer connections. No reservations are necessary. On Highway 134, off Route 54.

Meade County State Park: *Kansas*

This park contains some of the finest springs in Kansas, a lake of a hundred acres, a state hatchery, and a buffalo and elk preserve. Camping and picnic grounds; fishing and boating; also a beach. The park is situated twelve miles southwest of Meade on State Routes 23 and 98.

Niobrara State Park: *Nebraska*

The industrious Mormons, who always believed that character was developed by overcoming difficulties, built a millrace three quarters of a mile long in 1846 at this spot. The park consists of about 400 acres in a heavily wooded island at the mouth of the Niobrara River. A long clear-water lagoon courses the center of the island, providing water recreation. Cabins and outdoor fireplaces. On Highway 12.

Oakwood Lakes State Park: *South Dakota*

This was the favorite ceremonial ground of the Indians when Nicollet and Frémont were exploring the country. "Lakes of the Grand Lodge," the red man called the inviting spot, where oak and hackberry, ash and elm rimmed the shorelines. A log cabin, dating back to 1875, still stands in good condition as the pioneer home of "Old Spot" Mortimer and his squaw wife. Ten miles north of Volga on U.S. 14, the visitor will find here good picnicking and camping, with water diversions—but above all, a historic country worth exploring.

Peninsula State Park: *Wisconsin*

The peninsula here referred to is the Door County mitten-thumb which reaches out between Green Bay and Lake Michigan. Fine stands of virgin pine, hemlock, balsam, and hardwoods cover a slowly mounting slope that finally reaches the bluffs high above the bay waters. It is no rarity to see the white-tail deer and other game animals as one drives and hoofs it on road and trail. Dense growths of white cedar perching on the cool ledges tell the lover of trees that he is in true northern country here. Interesting fishing villages string along this north Door County waterfront. Camping and picnicking, water recreation, and horseback riding. Near Ephraim on State Route 42.

Pere Marquette State Park: *Illinois*

This, the largest of Illinois state parks, offers an unusual range of interests to the visitor. Prehistoric indian occupation; the visit of Father Marquette and Louis Jolliet in 1673; the beauty of well-timbered bluffs; fossil life in the rocks and ice-age wind-blown loess on the ridges; wildlife in abundance and hundreds of species of birds in the rich forest—what more can one ask for? There are many miles of foot trails and bridle paths, and trained naturalists during the season aid in the appreciation of the park's significance. Camping and picnic areas, a massively constructed rustic lodge and cabins. Six miles west of Grafton on State Route 100.

PIKE STATE PARK: *Ohio*

The park, six miles south of Bainbridge on U. S. Route 50, is of good size, but Pike Lake covers only thirteen acres. A nice sheet of water, though, and it is said that the bass, bluegills, and crappies are not too elusive. The best thing is to hire a rowboat and give a workout to those almost-atrophied muscles. You will not be run down by a motorboat, for there are none here. During the summer there is a natural history program for visitors; Ohio's efforts in interpretive services are notable.

POKAGON STATE PARK: *Indiana*

Lake James and Snow Lake, which provide water activities in Pokagon, are both of glacial origin, as are so many hundreds of others scattered throughout northern Indiana. The Potawatomi Indians occupied this region before the white man arrived. All that remains of the tribe, to which Father de Smet first brought Christianity, is the name of the inn that accommodates visitors the year around. But the camper is provided for, too, with a fine site on a wooded bluff overlooking Lake James. Winter sports are popular: Lake James becomes a great skating rink, and the hills furnish skiing slopes. The park lies on U. S. 27, a few miles north of Angola.

PONCA STATE PARK: *Nebraska*

East to West, the state of Nebraska slowly climbs up hill, from the oak-covered bluffs of the Missouri, through the sandhills, to the high Pine Ridge where folks talk of the "little Black Hills." This fine state park overlooks the "Big Muddy," and foot trails lead to look-outs where the historic river can be viewed. The variety of bird and wild animal life within this area is unusual, and fossil remains can be seen along the trails. Picnic and camping sites, swimming pool and cabins. Reached by Highways 9 and 12.

SAM A. BAKER STATE PARK: *Missouri*

Lake Wappapello, in the southeastern corner of the state, is famous for its fishing, especially for its black bass. This park lies just at its headwaters, with Big Creek as its eastern boundary. The bluffs along the creek are rugged and the view from the summit of Mudlick

Mountain well worth the trail climb. Well-forested, the park seems more out-of-the-world than it really is. There are cabins and picnic grounds, and a dining lodge. The folder speaks of "an area that has been set aside for the ones who wish to sink stakes in the ground and erect their own tents." And many do that very thing. On Highway 143, from Route 34.

Scenic State Park: *Minnesota*

In a state so rich as Minnesota in wild and beautiful park areas, this one is the most primitive of all. On a long peninsula between Coon and Sandwick Lakes is located one of the finest remaining virgin stands of Norway pine. Deer and other wildlife are abundant, and along the trails are flowers and plants that will be unfamiliar to those who come from farther south. The strange "pitcher plant" grows in the lower areas. Modern camp and picnic facilities. Boating, swimming, fishing, and many trails. On Highway 38 to Bigfork.

Scott County State Park: *Kansas*

In the museum at the University of Kansas, at Lawrence, the visitor sees many relics taken from an Indian pueblo in this site. When the heavy hand of the Spanish conquistador was laid upon the tribes in New Mexico, most of them remained in their homes to fight oppression as best they might; but a group migrated into Kansas and set up El Quartelejo. They occupied this site from 1650 to 1720. In this park, then, the visitor is offered good recreation facilities on a 115-acre lake and also a bit of archaeological lore. Many springs, rock gardens, foot trails, camping and picnicking areas. Twelve miles north of Scott City, off U. S. 83.

Spring Mill State Park: *Indiana*

Ralph L. Brooks, on behalf of the Indiana Department of Conservation, wrote a charming pamphlet in which he styled this delightful retreat from modernity "the Village that Slept Awhile." No greater tribute can be paid Spring Mill State Park than to say that it was one of the favorites of Colonel Richard Lieber, father of the Indiana park system. It is a reconstruction, but one that breathes the very spirit of frontier living and enterprise. And history here has a marvelous setting. The park preserves at least a hundred acres of virgin woodland, including white oak and tulip-poplar giants; caverns and underground rivers, too, that contain rare species of blind fish. Three miles east of Mitchell on State Route 60.

Tahquamenon Falls State Park: *Michigan*

Hiawatha slept here. Also, he built his canoe here, and his friend Kwasind, "the strong one," kindly cleared the river of its debris. Despite lumbering in the days when log-driving was a colorful activity, there are still patches of virgin pine, hemlock, spruce, and other northern trees; wildlife of all kinds is plentiful. The river flows through deep swamps and between high hills before pouring its flood into Lake Superior. This is an ideal camping park, with sites at the Lower Falls and near the river mouth. It is ideal for the man with a canoe. County roads from Newberry, Eckerman, and Sault Ste. Marie, off Highway 123.

Waubonsie State Park: *Iowa*

Here, in the hills of the windblown ice-age dust known as loess, there is an interesting transition of plant life. Looking at the cactus, yucca, and other desert and semidesert growth, the visitor is reminded of the southwestern part of the country; yet other plant life is that of the prairie land. The high ridges were once the council grounds of the Potawatomi Indians. Interesting hiking trails; excellent camping and picnic facilities. Seven miles southwest of Sidney, U. S. 275, Iowa 2, 239.

Wilderness State Park: *Michigan*

In many a state park, wilderness is relative. Here, when one passes through the entrance eleven miles west of Mackinaw City, wilderness is absolute, except for the fringe that makes visiting possible. Civilized man has showered this country with benefits by leaving it alone. All the northern wildflowers and trees and shrubs grow here as they have for numberless centuries; and deer, bear, and bobcat—occasionally a wolf, maybe—ply their trades in the forest and on the shoreline of Mackinac Straits. Camping and picnic facilities, and overnight cabins with fireplaces on the trail system. Off U. S. 31.

(I V)

THE WEST

Bastrop State Park: *Texas*

From the viewpoint of natural history, what makes this park significant is the fact that the pines that grow here don't belong in this region. This is what the biologists call an "island"—representing a forest growth that has defied changes in climatic conditions. Buescher State Park, twelve miles away, is connected with Bastrop by a scenic drive. This is a popular place with campers, for there is plenty of shade, and you know what that means in a land of scanty rainfall. Some pleasant rock cabins are grouped near a spring-fed lake. State Routes 21 and 71.

Beaver Dam State Park: *Nevada*

Thirty-five miles northeast of Caliente, Beaver Dam consists of 719 acres of satisfying scenery. Wonderful camping and picnicking possibilities, but no facilities for house trailers. Caliente is on U. S. Route 93.

Bottomless Lakes State Park: *New Mexico*

These six small lakes, ten miles east of Roswell on U. S. 380, are guaranteed to be bottomless. The name of the guarantor is not available; but anyway the visitor will probably use only the top twenty feet of Lake Lea, the only one where there is a lifeguard on duty and swimming is permitted. The other lakes are: Pasture, Figure 8, Devil's Inkwell, Mirror, Cottonwood. Fine stone buildings around Lake Lea provide various facilities, and there is a picnic ground.

CALAVERAS BIG TREES STATE PARK: *California*

This park offers sheer magnificence. Some of the finest specimens of the Sierra Redwood (the Big Tree, as it was called for so many years) exist in these north and south groves, situated about twenty-five miles northeast of Angels Camp. In summer the state provides a naturalist service, so that the camper and picnicker may not only see but come to know these greatest of living things. If any man can put hand upon the shaggy side of a tree that has seen 4,000 sunrises, without losing a fragment of his vanity, he may go far, but not necessarily in the right direction. Three miles north of Arnold on State Route 4.

CHERRY CREEK STATE RECREATION AREA: *Colorado*

Cherry Creek's impounded waters provide a lake of 10,000 acres, with boating, swimming, and picnicking about ten miles southeast of Denver, adjacent to State Route 83. This is an agreeable area greatly used by the people of metropolitan Denver.

CITY OF ROCKS STATE PARK: *New Mexico*

Go twenty-two miles northwest of Deming on Highway 260, then turn at the park sign into a rock wilderness formed of what geologists call rhyolite tuff. This is, of course, of volcanic origin, and is known here, as "Kneeling Nun." Among these strange rock formations one can picnic delightfully. On hot days, with low humidity, one cools off simply by getting in the shade of a rock. Well water and rest rooms are provided.

CONCHAS DAM STATE PARK: *New Mexico*

As yet, New Mexico's state parks are not numerous; but each one, as it is created, is equipped with modern facilities for the visitor. Ample provision is made for the camper and the picnicker around Lake Conchas, which is said to be the largest sustained water surface in the state. There are cabins and a lodge, and the fish in the lake offer a good variety. Twenty-four miles north of Newkirk on Highway 129; thirty-two miles northwest of Tucumcari on Highway 104.

Cove-Palisades State Park: *Oregon*

There are twenty-two miles of white waters within this canyon park, located five miles west of Culver on U. S. 97. Three rivers, the Crooked, the Deschutes, and the Metolius, come together in a region that especially invites those who have an interest in the geology of a great lava plateau, the second largest in the whole world. All three rivers are famous for their trout fishing, and fishermen may camp on an adjoining area after registering with the caretaker. There are fine picnic locations.

Davis Mountains State Park: *Texas*

Here you are in mile-high country, reached on State Route 118, five miles west of Fort Davis. This is the road that leads to the McDonald Observatory, where, in the clear atmosphere, astronomers study stars, planets, and the generous additions being made by modern science. This is ideal country to be seen from the saddle, but the hiker will enjoy it, too. You can picnic or camp here, or take rooms in an unusual adobe-type lodge, so constructed that most of the rooms have different scenic outlooks.

Dead Horse Point State Park: *Utah*

This area, at present under development, will offer one of the finest of panoramic spectacles: the sweep of Colorado River Canyon, high-colored on cliff, butte, and mesa. Northwest from Moab about twelve miles to a junction with a graded earth road; then twenty-two miles southwest. Arrows indicate direction. The road is difficult, and four hours should be allowed for the round trip from U. S. 160. Ample supply of water should be carried by the tourist. Not far to the north is situated Arches National Monument, administered by the National Park Service.

Flathead Lake State Park: *Montana*

The melting of glaciers and snowfields in the high mountains to the north and east produced this large and deep lake, where the state has provided camp and picnic sites, with facilities for boating and swimming. The fishing is at its best in June. For more than forty miles, U. S. 93 winds along the western shore, in view of the great Swan and Mission Mountains. There are camping and picnic sites twelve miles north of Polson, the town of the famous August "cherry harvest."

Fort Bridger State Park: *Wyoming*

Jim Bridger would have been surprised if anyone had called him James. This great figure in the story of western expansion, however, must not be regarded merely as an illiterate adventurer. Actually he was a man of shrewd common sense and outstanding ability. Jim's fantastic yarns became famous throughout the frontier. It was his way of getting even because, when he revealed the stark truth about nature's wonders in this region, nobody believed him. Very justly, mountains and towns have been named for this pioneer, who built a fort on Black's Fork of the Green River. Many of these buildings can still be seen just off U. S. 30 S. The pony express station still stands here.

Fort Churchill State Park: *Nevada*

This historic place is on a good gravel road that crosses from Weeks, on Alternate 95, to U. S. 50 between Silver Springs and Dayton. During the Indian campaigns this post, in ruins now, saw great activity as a part of the Overland Telegraph Line, with a Pony Express station nearby. There are campsites and picnic grounds just below the fort, across the railroad tracks by the Carson River.

Fort Phil Kearny State Historic Site and Related Sites: *Wyoming*

The blazing of the Bozeman Trail was seen by the Indians as a threat to their very existence, and they fought it bitterly. Fort Kearny, to help guard the trail, was on Piney Creek, about a mile northwest of U. S. 87 near the paved road that now leads to the town of Story. Nearby, the brave but unwise Fetterman and eighty of his men were ambushed and slain by the Indians. The Wagonbox fight took place not far away. No visitor facilities are offered here, but the tourist who spends some time in this locality is on rich historic frontier ground.

Fort Vasquez State Historical Monument: *Colorado*

Within an "island" formed by the divided Highway U. S. 85, thirty miles north of Denver and just south of Plattsville, is an adobe fort that harks back to the fur-trade days. In 1837 the Rocky Mountain Fur Company backed two trappers, Louis Vasquez and Milton Sublette, in the building of this fort. It was one of four such posts on the "Trappers' Trail," along the South Platte River. In 1842 the Arapaho Indians sacked it. Later it was a stop on the stage line between Denver and Evans. Parking, picnic facilities.

Garner State Park: *Texas*

The mountains to the north which the tourist sees when he drives along U. S. 90 near the town of Uvalde—Jack Garner's home place—contain this cheerful and interesting park, through which the clear stream of the Frio winds its way. The elevation here is just about 2,000 feet. Except along the stream banks the country is craggy, with cave shelters—wonderful hiking for those who have stout shoes and lively muscles. Mostly the visitors fish, or ride horseback. The trees along the river are towering—pecans, oak, and cypress. Plentiful wildlife can be seen here; this is a revealing spot for the amateur naturalist. U. S. 83 leads to the park entrance.

Guy W. Talbot State Park: *Oregon*

Sam Boardman, the "father of Oregon parks," used to love to tell how a certain majestic crag about four miles from the Crown Point overlook was threatened with destruction by a rock-crushing quarry job. The crag was to be brought down with one tremendous shot, and the tunnel was already loaded with ten tons of powder when the highway chairman sent a Paul Revere to stop the desecration. The powder is still there, but diluted in the water that flooded the tunnel. The beautiful Latourell Falls are worth a visit—a 250-foot drop over a volcanic bluff of the Columbia. Five miles west of Bridal Veil, on U. S. 30.

Hyde State Park: *New Mexico*

This high point in the southern end of the Sangre de Cristo mountains has long been a favorite of residents of Santa Fe and visitors to that Spanish-American city where English is so often spoken with an accent. The views from the turnouts on the mountain drive—up Ski Basin Road from the city—reveal the valley of the Rio Grande in all its expansiveness. Picnic sites and campsites, shelters and fireplaces; but this is a country where shelters are seldom required even by delicate souls. Ski country, of course. Eight miles northeast of Santa Fe on state Route 475.

Ichthyosaur Fossil Area State Park: *Nevada*

Picnicking and camping sites are available in this park, which preserves the fossilized remains of the great sea-going reptiles that swam in an ancient sea, part of the Pacific Ocean that covered this segment of Nevada in far-gone days. The park can be reached by U. S. 50, west of Austin, then south on State 21. This trip should not be attempted in the winter.

Jessie M. Honeyman Memorial State Park: *Oregon*

The rhododendrons of this park are famous even in a coastline which does not lack these lovely shrubs. The forest is dense, too, even for an ocean strip where soil and climate send trees toward the blue sky. Part of Woahink Lake is within the area, and all of Cleawox Lake. The park was justly named for a lady who for many years was a moving spirit in the preservation of the beauties of the state. The usual activities are available on the lake; and the overnight camping facilities for both tent and trailer have modern equipment. The park is just south of Florence, on U. S. 101.

Lake Walcott State Park: *Idaho*

East of Rupert, this area is accessible from U. S. 30 N. Facilities are available for boating, fishing, swimming, and picnicking on the shores of Lake Walcott Reservoir.

Lava Hot Springs: *Idaho*

Many tribes of Indians came here "to take the cure of the waters." Even inveterate enemies agreed that this place was a sanctuary, just as for many centuries the catlinite pipeclays of southwestern Minnesota were worked peaceably by various red peoples who did not love one another. The pool here is fed by at least thirty different springs, all of varying temperatures, so that in going from one end to the other one has the odd experience of passing from warm and warmer to cool and cooler. All around are the smokeholes of ancient volcanoes. A trailer park is maintained, and ample accommodations can be had in the adjoining village. On U. S. 30 N, east of Pocatello.

Lewis and Clark Caverns State Park: *Montana*

Next to Mammoth in Kentucky and Carlsbad in New Mexico, this great labyrinth in the Madison limestone is of first dimension. All the strange formations found in caves are to be seen here, and in addition, the "clusterite," which resembles a bunch of glistening grapes. Historic country is this region of the Three Forks. Before Lewis and Clark came, the Mountain and Plains Indians were continually at war, and here the two white explorers determined the true source of the Missouri River. The caverns are electrically lighted. Women visitors should wear flat-heel shoes. Picnicking facilities. Three miles off U. S. 10, east of Whitehall.

Little Round Lake State Park: *Idaho*

From May until October this area, eight miles south of Sandpoint, two miles west of U. S. 95, offers opportunities for fishing, swimming, boating, picnicking, and camping. There are ample campsites.

Makoshika State Park: *Montana*

Whether the badlands are bad lands depends upon what you wish to use them for. Montana has wisely set aside nearly 800 acres near Glendive where the traveler can enjoy this strangely eroded country that extends eastward into North Dakota. This is fossil country, as well as good hunting for the moss agate. In spite of the forbidding appearance, the grasses that grow in the badlands are nutritious feed for stock. A fine place to picnic and browse. Three miles east of Glendive on U. S. 10.

Moran State Park: *Washington*

It was the gift of this area by Robert Moran—the builder of the battleship Nebraska—which caused the Washington legislature to organize a state park agency in 1921. When one receives a magnificent present like this, nearly 5,000 acres on Orcas Island in the San Juan group of Puget Sound, with three lakes and a virgin forest, one is definitely engaged in preservation. The view from Mount Constitution has been compared with that from the mountains back of Rio de Janeiro in Brazil. Forest and alpine meadows are superb. A large number of campsites are available. Via ferry from Anacortes.

Mount Spokane State Park: *Washington*

About thirty-five miles northeast of the city of Spokane, this park is the state's largest—more than 24,000 acres. From the lodge one looks out into the state of Idaho and over "the inland empire." In summer, horseback riding is the thing; in winter, the dry powdery snow, characteristic of the eastern part of the state, provides good skiing conditions. Off U. S. 2.

Old State House State Park: *Utah*

The first Territorial Assembly of Utah, in 1851, chose Fillmore as the seat of government. Truman Angell, the architect of the Mormon Temple, drew plans for a three-winged domed capitol, but only one wing had been completed—a-two-story structure of red sandstone—when five years later Salt Lake City was chosen as the capital city. After various uses were made of this building, it returned to public ownership, and now houses a museum of pioneer artifacts. Fillmore is on U. S. 91 about midway between Cedar City and Provo.

Palo Duro Canyon State Park: *Texas*

Some modest Texans think that this 15,000-acre park is about the best there is; and they may "have something there," as the saying goes. Colonel Goodnight, of cattle fame, entered this spectacular erosional area in 1876, and if you like to see the strange forms that rocks—colored ones—can assume, you will be as surprised as the colonel when you look around this canyon. If you descend from canyon top to floor, you will have traversed a geological history of several hundreds of million years. There are fifteen miles of scenic drives, more miles than that of bridle paths, and twice as many more of foot trails. There is no lack of picnic and camping space; and there are modern cabins on the rim. On State Route 217, twelve miles east of Canyon.

Pioneer Monument State Park: *Utah*

In a visitor center here, on an elevated bench at the mouth of Emigration Canyon, you will find a large mural depicting the hegira of the Mormon emigrants from Nauvoo, Illinois, into the desert land that they made to blossom like the rose. After great hardships, the overlanders came out of the Wasatch Mountains and beheld the valley of the Great Salt Lake. A stone pylon, surrounded by bas-relief figures, shows scenes of Utah history, not only of the Mormon settlers but also of earlier wanderers. In Salt Lake City on State Route 65.

Ponderosa State Park: *Idaho*

From May to October, on the shores of Payette Lake, is offered a fine variety of recreation pleasures, including horseback riding, fishing, boating, swimming, and camping. Picnicking, too, of course. The area is northwest of McCall, which is a take-off and outfitting point for the vast primitive area that covers a large part of central Idaho. It is forested mainly by coniferous trees that for lack of access have escaped the lumberman's ax. On State Route 15.

Red Buttes Battlefield State Historical Park: *Wyoming*

The Red Buttes battle, when a little party of soldiers of the 11th Kansas Cavalry were all but wiped out by Indians, is commemorated with a granite marker bearing an Oregon Trail plaque. It was 1865, and Sergeant Amos J. Custard and his men were encamped with their three wagons on Willow Creek. A body of warriors composed of Sioux, Cheyenne, Arapaho, Comanche, and Blackfeet—a coalition that was indeed a novelty, for these tribes were seldom at peace with one another—swooped down upon them. Three men escaped by running to the river and going into hiding along its banks. The park is six miles southwest of Casper on State Route 220, four miles from the scene of the fight, which spot is marked by stones.

Robbers Cave State Park: *Oklahoma*

There were robbers here once. It was a fine hideout in a sandstone cliff, just the sort that Belle Starr, the James boys, and other dangerous people with six-guns would have sought, in which to sit quietly and think what next. Present-day robbers are of a different sort—the din of traffic and machinery, the nervous tension that robs us of nervous vitality, the worry of the market place. This park now has no robbers of either sort: it offers a restful big stretch of mountain charm in the San Bois. Six miles north of Wilburton on State Route 2. Horseback riding, hiking trails, water diversions, picnic areas and campgrounds; also fine housekeeping cabins.

Roman Nose State Park: *Oklahoma*

It will be obvious why the Cheyenne Indians loved this cheerful canyon valley, where a dam has supplied a precious water area craved by Oklahomans. Many tourists delight in just such a spare, dry-looking land as this, especially when it is only a step to good fishing and pleasant boating. No outboard motors are permitted. The lodge is small but especially pleasant, and would have greatly surprised, in its modernity, that acquiline-nosed Cheyenne chief for whom the area is named. As Roman noses were rather a habit with the Indians, perhaps this one happened to be very large. There are trails, picnic sites, and shelters. On State Route 8, seven miles north of Watonga.

Sutter's Fort State Historical Monument: *California*

The discovery of gold at Coloma on January 24, 1848, at the sawmill on the American Fork of the Sacramento River which was being built by John A. Sutter and James W. Marshall, touched off the great California gold rush. Merchants and blacksmiths and boardinghouse keepers moved into the fort to supply the needs of the miners, who flocked from all over the nation. Of the original fort there remains the two-story central building, built of oak beams and adobe. The outer walls and rooms are a reconstruction. The fine Indian museum in Sacramento is also an attraction. In Sacramento, at 28th and L Streets.

Tubac Presidio Historical Monument: *Arizona*

This is truly historic country. The town is the oldest founded by white men in Arizona. It was the rallying point of De Anza when he made his famous overland expedition from here into southern California, across the desert, finally to reach the Golden Gate of San

Francisco. On the west are the Diablito Mountains, with the Santa Ritas on the east: two valleys upon which Coronado had looked, when he marched from the south in his voyage of discovery. In Pima Indian language, Tubac means "the burned place"—significant of the Apache raids that made colonization difficult for the padres of Spain. The adobe houses and stores are grouped around a white-plastered church. On Interstate 19 north of Tumacacori National Monument; twenty miles north of Nogales, off U.S. 89.

Twin Harbors State Park: *Washington*

Perhaps one of the reasons for the popularity of this park for over-night camping is the presence of the famous razor clam. A good little essay could be written about digging clams. The sport differs from fox hunting in that the clam is good to eat; and from hunting the Kodiak bear in not being so dangerous. Only a small fraction of the country's population has ever seen a clam in its native haunts: what one gets in a restaurant is but a faint shadow of the shelled delicacy dug from a sandy beach or muddy estuary and eaten within the hour in your own camp. The clam digger enjoys the same sort of relaxation as a driver of oxen—lots of time to meditate. These 240 acres between Grays Harbor and Willapa Harbor offer a relaxing experi-ence. Twenty-one miles southwest of Aberdeen on State Route 13 A.

Valley of Fire State Park: *Nevada*

Somehow the very name of this park sounds like adventure, and the visitor who is willing to rough it in primitive country will not be disappointed. The red Jurassic sandstone has been weathered into fantastic shapes, and the ancient Indians apparently did a lot of writing and drawing on the faces of these rocks.

Visitors should carry water with them. Much of the road through the valley follows the Arrowhead Trail that connected Salt Lake City with Las Vegas. Campsites and picnic sites are available at several points. Reached by State Route 40 from Crystal on U. S. 40, or State 12 from U. S. 91.

Yuma Territorial Prison Historical Monument: *Arizona*

The neighboring Indians used to make pin money by capturing escaping prisoners from this unpleasant place of detention, situated on a granite bluff which at this point tries to intercept the passage of the Colorado River. The reward was $50 a head, and to stay in business the Indians invented plans to facilitate escapes. The adobe walls are six feet thick, but the doors and windows, as anywhere else, frequently leaked. There were cells for incorrigibles, and a dungeon block where prisoners were chained at safe distances, to keep them from killing each other. The prison is not in use now. On U.S. 80, end of highway bridge, south side of Colorado River.

APPENDIX A

STATE PARK PROGRAMS IN OTHER STATES

In the main text of this volume, where many outstanding state parks are described, certain states are not represented. For the most part the reason is simply that at the time of writing these states did not contain such a well-rounded system of recreation areas as to warrant their inclusion. However, it is gratifying to know that in most of these states there is at present a wholesome activity directed toward the achievement of desirable park systems. This is notably the fact in the Rocky Mountain region, where, because the impact of large centers of population has not hitherto been felt, or because of the resistance of commercial interests, or for some other reason, the state park movement has been tardy in taking hold. When this study was begun, there were forty-eight states in the Union. There are now fifty, and both of the latest stars in the flag contain spots of beauty, scientific significance, and historic quality which deserve preservation. In the following paragraphs will be found such information about plans for acquisition and development as is presently available.

Alaska. Before statehood, considerable thought was given to the exceptional recreation resources of this northern outpost. In one of a series of surveys prepared by B. Frank Heintzleman, then territorial governor, these sentiments were voiced: "We have to realize that as time goes on we will find more and more 'no trespassing' signs along our roadsides and on our boat lanes, air routes and hiking trails. We should undertake a program now that will assure the continued enjoyment of many of these places by Alaskans and their visitors. Because of the very richness of our present recreation resources we are in danger of taking no thought for their future preservation and thus losing through neglect as our population increases those spiritual, aesthetic and cultural values which are presently so abundant in pioneer Alaska. Without those values Alaska will be a poorer place than nature destined it to be. . . ." Alaska, singularly free from the burden of expensive land acquisition and "starting from scratch" with a vast amount of the accumulated experience of other states at its disposal, yet has "a pressing financial situation," as one might expect from its change of status, and will for the present direct its chief efforts toward the maintenance and limited expansion of campsites and wayside rest stops along the highways. A long-range program calls for study directed at the selection and classification of sites that will provide hunting, fishing, boating, swimming, and the preservation of and access to "historical sites and natural phenomena such as the Lake George area, Worthington Glacier and other areas."

Arizona. For many years the efforts of the citizens of Arizona who desired the establishment of a system of state parks were greeted with legislative rebuff. Certainly no state has been more richly endowed by nature with colorful scenery and scientific wonders, and also with possession of a prehistory and history of significance. It was possible for a small segment of the population, pioneer-minded people of unquestionable merits, yet convinced that the hoofed animal was still the state's greatest heritage, to stifle a park movement even when the governor himself presented a plan. However, in 1957 the opposition mellowed to the extent that a State Parks Board was established with an initial appropriation of $30,000. True, this was no great amount, but California began with less; even allowing for the change in the dollar's purchasing power over ensuing years, the barrier has been broken. Nor has the enthusiasm diminished, for $73,000 was set aside for the 1960-61 fiscal year, and work is ready to begin on the first stage of the capital improvement and restoration programs of Tubac Presidio, Tombstone Courthouse, and Yuma Territorial Prison State Historical Monuments. A planning division of the Board has been established, and a permanent landscape architect has been employed, so that, though the strict limitation of the size of areas that would be acquired was a disappointment, one may regard the situation in Arizona as altogether hopeful. A comprehensive inventory of sites has been compiled and criteria for a state park system adopted.

Colorado. At the time of the publication of *A State Park System for Colorado,* in 1959, this state had five historical areas, operated by the State Historical Society, and some fishing camps on reservoirs and streams maintained by the Game and Fish Department. Thus the *Report* of 1959 felt justified in making the flat statement that Colorado had no state parks. And this in a state which "has been blessed by nature with the potentials which can make it the 'outstanding recreation state in the Nation.'" Nobody who knows what nature has done for Colorado will rebel against this touch of flamboyance. In 1955 the Colorado legislature established a State Park and Recreation Board, consisting of seven members with six-year staggered terms. A state park director, a man of long experience in a similar capacity in another state, was chosen. In 1958 an extensive inventory of existing outdoor recreation resources was undertaken, and after analysis of this study, sixty-six of the more important areas were selected, based upon their location in respect to the need of recreation, their scenic or scientific quality, and their availability. The Board expects to follow the suggestions of this survey for some time to come, as the state park system takes form. Though the first aspect of the Board's work was the development of six waysides in the eastern part of the state, several units have been obtained by lease—one a few miles southeast of Denver from the Corps of Engineers; two others on reservoirs in western Colorado from the Bureau of Reclamation; others from the Denver Water Board. The 1959 General Assembly appropriated $100,000 for land acquisition. For such acquisition and for development there has been transferred to the Board the income from the Internal Improvement and Saline Land Funds. The progress so far made in Colorado seems to promise well.

Delaware. This state has not yet achieved any considerable stature in the field of state parks, but it has the distinction of owning fourteen and a half miles of its ocean shoreline, which may be used in accordance with a high concept of management. In a time when the seaboard states are faced with a rapidly vanishing shoreline, this foresight of Delaware gives strength to the entire state park movement.

Hawaii. "A tangled ownership pattern of land areas," and the fact that more than half the land of the islands—much of it potentially valuable as park areas—was held in private ownership, faced the Territory in 1959 when its planning office issued a brochure on the subject not long before statehood came about. A Division of Territorial Parks was established in 1949, but no funds were ever made available for it. After statehood, the administration of state parks and historic sites was vested in a Division of State Parks in the Department of Land and Natural Resources. As to the culturally significant historic sites in the islands, an advisory council board has been appointed. The need for state parks in Hawaii is widely recognized. In 1843, when Kamehameha III uttered the words "Ua mau ke ea o ka aina i ka pono" (the life of the land is perpetuated by righteousness), there was hardly such a thing as urban life in the islands. Now, according to the report of 1959, "approximately 111 square miles of land have disappeared under asphalt and concrete on the Island of Oahu." The state administers twenty state parks embracing more than 6,000 acres.

Kansas. Two agencies in this state have the responsibility for provision of park and recreation areas: the Forestry, Fish and Game Commission, and the State Park and Resources Authority. At the present time fifty-seven areas are designated as state parks, lakes, and recreation areas, all of them being manmade impoundments providing fishing and other water activities. Since, within the next few years, the major effort of the Park Authority will be devoted to the provision of recreation facilities on reservoirs constructed by federal agencies, the preservation of significant natural and historic areas will be deferred.

Mississippi. The perfection of the Gulf coastal beach strip in this state is world famous. It has been heavily built up and occupied by private owners; however, there appears to be some chance of a state park along this shoreline. No information was available which would lead the author to suppose that a visit to one of the fifteen state parks would be fruitful. A not-unfriendly observer wrote: "The state park program here is not keeping pace with that of many other states."

Utah. A handsomely printed and illustrated brochure, issued by the Utah State Park and Recreation Commission in 1959, marked the first step in a program which, if sufficiently backed by the public, would preserve the rich heritage of scenic, historic, and archaeological treasures, "values which are now being thoughtlessly destroyed, dissipated or ignored." The high concept of the group which produced this report can be judged from a single quotation: "How can we best weigh the aesthetic gains inherent in maintaining the pristine beauty of a mountain-side vista, as against the physical and economic benefits of constructing a ski-lift on that same slope? How can we weigh present dollars-per-acre land costs against the recreational needs of grandchildren who will enjoy, many decades hence, the parks we establish today?" The report, after a brief discussion of the whole recreation problem, in Utah and elsewhere, deals with the existing state parks, which are four in number and small in extent. It also recommends projects for immediate acquisition and development: several areas located within a short distance from the major metropolitan centers; a major recreation area in the beautiful Wasatch Mountains; others in the Oquirrh Mountains, at the North Fork of the Ogden River, the Mantua Area, Bear Lake, Circle Cliffs Petrified Forest, Cove Fort, Dead Horse Point, and several more, not forgetting an adequate chain of roadside rests. The third section recommends projects "for early action." No one who looks at the illustrations of this report can fail to realize what a storehouse of beauty, natural phenomena, and outstanding history lies within the borders of this state. In some instances the time is now, or never. Petrified wood of the finest quality is being hauled away by the truckload. Later, the Commission expects to recommend recreation projects for Great Salt Lake. Since issuance of the brochure, the legislature has made substantial provisions for acquisition and development, including authorization to expend not more than $1,173,648 for installment purchase of lands for the highly significant Wasatch Mountain State Park east of Salt Lake City.

Wyoming. At the present time the state park system consists of eight Bureau of Reclamation reservoirs, where the state administers recreation facilities for picnicking, camping, and boating. In addition, thirty-three historical areas are administered by the State Archives and Historical Department. There is interest currently in a long-range plan for a system which will include scenic, scientific, and historic areas. "We are just getting started," says an informant, "and we expect to show considerable progress in the years just ahead."

APPENDIX B

STATE PARKS*

Name of State	*Number of Areas*	*Total Acreage*
Alabama	47	42,658
Alaska	65	3,094
Arizona	4	174
Arkansas	16	19,341
California	179	704,912
Colorado	18	11,034
Connecticut	75	22,222
Delaware	6	3,758
Florida	52	121,677
Georgia	59	55,150
Hawaii	20	6,245
Idaho	25	25,561
Illinois	86	52,562
Indiana	35	51,129
Iowa	91	29,728
Kansas	63	110,808
Kentucky	33	36,878
Louisiana	18	12,240
Maine	32	212,905
Maryland	21	23,879
Massachusetts	45	32,916
Michigan	83	185,980
Minnesota	74	100,862
Mississippi	15	13,634
Missouri	37	72,313
Montana	24	9,329
Nebraska	76	69,493

* Includes parks, recreation areas, monuments, historic sites, parkways, waysides, and other related areas administered by state parks and state historical agencies. Waysides administered by state highway departments and state forests are not included. (From State Park Statistics—1961)

Name of State	*Number of Areas*	*Total Acreage*
Nevada	11	10,180
New Hampshire	43	43,838
New Jersey	41	22,737
New Mexico	17	4,365
New York	143	2,567,256
North Carolina	21	37,047
North Dakota	66	5,191
Ohio	113	90,019
Oklahoma	37	59,119
Oregon	180	60,898
Pennsylvania	157	167,298
Rhode Island	75	8,490
South Carolina	25	46,248
South Dakota	143	94,315
Tennessee	20	132,175
Texas	60	62,271
Utah	18	25,677
Vermont	39	17,331
Virginia	20	29,861
Washington	157	75,724
West Virginia	25	44,390
Wisconsin	40	19,835
Wyoming	42	152,074
TOTAL	2,792	5,799,057

APPENDIX C

AGENCIES ADMINISTERING STATE PARKS AND RELATED RECREATION AREAS

ALABAMA
Department of Conservation
DIVISION OF STATE PARKS, MONUMENTS AND HISTORICAL SITES
State Administrative Building
Montgomery 4

Alabama Museum of Natural History
University, Tuscaloosa

ALASKA
Department of Natural Resources
DIVISION OF LANDS
344 6th Avenue
Anchorage

ARIZONA
ARIZONA STATE PARKS BOARD
State Capitol Building
Phoenix

ARKANSAS
ARKANSAS PUBLICITY AND PARKS COMMISSION
State Capitol Building
Little Rock

CALIFORNIA
Department of Parks and Recreation
DIVISION OF BEACHES AND PARKS
1125 Tenth Street
Sacramento 11

COLORADO
STATE PARK AND RECREATION BOARD
221 State Services Building
1525 Sherman Street
Denver 3

The State Historical Society of Colorado
East 14th Avenue at Sherman Street
Denver 2

CONNECTICUT
State Park and Forest Commission
PARK DEPARTMENT
165 Capitol Avenue
Hartford 15

DELAWARE
STATE PARK COMMISSION
3300 Faulkland Road
Wilmington 8

Note. The agency, division, or unit in each state in which primary responsibility for state parks is vested is indicated by capital letters.

Public Archives Commission
Hall of Records
Dover

State Highway Department
Box 151
Dover

FLORIDA

Florida Board of Parks and Historic Memorials

FLORIDA PARK SERVICE
P. O. Drawer 3697 M.S.S.
Tallahassee

Stephen Foster Memorial Commission
White Springs

GEORGIA

State Division of Conservation

DEPARTMENT OF STATE PARKS
7 Hunter Street, S. W.
Atlanta 3

Georgia Historical Commission
116 Mitchell Street, S. W.
Atlanta

Franklin D. Roosevelt Warm Springs Memorial Commission
Warm Springs

Jekyll Island State Park Authority
214 State Capitol
Atlanta 3

Stone Mountain Memorial Association
209 Agricultural Building
19 Hunter Street, S. W.
Atlanta 3

HAWAII

Department of Land and Natural Resources

DIVISION OF STATE PARKS
P. O. Box 621
Honolulu 9

IDAHO

State Board of Land Commissioners

DEPARTMENT OF PUBLIC LANDS
Room 120, State House
Boise

ILLINOIS

Department of Conservation

DIVISION OF PARKS AND MEMORIALS
100 State Office Building
Springfield

INDIANA

Department of Conservation

DIVISION OF STATE PARKS
State Office Building
Indianapolis 4

IOWA

State Conservation Commission

DIVISION OF LANDS AND WATERS
East 7th and Court Avenue
Des Moines 8

KANSAS

KANSAS STATE PARK AND RESOURCES AUTHORITY
801 Harrison
Topeka

Forestry, Fish and Game Commission
Pratt

Kansas State Historical Society
State Capitol
Topeka

KENTUCKY

DEPARTMENT OF PARKS
Capitol Annex
Frankfort

Breaks Interstate Park Commission
(Kentucky and Virginia)
Pikeville

LOUISIANA

STATE PARKS AND RECREATION COMMISSION
Old State Capitol Building
Baton Rouge

MAINE

STATE PARK COMMISSION
New State Office Building
Augusta

Baxter State Park Authority
P. O. Box 488
Millinocket

MARYLAND

Board of Natural Resources

DEPARTMENT OF FORESTS AND PARKS
State Office Building
Annapolis

Maryland Tercentenary Memorial Commission
Old State House
St. Marys City

MASSACHUSETTS

Department of Natural Resources

Division of Forests and Parks

BUREAU OF RECREATION
15 Ashburton Place
Boston 8

Department of Public Works

Division of Waterways
100 Nashua Street
Boston 14

Deer Hill State Reservation Commission
Office of County Commissioners
Northampton

Mount Everett State Reservation Commission
609 West Street
Pittsfield

Mount Greylock State Reservation Commission
154 Pleasant Street
Dalton

Mount Sugarloaf State Reservation Commission
Court House
Greenfield

Mount Tom State Reservation Commission
Hamden County Court House
Springfield

Purgatory Chasm State Reservation Commission
Sutton

Wachusett Mountain State Reservation Commission
Princeton

Walden Pond State Reservation Commission
Court House
Cambridge

MICHIGAN

Department of Conservation

PARKS AND RECREATION DIVISION
Stevens T. Mason Building
Lansing 26

Mackinac Island State Park Commission
Mackinac Island

MINNESOTA

Department of Conservation

DIVISION OF STATE PARKS
353 Centennial Building
St. Paul 1

Minnesota Historical Society
State Capitol
St. Paul 1

MISSISSIPPI

STATE PARK COMMISSION
1104 Woolfolk Building
Jackson

MISSOURI
STATE PARK BOARD
1206 Jefferson Building
Jefferson City

MONTANA
State Highway Commission
STATE PARKS DIVISION
Highway Department Building
Helena

NEBRASKA
Game, Forestation and Parks Commission
DIVISION OF STATE PARKS
Lincoln 9

NEVADA
STATE PARK COMMISSION
State Capitol Building
Carson City

Nevada State Museum
Carson City

NEW HAMPSHIRE
Department of Resources and Economic Development
DIVISION OF PARKS
State House Annex
Concord

NEW JERSEY
Department of Conservation and Economic Development
Division of Resource Planning
BUREAU OF PARKS AND RECREATION
520 E. State Street
Trenton 25

NEW MEXICO
STATE PARK COMMISSION
P. O. Box 958
Santa Fe

Museum of New Mexico
P. O. Box 1727
Santa Fe

NEW YORK
Conservation Department
DIVISION OF PARKS
State Campus Site
Albany 1

Allegany State Park Commission
Red House

Central New York State Parks Commission
Clark Reservation
Jamesville

Finger Lakes State Parks Commission
R. D. 3
Trumansburg

Genesee State Park Commission
Letchworth State Park
Castile

Long Island State Park Commission
Belmont Lake State Park
Babylon, Long Island

Niagara Frontier State Park Commission
320 Riverway
Niagara Falls

Palisades Interstate Park Commission
(New Jersey and New York)
Administration Building
Bear Mountain

Taconic State Park Commission
Staatsburg, Dutchess County

Thousand Islands State Park Commission
832 Washington Street
Watertown

Division of Lands and Forests
State Campus Site
Albany 1

East Hudson Parkway Authority
County Office Building
White Plains

Education Department
Division of Archives and History

State Education Building
Albany 1

NORTH CAROLINA

Department of Conservation and Development

DIVISION OF STATE PARKS
Box 2719
Raleigh

Department of Archives and History

Historic Sites Division
Box 1881
Raleigh

NORTH DAKOTA

STATE HISTORICAL SOCIETY OF NORTH DAKOTA
Liberty Memorial Building
Bismarck

OHIO

Department of Natural Resources

DIVISION OF PARKS
Hanger Building
1500 Dublin Road
Columbus 12

Ohio Historical Society

Division of Properties
Ohio State Museum
Columbus 10

Akron Metropolitan Park District
2077 Newton Street
Akron 5

OKLAHOMA

Oklahoma Planning and Resources Board

DIVISION OF RECREATION AND STATE PARKS
533 State Capitol
Oklahoma City 5

Will Rogers Memorial Commission
Will Rogers Memorial
Claremore

OREGON

Oregon State Highway Department

STATE PARKS AND RECREATION DIVISION
301 Highway Commission Building
Salem

PENNSYLVANIA

Department of Forests and Waters

DIVISION OF STATE PARKS
408 Educational Building
Harrisburg

Water and Power Resources Board
Harrisburg

Bushy Run Battlefield Park Commission
Bushy Run Battlefield
Jeannette

State Park and Harbor Commission of Erie
Erie

Washington Crossing Park Commission
Washington Crossing

Brandywine Battlefield Park Commission
Box 227
Chadds Ford

Valley Forge Park Commission
Valley Forge

Pennsylvania Historical and Museum Commission

Bureau of Museums, Historical Sites and Properties
State Museum Building
Harrisburg

RHODE ISLAND

Department of Public Works

DIVISION OF PARKS AND RECREATION

State Office Building
Providence 3

SOUTH CAROLINA
South Carolina State Commission of Forestry
DIVISION OF STATE PARKS
506 Calhoun State Office Building
Columbia

SOUTH DAKOTA
Department of Game, Fish and Parks
DIVISION OF FORESTRY AND PARKS
Pierre

Custer State Park
Hermosa

TENNESSEE
Department of Conservation and Commerce
DIVISION OF STATE PARKS
203 Cordell Hull Building
Nashville 3

TEXAS
TEXAS STATE PARKS BOARD
P. O. Drawer E, Capitol Station
Austin

Fannin State Park Commission
P. O. Box 3
Fannin

San Jacinto State Park Commission
P. O. Box 25125
Houston 5

UTAH
STATE PARK AND RECREATION COMMISSION
19 West South Temple
Salt Lake City 1

VERMONT
State Board of Forests and Parks
DEPARTMENT OF FORESTS AND PARKS
Montpelier

The Vermont Board of Historic Sites
Montpelier

VIRGINIA
Department of Conservation and Economic Development
DIVISION OF PARKS
1106 Travelers Building
Richmond

WASHINGTON
STATE PARKS AND RECREATION COMMISSION
522 South Franklin Street
Olympia

WEST VIRGINIA
Department of Natural Resources
DIVISION OF STATE PARKS AND RECREATION
State Office Building
Charleston 5

WISCONSIN
Wisconsin Conservation Department
FORESTS AND PARKS DIVISION
Box 450
Madison 1

State Historical Society
Historic Sites Division
816 State Street
Madison 6

WYOMING
WYOMING STATE PARKS COMMISSION
Boysen Route
Shoshoni

State Archives and Historical Department
State Office Building
Cheyenne

INDEX

(S.P.=State Park. S.F.P.=State Forest Park. S.R.=State Reservation. S.M.=State Monument. H.S.=Historic Site. S.R.A.=State Recreation Area. M.S.P.=Memorial State Park. H.S.P.=Historic State Park. H.S.M.=Historic State Monument.)

A NOTE ON THE TYPE

THE TEXT *of this book is set in* ELECTRA, *a Linotype face designed by* W. A. *Dwiggins* (1880-1956). *This face cannot be classified as either modern or old-style. It is not based on any historical model, nor does it echo any particular period or style. It avoids the extreme contrasts between thick and thin elements that mark most modern faces, and attempts to give a feeling of fluidity, power, and speed.*

Composed, printed, and bound by
The Haddon Craftsmen, Inc., Scranton, Pa.
Typography and binding design
based on originals by
W. A. DWIGGINS

A NOTE ABOUT THE AUTHOR

Since 1935 Freeman Tilden, who began his career as a newspaperman and continued as novelist and playwright, has devoted his entire time to writing and lecturing on conservation. Since 1940 he has served as consultant in the office of the Director of the National Park Service, and his book, *The National Parks,* is generally considered the standard work on that fascinating subject. Its publication led to a long-range study of park interpretation for the Service; the resultant book, *Interpreting Our Heritage,* is regarded as the "bible" of professionals engaged in such work. Freeman Tilden was born in Malden, Massachusetts, and resides in New Hampshire or Florida or Washington, D.C. He and his wife, a Vermonter, have four grown children.

August 1962

NORTH PLATTE COLLEGE LIBRARY
NORTH PLATTE, NEBRASKA